ELEVEN GODS
AND A
BILLION INDIANS

ELEVEN GODS AND A BILLION INDIANS

THE ON AND OFF THE FIELD STORY OF CRICKET IN INDIA AND BEYOND

Boria Majumdar

**SIMON &
SCHUSTER**

London · New York · Sydney · Toronto · New Delhi

A CBS COMPANY

*For Sharmistha—we have shared the
dressing room for two decades!*

CONTENTS

PART THREE

PART FOUR

PART FIVE

PROLOGUE

Not Just a Sport

20 March 2017. The last and final day of the Ranchi Test match between India and Australia, with the series tied at 1–1. Australia is overnight 23 for 2 and still trailing by 129 runs after a monumental effort by Cheteshwar Pujara and Wriddhiman Saha had given India a 152-run lead in the first innings. The ball is turning and spinning off the rough and most people following the match feel that with R. Ashwin and Ravindra Jadeja bowling brilliantly, India can take a series defining 2–1 lead, with only the fourth and final Test at Dharamshala remaining. Unlike what the norm is these days with regard to Test matches, there is serious interest in this one—and the series in general—owing to the fierce competitiveness exhibited by both teams through the high-octane cricket the series has produced so far. Australia's captain Steven Smith's 'brain fade' and his Indian counterpart Virat Kohli's veiled attack that called his opposite number a cheat (without ever using the word, though) added to the excitement, with the Australian papers going to the extent of calling Kohli the 'Donald Trump of cricket'.

It was just how an India–Australia series should be. Intense, passionate and, at times, over the top.

At about 8 a.m. in the morning, I noticed a couple of missed calls from a very senior official of the Board of Control for Cricket in India (BCCI), the governing body of the game in the country. I had put in a formal request to interview one or two of the players at the end of the series and assumed he was calling in that regard. The official in question had conducted the affairs of the BCCI with efficiency since the Supreme Court had appointed a Committee of Administrators (CoA) to oversee the BCCI's functioning on 30 January 2017 and, contrary to peoples' expectations, there had been very few hiccups in the running of the sport. When I returned the call, he picked up after one ring, stating: 'We have sent a detailed note to the ICC [International Cricket Council], which is now in the public domain. Do take a look. It lists our objections to the proposed financial redistribution plan and spells out why we are opposed to it. It will also show you that we are committed to protecting the BCCI's interests at any cost, contrary to what is being said by some in the media.'

Under normal circumstances, it would have been absolutely fine for him to tell me what he did. He knew I had an interest in the subject. He was doing his job and was committed to upholding Indian interests at the ICC, the global governing body of the game. However, with the India–Australia Test match poised for a very interesting finish, I expected him to, at the very least, mention the match, or refer to it in some form. But he did not. And, to be honest, it wasn't surprising.

The Test match, suffice to say, wasn't his priority. Yes, India was playing Australia in one of the most high-profile Test series of our times but the BCCI was pre-occupied with other, what they called, 'pressing concerns'.

They were concerned about votes, threats to other boards,

obtaining a few hundred million dollars more at the ICC and holding on to power.

To write an accurate historical account of Indian cricket one needs to first understand that it is not simply a history of what is happening on the field. That is only a part of it. What is played off the field is equally important and fascinating. These two stories, which run concurrently on and off the field, make Indian cricket what it is. Unless one is able to comprehend and make sense of both these strands, running parallel to each other, one wouldn't be able to fathom why the BCCI official did not refer to the India–Australia Test in the course of that conversation.

It is important to take readers a little further back to elucidate upon this point. Jagmohan Dalmiya, the then BCCI president and arguably one of India's best sports administrators of all time, had just passed away in Kolkata after a sudden deterioration in his condition on 20 September 2015. It had come as a shock to everyone, and people had started flocking to the B.M. Birla Heart Research Center in Alipore to pay their last respects. Former India captain Sourav Ganguly, a very close friend of the family, was one of the first to arrive at the hospital and was playing a key role in overseeing how events leading up to performing of the last rites should move from thereon. That's when a fairly well-known figure in the Indian cricketing circles came up to him and said, 'You need to take over the reins of the Cricket Association of Bengal [CAB] now if you are keen. This is your best chance.' Ganguly's face contorted with disgust the moment the statement was made. He chose not to respond and when we made eye contact a few seconds later, I realized he was upset and frustrated. That it was still bothering him was evident when he later said to me, 'Mr Dalmiya's body is still here. It is not even one hour since the tragedy and look what people are saying! It is just unfortunate.'

It was, indeed but, as Ganguly knew well, it was typical of the Indian cricketing world.

Power tends to corrupt, and absolute power corrupts absolutely.

The next morning, Mr Dalmiya's body was kept at his Alipore home until about midday for people to come and pay their respects. Almost everyone from the BCCI turned up. Anurag Thakur, the then BCCI secretary, was one of the first officials to visit and he conducted himself with the utmost dignity and integrity. Avishek Dalmiya, Mr Dalmiya's son and now the secretary of the CAB, came up to me in the course of the morning and mentioned that a number of senior BCCI office-bearers were on their way to pay their respects. Each of them was coming to Eden Gardens, Mr Dalmiya's second home, from where the family would then proceed to the cremation grounds. A huge crowd had gathered at Eden Gardens and it was heartening to see the chief minister of West Bengal, Ms Mamata Banerjee, accord Mr Dalmiya a 21-gun salute for his services to Indian sport. It was a fitting tribute for all he had done for cricket in this country. Moments before the national anthem was played, the entire BCCI top brass had reached Eden Gardens and, having performed the last courtesy, retreated to the home team's dressing room at the ground level of the club house. The conversation there, in the presence of one of the CAB joint secretaries, was all about who will succeed Mr Dalmiya and how it was important to stop N. Srinivasan from trying to make a comeback.

Outside, the gun salute was being offered to the just-departed BCCI president while inside his colleagues were busy plotting their next move to replace him. Again, it wasn't surprising to witness these contrasting scenes, for that's how Indian cricket has been governed for years. The Board has evolved into an INR 20,000-crore behemoth and thanks to the super-lucrative Indian Premier League (IPL), the control of Indian cricket has become one of the most coveted professions in the country.

However, this is not to say that the two strands I mentioned earlier, which run parallel, do not feed off each other or come to a head on occasion. Indeed, they do. All the time. On 6 January 2017, only days after the Supreme Court verdict had changed the face of the BCCI, ousting the president and the secretary and disqualifying many others, the Indian team for the one-day international (ODI) and T20I series against England was due to be selected. With M.S. Dhoni stepping down from captaincy, the selectors also needed to formally appoint Virat Kohli as captain across all three formats of the game. Given that this series against England was to be the last ODI assignment before the ICC Champions Trophy in June, it had assumed far more significance than any run-of-the-mill bilateral ODI contest. Selections were scheduled to be convened at around 1 p.m. at the Cricket Centre in Mumbai. Just minutes before the process was about to start, news trickled in that the meeting had been delayed. For the first few minutes it wasn't clear what was causing the delay. Only later did it become known that the Board's joint secretary, Amitabh Chaudhury, who, at that point, was understood to have been ousted by the Supreme Court verdict, had called Rahul Johri, the CEO, stating that he was the convenor of the meeting in the absence of Ajay Shirke, the secretary (who had also been ousted). It was also mentioned he would only reach Mumbai that evening to convene the selection committee. Why Chaudhury did what he did is not known. Even if he wanted to convene the meeting, logic states he should have been in Mumbai. He was very much in the know that the selection meeting had been scheduled on that day and there could be nothing more important for the Board's office-bearers than selecting the national team.

On receiving his call, Johri, who had been asked by the Supreme Court-appointed Lodha Committee to convene and preside over the meeting, contacted the secretary of the Lodha Committee, advocate Gopal Sankaranarayanan, for advice. Even though Chaudhury was disqualified to preside over the meeting, only upon being told by Sankaranarayanan that he could proceed with the meeting did it go on. While this entire drama was being played out, the selectors, led by M.S.K. Prasad, were waiting in a room on the third floor of the Cricket Centre awaiting clarity. In all, they had to wait for a little under three hours before they could finally select the team. Two of the selectors, while not wanting their names to be revealed, confirmed that they had received calls from a few BCCI office-bearers threatening them not to go ahead with the meeting. Eventually, the meeting, which was to start at 1 p.m., started at 3 p.m. and the formal announcement of Kohli being appointed as captain of the ODI team happened at 4 p.m.

There were, however, other aspects to the drama. Just around the time that the selection committee meeting was about to start, the BCCI received a notification from the Tamil Nadu Cricket Association stating they were unable to offer grounds for the India–England U-19 series that was to be held in February 2017. The timing of this communication is of significance. Whether it was deliberately sent at the same time or was simply a matter of coincidence will never be known. But the communication was enough to add to the confusion and throw the administrators off gear.

Even after the meeting was over, a section of the ousted BCCI office-bearers were of the opinion that the team selection had been illegal and wanted to move court for further clarification on the matter. However, good sense ultimately prevailed and the move was scuttled. Else, the Supreme Court would also have had to decide if Kohli should captain Team India!

Despite all the drama off the field, two things have remained constant for a while. One: India's performance. The team has done well consistently, very well in home conditions, in fact, and has shown signs of being competitive overseas under Kohli's leadership. India made the semi-finals of the 2015 World Cup with commendable wins over Pakistan and South Africa, and put in impressive performances en route to beating Australia to make the semi-finals of the World T20 at home the following year. In Tests, India finished 2016–17 as the top-ranked team in the world, with series wins over the West Indies, New Zealand, England, Bangladesh and Australia. Thereafter, Kohli led India to the finals of the Champions Trophy in England in June 2017, and an impressive ODI series win in South Africa in February 2018.

Off the field, there seems to be a semblance of order behind all the chaos. At the time of the appointment of the CoA by the Supreme Court on 30 January 2017, the first concern voiced—by the public and the media alike—was how these people, who had little or no experience in administering the game, would run cricket in India. Could a motley bunch of four individuals, among whom only one had a cricketing background, ensure that action continued without a hitch? Was the CoA capable of conducting tournaments like the IPL? Added to these apprehensions was the issue of the CoA failing to protect India's financial interests at the ICC. With the ICC intending to go ahead with the financial redistribution plan, first mooted in 2016 when Shashank Manohar took over the reins of the world body, this question was foremost in the minds of the former office-bearers ousted by the court, individuals who were out to prove their importance in the running of Indian cricket. Finally, it wasn't clear amidst all this fluidity if the CoA and the Board's chief executive officer (CEO) would be able to inspire confidence in marketers to invest in Indian cricket going forward. This concern became acute when industry leaders like Star India declared their intention not to bid for a renewal of the shirt sponsorship rights for the national team, a property that had been with them for the past four years. With key tournaments like the Champions Trophy round the corner, and the on-field performance of the team at its best ever, Star India's declaration to not participate in the tender was surprising but, as later expressed by its CEO, Uday Shankar, largely driven by the volatility surrounding the game in the country. Clearly, it was a test for the CoA and the professionals holding office in the BCCI to ensure that the most-followed sport in India didn't run into a protracted state of financial and administrative stalemate.

Defying all concerns, the Board managed to up the shirt sponsorship value by a whopping five times with OPPO Mobiles India, the smartphone manufacturer, stepping in to replace Star. The value, for the record, is four times what Cricket Australia (CA) gets from shirt sponsorship for its national team. The IPL auction was staged without a hitch in Bengaluru and, for the first time in years, the spectacle itself was conducted without any major controversy erupting during or in the immediate days following the close of the tenth edition of the tournament. The ICC–BCCI standoff, too, was eventually settled, with the BCCI managing to get a USD 405 million share from the ICC as per the new financial model—more than double of what the England and Wales Cricket Board (ECB), the second-biggest earner, gets from cricket's apex body. Above all, despite early apprehensions, the Indian team participated in the Champions Trophy without further drama. The moot point is that the BCCI's operations never came to a standstill.

However, this is not to suggest that the going was always smooth; that has never been the case with Indian cricket. The day India landed in England, under the stewardship of captain Kohli and head coach Anil Kumble, to defend the Champions Trophy title, an announcement seeking a new head coach for team India was made. This came at the back of a story that all was not well between the captain and the coach. Despite emphatic on-field performances, Kohli and Kumble weren't getting along, and sources within the BCCI suggested there had hardly been any communication between the two of them for months. Kumble, who was initially keen on an extension, was informed by the CoA that they were left with little option but to open a new search and the issues between the captain and the coach needed to be settled before an extension was possible. While much of it (in fact, all of it) was already out in the media, the BCCI acting secretary Amitabh Chaudhary, upon landing in England, dismissed the whole episode as media speculation, even trying to suggest that it was the media that had cooked up the story and was now blowing it out of proportion. Within days of Chaudhary's denial, Ramachandra Guha, member of the CoA, resigned from his position, citing the treatment meted out to Kumble as one of the reasons. His media statement was a formal ratification of the crisis. Guha, who made some pertinent points in his note, should have been questioned about the timing of his resignation. With the team in England, in the middle of the second-most important cricket tournament in the world, he may have waited a week or two before making his frustrations public. Things came to a head when members of the BCCI's Cricket Advisory Committee were forced to meet in London, right after India's match against Sri Lanka, to deliberate on the next coach. India had lost to a much-lesser Sri Lankan side and to suggest that the dressing room hadn't been impacted by the goings-on and had remained insulated was unreasonable. How could the players not have been impacted by an ongoing public spat between their captain and the coach? How could they not have been bothered when the search for a new head coach was on in the middle of the Champions Trophy? How could they have kept their focus on the task at hand?

To their credit, Kohli and the boys put up a brilliant performance against South Africa at the Oval on 11 June and made the semi-finals in style. Thereafter, India stormed past Bangladesh in Birmingham to make their second consecutive Champions Trophy final. Yet again, Indian cricket was continuing to surprise one and all. The team, despite issues in the dressing room, was showing no signs of discomfort on the field and was getting ready to play Pakistan in a much-hyped final. Players were in denial mode, at least publicly, and even a meeting between the captain and the Cricket Advisory Committee—consisting of Sachin Tendulkar, Sourav Ganguly and V.V.S. Laxman—to try to diffuse the captain–coach crisis a day before the final was considered par for the course. It was only after India lost to Pakistan did most people revisit the dressing-room crisis and suggest that the Kohli–Kumble rift wasn't possibly the best thing to have happened in the middle of the tournament. Kumble, who resigned a day after the Champions Trophy final, alluded to his deteriorating association with Kohli in a post on social media, stating that the relationship had become 'untenable'. His assertion led to an instant outburst, with the captain being trolled on Twitter as an egotist and control freak. Coming on the back of the defeat in the final, people decided to take pot-shots at Kohli, without knowing his side of the story or what had really transpired to push things beyond repair. The team was subsequently on its way to the West Indies and did so without a head coach. In the series that followed, India once again played quality cricket to defeat the West Indies 3–1 on their soil in the five-match ODI series to seal yet another away series victory. The coach hunt was on alongside, and there was speculation that the team had communicated its preference to the BCCI.

It has to be acknowledged that the BCCI's handling of the Kohli–Kumble affair was poor. The story had come out at the worst possible time and thereafter, the BCCI wasn't able to stem the media scrutiny that followed. Whether the off-field rumblings influenced India's on-field performance in England can never be definitively proved but what is certain is that in trying to understand a comprehensive history of the game in India, one needs to document the two parallel strands running side by side in cricket. Both make the game what it is, a cash-rich industry that attracts the high and mighty and brings out a kind of passion that is seductively intense and, at times, beyond comprehension. It is perhaps the only sport where the West looks to the East. The IPL—regardless of whether we like it or not—is a global template.

How do you explain 5,000 Indians screaming 'Sachin! Sachin!' outside Tendulkar's Bandra home on 15 February 2015—the day of the India–Pakistan game in the World Cup in Australia, despite the fact that Sachin wasn't even a part of the tournament, having retired in November 2013? These are the men and women who make this game the phenomenon it is and that's what makes a study of Indian cricket worthwhile. These fans, spread across the country and numbering in millions, encourage marketers to invest in the game and make the IPL one of the most valued franchise-based tournaments in the world. With their painted faces, these gung-ho fans are symptomatic of a new resurgent India that unabashedly expresses itself through Indian cricket on the world stage. They travel the world to support the team and aren't overawed by any kind of impediment. In England, they outnumber the English fans at Lord's, and at Melbourne, they are significantly more in number than Australian cricket supporters. They are the huge blue billion that give the Indian cricket industry teeth and muscle.

From the time when players had to depend on Air India employees to bail them out when touring abroad in the 1960s to today, when the skipper signs endorsement deals of over INR 100 crores each for eight years with leading global brands, this is a story of a sport which represents the complexities of contemporary India as an aspiring global superpower.

Before getting on with the story, it must be stated that it has never been a unilinear narrative but rather a story that has been mediated at every stage by unexpected twists and turns and is now a dynamic, everyday narrative that can never be captured in all its nuances. Further, not everything that one has seen or heard in the last two-and-a-half decades of association with Indian cricket can be backed up by incontrovertible proof. For example, which are the players included among the thirteen names that remain in a sealed envelope with the Supreme Court of India and who are yet to be investigated for corruption? Does this list include icons who have massive fan followings in the country and beyond? Will these names ever come out? Will anyone mention any of these names in the public domain based on information available from that much-abused word: 'sources'? Besides, can such information ever be backed up with sufficient proof?

Most who write on cricket in India will say they know some of the names listed in the envelope. And most, as it may be, would be right. However, has anyone seen the contents of the envelope and can anyone ever put these names out in the media without the consent of the apex court? And should it not be asked why the court will not allow these names to be revealed if such a thing allows for a cleansing of the game? While administrators were pulled up and penalized for possible wrongdoing, why is there a different yardstick in place for players?

Tendulkar, whose autobiography *Playing It My Way* I have co-written, said it well. 'Yes I was pained by match-fixing. [I] was angry, very angry, in fact. But when people asked me why did I not speak up and give names, the answer is I had no idea who was doing it and how. As a player all I was interested in was winning cricket matches for India. That's all that mattered to me. Play the sport with distinction and integrity.'

However, this did not pre-empt me from questioning Tendulkar over and over again. Did the team not suspect any wrongdoing and, if so, how was that even possible? And, if they did, how did they deal with it? How disappointing was it to come to terms with the fact that matches or results had been influenced, and did it ever cause a sense of disillusionment? And did he ever have a sense that the game would again be back in all its glory?

Even after India lost to Pakistan in the Champions Trophy final, questions were asked about the defeat. Social media was abuzz that something murky had gone on behind the scenes. It is important to acknowledge that such inane speculations, based on completely unfounded and unsubstantiated allegations, will forever be a feature of Indian cricket going forward. Every unexpected result, more so if it is an adverse one, will be met with a sense of doubt by the ever-passionate Indian fan. The same fan, however, will spend a whopping £1,000 or more for a hospitality ticket the next time India faces Pakistan in an ICC event. That's what Indian cricket is all about. It is a phenomenon that has more than a billion Indians addicted to it. No other sport comes near it in popularity and no sport will, at least in the next two decades. Its power is such that the Indian political class is eternally attracted to it and remains associated with it, even if it is from behind the scenes. Every business tycoon wants to own an IPL team, for it is the ticket to a world of glamour and media attention that thousands of crores of rupees can't buy. It is religion to over a billion Indian men and women.

When the Indians returned home after a dismal World Cup campaign in 2007, M.S. Dhoni had to make the Tollygunge Club in Kolkata his home for five days. He couldn't risk going back to Ranchi. Four years later, when he won India the World Cup, all of Ranchi was his. They couldn't wait for him to come back.

This is the story of Indian cricket, uniquely Indian in every sense.

PART ONE

THE CURSE OF FIXING
PRELUDE TO THE MODERN GAME

It was the eve of the Champions Trophy group-stage match between India and Pakistan on 4 June 2017, and Mohammad Azharuddin, the former Indian captain and a legend of the game, was in Birmingham to do television expert duties for Aaj Tak and India Today. On 3 June, the day before the match, India Today did a special show, from opposite the Edgbaston Cricket Ground, on the high-octane clash, bringing on board multiple experts. Just as the show finished did it transpire that Azharuddin did not have tickets for the game the next day. As a former India international player who has captained India in three World Cups—1992, 1996 and 1999—it was odd that he would have to struggle for tickets. Another former player, surprised to hear this, suggested to the producers of the show and to the India Today crew that he would speak to the ICC and arrange tickets for Azharuddin. The problem, we all thought, was sorted. However, till late evening, Azhar did not have his tickets and when the player who had agreed to help was asked what happened, he looked uncomfortable. The truth was that the ICC had refused to entertain the request simply because it was Mohammad Azharuddin.

Despite being cleared by the Indian judiciary, the allegations of his involvement in wrongdoing continued to haunt him. It is improper to go into the morality of this issue. Rather, I won't. Was the ICC being unfair? Was it a case of different parameters for different people? And could Azharuddin and some of the others, who were implicated at the turn of the millennium, ever consider this issue a completely closed chapter?

These are questions, yes, but there are no real answers.

Azharuddin—one of my favourite Indian batsmen of all time— had filed a case in 2001 against the ban imposed on him the previous year, and finally got a verdict in his favour in 2012. Ajay Jadeja, the former India batsman, too, has been cleared of the match-fixing taint and so has the wicketkeeper-batsman Nayan Mongia. Legally, the trio have won the battle. The question, then, is simple—have they been cleared because there is no conclusive proof or was the entire saga blown out of proportion by an evolving 24x7 media between 1997–2000? Why should cricketers suffer the outcome of an extreme media reaction? Or is it a case of truth being concealed forever?

Frankly, it might be a bit of both. The Hansie Cronje-scandal, for example, could not have occurred in isolation. Hansie's confession is in black and white. The media exposés are a fact. Books, some of them painstakingly researched, exist and will forever be out in the public domain. Testimonies were recorded, investigations conducted and men were found guilty. Something was, indeed, going on and players were surely involved. They are the principal actors in this spectacle called cricket. A senior journalist in India lost his job in the process and a few others were questioned. It was murky. Credibility was at stake and the game was vulnerable in the absence of a pre-emptive mechanism. Authorities were caught by surprise; instead of taking the crisis head on and try and cleanse the rotten underbelly, they turned rabbits and closed their eyes, feigning ignorance.

Was it an overreaction of sorts—a real *good story*, as we understand today in the context of 24x7 media? To an extent, it perhaps was. The news magazine exposé is a case in point. While it was spearheaded by some of India's finest journalists and done with precision and passion, it was essential for the news magazine which broke the story of match-fixing in 1997 to be able to sustain the campaign at the time. One of the founders of the magazine, speaking to me on condition of anonymity, suggested that they needed a cover story that would completely take competition by surprise. The match-fixing exposé was a brilliant story. While the magazine had India's worst-kept secret on the cover, its singular rival had a story on Sitaram Kesri, the Congress president. The result was a no-brainer. The news magazine needed Manoj Prabhakar, the former Indian all-rounder, as much as Prabhakar needed an outlet to expose the rot. It was a marriage of convenience between the two parties. But then, did Justice Yeshwant Vishnu Chandrachud, the retired Chief Justice of India—who headed the one-man investigation commission instituted by the BCCI to investigate the match-fixing allegations—not treat Prabhakar's testimony with the seriousness it deserved? Was a 30-minute meeting with Prabhakar good enough to get to the root of the problem? And by suggesting that Mongia disagreed with Prabhakar on the 1994 India–West Indies ODI in question, and hence there was no problem, did Justice Chandrachud approach the crisis rightly?

However much we try and probe, this will forever remain a grey area in the history of Indian cricket. Nothing except Cronje and his death is in black and white. Testimonies were changed, the truth concealed and cricket came out of the whole issue scarred and jolted.

Sample this: A senior journalist who is a good friend of mine and has covered the game for three-and-a-half decades was in the Caribbean in 1997 to cover India's Test series against the West Indies. In Antigua, he was struggling for accommodation and, for a night, had no option but to request another journalist friend to bail him out. The friend in question readily agreed. Such things happen and are hardly uncommon.

'Navjot Sidhu was not playing that Test match. I had done my copy and it was fairly late when I mentioned this to the friend I was staying with. It wasn't anything earth-shattering and I just happened to mention it. But his reaction was startling. He started pacing up and down the room and looked anxious. His mood and body language had changed. And eventually he ended up making a few calls to people very late into the night,' mentioned my friend, after much cajoling.

Three people were sharing the apartment in Antigua. While one of them was fast asleep, my friend couldn't sleep after seeing the reaction the piece of information had elicited. 'At around 2.30 a.m., I could hear a phone conversation going on in the drawing room. It was odd. Why would anyone make calls that late at night? When I asked if anything had happened, I was told the story had to be passed on. It wasn't the age of 24x7 media, but I decided to leave it at that.'

A few months later, this incident was reported in *Outlook* magazine. My friend, however, hadn't shared it with *Outlook*. The person speaking on the phone wouldn't have. So was it the third journalist, whom they had suspected to be asleep, the one to provide this information? Was he an undercover investigator of sorts trying to blow the lid on corruption?

Again, there are plenty of such questions without any real answers.

The grapevine has it that journalists would regularly speak to bookies and pass on information. This was done in exchange of fairly decent sums of money. While betting and passing on information never amounted to fixing—it is important to make a distinction between the two—passing on team information did constitute an act of corruption.

Stories like the above are aplenty. Almost every journalist who has covered cricket in the 1990s has his or her own story on fixing to tell. While some journalists like G. Rajaraman have written a book on the subject, others have written magazine pieces and newspaper op-eds. There are still others who know more truths about the scandal than most but continue to feel apprehensive in talking about colleagues. The *Outlook* exposé quotes Kamal Bindra, wife of the cricket administrator I.S. Bindra, multiple times. It is clear that she was cagey and, after a point, refused to divulge more.

The trail turned cold, with the BCCI deciding to turn a blind eye.

A very senior sports-marketing professional, who had set up his firm in the mid-1990s, narrated some rather fascinating stories to me at the time of writing this book. However, like most others who have shared information with me about the fixing episode, his condition was that he could not be quoted. He mentioned a friend of his from a Delhi college visiting Jadeja's room on multiple occasions during a particular series. There was no ICC Anti-Corruption and Security Unit (ACSU)—cricket's independent watchdog—back then, and visitors weren't subject to any security checks in Indian cricket in the 1990s. As long as the player was comfortable meeting with the visitor, no one was stopped. And the visitor in question was a schoolmate of Jadeja. The visitor had, in turn, mentioned to the sports-marketing professional that the people hovering around the cricketers weren't the best kind. They looked shady and it was all a kind of veil. Again, that's where the trail dies. The veil never lifted. Not much information is available on these individuals being alluded to. Rather, what we do know is that the political class did get involved. The press conference by the activist and president of the Samata Party, Jaya Jaitley, on the corruption issue, is a case in point. Jaitley, it was reported, was standing up for her daughter, Aditi Jaitley and her friend Ajay Jadeja. Given her proximity with the defence minister of the country, Jaitley's interference became the subject of much political gossip in the capital. But that's where it ends. There are opinions galore, but no conclusive evidence. There is gossip aplenty, but no concrete follow-up. There's been endless talk, but little action to show for it all.

Since then, as I already mentioned, the judiciary has cleared Azharuddin, Jadeja and Mongia of all allegations levelled against them and the case now stands closed.

The same sports-marketing professional mentioned above also said that one of the players he is close to—who is now a legend of Indian cricket—once told him that senior cricketers had instructed him to be careful on the West Indies tour of 1997. Sharing of rooms among players was a practice back then and the player in question was warned about his roommate and told that he should step out of the room if he saw anything suspicious. If this is indeed true, the players, too, had suspected wrongdoing. They knew, or suspected at least, that questionable activities were being conducted. Why they did not speak to the BCCI or chose to remain silent on the issue is a matter of conjecture. Was it because they were scared of stirring a hornet's nest? Was it because they were aware that the BCCI would not look at such complaints favourably? Or was it because of that vital cog in the wheel that was missing—conclusive proof?

Was the BCCI aware of such things? Were Jagmohan Dalmiya, A.C. Muthiah, I.S. Bindra and Raj Singh Dungarpur, men who controlled Indian cricket at the time, interested in going into the deep end of the matter? Did the lure of television money and a fear of controversy prevent them from doing so? Could stories—which keep flying around, most of them being based on hearsay—be relied on or taken seriously?

Will we ever know who the actors were? With Cronje dead, all that is left of it is a cold trail. How was the process orchestrated? Was it similar to what was done in 2013 with the IPL spot-fixing scandal? Did journalists and team support staff act as conduits, as is often speculated? Finally, was the investigation under Justice Chandrachud a fair one or was the investigator keen on concluding that the glass was half full rather than half empty? Was such an approach a defence mechanism prompted by an anxious BCCI and has it hurt the game in the long run?

It was a shady world, no doubt, and answers to these questions will forever be subjective.

All that we can conclusively say is that match- or spot-fixing—trying to influence the outcome of a match by paying players—was a mid-1990s phenomenon in cricket. The toss-related incident involving Asif Iqbal and G.R. Vishwanath in 1978–79 at Eden Gardens notwithstanding, fixing was the by-product of cricket's transformation into a big-money sport in India and across the world. Yes, there have been instances of players selling out in cricket in the past as well but such instances can never be equated with the attempted systematic fixing of matches that started in the 1990s. Such attempts were a product of the television and mobile phone revolution, which made sure that almost every cricket match played in the world was televised in India and followed in real time using digital technology. Real-time-information flow was the key and could only happen in the aftermath of the economic liberalization of 1991. For instance, Ranji Trophy games aren't attractive for a bookie; they can never be. Most of them aren't televised yet and the stakes involved aren't as high as an IPL or an international contest.

For me, personally, the match-fixing crisis was a deeper challenge. I had just started a PhD on the history of Indian cricket when the Cronje scandal broke out. All of a sudden, every cricket-related activity was under suspicion. No match was considered clean. Icons were turning into fallen mortals overnight. Fans were distraught and angry, and determined to not watch the game any more. Cricket just wasn't the same. And here I was starting a doctoral dissertation on a sport that was perceived rotten. Was the dissertation on cricket or on a staged charade? Was I writing a 100,000 word-epitaph? Were the matches I was planning to comment on being played for real or were they fixed? Self-doubt began creeping in. I remember a meeting with my supervisor David Washbrook, where we discussed if there was any sense in pursuing the dissertation further. All dressed-up and nowhere to go, I was a fan and analyst impacted in the strangest manner. And, clearly, I wasn't alone. There were thousands like me all over the world whose belief had been shaken and confidence stirred. The impact of match-fixing wasn't simply restricted to the game and its immediate actors. The tremors were felt across the fraternity and caused irreparable damage.

I was hanging on to Sachin Tendulkar, Sourav Ganguly, Rahul Dravid, Javagal Srinath and Anil Kumble. All five of them are of nearly the same age and my understanding of cricket had been shaped by them while I was growing up in urban Kolkata. Tendulkar, Ganguly and Dravid stood for the fact that not all was lost. Cricket could still be a religion of sorts with the players as its deities. Sachin's 136 against Pakistan in Chennai, braving an excruciating back pain, was for real. Ganguly and Dravid's partnership in Taunton in the 1999 World Cup played out before our eyes. These two performances were two of India's best showings ever. Kumble picking up all ten wickets at the Feroz Shah Kotla Ground against Pakistan was proof that god doesn't play dice and that the sport was still for real, not reel. Could they have done more to help the doubting fan? Perhaps, yes. But then, as Sachin keeps saying, he could only have spoken if he knew who was/were involved in those malpractices. He was in his own little cocoon, trying to win games for India, losing his mind for failing to win matches that should have been won while trying to unravel the mystery. He was a player and not an investigator and, as Ganguly says, 'was determined to rescue the sport from the throes of this unprecedented crisis'.

I have known Ganguly since 1992. He could never fix matches. With him as the new captain of India and with people like Tendulkar, Dravid and Kumble in the side, the crisis had to pass. The values they stood for was balm for a troubled nation. And for cricket at large.

And then there was county cricket. Or, put more aptly, local cricket in Oxford. There were no spectators. Rather, less than 100, sometimes even 50, with some of them busy sipping their apple cider on lovely sunny Oxford evenings as a match was being played. Most were oblivious to the cricket at the Oxford University Club grounds in front of them, a facility that would give most of India's Test match venues a run for their money. Surrounded by trees and adorned with a beautiful little pavilion and clubhouse, it is the near-perfect English club ground. Importantly, both for the players and the ones present, there were no cameras, no dubious people lurking around and no big prize for winning the game.

Just as the clock struck 5 p.m., players started trickling in with their kit bags to the club, gradually making their way to the changing rooms to get into their gear. It was release at the end of a long, hard day in the laboratory or at the Bodleian Library. For the many sitting and relaxing in the lobby, watching television or even working, the players did not make any difference. It was cricket as it had evolved two-and-a-half centuries ago. To quote Edmund Blunden, 'The game which made me write at all, is not terminated at the boundary, but is reflected beyond, is echoed and varied out there among the gardens and the barns, the dells and the thickets, and belongs to some wider field.'

For someone searching for reassurance, this was a rare departure. Watching cricket for the love of the game, knowing it was the unadulterated sport being played out in front of me.

It was a throwback to Neville Cardus, to R.C. Robertson-Glasgow and Hugh de Sélincourt. With the sun melting away and giving way to a lovely British early-summer evening, the game meandered on at its own pace. There was no frenzy, no urgency, no deadlines. It was a throwback to the past, as if I was studying a rare relic.

Come to think of it, these very hallowed grounds of Oxford and Cambridge had provided English cricket with some of its greatest stalwarts in the early twentieth century. Eton and Harrow, followed by Oxford or Cambridge, was the norm for the English upper-classes and cricket was a staple for these gentlemen, who travelled the world to try and evangelize and hold the empire together. They wouldn't fix matches or even dream of doing so. Rather, they introduced the game to us in India in the mid-nineteenth century, something we very generously appropriated and indigenized over time. Oxford was not an aberration. In England, there were more than 100 games played every afternoon; games which had little significance in terms of results. These were a reminder that not always does one need to make millions from the game, or make a living out of it at all.

The dissertation, I realized, did make sense after all.

So, how do we reflect upon match-fixing in the long history of cricket? Was it really a case of a few bad apples falling prey to the lure of a quick buck, or did the rot run far deeper than will be ever revealed? And, how did cricket come out of it in the long term?

Mark Waugh and Shane Warne, pulled up for passing information to bookies, continue to be revered; one a selector and the other a commentator and Australian cricket's best all-time brand. Azharuddin and Jadeja are both television experts, as is Nayan Mongia. All of them have been cleared of wrongdoing by the highest judiciary. Cronje is dead while Nicky Boje and Roger Telemachus have simply faded away. The game itself has moved on, as have the players and administrators. Only we fans have never fully been able to digest it. Every now and then, there is a throwback to fixing. To us, these instances remain as unresolved investigations and, as a result, are unsatisfactory. Our game was violated and justice wasn't done. It has left us all paranoid. At the slightest hint of spot- or match-fixing, we get worried. Rumours start flying thick and fast. Social media is thrown into a tizzy. The game, unsure and under-prepared, wasn't able to deal with the crisis in the past. It tried looking away when it should have faced it head on. Cleansing, and not a cover-up, should have been the aim, and because this virus wasn't cleansed; it remained benign for a while, but with the potential to turn malignant. The tumour wasn't operated upon and, in 2013, Indian cricket paid the price for it yet again. The stakes were bigger, since the game is now a billion-dollar industry. As a result, the malignancy was even more potent and destructive.

The more immediate need, however, was taken care of. With a thrilling India–Australia series played out in March 2001, spearheaded by Sourav Ganguly, V.V.S. Laxman, Rahul Dravid, Sachin Tendulkar and Harbhajan Singh, all of whom turned gladiators against the world's best and most-feared cricket team, the game soon found its new redemption song. Good, we thought, had prevailed over evil. But history had another tale to tell.

REDEMPTION SONG: INSPIRE AND IGNITE

THE MIRACLE OF 2001

A few things are taken for granted when it comes to Indian cricket as we know it today. Irrespective of which part of the world the Indian team is playing in the team always has a huge crowd support backing them. In the World Cup match against South Africa in 2015, among the 87,000 spectators present at the Melbourne Cricket Ground (MCG), close to 85,000 were Indians. This wasn't an aberration. In 2009, the then England captain, Paul Collingwood, famously alluded to this reality when fans booed his team as they made their way from the nursery ground to the main pitch at Lord's to take on M.S. Dhoni's India. The majority of the spectators, a disappointed Collingwood lamented, was supporting India.

The second thing we take for granted is the cash-rich nature of the sport in India. Indian cricket players are the highest-paid sports stars in the country and earn considerably more than cricketers from other nations. Some of them feature in the list of highest-paid sportspersons in the world. With the BCCI growing richer by the day, earnings of Indian players will only go up in the months and years to come.

Finally, we see an expression of India through the prism of cricket. Even at the cost of sounding dramatic, it must be said that the situation may be likened to a famous sequence in the Bollywood blockbuster *Deewar*. When Shashi Kapoor, a police officer with a meagre income, is asked by his more prosperous elder brother Amitabh Bachchan what he has to show for himself and all his efforts, a confident Kapoor says, '*Mere pass maa hai.*' When we talk of India on the global sporting stage, it is this one sport where India rules. We have the best players, the best league, the richest board and the muscle to dominate world cricket, with England and Australia playing catch-up. Aggressive nationalism, a feature of contemporary India and one that defines the modern Indian youth, finds expression in cricket. This is what explains the humongous social media followings—most running into millions—of India's leading cricketers, who are considered symbols of a resurgent and aggressive modern India.

Each of these features, which define Indian cricket at the moment and have become integral to the game in India, are of fairly recent vintage. The BCCI was a loss-making institution till the early 1990s. The story of the financially robust board that we now take for granted is actually a two-and-a-half-decade-long phenomenon, more so of the last 15 years, starting with the Australia tour of India in 2001. With match-fixing having eaten into the edifice of the game, world cricket was faced with its biggest crisis in years. Advertisers who had invested huge amounts in the game were all of a sudden left with no option but to move away from cricket. While in other cricket-playing nations Olympic sports benefitted as a result, in India, the move away from cricket helped reality TV shows, for that's where the advertising revenue went in the absence of any real competition from Olympic sports. Shows like *Kaun Banega Crorepati*, with the Hindi film industry's megastar Amitabh Bachchan at the helm, was one of the prime beneficiaries of the match-fixing scandal.

Cricket, in 2001, needed new oxygen to continue as India's foremost national passion. Faith of its fans had to be restored, and new fans needed to be brought in. The idea that India could continue to express itself through cricket needed to be reinforced. That's exactly what happened with the India–Australia series, when cricket nationalism reached a crescendo at the back of some incredible on-field performances from the Indian team. Since then, cricket, it can be said, has never looked back as a sport, even in the face of the IPL spot-fixing scandal and subsequent judicial intervention.

The Australia team that was scheduled to tour India in 2001 had taken on and decimated the very best in the world. Having won 15 Test matches in a row, they were coming to India to conquer what captain Steve Waugh had labelled as the team's final frontier. His was a team that can easily go down in cricket history as one of the best ever and the Indians, under newly appointed skipper Sourav Ganguly, were evidently the underdogs going into the contest. With Javagal Srinath and Anil Kumble, India's two best bowlers, out because of injury, the task ahead for Ganguly and his boys was monstrous. To get past the likes of Waugh, Matthew Hayden, Justin Langer, Ricky Ponting and Adam Gilchrist, India needed to make a very special effort. More so because there was no one on the horizon who could run through this famed Australian batting line-up. In the bowling department, Glenn McGrath, Jason Gillespie, Michael Kasprowicz and Shane Warne were performing at their best. Considering the immensity of the challenge that lay ahead, batsmen like Sachin Tendulkar, Rahul Dravid, V.V.S. Laxman and Ganguly himself needed to collectively punch above their weight to prove to be competition for the Australian team.

The first Test match in Mumbai was evidence of how good the Australians were. Riding on centuries from Hayden and Gilchrist, and terrific bowling spells from McGrath, Gillespie and Warne, Waugh's team breezed past India inside just three days. 'They were really good,' says Ganguly, reminiscing about the opposition's collective display of might. 'We were left wondering how and what we needed to do to take them on. Seriously speaking, I was searching for answers. They had all their bases covered and we needed something out of the ordinary to happen to be able to beat them. And Kolkata [where the second game was played], in that sense, was a freakish Test match. If you seriously ask me how it happened and how we managed to get over the line in Kolkata after being 128/8 on day two, responding to Australia's 445, I will have to tell you it was a miracle and it was [an] intervention from above. Such miracles rarely happen in cricket.'

Coming into Kolkata, not even the most ardent Indian fan had given the hosts a chance. Australia, it seemed, was fast imposing itself, and it was no contest. Yes, Harbhajan Singh had bowled beautifully in Mumbai, but, for a youngster, it was hard to believe how time and again he could strangle an Australian batting line-up considered the best side of all time.

Even at the Eden Gardens, all was going to plan for the Australians. At 252/4 on day one, Australia was poised to post a big total, much before Harbhajan accomplished the first miracle of the series: A hat-trick—the first Indian to do so. It was as if the massive Kolkata crowd had suddenly awakened from their slumber. A quiet stadium started to make real noise, and all of a sudden, it was a contest. India had staged a comeback and, if they could polish off the tail quickly, things could still happen for Sourav's men. Unfortunately, for India, though, the tail wagged and Waugh farmed the strike quite adroitly to take Australia to 445, scoring a brilliant century in the process. For India, pitted against a buoyant Australian bowling attack, it was a tall ask. And when the top order collapsed for the third time in a row, it seemed that Australia would easily get to their 17th consecutive Test win—the first such feat by any team in world cricket.

India displayed some pluck on the third morning, thanks to Laxman, who scored a gritty 59 and was the last man to get out.

Australia, leading by 274 runs, enforced the follow-on. 'We had the measure of the Indians so far in the series and the bowlers were confident of doing it one more time. I had no hesitation in asking the Indians to bat again,' says Steve Waugh, recounting the horror that was to follow.

In an inspired move, India decided to push Laxman to number three—a decision that transformed Indian cricket forever. 'It was decided that the way V.V.S. batted [in the first innings], we were better off sending him at three. Rahul could bat at six, and it was something that could unsettle the Australians,' Ganguly narrates with a smile. 'But no one could anticipate what followed. Even when I got out and we ended day three at 254/4, it was Australia's game. I have to say what followed was the best-ever partnership in the history of Indian cricket. We did not lose a wicket through the fourth day and scored 335 runs in the process. Rahul and Laxman were both on drips in the dressing room; by the end of it all, they had lost so much fluid. However, despite the exhaustion and the cramps, they kept backing themselves. Australia literally could not believe what was going on,' recounts Ganguly.

Laxman's 452-ball 281—his Sydney 167 in 2000 notwithstanding—marked his maturing as a cricketer. 'I was batting well throughout the Test match and when asked to bat at three in the second innings, I must say I felt good about it. Here was an opportunity to make the most of the good form. As the partnership with Rahul progressed and we had scored a 100 together, we started to believe we could just carry on and on. We knew we had to play out the new ball and some key spells and that would put the pressure back on the Australians. The plan worked and though it was tiring, we kept pushing each other on because something really special was about to happen,' mentions Laxman, sitting outside the very same dressing room at the Eden Gardens and reminiscing about the innings.

During the course of the innings, Warne was treated with disdain, and each time Laxman danced down the pitch to play against the turn through the off-side, the crowd erupted for him. The gladiator had his audience; a mass of humanity, who had started to believe in miracles, were on their toes. Australian shoulders had dropped by the end of day four, and it was clear that India would no longer lose the Test match. Winning the game would assume significance for the home side at so many levels. One, not only would it mean a victory against the mighty Australians, but also correspond to ending the opponent's undefeated streak. Did anyone, however, really believe that the three-match series would go into the decider in Chennai, tied at 1–1? Perhaps not. Riding on Laxman's 281 and Dravid's 180—an answer to all his critics who had doubted his ability—Ganguly declared in the morning session of day five, setting Australia a target that most teams wouldn't want to go for on a turning surface. This Australian team, however, was different. They were the best in the world and would never shy away from a challenge. Harbhajan was bowling the best he has ever bowled in his career and it was a contest every cricket fan who was there at the Eden Gardens would forever cherish.

The press box—it was my first time at the Eden Gardens media centre—was full of emotion. Australian journalists could not believe what they had witnessed and still felt Waugh and his team could hold on. The Indian journalists, on the other hand, had finally found their voice. Quiet and sneered at for two days, they started to cheer every Australian wicket that fell.

When the Indians dropped Waugh just at the stroke of tea, it seemed a draw was the most likely result. The Australian captain went back unbeaten and, with seven wickets still remaining to be taken, it seemed a task too steep to accomplish even for Harbhajan, who was bowling like a man possessed. 'The gods thought differently,' says Ganguly, sporting a smile. 'Moments after tea, Steve Waugh gave us another chance and this time, we did not mess up. With Steve out, we had started to believe it could be done. And when things weren't happening for a while, I decided to go to Sachin just to try him out for an over or two. The plan was to keep things tight from one end and bowl Harbhajan right through from the other because he was my key weapon to pick wickets. Sachin, who always had the ability with the ball, bowled a magical five-over spell and picked three wickets, making it game, set and match for us. The googly with which he got Shane Warne out could have got any batsman in the world.'

Tendulkar, who had not done much with the bat during the two innings, falling for just 10 in both innings, was itching to contribute with the ball. 'I knew I had one or two overs to make an impact and thought to myself that it was best to mix it up against Hayden and Gilchrist because conventional wisdom suggested I would only bowl off spin against the left-hand batsmen. And once I managed to get Hayden and Gilchrist out and Warne walked in, I made up my mind to try and bowl a googly to him. He wouldn't be expecting it and it was my chance to pick up a third wicket. The ball wasn't as full as I would have wanted but Warne was done in by the turn. And when it hit him back in his crease, I knew I had him plumb,' recounts Tendulkar.

Finally, when Harbhajan trapped McGrath's lbw—a decision that will forever be contested in the annals of world cricket—100,000 people at the Eden Gardens collectively erupted. The noise was deafening, the passion seductive. Match-fixing was a thing of the past. Cricket in India had been given a new lease of life, and Ganguly's team had accomplished a feat none had in world cricket. That the Australians could be beaten was finally a proven reality and, as Ganguly says, the Indians went to Chennai for the decider believing that the momentum had turned in their favour.

The Test match captured peoples' imagination at all levels, evident from an incident that took place that evening, four hours after the match had ended. Umpire S.K. Bansal, who was officiating when the last wicket fell, was returning to his hotel when his driver took a wrong turn into a one-way street. Within minutes he was stopped by a traffic constable on duty and asked to hand over his license for breaking traffic rules. The driver, uncertain and afraid, looked to Bansal for support. Bansal, the story goes, stepped out of the car to request the cop to let the driver go and apologized on his behalf. Seeing him, the cop for a moment was left wondering who he was and then asked if he was indeed THE S.K. Bansal who had given Glenn McGrath out! Upon knowing that he was indeed, the cop asked the driver to carry on, saying that for Umpire Bansal, all rules could be changed that evening!

This story, which has been narrated to me by several people and corroborated by Bansal himself, tells us a lot about how the victory was perceived in Kolkata at the time. Cricket, it would not be an exaggeration to suggest, was back overnight as front page news. Harbhajan, Laxman and Dravid were being celebrated as national saviours and the spectre of match-fixing, still fresh in public minds, had taken a backseat. You just can't fix a match like the one played out at Eden Gardens and bat and bowl the way the Indians did. It was cricket of a very different level and a Test match like that one could never be scripted. Laxman dancing down the track to Warne and hitting him past mid-off and mid-on; Harbhajan bowling like a dream; and finally Dravid batting as if peoples' lives were dependent on him—were exactly the kind of performances cricket needed to regain credibility. Thanks to the Eden miracle, it happened.

Moving on to Chennai for the third and final Test of the series, the Indians were a changed lot. They knew Australia could be beaten and also knew the impetus had firmly shifted in the aftermath of the Kolkata win. Steve Waugh and his boys were jittery and were bound to take a little time to come to terms with what had happened. But the Indians also knew that Australia would come hard at them. They were hurt and wounded and would retaliate. 'I just asked the boys to play their best for we had seen what our best was capable of. That we could beat the Australians was now known to the world and there was no reason to feel overawed. Hayden was playing the series of his life and it was important to get him out. More importantly, we had to bat well and make sure we put the Australians under pressure,' says Ganguly.

Yet again it was Harbhajan who stood up for India with the ball. A Hayden double ton notwithstanding, Harbhajan ran through the Australian line-up and made sure that a good batting effort was all India needed to set up the match. And this time, Tendulkar came to the party. Scoring a much-needed century, Tendulkar led India to a mammoth 500-plus score and gave his side a handy lead of over 100 runs. With Australia finding it hard to play against Harbhajan in the second innings as well, all India needed was a little more than 150 in their second innings to win the match and the series. Just when people thought it was all over, the Australians did make one final comeback. Getting Tendulkar, Laxman and Ganguly in quick succession, they gave themselves a chance to close the game. Sameer Dighe—Sam Dig to his friends—who was playing this match ahead of injured regular wicketkeeper Nayan Mongia, had to bring all his grit and batting skills to the fore to finish the contest. 'It was tense. The entire dressing room was on edge and I must confess I was nervous as hell. You had to feel the nerves; the stakes were so high. We were close and it was very important that I stayed out there and finished things. To come as close and not get over the line would spell disaster for Indian cricket. There was a lot of chirp out in the middle and the crowd was also making a lot of noise. In hindsight, I can tell you it was the ultimate high of my cricket career. You may say I got just 22 but while chasing 155 each of those runs were worth their weight in gold. Finally, when Harbhajan completed the second run after a nudge to point, it was as if we had won everything in life. We, as a team, had accomplished what no other cricket team had done and this victory will forever be pivotal in the history of our cricket,' Dighe said, recounting his moment of glory as an Indian cricketer.

From being tormented in Mumbai to winning after having followed-on in Kolkata to finally closing out the series in Chennai, India under Ganguly had given back world cricket its greatest attribute: Credibility. That it was not all fixed was driven home in emphatic style. Seeing full stadiums for Test matches was a serious message for sponsors and many of them started getting back to investing in the game. India's poor run at the Sydney Olympic Games helped. Cricket had survived the match-fixing scandal. New heroes like Laxman, Harbhajan and Zaheer Khan emerged on the horizon and fans celebrated the positivity that accompanied these on-field performances.

Aggressive 'cricket nationalism', which is now an acceptable feature of contemporary Indian life, was starting to reappear on the horizon after an interlude of 12 months and that's what made corporate India look at the game again with zest. It was this steady corporate interest, which eventually made the IPL, conceptualized and executed by Lalit Modi, a reality in 2008.

Interestingly, the aggressive brand of nationalism that I refer to here wasn't particularly new to the game in India. Nor was it a 1990s phenomenon. In fact, expression of Indian-ness on the cricket field and appropriation of the game for nationalist purposes can be traced back to the 1830s, a time when the game hadn't yet taken firm roots in the country. From the very beginning, the cricket field in India was a contested terrain with sepoys, the first entrants, using it to challenge their colonial masters and, on occasion, defeat them. Appropriation of cricket for nationalist needs predates the 1857 rebellion and throws up the question of whether the Oscar-nominated film *Lagaan* indeed had real-life parallels—to the earliest cricket gladiators of India.

WHEN THE SEPOYS BATTED
FOR INDIA

Historians have forever debated the reasons behind the confidence of the sepoys that prompted the defiance of 1857, commonly accepted as the first landmark anti-colonial uprising in nationalist historiography. I aim to suggest that the confidence behind the act of defiance that resulted in 1857 may, in part, have been acquired on the cricket field. Playing cricket against the colonial masters in the 1830s and 1840s, Indian sepoys had already successfully thwarted English superiority in the latter's own sport.

It is an interesting question as to why the sepoys, and later some Indian princes and middle-class patrons, readily appropriated the British masculine games of cricket and football. From a pragmatic point of view, it may be surmised that they saw in them a worthwhile cultural tool to reassert their hurt self-esteem and injured masculinity. On the other, cricket and football had the potential to be assimilated as means of crossing swords with the British imperialist. At a time when the ills of an unequal political and economic structure threw up contradictions, which quite naturally had a deep impact on the social psyche of the Indians, sport might have provided a level playing field. Failing to attain power and prestige within the army or in society, the sepoy, and later the middle-class Indian nationalist, searched for apolitical ways to counter British humiliation.

I also propose, as an extension, that such faith acquired on the sporting field may have urged Indian nationalists in the post-mutiny period to appropriate European sport as a means of resistance. With military uprisings no longer an option and the British firmly entrenched as the paramount power in India, the sports field assumed increased significance in the second half of the nineteenth century.

Finally, it can be argued that such proto-nationalist activities on the sporting field shaped colonial sporting policy in the post-1857 period. On the one hand, the British encouraged the organization of Indian cricket along communal lines—a straightforward outcome of 1857. On the other, it was the colonial policy of bringing the princes back to the forefront of administration after 1857 that resulted in cricket being appropriated by the native aristocrats, who had both the means and the motivation. Had this not been the case, Indian cricket, like its earliest English counterpart, which was organized and controlled by peasants from south-east England, would have remained a more representative sport. Aristocratic appropriation of cricket was something the colonial state envisaged. With the princes acting as compradors, it was in British interest to position them as leading patrons of Indian cricket. This allowed the colonizers to use cricket as a tool for acculturation, a means to douse subversive native sensibilities. However, a caveat needs to be introduced here. Deliberating on the nature of princely patronage of cricket, it was assumed that all princes would see cricket as a means to link themselves to the English aristocracy. It is a different matter that some of them, like the Maharaja of Natore in Bengal, were determined to set up cricket teams comprising only Indians as a direct challenge to the colonizer, something dealt with in other parts of the book.

In fact, the spread of European sport in colonial India went hand in hand with its cultural indigenization. Historians of Indian football note that Calcuttans, with the rest of India in their trail, were the only people in the world to indigenize football skills and technique, playing barefoot, as they did from the very beginning. The Bengalis imparted to the game a distinctive Indian touch. From the very beginning, Mohun Bagan, the leading Bengali club, played barefoot, keen on cashing in on the speed and footwork of this method, and despite failure against booted teams on rainy grounds, never thought of wearing boots. The barefooted jugglery of Indian legends like Gostho Paul, the Bhaduris, Syed Abdus Samad and Umapati Kumar against booted European teams, even on slushy surfaces, was a constant source of pride for the Bengali nationalist. The barefooted genius of the Indians made P.B. Clark, the captain of the visiting Islington Corinthians, an amateur British side, remark in 1938: 'Indians alone play real football, what they call football in Europe is after all only bootball.'

So, when did the Indians' tryst with cricket begin? In trying to answer this question, chroniclers have invariably turned their attention to Bombay (now Mumbai). I did the same in my doctoral dissertation at Oxford and in most of my early writings on the history of Indian cricket. We have all been unanimous in suggesting that the formation of the Oriental Cricket Club in Bombay by the Parsis, in 1848, marked the start of organized cricket in India. This was followed by the formation of a spate of Parsi cricket clubs in the 1850s and 1860s. There were stray attempts earlier—such as the one in 1839, when a school teacher, Boswell, tried to introduce the game to his students in Bombay, but such efforts were few and far between. It was the Parsi initiative, all scholars of Indian cricket agree, that started what is today the nation's most relentless obsession.

However, as is often the case with history, new findings contest the old and make for fascinating new revelations. One such startling revelation is that Indian cricket was born amidst native sepoys who had established themselves as players by the middle of the nineteenth century. News reports published in the *Sporting Intelligence Magazine* brought out by the editor of *The Englishman* newspaper between 1833–1850 say as much.

In a detailed account of a match played at Sylhet on 3 March 1845, the reporter states, 'You will oblige me by giving a place in your columns to the account of a match played here . . . [between] the European officers and the sepoys of the light company against those of the other companies of the 28th regiment.' The rest of the report is even more startling: 'The most enthusiastic European cricketers could not have played with more energy and cheerfulness than the native sepoys did. I am not a cricketer myself, but invariably attend as a spectator when the natives are playing; the knowledge that the officers, whether playing or not, take an active interest in their performances gratifies the sepoys.'

Interestingly, the sepoys had acquired prowess in even the most difficult of skills, such as, wicketkeeping: 'Among the sepoys, I observed one or two who bowled well, some who were very good wicket-keepers, and others who caught well . . . and as fielders, few Europeans can surpass them.' The report singled out sepoy Lungum for his extraordinary batting prowess and declared that in a season or two, the native sepoys would be equipped to handle the best European talent in India.

From other reports published in the same magazine we come to know that sepoy cricket was well developed across the Indian heartland. On the other hand, sepoys hardly played cricket in the south, where the game continued to be a preserve of the English soldiers in the army. Similarly, in Bombay, sepoy cricket was hardly developed. Places where it was fairly well-developed were Barrackpore, Dum Dum, Agra, Cuttack, Midnapore, Sylhet, etc. It may be a mere coincidence that the cities and towns where sepoy cricket was fairly well-developed were those which were prominent in the uprising of 1857.

The well entrenched nature of native cricket across the heartland
is evident from multiple reports published in the *Sporting Intelligence
Magazine* over the years. About native cricket in Agra, a report
published in 1843 states that though the match was well contested,
the fielding and bowling of the natives were 'inferior to that of their
antagonists'. The reporters declared that while the native bowlers
bowled round-arm, they did so without sufficient practice and were
unable to deliver the balls with any consistency.

In yet another report, sent in from Cuttack, the scribe comments:
'. . . you seem to be little acquainted with this land of the Oriahs
and the sporting characters that are to be found in it . . . Now that
the cold weather is setting in, sufficient hands can be mustered for
witnessing that scientific, manly and truly English game.' The report
was accompanied by the scorecard of the first match of the season,
according to which, one of the teams had in their ranks three native
players.

The early popularity of cricket among the sepoys was ascribed to
cricket's potential as healer of the difference between the European and
the native. One of the reports draws attention to this aspect of the
sport—'Cricket is essential in improving one of the great defects, so
often complained of, the distance of the Europeans in the intercourse
with the native.' It goes on to suggest that European officers, from
the senior to the junior, encouraged the game, either as spectators
or players. 'Were they not to do so . . . I fear the sepoys would not
long continue to play.' The writer suggests that while there were
many tangible products of Britain's colonial legacy, one of the most
striking and influential was cricket. Since the start of the nineteenth
century, cricket had been a significant determinant of the relationships
established between the colonizer and colonized, helping to reduce the
potential for conflict between two very different cultural traditions.
The reporter, to draw a contrast with an indigenous sport, cites the
example of hockey on horseback. Hockey, it is mentioned, was a

very popular Manipuri pastime, played on horseback or ponyback. 'It might be supposed that sepoys would take an interest in it; for the natives of the upper provinces are generally admirers of good horsemanship, and no little skill is required in playing mounted hockey.' However, the sepoys seemed to take no interest in it, possibly because it lacked that spirit of intimacy with their superiors that they seemed to have begun to value.

But not always did the spirit of sportsmanship last. In an article titled, 'Sepoy cricket at Sylhet', a reporter writes that the match between two regimental sides, one of them containing no less then eight native cricketers, was perhaps the best-contested and most acrimonious encounter of the season. He singles out sepoy Soophul for praise, describing his bowling as 'first rate.' This transformation was inevitable and was rooted in the very nature of sport. As the Australian scholar Brian Stoddart has argued, 'In the very success of this socially segmented and skewed imperial ideology . . . lay the origins of some major complications for the empire and what became of its post-colonial commonwealth. These complications emerged from an enormous contradiction that existed within the imperial construction of sport . . . Sport was promoted as an instrument of apparent trans-cultural unity but within it were several strands of potential conflict.'

Thus it is hardly surprising to note that within the confines of the army, the 'games ethic' was successfully subverted on occasions. Sepoys, already peeved with discriminatory treatment meted out by the colonial state, initiated this process of subversion. To that extent, the history of the appropriation of the games ethic within the ranks of the Indian army can be seen as part of a nationalist enterprise.

In fact, all of the cricket matches, which pitted the native sepoys against European officers of the regiment, are of special interest. To draw a parallel, such matches assumed proto-nationalist proportions of the kind depicted in the blockbuster Hindi film *Lagaan*. That the cricket field had already become an arena for assertion of native strength against European dominance is fascinating in the light of what happened in 1857.

Interestingly, the British had learnt their lessons from the occasional defeats against the sepoys and such matches were a thing of the past by the mid-1850s. In fact, British refusal to play against the Indians became a norm in some provinces by the second half of the nineteenth century. Repeated urgings by the Town Club in Calcutta for a bilateral contest was turned down by the exclusively European Calcutta Cricket Club and it was only in 1895 that they acceded to the request of Saradaranjan Ray, founder of the Town Club, for a match.

This is very similar to the case of hockey in the early decades of the twentieth century. With the possibility of India beating Britain rife in hockey between 1928 and 1948, the British refused to play against their own colony. In fact, Britain did not participate in Olympic hockey contests in the years 1928–36, knowing that the Indians were favourites to win the gold. This is especially interesting because Britain had won the Olympic gold in field hockey in 1904 and 1920 respectively, the only years when hockey had been played before 1928, when India did not participate. When Britain did play against India in 1948 they were trounced 0–4, a major confidence boost for the newly independent Indian state. Such a boost did not happen immediately in cricket—the Indians defeated the English for the first time in a series only in 1960. While British refusal to play against India in hockey draws attention to the seriousness of sporting contests between the colonizer and the colonized, it also reinforces the value of the British policy of allowing native princes to consolidate their hold over Indian cricket.

By the middle of the nineteenth century, the games ethic in India had come a long way. From being a preserve of the European imperialist and an English public-school code, its appropriation created an arena of competition between the British and the Indians, in turn breeding among the Indians a sense of confidence, which might well have flowed into contexts far more serious than the sporting field. But to suggest that Indian sporting clubs of the 1840s and 1850s, from their very inception, began to reflect or represent purely nationalist instincts on the sports field is perhaps erroneous. Nonetheless, from the middle of the century, sports had become a new and unique cultural nationalist force among sections of Indian society, although the approach of different segments of society to it was hardly uniform. It is thus fair to suggest that the answer to the confidence on display in 1857 may be hidden in the idiosyncrasies of a game in which the English had been successfully challenged by Indian sepoys two decades before the Mutiny happened. It may also be argued that British policy in the wake of the 1857 uprising— divide and rule and preferring the prince over the peasant—shaped the evolution of Indian cricket, football and hockey in the late-nineteenth and early-twentieth centuries.

Finally, it is evident that sport, which has been accorded little merit in studies of Indian history, was of major significance in discourses relating to the disciplining of the indigenous population and in subsequently stimulating resistance against the colonial state. The games of cricket and football, especially, were considered by the colonizers to carry with them a series of moral lessons, relating to hard work and perseverance, team loyalty and obedience to authority and, indeed, involving concepts of correct physical development and 'manliness'. As such, they were used as key weapons in the battle to win over local populations and to begin transforming them from their 'uncivilized' and 'heathen' state to one where they might be considered 'civilized' and 'Christian'.

The pre-eminent role of the games ethic in India was most evident in the case of the Indian army. In the early-1830s, British generals and commanders of the Bengal army fought hard against indigenous religious customs and social habits to introduce cricket and other European sports among the Indian sepoys, mostly from high-caste Hindu backgrounds. Despite initial resistance from the sepoys, their superiors were successful in advancing the game among the local soldiery, who, on their part, were introduced to a new code of ethics. Cricket, for the English commanders, was a moral means to serve a wider imperial end. In fact, it has been rightly argued that bureaucratic and military coercion were not the only reasons why Britain was able to hold on to its vast empire for as long as it did. Cultural power—ideas, beliefs, rules and conventions concerning social behaviors, carried throughout the empire by the British—also contributed to their ability to control the colonized.

Interestingly, most English garrisons within the British Indian army were modelled in the spirit and ethos of the English public school. Numerous games of cricket and soccer were played by Indian soldiers across the country. Almost every leisure hour was utilized by soldiers to sharpen their sporting skills and, more often than not, these games became arenas of intense rivalry. The love for cricket cultivated had a much wider impact on local society. Indian sepoys, in emulation of their superiors, took an active interest in the game, and by the 1840s, cricket had gained the reputation of an egalitarian agency, which alone transcended the divisions of colonial social order.

OVERCOMING THE ODDS OVERSEAS

Although the sepoys had made the sport a level playing field in the 1840s, Indian national teams after independence failed to conquer overseas shores for the best part of 70 years. Successes in 1971, in the Caribbean and in England, and thereafter in 1986 in England notwithstanding, India, till the late 1990s, was a poor traveller. Except a 1–0 series win in Sri Lanka in 1993, away wins were few and far between. India lost 0–1 to England in 1990, 0–4 to Australia in 1992, 0–1 to South Africa in 1992, 0–2 to England in 1996, 0–1 to the West Indies in 1997, 0–2 to South Africa in 1996–97 and 0–3 to Australia in 1999–2000. Despite having players of the calibre of Sachin Tendulkar, Rahul Dravid, V.V.S. Laxman, Anil Kumble, Sourav Ganguly and Javagal Srinath in the team, the poor away record was something Indian fans had reluctantly come to terms with. Every away tour was met with a sense of inevitability and all there was to celebrate was individual performances. Failure to chase down totals like 120 in Barbados in 1997 was inexplicable and will forever constitute the lowest point of Tendulkar's captaincy.

Ganguly, made full-time captain close to a year prior to the

Australia series in early 2001, was determined to change this poor away record.

'Something had to be done. It was unacceptable to me that we travelled abroad to always come back second best. In fact, we had the mindset that it was beyond us to win overseas, and even a draw was an acceptable result,' Ganguly says as we settle down in his sprawling drawing room with his favourite biryani at his Behala house in South Kolkata.

The setting is ideal. This mansion is where Ganguly grew up wanting to make a name for himself in cricket. And the drawing room is a testimony to that ambition. 'Awarded to Sourav Ganguly, Member of the Bengal Ranji Trophy team', reads one of the trophies adorning his cabinet; the year of the tournament almost impossible to decipher, having faded away with time.

Seeing the trajectory of my gaze, Ganguly is quick to point out that it is one of the trophies he received after Bengal won the Ranji Trophy, India's premier domestic competition, in 1990.

'From playing in that match against Delhi as a teenager to captaining India to being dropped and now to president of CAB, it has been quite a journey,' he smiles and says, as he asks one of the many staff working in his administrative office next door to get me some *mishti doi*, a sinful delicacy that we Bengalis find impossible to resist.

As we tuck into our biryani and chicken rezala, so very different from the biryani you get in other parts of India, I remind Ganguly that I had requested him (and he had agreed) that in the next two hours he couldn't fiddle with his iPhone. Yes, if there is an important call, he could take it but otherwise, I would need his undivided attention.

'*Chawlo, shuru karo* (let's begin),' he says and places the phone with the silver back facing frontwards on his rather cluttered desk. It is an attempt to stop gazing at the device from time to time, a practice that has inadvertently become integral to our existence in present times.

'So, how did you go about changing such a mindset?' I ask him. While the players remained the same, something different was done in the period between 2001 and 2005 which resulted in India starting to perform consistently well overseas. And that's what will be the enduring legacy of Ganguly as captain of the Indian team.

Listening to people sing his praises is nothing new for Ganguly. Fondly called '*Dada*' by thousands of Bengalis and Kolkatans, he is still the second-most popular Bengali after Chief Minister Mamata Banerjee—even after a decade since his retirement. And if I may say so, that he loves the attention and the praise. Above all, he loves being *the* Sourav Ganguly.

Today, however, is different. I am praising Ganguly, the captain, and not the batsman, the commentator or the CAB president. And this, still, makes a difference to him. Having spent a good part of his life in transforming Indian cricket, Ganguly still enjoys talking captaincy, especially if one is willing to dig deep and understand what he did differently.

I have known Sourav for close to 25 years now. He was a senior at St Xavier's College, Calcutta (now Kolkata), and the one thing that has always been foremost with him, for good or bad, is a sense of self-belief. He takes time in picking his people but once he does so, he backs them with his life. His captaincy philosophy was no different. With players like Virender Sehwag, Zaheer Khan, Harbhajan Singh, Yuvraj Singh and a host of others, including M.S. Dhoni, Ganguly backed them because he thought each of them could do a job for India. Moving away from favouritism and regional selection, Ganguly made sure that youngsters from all across the country made the Indian team and were given a fair run to prove themselves. And, in doing so, he backed his instincts more than anything else. Take the case of Dhoni, for example, arguably India's best white-ball captain and finest finisher of all time. Ganguly had heard of him as an unorthodox big-hitting batsman-wicketkeeper in 2002–03. Most would have wanted to see him first before speaking about him to the selectors. Not Ganguly. 'A number of people I had regard for, like Raju Mukherjee and Prakash Poddar, who were Talent Research Development Officers appointed by the BCCI, mentioned Dhoni to me. [They] said here is a player who could hit the ball long with effortless ease and could be a big-match player. I remember speaking to the selectors and requesting them to pick him for India A. They asked me who this player was and if I had seen him. I said, "No, I have not, but I don't want to waste precious time." I insisted Dhoni be given a chance and his performances in the next twelve months made sure we could go ahead and pick him in the senior India team for the Challengers in February 2005.'

Ganguly played and captained this tournament and made sure Dhoni was in his team as batsman-wicketkeeper. 'In a match against India B, a team that had an in-form Ashish Nehra as the frontline seamer, Dhoni scored a blistering 100, even hitting Nehra to the roof of the Wankhede Stadium. There was no doubt he was a special talent and it was only a matter of time before he played for India. Captaining him, I could sense he was different and was clear that he should not change his style. I am glad he has done justice to his potential for India.'

If it was Dhoni in 2004–05, it was Sehwag, yet another match-winner for India, who came of age in 2001. It was in Sri Lanka, in 2001, that Ganguly first went to Sehwag and asked him to open the batting in one-day cricket. This was ahead of the last group-stage clash against New Zealand in the tri-series, a tournament which India could hope to win only after defeating New Zealand and sealing a spot in the finals. With Tendulkar sitting out with an injury, Ganguly decided it was time to do what he had been thinking of for a fairly long time. Sehwag, who had a modest start to his career, had scored 169 runs at an average of 15.36 in the 14 ODIs he had played since his debut in 1999 and had, therefore, reacted to Ganguly's proposal with reluctance. He was apprehensive about facing the new ball and, more pertinently, scared of failure. That's where Ganguly came in. As captain, he assured Sehwag a fair run at the top and also said that in case Sehwag was unsuccessful as an opener, it was his responsibility to give him a go in the middle-order. This meant Sehwag could bat at the top with freedom and without having to think of his position in the side. Ganguly, who wielded serious authority as captain, could indeed do what he had said. The result was immediately evident when Sehwag went out to open with Ganguly in this important clash. Smashing a 70-ball 100, this innings marked the arrival of Virender Sehwag, the next big-batting star for India. Hammering a boundary off the second ball he faced, Sehwag was never circumspect during his innings. Having conceived and executed the plan to perfection, the decision to open with Sehwag gave captain Ganguly a lot of satisfaction.

'He played a rank bad shot in the final and I was very upset with him. We lost the final to Sri Lanka and the next morning he came to see me at 5.30 a.m. before he left for the airport on his way back to Delhi. I was in no mood to talk to him and said I will call him later. He needed to know his captain was not pleased with the way he batted in the final,' Ganguly quips just as the phone starts buzzing. He looks at the caller and says to me that he has to take it. As I do my best to focus on my notes, I hear him speak on the Lodha Committee reforms and something to do with the next BCCI Special General Meeting (SGM).

As he looks at me at the end of the call, I know I have temporarily lost him. He is fidgety and is invested in a WhatsApp message he has received. 'Every single day I come home at 10 p.m., you know,' he says with a slight shake of the head. 'Administration drains you.'

'So, will you say it was easier being captain of India?' I ask, desperate to get him back to Sehwag.

'Oh, absolutely,' he says and goes on to add, 'I had the most dedicated bunch of boys one could ask for.'

'Sehwag, for example was a gem. He had no fear, you know, and that was his biggest asset. That's what prompted me to think he will make a fine Test opener if persisted with.'

Ganguly, to my relief, is back where I want him to be.

By his own admission, his mind had already started to tick in Sri Lanka at the time of the tri-series final. The Indian team was due to travel to South Africa towards the close of 2001, and the mediocre performance of the Indian openers in the tour further strengthened his resolve. Sehwag was being wasted in the middle-order in Test cricket, Ganguly realized. He was one who could win you matches and ought to be asked to open the batting.

'On his day, he will get me 80 off the first 10 overs. That's all I wanted of him. He would not allow the bowlers to dictate to him at the start of the match, and if he survived the initial few overs, he would get me runs at a blistering pace and set the game up for the team. At the time, [Matthew] Hayden and [Justin] Langer were redefining Test-match-batting for Australia, scoring at over four runs an over. We needed to do something similar to be successful overseas. Just trying to block and survive the new ball wasn't going to work, and I was determined to experiment with Sehwag at the top.'

Ganguly went to Delhi upon his return to India and met up with his opening partner-to-be in ODI cricket and mentioned the plan to him. He wanted to take Sehwag into confidence before announcing the plan to the world. Sehwag, understandably, was apprehensive. After all, this was Test cricket being talked about. The first hour always belonged to the bowlers and, more so, in England. Add the constant presence of multiple slip fielders, coupled with the conditions on offer, and opening in Test cricket was something Sehwag had not thought of in his wildest imagination. However, his captain had already made up his mind about wanting Sehwag to open in English conditions against the swinging ball.

'I could sense he was uneasy, not that I expected anything different. Opening the batting in Test cricket wasn't easy and he had never opened in a first-class match. I told him he had to do it. I reminded him he was apprehensive when I had suggested he bat up the order in one-day cricket. Opening the batting in the 50-over game had made him a very different player, and I was confident it will be the same in Test cricket.'

Sehwag, who shared a great rapport with Ganguly, opened up to his captain and confessed that he feared getting dropped on account of not being able to score runs at the top of the order. At a time when he was trying to establish himself as a Test player, Sehwag felt this move could have an adverse impact on his career. Ganguly, however, assured him that he will be given a run in the middle order before he was left out and suggested he open the batting without having any inhibitions about the outcome.

'I was backing my instincts. The more I thought about what our real problem was, the more I was convinced we needed to lay a claim to the game on day one itself. And it was only possible with someone like Sehwag at the top of the order. I knew it was an experiment but, in my mind, it was a punt with a real chance of success. Sehwag had exceptional hand-eye coordination and was not scared to go out and face up to any bowler in any condition. He was exactly the kind of player I needed for the challenge.'

When I ask Sehwag about this conversation, he is characteristically tongue-in-cheek. 'Sourav said to me I was successful as an opener in 50-over cricket and could have similar success in Test cricket. I thought to myself, he and Sachin had much more success than anyone in history opening the batting in 50-over cricket; then why on earth was I being singled out! Why don't they open the batting in Test cricket also and leave me to bat in the middle order? But he was my captain and I could never say it to him,' Viru says, bursting out laughing.

Having spoken to Sehwag, Ganguly discussed the move with team coach John Wright and it was decided that the experiment would be tried out in England. Against a bowling attack that featured the likes of Matthew Hoggard, Steve Harmison, and Andrew Flintoff, it was a gamble, and Sehwag with a 96-ball 84 at Lord's, justified the decision in his very first innings as opener. He followed up the Lord's half-century with a first-innings hundred in Nottingham in the second Test. Ganguly's insistence on Sehwag assuming the opener's role was proving to be a risk every bit worth taking.

Sehwag—more than Hayden and Langer—subsequently went on to redefine the art of opening the batting in Tests and played a stellar role in leading India to the pole position for the first time ever in 2009. His innings of 195 against Australia at the MCG on day one of the Boxing Day Test in 2003 will always rank as one of the best innings played by a visiting player on Australian soil. Suffice to say, Sehwag, the opener, turned out to be one of the biggest match-winners for India between 2002 and 2009.

Ganguly forever believed that India's strength was spin bowling both at home and overseas. He was always keen on playing Harbhajan and Kumble in tandem if the opportunity presented itself. Playing two spinners prompted him to bat first on a green pitch at Headingley in August 2002, a decision that would give his spinners a crack at England in the second innings. He was backing his batsmen to step up and put up a challenging score in difficult conditions and set up the game for the bowling unit. It was aggressive captaincy and a departure from what Indian captains were used to doing on foreign soil.

'I must tell you, Ian Botham looked at me with disbelief at the toss when I announced my decision to bat first. He couldn't come to terms with the decision! Thankfully for me, Rahul played exceptionally well and then both Sachin and I followed up with hundreds to bat England out of the game. Each of the bowlers then did the job for us, with Anil and Harbhajan sharing eleven wickets between them. This win will always rank as one of our best wins in England,' Ganguly asserts.

The Test series was preceded by an emphatic win in the NatWest tri-series against England and Sri Lanka and yet again the architects were two youngsters Ganguly was instrumental in getting into the team—Yuvraj Singh and Mohammad Kaif.

He had first heard of a very young Yuvraj Singh from former India player Ashok Malhotra. Ashok had seen serious promise in Yuvraj and promptly informed Ganguly about this talented youngster from Punjab. Ganguly, in the absence of a match at Eden Gardens, flew to Delhi to see Yuvraj bat to get a sense of how good he was.

'What I saw impressed me a lot. He had this free flow of the bat and could hit the ball a long way. I was seeing the answer to my middle-order woes in the one-day game. Yes, he was young and not a finished product yet, but he was good enough to play international cricket. We picked him for the second edition of the ICC KnockOut Trophy in Nairobi in 2000 and he started his career with a sensational innings of 84 against Australia that knocked the world champions out of the tournament.'

In the NatWest tri-series final, Yuvraj and Kaif stitched together a superlative rearguard 121-run sixth-wicket partnership to clinch a thriller at Lord's. Sensing something incredible was unfolding, most Indian players refused to move from their positions in the dressing room through the innings. No one left the room for even a bio break and it was only after the match was won did normalcy resume. What emerged as a lasting image from among the euphoric celebratory moments that ensued had the captain at centre stage. To commemorate the occasion, Ganguly did something that has since made him a part of Lord's folklore. A traditionalist of sorts, belonging to a conservative upper-class Kolkata family, it was unthinkable to see Ganguly take off his shirt and wave it like a torch standing bare-chested on the Lord's balcony. Yes, it was done in response to what Andrew Flintoff had done in Mumbai a year earlier, but that Ganguly, a soft-spoken Bengali, could do what he did was in itself a statement of what this team was capable of. This was a team that wasn't going to be constrained by traditional values and ideas and was willing to express itself anywhere in the world. Ganguly, with shirt in hand, exposing the many threads he wears round his neck for religious reasons, presented a peculiar paradox. Here was a typical god-fearing Bengali, who was willing to shed all his conservatism to convey to the world that this was a very different Indian team that he was leading, one that was willing to give it back to the opposition if there was provocation.

Ganguly, it must be said, did not have the quintessential sportsman's physique in 2002. He wasn't showing off his six-pack. He wasn't a Virat Kohli who spent hours in the gym working on his body. Yet in that one moment of ecstasy, when Kaif and Zaheer completed the second run clinching the two-wicket win for India in the final over, he ripped open his shirt and started waving it for a good 20 seconds, much to the shock of all Marylebone Cricket Club (MCC) members present. Here was an Indian captain who, in a sense, was subverting everything that Lord's stood for. And what is important is that he did so knowingly. He was aware it was the Lord's balcony. He was aware cameras were on him and, in hindsight, he would never do it again, something he says time and again. But this rather outrageous gesture went a long way to breaking barriers and giving the Indian team its new-found identity.

'I knew this was coming. We have discussed this many times before, haven't we? Yet something told me you will not leave without asking the NatWest question. Let me make it clear once and for all to you and all the readers: I won't do it ever again. The thing just happened and I am embarrassed to see the picture each time it is shown on television. Trust me, a bare-chested Sourav Ganguly at the

Lord's balcony isn't how I like to see or imagine myself. You all call it iconic. I don't. I know it has become a tourist thing at Lord's. People come to see where Ganguly opened his shirt! Not the most pleasant thing but that's what sport does to you. In that one moment every possible emotion must have flooded my mind. There was relief and ecstasy in winning, recollection of what Andrew Flintoff had done and a vent of frustration of sorts for not having won overseas for a long time. But the man who opened his shirt is not how I want to be remembered in India's cricket history I did also score a few runs at Lord's and have my name in the honours board. It seems you all have conveniently forgotten that side of me!'

Incidentally, his wife Dona loves that Sourav did what he did. 'I think it was great of him to do it and I quite liked it,' says Dona when I ask her the same question. Sourav, left stumped, can just smile.

The trend that started with the NatWest tri-series in England continued at the World Cup, co-hosted by South Africa, Kenya and Zimbabwe, in February–March 2003. Coming at the back of a poor New Zealand series, India suffered a heavy defeat at the hands of Australia, without mounting a challenge. This triggered a serious reaction from fans back home and players' houses were attacked and pelted with stones. Eventually, senior players like Tendulkar had to appeal to fans to keep faith and promised to turn things around in the rest of the tournament.

The defeat to Australia at Centurion, in India's second game of the tournament, acted as a catalyst in getting the team together. What followed was a run of eight straight wins, leading up to make the final. England, Pakistan, New Zealand and Sri Lanka were all beaten. However, much was left in the tank, and it once again took Australia to stop India's run in the final, where Ganguly's team lost by 125 runs.

Despite the loss, the streak of eight wins marked a momentous journey for India in South Africa; the victory against Pakistan at Centurion will forever hold special significance for the team. The ground, as admitted by almost all of the players I spoke to, was full over two hours prior to the start of play. Fans from both sides had made their way to the venue and it contributed to one of the most electrifying atmospheres witnessed at a game of cricket in recent times. Played against the backdrop of the Kargil War, it was, in every sense, more than a game. A kind of nationalist assertion, which we commonly associate with sport these days, typified the contest and every Indian player who played a part in the win, remembers it with fondness.

This is how Tendulkar, star of the show at Centurion, remembers the occasion: 'The first time I was told about this match was exactly a year earlier when some of my friends had mentioned the India–Pakistan encounter at Centurion Park on 1 March 2003. It was a huge game for both teams. The intensity was such that I could not sleep in the last three nights leading up to the game. In my mind, I was continuously rehearsing the shots I would play against the Pakistani fast bowlers. I felt as though I was in the zone I would like myself to be in before an encounter like this. The dressing room atmosphere was charged up and every player who played in this match was feeling the tension. If there was ever a match we wanted to win, it was this one. The nation would brook no failure and, [for] many of our fans, this was the final. It really did not matter to them what happened in the rest of the tournament if we managed to beat Pakistan at Centurion.'

India did go on to win the contest and Tendulkar, many will agree, played one of the best innings of his career in this match. Chasing a formidable total, Tendulkar, taking first strike, mounted an unprecedented assault on the likes of Wasim Akram, Shoaib Akhtar and Waqar Younis. While Tendulkar's perspective on the innings is well known and has been documented at length in his autobiography,

Playing It My Way, Shoaib Akhtar, the man at the receiving end of the onslaught, also helps put it in context.

'We had a very good score on the board and each of us were charged up. We knew if we managed to get Tendulkar early, we could have India under pressure. I was bowling really fast and was confident of my ability. But that day was different. Tendulkar, literally, was batting like a man possessed. When I bowled him outside off stump, he just dispatched me over third man for six. As a bowler, you tend to wonder, "Hey what is this man doing! How did he do that?" I tried to compensate and bowled on middle and leg stump and this time he whipped me to the on-side for another boundary. I exchanged a glance with the captain, for there was little I could do as a bowler. My only option was to bowl full, and this time Tendulkar just pushed at the ball. It was no more than a gentle push but the timing was such the ball went past the mid-on fielder to the boundary. If the world's best was batting like the world's best and more, there's hardly much that you can do.'

With wins against Pakistan, Sri Lanka, New Zealand and England, Ganguly's India had most definitely proven themselves to be capable challengers to Australia for the world title. However, the final was one of the most one-sided contests ever witnessed in the decider of any World Cup. Australia pummelled India to go home with their second consecutive world title.

'We were simply outplayed,' says Ganguly. When I ask why and what went wrong in the game, Ganguly, the quintessential optimist, is candid. 'They were just too good,' he says with a wave of his hand. 'The gap between us and the rest of the teams was this much'—he uses his hands to drive home the parallel—'and the gap between Australia and us was just a little less.' The wound of the 2003 final, it is apparent, is still raw but the result, it must be conceded, followed the expected script. This was the closest Ganguly could get to a world title and Tendulkar, despite being named Man of the Tournament, could hardly celebrate the achievement. The World Cup, the valiant run notwithstanding, was unfinished business—for Tendulkar and the team.

If Ganguly's India came close in South Africa, only to falter at the last hurdle, they had another opportunity to showcase their progress as a team during the year-end tour of Australia. No visiting team had been able to match the Australians in Australia and much to the chagrin of the Indian players, many in the BCCI had written the visiting team off even before they set out on the tour.

'It was a very important tour for us as a team; more so, for me, as captain. We were playing the world's best cricket team and I was determined to leave a mark. I had toured Australia twice before in 1992 and 1999 and each time we had lost rather poorly. In 1999, I had felt good about my batting but was not able to convert starts into big scores. And Australia is one such country where, if you start losing games, it is almost impossible to stem the tide. The players, fans and media, all start getting on top of you and once you're left behind, all you can do is play catch-up.'

The first Test at the Gabba will surely be ranked as captain Ganguly's finest hour. Faced with an Australian first innings total of 323, India, in no time, was reduced to 62 for 3. With Sehwag, Dravid and Tendulkar back in the hut, Ganguly had to stand up to what he professed. He had to play fire with fire. And he did. The harder the Australians came at him, the more positive Ganguly turned in his approach en route to a gritty 144.

'I had no option but to be positive. You had to fight the Australians in their own game and beat them if you wanted to make a statement. Most teams got steamrolled and did not push back when the Australian bowlers came hard. That's what we did all series. In Brisbane, it was Laxman and me, in Adelaide, it was Rahul and Laxman and in Melbourne, it was Sehwag. Finally in Sydney it was Sachin. The entire series we did not take a step back and that's what worked for us.'

Deep Dasgupta, part of the team in Australia and an astute observer of the game, made some interesting observations about this dramatic Indian turnaround in overseas conditions. The team, Deep says, travelled with a very different mindset. They weren't afraid of losing and they weren't afraid of taking risks either. Each time the Australians sledged, the Indians would give it back. At every step, the visitors refused to back down. Ganguly's knock of 144 had a huge catalytic effect on the team and the fact that the Indians managed to eke out a first innings lead at the Gabba was considered a moral victory of sorts. Even after Zaheer Khan pulled out injured, there was no perceived dip in morale on the Indian side. In Adelaide, India's four-wicket victory involved one of India's finest brands of cricket of all time. Australia had ended the first day at 400/5 and there was every reason for India to feel deflated and, perhaps, give up. However, they refused to succumb to pressure and, instead, came back firing on all cylinders the next day. Every player in the team believed they were game for the challenge and even after the Australians had scored 550 plus, their shoulders did not droop.

'This was our series to stand up and be counted. Whatever the Australians got, we knew we could get more. Yes, I wasn't playing but that did not mean I was not involved. Every member of the touring party was involved. It was a collective effort and the win in Adelaide and the Test match in Sydney will always be among my best memories as a Test cricketer,' says Deep.

Dravid, the architect of the victory in Adelaide, played the match of his life, scoring 233 and an unbeaten 72. A fierce competitor all through his career, Dravid played the best cricket of his career in Australia in 2003–04 and, with Tendulkar playing one of his most determined innings in Sydney in the fourth and final Test, this was a series that India should have won. Batting for ten hours, while not playing a single cover drive in an innings of resolute determination, Tendulkar finished the first innings with an unbeaten 241, setting the match up for a likely win for his side. Although a draw eventually meant the series ended in a 1–1 tie—the Australians holding on to ensure their captain, Steve Waugh, did not retire on a losing note—India convincingly emerged the more dominant of the two sides through the four-match series.

The Australia series was followed by a historic run of victories in 2004 in Pakistan, where, for the first time in 50 years, India won both the ODI and Test series. A series that had created unprecedented hype in both the nations, and around the world, witnessed India play committed, aggressive cricket right through. The Indian win, however, was somewhat marred by a public spat between Tendulkar and Dravid, a dispute that resulted from stand-in captain Dravid's decision to declare in Multan when Tendulkar was batting on 194. Tendulkar, miffed at the call, has talked about it fairly openly in his autobiography and elsewhere:

'At tea time, I asked stand-in skipper Rahul Dravid and coach John Wright what the plan was. I was informed that we were looking to give Pakistan an hour to bat and would put them in with 15 overs left on the second day. It was a perfectly sensible plan and I went about my business after tea with this in mind. This meant the ball would be considerably new the following morning and would also allow our fast bowlers to have a go at the Pakistan batsmen in the second afternoon itself.

A little more than half-an-hour into the post tea session, Ramesh Pawar, who was substituting in that game, came in and asked me to accelerate. I even joked with him saying I was aware that we needed quick runs but with the field totally spread out there was only so much we could do. For the non-striker, the field was in and maybe Yuvraj, who was batting with me, could go after the bowling. Thereafter, he [Pawar] came out again in some time and asked me to get my double hundred in that over itself as Rahul had decided to declare. I was batting on 194 and was startled to say the least. Interestingly, Yuvraj was on strike at the start of the over and he blocked the first two balls before picking up two runs off the third ball. He once again blocked the fourth ball and was out the fifth ball. I had not faced a single ball in that over and was awaiting my turn to go for a big shot and get to my double hundred before we declared. Just as I could see Parthiv Patel come out, I saw Rahul gesturing us to go back to the pavilion. He had declared the innings with me batting on 194. I was shocked. Just at the start of the over, I was told that I needed to get to the double hundred quickly and since then I had not faced a single delivery. Yet we had declared the innings with 16 overs still to be played in the day, one more than what we had agreed at tea time. It was day two of the Test match and not day four like it had been in Sydney, a couple of months earlier. Disappointed, I made my way back to the dressing room and could sense that the whole team was shocked at the decision.'

Ganguly, too, was shocked at the decision. When asked if he had a part in the call, he categorically denied any involvement. 'It was not my call. I was not party to the decision and must say Sachin was very disturbed by it. I should also say I was relieved Rahul and Sachin managed to put it past them in Multan itself and there was no residue of the ill-feeling going into the next Test.'

This was a rare occasion in Indian cricket that a disagreement between two stalwarts came up for public discussion. One can only wonder what would have happened if social media, most notably Facebook and Twitter, was around at the time. That this would be trending for days on end is simple enough to conjecture.

With the series win in Pakistan under Ganguly, the process that had started in England with the NatWest Tri series win and the win in Headingley was now complete. India was no longer a team that could be dismissed as poor travellers. Finally, we were competitive overseas.

In conclusion, it must be said that the transformation of the Indian side under Ganguly cannot be treated in isolation. It was part of a larger change in the Indian mindset at the turn of the millennium. In fact, it could be linked to an Indian takeover of world cricket of sorts. Jagmohan Dalmiya, a Marwari businessman, who did not speak the most fluent English, possessed the mojo to take over the reins of the ICC in 1997 and transform cricket's finances overnight. To Dalmiya, it did not matter whether or not he was from Oxbridge or a product of the English public school system. All he knew was to make money for the game at a time when cricket needed it as badly as it ever did. He did not hesitate in making Bangladesh a Full Member of the ICC by according it Test status in 2000 because it enabled India to have one extra vote in the ICC's boardroom and push through the agenda that every third 50-over World Cup should be in the sub-continent. The days of the English and Australian veto were long gone and Ganguly, in many ways, was a product of his times. To him it wasn't a big deal to make Steve Waugh wait for 30 minutes or more at the toss at Eden Gardens in 2001. Yes, the official reason given was that Ganguly had forgotten his blazer in the dressing room. For the record, it wouldn't take someone like me, unfit and out of shape, more than five minutes to walk back and get the blazer! Thirty minutes to fetch the blazer is no more than a excuse. So what if Waugh had to wait? The Indians had been forced to endure many such things in the past. Now, the tables had been turned; roles had been reversed. It was time to give it back to the opposition and it was best if Waugh, Nasser Hussain and the others did not make much fuss about it. Hussain showed his opposite number his shirt number when he reached his century in the NatWest final in July 2002. Ganguly responded by performing his famous bare-chested shirt-waving act at the Lord's balcony. The two remain good friends to this day and Hussain famously has coined the phrase 'Ganguly time' to take a dig at Ganguly's sense of punctuality! English administrative staff had complained to Dalmiya in January 2002 that they did not have enough new practice balls ahead of their match at Eden Gardens. All Dalmiya did was order his men to give them some more old used balls. Take it or leave it was the message.

This India was radically different to the one that would consider Lord's the Mecca of cricket and allow MCC stewards to ride roughshod over its players in the name of tradition. The Indian side was fast turning into a globalized, consumer-culture-driven unit where materialism and money was starting to talk, and do so loudly. Ganguly simply played the part of the global spokesperson of this new-look India in 2002 in England. That he wasn't the least bit insecure was evident when he recommended Greg Chappell's name to be the next India coach in 2005. Whether it was Chappell, or anyone else at the helm, Ganguly wasn't overawed. It simply did not matter to him. Rather, he was obsessed with the cult of excellence at the expense of anything required to achieve that sting in the Indian team. That it turned out to be a clash of cultures with Chappell is a different matter altogether. The empire did strike back with Chappell and did gain temporary ascendancy in 2005 but ended up being banished altogether from the Indian cricketscape in April 2007 after a disastrous World Cup campaign in the Caribbean. To this sordid chapter we will next turn.

On Ganguly, however, I will leave the last words to former Australia skipper Michael Clarke. Clarke, one of the best captains of his era, has forever been a Ganguly fan for his aggressive style of conduct on the field. One of Clarke's favourite anecdotes goes thus: Ganguly and Ricky Ponting were out at the toss during one of the matches in India—Clarke doesn't specifically remember which one—and Ponting had the coin in hand. Just as he flipped the coin, Ganguly, if Clarke is to be believed, said, 'Head-Tail'.

'Trust me, mate, that's what Ricky told me,' Clarke says, cracking up. 'Ricky said he couldn't fathom what had happened with Dada having said Head-Tail. [And, apparently it was said at the speed of lightning.] It had taken Ricky a second or two to come to grips with the situation and by that time the coin had come down. Ganguly just picked it up and said to Ricky, "We'll bat" and walked off. India had won the toss and were batting. Ricky did not really know what to do or say and all he did was tell us in the dressing room exactly what happened at the toss.'

With each sentence, Clarke's laughter gets louder and all of us, his auditors keeping him company, can't help but join in. While making every room for exaggeration, this story sums up Ganguly's nous as captain and explains how a very traditional Bengali *bhadralok* (gentleman) transformed Indian cricket forever.

My colleague Rahul Kanwal, one of India's leading journalists, once asked Ganguly if he indeed had said 'Head-Tail'. To Rahul's surprise, Ganguly answered in the affirmative.

CHALLENGING THE CHAPPELL SHENANIGANS

It was all going well for Sourav Ganguly and Indian cricket until the arrival of Greg Chappell. India had beaten world champions Australia at home in 2001, won the NatWest tri-series and a famous Test at Headingley in England in 2002, and had drawn 1–1 in a Test series against Australia on Australian soil in 2003–04, before beating Pakistan in their backyard in March–April 2004. The reversal against Australia, at home in late 2004, and the dip in form in early 2005 notwithstanding, Indian cricket under Ganguly and John Wright was in reasonable health. On the back of some good results, Ganguly was keen to take his team to the next level and Chappell, he felt, was a possible answer to do so. Ganguly and Chappell were good friends and the former had great respect for his understanding of the game. He had even written the foreword to one of his books, *Greg Chappell on Coaching*. A few months ahead of the Indian tour to Australia in December 2003, Ganguly, determined to change India's poor record Down Under, decided to spend time with Chappell to get himself tour-ready. Impressed with Chappell's insights, especially the suggestion that one should not bat expecting bouncers in Australian conditions, Ganguly asked Chappell if he was interested in a long-term role with the Indian team if the opportunity presented itself. Chappell, understandably, was keen. Coaching India was the most high-profile job in world cricket and he was eager to take up the challenge.

'John Wright was at the end of his tenure and had made public his intentions of not seeking an extension. The situation was ripe to get a new coach. Having trained with Greg in Australia, I felt he could take Indian cricket to the next level and recommended him for the job in April 2005,' says Ganguly of a decision he regretted later.

The statement has a note of resignation attached to it. Each time he speaks of Chappell and his stint in India, Ganguly knows he had blundered. A great judge of men had made a serious error in judgement, which could have ended his career. That it did not was partly fate and partly the steel that Ganguly had infused in the Indian team during his period at the helm. It was steel that separated men from the boys and allowed Ganguly to stand up to Chappell when the odds were heavily stacked against him. In this classic manager-versus-superstar clash, Ganguly did have a final ace up his sleeve—his ability, backed up by self-belief on the 22 yards with a bat in hand. Unlike David Beckham, whose football skills had deteriorated when the Manchester United boss, Alex Ferguson, wanted him out of the team, Ganguly could still go back to the basics and come back stronger in a hostile environment such as South Africa against the likes of Shaun Pollock, Makhaya Ntini, Jacques Kallis and others. Ganguly's life is classic Bollywood—an ageing legend who knew he had a few final hurrahs left. A biopic if the directors in Bollywood have the time to read the next few pages of unadulterated drama.

With Jagmohan Dalmiya still in power at the BCCI, and given Ganguly's proximity to the BCCI and former ICC boss, it was no surprise that Greg Chappell emerged as the top man for the job based on Ganguly's recommendation in April 2005. Other candidates in the fray included Tom Moody, Mohinder Amarnath, Dav Whatmore and John Emburey. A veteran cricket administrator still associated with the game confirmed to me that some senior players like Rahul Dravid preferred Moody to Chappell. 'When we asked Rahul who he thought was best-suited for the job, he mentioned Tom Moody but went on to add that eventually it was Ganguly who would take the call,' says one of Indian cricket's perennial go-to men. It is quite an irony that Ganguly, who was instrumental in getting Chappell to India, ended up having a bitter fallout with him, while Dravid, who had initially preferred Moody over Chappell, ended up becoming close to the Australian.

At the time when Chappell assumed charge as head coach in July 2005, Ganguly was serving a six-match ban imposed on him in March 2005 for slow over rate. Dravid was interim captain and it was for the Zimbabwe tour in September 2005 that Ganguly was once again given back the reins of Indian cricket.

'Something from the very start of the tour was not right. I don't know what had happened but something definitely had gone amiss. I think some people who Greg had become close to may have told him that with me around, he would never have his way in Indian cricket and that may have triggered a reaction. Whatever it may have been, he was not the same Chappell in Zimbabwe compared to the one who had helped me get ready for the Australian tour in December 2003,' Ganguly states.

While Chappell's side of the story is out in the public domain, and his issues with Ganguly mentioned in detail in a confidential email to the BCCI written at the end of the Zimbabwe tour—a story broken by senior journalist Gautam Bhattacharya—Ganguly's side of the story has never been written about fully. 'It will again create unnecessary controversy,' he says when I ask him to clear the air on Greg Chappell. Readers, I insist, need to know what exactly happened and a definitive history of Indian cricket must document what had gone on between him and Chappell. With Ganguly, it is never easy to understand if he is in agreement but gradually, after some more cajoling over tea and some excellent *bhujia*, which Dona, his wife, has sent down to us, he starts giving me his side of the story.

'It all started with a side game in Zimbabwe against the Zimbabwe A team. I was hurting from a tennis elbow and the injury was starting to bother me yet again while I was batting in this match. It was an inconsequential side game and the best thing for me was to walk out and nurse the injury. Greg wasn't around in the dressing room when I had retired hurt and it was only after a while that he came back to ask what had happened to me. I said I had a painful elbow and with a Test match coming up did not want to risk playing on. He was unrelenting. To my surprise, he insisted I go out and bat and I was forced to tell him I wouldn't because I was in good touch and did not want to jeopardize my chances of playing the Test match. I even said that the pain notwithstanding, I was sure to turn up for the Test.'

Ganguly's version stands in contrast to Chappell's portrayal of events in the practice game in Mutare. In his email to the BCCI written at the end of the tour, Chappell talks about this match at length. 'Sourav batted in the match against Zimbabwe "A" team in the game in Mutare. I am not sure of the exact timing of events because I was in the nets with other players when Sourav went in to bat, but the new ball had either just been taken or was imminent when I saw Sourav walking from the field holding his right arm. I assumed he had been hit and made my way to the players' area where Sourav was receiving treatment from the team physiotherapist, John Gloster.

'When I enquired as to what had happened Sourav said he had felt a click in his elbow as he played a ball through the leg side and that he thought he should have it investigated. Sourav had complained of pain to his elbow at various stages of the one-day series, but he had resisted having any comprehensive investigation done and, from my observation, had been spasmodic in his treatment habits, often not using ice-packs for the arm that had been prepared for him by John Gloster. I suggested, as had John Gloster, that we get some further tests done immediately. Sourav rejected these suggestions and said he would be "fine". When I queried what he meant by "fine" he said he would be fit for the Test match. I then queried why then was it necessary to be off the field now. He said that he was just taking "precautions".

'Rather than make a scene with other players and officials in the vicinity, I decided to leave the matter and observe what Sourav would do from that point on. After the loss of Mohammad Kaif, Yuvraj [Singh] and [Murali] Karthik to the new ball, Sourav returned to the crease with the ball now around 20 overs old. He struggled for runs against a modest attack and eventually threw his wicket away trying to hit one of the spinners over the leg side.

'The next day I enquired with a number of the players as to what they had thought of Sourav's retirement. The universal response was that it was "just Sourav" as they recounted a list of times when Sourav had suffered from mystery injuries that usually disappeared as quickly as they had come. This disturbed me because it confirmed for me that he was in a fragile state of mind and it was affecting the mental state of other members of the squad . . . When we arrived in Bulawayo, I decided I needed to ask Sourav if he had over-played the injury to avoid the danger period of the new ball as it had appeared to me and others within the touring party that he had protected himself at the expense of others. He denied the suggestion and asked why he would do that against such a modest attack. I said that he was the only one who could answer that question,' Chappell writes.

He goes on to conclude, 'I was so concerned about the effect that Sourav's actions were having on the team that I decided I could not wait until selection meeting that evening to inform him that I had serious doubts about picking him for the first Test. I explained that, in my view, I felt we had to pick Kaif and Yuvraj following their good form in the one-day series and that Sehwag, Gambhir, Laxman and Dravid had to play. He said that his record was better than Kaif and Yuvraj and that they had not proved themselves in Test cricket. I countered with the argument that they had to be given a chance to prove themselves on a consistent basis or we would never know. I also said that their form demanded that they be selected now.'

In Sourav's' version, however, the discussion was never restricted to him or his place in the Test team. 'Greg came to me one evening and showed me a team he had picked for the Test match. Some key players were not in his playing XI and I was a little taken aback at what he was trying to do. I rejected his suggestions and said to him clearly that the people he wanted out had done great things for Indian cricket while he had just been there for three months. He needed to spend more time to fully understand the situation before he started taking tough calls. He, it was clear to me, was in a hurry to make the team "Greg Chappell's team". The problem with some coaches is that they come with a preconceived notion. They have a pattern in their mind and unless you fit the pattern you are out. These people are very rarely successful and have had to give way soon enough. Good coaches are those who come with a free mind and adapt to the system they are exposed to.'

Chappell, it is known, had asked Sourav to stand down from captaincy two days ahead of the first Test at Bulawayo, a suggestion that was understandably not well received by the Indian skipper. Coming two days before the Test started, it had the potential of impacting team morale. The captain–coach divide was out in public when Ganguly spilled the beans at a press conference during the Test match.

'I got a hundred in the Test match and had batted for nearly six hours. Soon after I was back in the dressing room and was icing my elbow did Greg come and ask me if I had any pain. I said to him how does it matter for I had just scored a hundred. With or without pain, I had done a job for India.'

Angry and frustrated, Ganguly opened up in front of the press when asked if Chappell had asked him to step down ahead of the Test match.

Amitabh Chaudhary, manager of the team in Zimbabwe and BCCI secretary in 2016–17, helped me put the events in sequence. Chaudhary, a career bureaucrat, is one of those BCCI members who is articulate and eloquent. Sitting at the ITC Sonar in Kolkata over coffee, he has a wry smile on his lips when he mentions to me, 'It is impossible to forget the tale of events in Zimbabwe in 2005. I remember the whole thing frame by frame and can still visualize every little detail. I was sitting in the dressing room with my feet up on the balcony, writing something when the team was out practising. That's when I could see Sourav come into the dressing room,' Chaudhary says.

He did not make much of it because players, every now and then, would come to the changing room to do minor things. In this instance, however, Ganguly stayed back for an inordinately long period of time and only because of that did Chaudhary become curious. 'I went back and asked Sourav what had happened. He was leaning on the glass front overlooking the ground and had a look of shock on his face.

'"The coach tells me I don't have a place in the playing XI," Sourav told me. I wasn't expecting anything like this and it took me a minute or so to understand the significance of what he was saying.'

Once he had composed his thoughts Chaudhary suggested to Sourav that the coach had no right to take a call on the captain and this was not something within his remit. Thereafter, he also suggested to Ganguly that it was best to take vice-captain Dravid into confidence on the whole issue and figure out where he stood on it.

'Sourav agreed, and I went out to the field to attract Rahul's attention. When Rahul met my eye, I indicated to him that we needed to have a word and it wasn't possible on the ground. Rahul and I walked back to the dressing room and I asked Sourav to tell Rahul exactly what Greg was suggesting. And once Sourav had done so, I mentioned to Rahul that this was not something Greg could or should have said and it was beyond his jurisdiction. He was not in a position to change the captain or vice-captain in the middle of the tour.'

Dravid, Chaudhary confirmed, agreed with his view and it was decided that the manager would speak to the coach and diffuse the situation.

'When I spoke to Greg, he did confirm to me that he had suggested to Sourav exactly what had been reported to me. He was holding his ground till I informed him that he was not the one to take this call. I also said to him that Sourav continued to be captain and will indeed play in the Test match.'

In Chaudhary's version, it was after a couple of hours that Chappell saw sense in what was being said and resigned himself to the situation. He even apologized to Ganguly and Dravid and the matter, Chaudhary was confident, was dead and buried.

'The dressing room was one with a transparent glass front and you could see everything from outside. The Indian media had seen us talking and whispers had started about what could possibly be the subject of conversation. Why should the manager talk to the captain and the vice-captain when the team was out practising? But with captain, vice-captain and now Greg all in sync, I was confident the matter was over.'

Clearly, it wasn't and snowballed into a major controversy once the tour was over and Chappell's email to the BCCI was out in the public domain.

Before I go to Sourav's response on the Chappell email, it is important to state once and for all that the email wasn't leaked. It was a superb newsbreak and Gautam Bhattacharya deserves credit for breaking the story. How he managed to do it has remained a secret for a decade and it was after much prodding that he agreed to explain his side of the story.

'That not all was well between Sourav and Chappell was known to a number of us in the media. If I remember right there was also an agency copy on the brewing misunderstanding between the two,' says Gautam when I sit him down on the issue. 'It was only natural that I would want to probe the matter further. And that's how I got the story. It was a tip-off from Zimbabwe and I can tell you it was a player who let out the secret to a source that Chappell had written this email against Sourav [Gautam wouldn't reveal the name of the player and I must say I respect his decision not to]. And I must also tell you that the very same fact was corroborated to me by another source associated with the team in Zimbabwe. The significance of the story was such that I just could not go ahead and do it without getting it confirmed by the BCCI. I clearly remember there was a BCCI meeting at the Taj Bengal Hotel in Kolkata the next day and the hotel lobby was full of journalists. I could not go to Dalmiya because if he requested me not to do the story, I would find it impossible to go ahead, given the nature of our relationship. So Dalmiya as a possible source was out. I finally got my opportunity, believe it or not, in the washroom of the Taj Bengal when Ranbir Mahendra and I were the only two people there. To be honest I had followed Ranbir to the washroom and like a journalist often does innocuously asked him if this email was likely to become a major thorn for the BCCI. Mahendra, to my relief I must say, confirmed the story and, in fact, added to my understanding and gave me a few more points alluded to by Chappell in the email. My story was right and all I needed now was further meat. I then approached Gautam Dasgupta, senior CAB official and who has wrongly been

maligned all these years for giving me the story. Dasgupta was
startled to know I had prior knowledge of the email and, in fact,
repeatedly requested me not to write anything. He also asked me
to speak to Dalmiya once before I decided to publish anything
on the issue. To set records straight let me also tell you, Dasgupta
called me as late as midnight that day and urged me not to publish
anything about the Chappell email. I feel bad when he is picked out
by people as my possible mole for he was the one who did his best
to stop the story from getting published. Once I had the details of
the story in place, I called Sourav in Zimbabwe and mentioned the
email to him. To my complete surprise he mentioned to me that he
was aware of it. I was startled to say the least. Sourav informed me
that it was Virender Sehwag who had notified him about the email
having read it while he was on his way to practice at Harare after
taking a bio break. How Sehwag had managed to see it, however,
I don't know. Nor did Sourav tell me about it. What I do know is
Sourav knew about the email and was fully aware of its contents.
As a result I asked Sourav to react to my story but he refused to
do so. All he said was if Chappell wanted all of this to be played
out in the media it was his choice, but Sourav would not want to
discuss such confidential issues in the public domain. He preferred
to give his point of view to the BCCI when he was asked to do so.
I respected his stance and went ahead with the story the next day
and must say it will forever rank as one of the biggest stories I have
done in my journalistic career,' recounted Gautam.

I did ask Sehwag for a corroboration of Gautam's version of
events and he did confirm that he had seen Greg's email, or at least
a part of it, and had reported back to Sourav. Sehwag was on his
way back to the dressing room for a bio break when Chappell was
writing the email to the BCCI. And when Sehwag came out of the
washroom and sat next to Chappell for a few minutes before going
back to the ground did he notice what was being written.

It was undoubtedly a huge story and took the cricket world by storm once it was published.

Reacting very strongly to some things Chappell had mentioned in his email, Ganguly goes on to tell me, 'He mentioned in the mail that I had this habit of pacing up and down the dressing room and it had the effect of unnerving the rest of the players. As a matter of fact, V.V.S. had this habit of dozing off in the dressing room before he batted. That's how he has always been. In Zimbabwe, Greg literally shouted at him one day as he was dozing off. He said V.V.S. was lazy and India was suffering as a result. Laxman was stunned at the rebuke and most in the dressing room felt uncomfortable in seeing a senior player being spoken to like this. Things were going from bad to worse.'

That Laxman wasn't treated well by Chappell has also been corroborated by Sachin Tendulkar. 'On one occasion, he asked V.V.S. Laxman to consider opening the batting. Laxman politely turned him down, saying he had tried opening in the first half of his career because he was confused, but now he was settled in the middle-order and Greg should consider him as a middle-order batsman. Greg's response stunned us all. He told Laxman he should be careful, because making a comeback at the age of 32 might not be easy. In fact, I later found out that Greg had spoken to the BCCI about the need to remove the senior players.'

The temporary truce arrived at in Zimbabwe did not last long. The leaked email meant the captain–coach spat caused the BCCI more embarrassment as the team returned to India. In an attempt at damage control, the BCCI summoned the two to a meeting in Mumbai attended by the top management and three of India's former captains: Srinivas Venkatraghavan, Sunil Gavaskar and Ravi Shastri.

'We were asked to bury the differences and move on. That was the best thing for Indian cricket under the circumstances. Greg wanted to see me for a personal chat at the end of the meeting but I refused. I was angry at what he had done and for having embarrassed us both. Bringing out dressing room talk in public wasn't the best thing for team morale and that's what had happened. I said as much to him and informed him that I would see him in a few days and it was best I had a little time to myself. That meeting, however, did not take place as I was not picked for the forthcoming ODI series against Sri Lanka on grounds that I had not fully recovered from the elbow injury,' Ganguly says while describing the completely unexpected turn of events.

The pain in the elbow had not fully gone away and Ganguly decided to skip the Challenger Series ahead of the next ODI contest against Sri Lanka. To his surprise, he was not picked despite being India's most successful ODI player in the nine years from 1996–2005. 'I called Greg to ask why I had not been picked and was told I had to first prove my fitness and only then could I make a comeback to the team. He said I had missed the Challenger Series and he was not clear if I was fully fit. It was surprising because the Challenger had never been looked upon as a selection trial. I had scored more ODI runs than anyone in the team in the last few years and it was a shock to see my name not in the list. It was the first time I felt Greg was trying to end my career. At 33, I knew I had years of cricket left in me and immediately went back to playing domestic cricket to prove my fitness. I can also tell you that I was angry at what was happening. More because I felt helpless. One day I was so angry that I just went to Eden Gardens and started running. I eventually stopped after doing 21 laps of the Eden Gardens which will be at least ten kilometres. I had no idea I had run 21 laps and only realized when someone pointed it out to me.'

Ganguly did reasonably well against a strong North Zone attack and got a hundred. In fact, on 30 November, when the Indian team was playing South Africa in an ODI in Kolkata, he was away in Maharashtra playing domestic cricket. He scored 159 after picking up

5/75 but it wasn't considered good enough for a spot on the team that was to tour Pakistan. Jagmohan Dalmiya, Ganguly's patron and backer in the BCCI, had lost the BCCI elections to Maharashtra strongman Sharad Pawar and there was more at play than simple cricketing ability.

Though Ganguly was eventually picked for the Pakistan tour at the back of some hectic behind-the-scenes parleying within the BCCI—including a meeting with the newly elected BCCI president Pawar, who had beaten the Dalmiya camp's Ranbir Mahendra in the elections—he did not get too many opportunities in Pakistan to prove Chappell wrong. Rather, what the country remembers is a hostile conversation between Ganguly, Dravid and Chappell on the morning of the first Test at Lahore—a conversation in which Ganguly was seen animatedly arguing his point of view. 'In Pakistan, the talk was about opening the batting. Greg had made it clear to me that Rahul was to bat at number three, Sachin at four, Laxman at five and Yuvraj at six. The opening slot was vacant and I was told that was the only spot available. I was more than happy to take up the slot and the challenge. On the morning of the first Test, I had an argument with Rahul on this, which, we did not know, was being shown on television.' Ganguly informed Dravid there was absolutely no need to change the batting order for him and that he was happy to open the innings. He had opened the innings in one-day cricket and it had changed his career forever. 'I believed I could get runs opening the batting in Test cricket and there was no need for the team to make an adjustment in trying to accommodate me in the middle.' Dravid, however, was adamant it wasn't the best thing to do and would send the wrong signal that he was forcing Ganguly to open on his return to the team. He eventually announced his decision to open the innings himself with Ganguly batting at number five. 'Greg did not say much and concurred with Rahul that he should open and I would go in at number five.'

Despite being included in the team for the first Test, Ganguly was not required to bat, with the match meandering to a dull draw. Sehwag stole the headlines with a blazing 254 with Dravid scoring 128 not out. Ganguly was left out of the side in the second Test with India opting to play an additional bowler and was eventually brought back for the third and deciding Test match in Karachi. In a match India lost rather tamely, Ganguly did not do too badly, scoring 34 and 37 in the two innings and picking up the wicket of opener Salman Butt in Pakistan's second innings. As proof of his statement—'Greg Chappell did not want me to continue'—he was dropped subsequently for the ODI series against England and the tour of the West Indies only to make a comeback for the year-end Test series in South Africa. In the interim, India had won ODI contests against Pakistan, England and the West Indies but were pummelled in South Africa 5–0. And while they beat the West Indies away from home in the Test series—only for the second time in India's history—it was largely owing to the individual brilliance of captain Dravid. In difficult circumstances, Dravid led from the front in Jamaica with a gritty 81 and later 68 in two innings in a relatively low-scoring game.

Unceremoniously booted out of the team, Ganguly spent the whole time pushing himself and scoring runs and picking wickets in domestic cricket eyeing one final comeback, if possible. 'I had seriously started to doubt if I would ever again be recalled. Greg did not want me and self-doubt had started to creep in. I knew there was cricket left in me but until I was given an opportunity, there was very little I could do. I pushed myself hard in these months and did all I could to make myself a better player. If I did get an opportunity, I had to make it count.'

The opportunity finally came in the Test series in South Africa in December. However, a very senior photojournalist who had covered Ganguly's career since 1996, called him and asked him not to go to

South Africa. He was sceptical of Ganguly's chances of success and said South Africa had the best fast bowling attack in the world and it would not be easy against four fast bowlers. 'I remember saying to him I appreciated his concern but if I had to play a few more years of international cricket, I had to do well in South Africa in difficult conditions. You can't be scared and get away in international cricket. You will soon be exposed and I was not one to run away from this challenge.'

The next few weeks can be labelled as the most interesting phase in the Ganguly-versus-Chappell face-off. The Indian team was in Potchefstroom when Ganguly boarded the flight to South Africa and, on landing, went straight to the ground to join the team practice. 'Greg was cold, not that I expected anything else. It actually worked well for me. I knew it was just me out there in the 22 yards with my bat. I could approach the situation with a very clear mind and must say it helped me become a better player. I had overcome every sense of fear and my mind was free from all clutter. In the practice game, I went in to bat at 69/5 on a wicket that had a very healthy layer of grass and scored a valuable 83.'

There is visible excitement in Ganguly's voice as he talks about this innings. Speaking appreciably faster than at the start of the conversation, he says he felt overjoyed and was eagerly looking forward to playing in the Test match, having got runs under his belt.

Dileep Premchandran, who has closely followed and covered Indian cricket for a decade and more, describes this comeback thus: 'A fellow journalist and I were in Chappell's room at the team hotel. He had opted not to take the team bus to practice, so that he could field a phone call from the [BCCI] . . . Chappell, a man who could talk passionately and at length about the sport he had graced three decades earlier, was clearly on edge. When he did eventually pick up the phone, his responses were almost monosyllabic. When he hung up, he turned to us and said just three words: "He's back."

'The "he" in question was Sourav Ganguly, instrumental in Chappell being chosen as coach, but deposed as captain within a couple of months of him taking over. The Chappell–Ganguly feud was the ugliest Indian cricket had seen, and its after-effects were being felt more than a year later. When Ganguly eventually arrived, in time for a pre-Test series tune-up in Potchefstroom, the two exchanged a handshake as ginger as that which two South African-born English batsmen exchanged after Textgate more than half-a-decade later. Ganguly would go on to be India's leading run-scorer in a 2–1 loss . . .' writes Premchandran.

In the Test match at the Wanderers, Ganguly walked in with the score at 110/4. The top order had been creamed up and the South African fast bowlers were making the best use of the conditions on offer. India badly needed a partnership to remain competitive and Ganguly was the last recognized batsman to go in to bat. The similarities with his debut match were uncanny. In England, in 1996, he was sent in to bat at number three in very difficult circumstances, with the team struggling against the moving ball. One failure and it could all be over for him. Labelled a 'quota' player who had been pushed in at the behest of Dalmiya, Ganguly had to prove himself at the only available opportunity.

In South Africa, he was yet again back to square one. He was no longer the boss who could call the shots. He had made it back to the team against the wishes of the coach and a failure at the Wanderers could mean curtains for his Test career. To everyone's surprise, much like England 1996, he played a solid hand of 51 not out. Against a very good South African pace attack in helpful conditions, this half-century turned out to be a very important innings in the context of the match, which India went on to win by 123 runs. 'Most of my teammates were very happy for me and I must say Greg, too, did come and congratulate [me]. All he said was "I do not know what happened in the last few months was good or bad but welcome."

All I did was smile back at him. Words were not needed,' he says with a wry smile.

India went on to lose the next two Tests and, as Ganguly suggests, 'The team was not in the best mental space. Almost every senior player in the team was unhappy and felt claustrophobic. Players who may have earlier felt that I was the problem element now knew what the reality was. Sachin, Sehwag, Harbhajan, Laxman, Zaheer were all unhappy with Greg and surprised at what he was trying to do. Greg kept telling some of his friends in the media that they had forever overhyped Sachin as god and he was never as good as he was made out to be. It was shocking to hear these stories and what all he was doing. He would get dressing room talk recorded for a documentary being made on him and no player could freely express himself with Greg around.'

That Ganguly had reasons to be concerned was confirmed by Harbhajan Singh. '*Main yeh nahi janta ki woh kyun aaya tha* [I'm not sure why he came to India]. Our cricket did not move forward under him. Rather, we went back by a few years as a result of all he did to Indian cricket. He instilled a fear factor among the boys and no one was comfortable. He wanted us out of the team and even targeted Sachin! It was a forgettable period in our cricket,' says Harbhajan while recounting the Chappell era in Indian cricket.

Sehwag and Laxman, two other cricketers whom I spoke to in the course of writing this book, had similar things to say about the time. While Sehwag was more aggressive and forthright, much like his social media avatar, Laxman, a measured and composed individual, also had some scathing observations to make about the Australian who had once wanted him out of the team.

Tendulkar, normally soft-spoken and politically correct, was visibly upset and angry each time I brought up the topic of Chappell in the course of co-writing his autobiography, *Playing It My Way*. I remember asking him why Chappell was such a sore point in the course of one of our conversations and for the first few seconds all he could do was stare at me. He was angry and was trying to compose himself before he started speaking again. Tendulkar, as people who know him well will testify, rarely loses his cool and this was one rare occasion. 'Greg had pushed our cricket back by at least four years,' he said and went on with his outburst. 'Someone like Greg should never talk about ethics. He would give out dressing room talk to the media and often got team meetings recorded for his own documentary. I had suggested to the BCCI not to send him with the team to the Caribbean for the 2007 Cricket World Cup. This was based on a premonition it will all end badly for us with him around. It wasn't possible for the BCCI to do so and the campaign ended in a disaster.'

Tendulkar, who was pushed down the batting order with Chappell in charge, was forced to bat at number four in the 2007 World Cup, a campaign that will rank as the worst in India's cricketing history. While it is unfair to blame Chappell alone for the failure, it has to be said that a team which is not in the right mental frame ahead of a big tournament has very little chance of doing well. While the loss to Bangladesh in the tournament-opener was a shocker, India was below par in the knockout game against Sri Lanka and failed to make the second stage of the competition.

What came as a huge surprise to me was Tendulkar saying Chappell had come to his house a few months before the World Cup to ask him to take over the captaincy. This is how the incident has been described in his autobiography: 'Just months before the World Cup, Chappell had come to see me at home and, to my dismay, suggested that I should take over the captaincy from Rahul Dravid. Anjali, who was sitting with me, was equally shocked to hear him say that "together, we could control Indian cricket for years", and that he would help me in taking over the reins of the side. I was surprised to hear the coach not showing the slightest amount of respect for the captain, with cricket's biggest tournament just months away. He stayed for a couple of hours, trying to convince me, before finally leaving.'

Chappell, however, has contested the claim saying, 'During those years, I only ever visited Sachin's home once, and that was with our physio and assistant coach during Sachin's rehabilitation from injury, at least twelve months earlier than what was reported in the book. We enjoyed a pleasant afternoon together but the subject of captaincy was never raised.'

Having known Tendulkar well for a decade-and-a-half and having worked with him on the autobiography for close to four years, I find it hard to believe that Tendulkar would have 'lied' about Chappell and the incident was a complete figment of his imagination, as Chappell claims it was.

Soon after the publication of Sachin's autobiography, Ganguly, in an interview to Rajdeep Sardesai, had this to say: 'In 2005, when I lost my captaincy, the issue was [the] same. And in 2007, just before the World Cup, the issue was [the] same. I really feel sad for Dravid, because it is not right when you have a captain and then you go behind his back and ask or talk to somebody about captaincy. Am sure he did the same thing when I was the captain, he did that with Rahul. It's a very sad situation for anyone and I really feel sorry for Greg Chappell and Indian cricket, that they had to go down to this level.'

Eventually, Chappell was asked to resign from his position as India's coach in the immediate aftermath of the 2007 World Cup disaster. Senior players led by Tendulkar complained to BCCI president Pawar that Chappell wasn't helping the team and fans were fast losing patience. In all honesty, the BCCI had no option but to sack Chappell.

It has now been a decade and more since Greg Chappell's removal as India coach. That he is still bitter about the whole episode and has not been able to forget the humiliation he had to bear is borne out from time to time. Commenting on Anil Kumble's appointment as India's coach in June 2016, Chappell suggested to *The Hindu* in an interview that 'Anil Kumble's appointment is inspired. He [Kumble] was the heart to Rahul Dravid's soul of the Indian teams in which they played with such distinction. If they had been blessed to have been surrounded by other selfless individuals whose only aim was to serve the team, the Indian teams in which they played would have been impossible to beat.'

This was clearly an attempt to indict Ganguly, Tendulkar, Sehwag, Zaheer, Laxman and Harbhajan, players Chappell had issues with and wanted out during his tenure as coach. However, it must also be said that despite his statements in the media, each of which is meant as a veiled defence of sorts, his tenure as coach between 2005 and 2007 will be remembered as a period when egos took centre stage to the detriment of the game.

It can also be argued that in the game Chappell was playing—to take control of Indian cricket—he was always fated to lose. Cricket, unlike football, is not yet ready to accept a manager or coach as the real boss. It is, unlike football, very much a captain's team. It was Ganguly's India that lost to Australia in October 2004. Ganguly's India won in Pakistan in 2004 and beat England at Headingley in 2002. John Wright, who was integral to the success of this team, was always a man in the background. Even for inspired decisions like sending Laxman to bat at number three in the second innings of the Kolkata Test match in March 2001, Wright was never given full credit. It is in the very nature of the game to credit a captain for a decision he takes but to credit the team for a decision inspired by the coach. Chappell, during his period as head coach, tried to change this and paid the price for it. Taking on legends like Tendulkar and Ganguly could never have been easy and it was only a matter of time before Chappell faced the ire of the BCCI. That he did all he did—record dressing room talk for his documentary and speak about Tendulkar to a select few in the media—hastened his dismissal. In a way, Chappell was self-destructive. He was taking on icons like Tendulkar and Ganguly without sound logic backing his reasoning. He wanted to drop Zaheer Khan, who, within months of Chappell's ouster, went on to win India a famous Test series in England under Dravid. Zaheer, for the record, was the Man of the Series. He further targeted Harbhajan, who turned out to be one of the architects of India's win in the World T20 in South Africa in September 2007—a tournament that heralded a revolution of sorts in Indian cricket. Finally, he was against Laxman batting in the middle-order, a position he dominated over the next four years till his retirement in 2012.

It is very rare that Tendulkar speaks with such venom. But when he did in April 2007—with Ganguly, Laxman, Zaheer and Harbhajan all backing him—Chappell was a dead duck.

That other coaches too have had to give way—John Buchanan in 2009 and more recently Anil Kumble in 2017, in slightly different circumstances—proves beyond doubt that in the Indian cricket set-up, the coach is better off leaving the captain to enjoy the limelight with the rest of the players. Speaking out or courting controversy or pushing their own vision, disregarding the captain's, doesn't always work. John Wright, Gary Kirsten and now Ravi Shastri understand this well.

THE CURIOUS CASE OF THE
CAPTAIN-COACH COMBINE

It was sometime in the afternoon on 25 March 2009 that my phone started ringing and refused to stop. It was my mother-in-law's birthday and I, busy with family duties, could not answer at first go. In five minutes, there had been eight missed calls from a particular number, and the moment I called back, a panicky voice said to me from the other end, 'Sir, Sourav has spoken to a rival news channel.'

'What has he said?' I asked. 'Has he said anything of significance? Why do you sound so tense?' Not a word of what I was saying seemed to register with the young reporter at the other end who just kept mumbling, 'Sir, we need Sourav.'

Without any idea of what he had said and in what context, I started calling Ganguly. It was on the fifth or sixth attempt that I finally got through. 'Yes, Boria,' was all he said, in a terse voice. Something did not seem right. Rather than trying to take a chance I asked him where he was. Making conversation on the phone was a risky proposition and I was better off trying to see him and get him to open up. 'At home, but don't tell anyone.' That was all Ganguly said before he disconnected the line. I quickly called the channel's cameraperson and set out for Behala, an hour's commute from my own place in North Kolkata. It was enough time for me to figure out what Ganguly had said and in what context. After making a few calls and looking it up on the Internet, I learnt that Ganguly had been part of a Kolkata Knight Riders (KKR) press conference alongside John Buchanan where, for the first time, a buzz doing the rounds in Kolkata was made public. Ganguly was no longer the captain of the Knight Riders. Buchanan, the KKR head coach, one with a penchant for out-of-the-box ideas, had come up with yet another of his revolutionary thoughts—the multiple-captaincy theory. All he had said at the press meet was that KKR will have multiple captains for the forthcoming IPL season in South Africa and that Ganguly wasn't going to be the sole leader going forward. Buchanan, it was clear, had the backing of the management and Ganguly, once again, was faced with a Greg Chappell-like situation.

Speaking to a few who had attended the presser, I learnt that it had bordered on the bizarre. Buchanan was the one who did all the talking and all Ganguly did, sitting next to him, was look at the ceiling and scratch his face every now and then. He, I was told, looked disinterested, and only when he was asked if he was upset at what was going on did he say with a smile that he was not. This was Ganguly, of course. If he does not agree with you he will just cocoon himself and block you off rather than get into a confrontation. Good or bad, that has been his style over the years. Immediately after the press conference was over, he had come out and said something to a journalist from a rival news network. While I did not know what the comment was, I was aware it was 'Big Breaking News' on the network. When I called the journalist who had spoken to Ganguly, all he said was, 'Dada looked unhappy and frustrated.'

After an hour of wading through mid-afternoon Kolkata traffic— always the worst with schools letting out at multiple locations—I reached Ganguly's house on Biren Roy Road. The security guards at the gate asked me to call him and only then would they let me in. They had seen me a few hundred times but the ritual always remained the same. One had to call Ganguly and only after he instructed the staff at the gate were you allowed in. Ganguly was in a white *kurta* and *pajama*, one of the very few times I have seen him in traditional Indian attire on non-festive days. He had just showered but the look of exhaustion hadn't left him. Even when he smiled and asked if I wanted a cup of tea, it was as if his mind was somewhere else. This wasn't the Ganguly I had been used to seeing; something was definitely wrong. My request for an interview was initially met with reluctance and that was the first sign he was apprehensive. Ganguly has never been one to say no to me for an interview, and it was only after much cajoling that he finally agreed. He asked me to instruct my cameraperson to set up next to the swimming pool at his in-laws' house, which is next door. He walked in close to 15 minutes later and just as we were getting miked-up for the interview, he called me aside saying he needed to speak to me confidentially before he went on air.

'Look, I have been asked not to speak on the captaincy issue,' he said. 'I can't say much at all, for it will only escalate the situation further.' I asked him if he had been consulted before Buchanan addressed the press and he said he hadn't. 'Did you not know what Buchanan was planning to say at the press conference?' I asked again. Clearly, I was pushing him. Once again, the answer was a clear 'No'. This had all the makings of big news: Ganguly saying on camera that he wasn't consulted by Buchanan about his radical multiple-captaincy theory and that he wasn't informed he would no longer be captain and it was only at the press conference that he was made aware of the development. I told Ganguly I needed him to say this on camera. However, he was clear he couldn't. Thereon, I said to him that I would still ask if he had been consulted. All he needed to do was shake his head, to convey that he hadn't. That would be enough of an answer for me. We decided we'd do the same about the captaincy issue and all he needed to give me was a nod of the head. He was hesitant, but agreed eventually. He was smarting, with frustration evident on his face, and needed a way to vent his anger. The interview happened without a hitch and within minutes of being aired, it spread like wildfire. Ganguly fans burnt Buchanan effigies the next day and Kolkata—for a second time after December 2005, when he was dropped from the touring Indian team to Pakistan—was on the boil.

Buchanan, however, was unperturbed. With the IPL moving to South Africa, he was aware he wouldn't have to deal with irate Ganguly fans at Eden Gardens. Taking advantage of the relocation, Buchanan went ahead with his plans of executing the multiple-captaincy theory. In hindsight, Ganguly finds it bemusing. 'None of us knew what was going on,' he says with a chuckle. 'In one of our practice sessions, John had placed Brad Hodge at midwicket, Andy Bichel on top of the sightscreen at one end, he himself was perched on the other end and there was a fourth person standing where deep cover would be. Each of them would follow John's signal and relay it to the on-field captain, Brendon McCullum, in this case, who was to follow the signal and instruct the bowler accordingly. If the signal was a finger next to the ear, it would mean a bouncer and so on. I had never seen anything like this on the cricket field and I wasn't sure if Brendon had either.'

Having spoken to other KKR players, it is clear they were equally confused. Ashok Dinda, the Indian fast bowler, who was one of the successes for KKR in IPL season one, was the most puzzled. On one occasion, when Dinda was walking back to bowl, he saw the captain signal something to him. Interestingly, the bowler, in Buchanan's scheme, had no agency to decide what delivery he would bowl. All he needed to do was follow the coach's signal. Dinda mistakenly assumed that he was being asked to bowl a yorker when Buchanan actually wanted him to bowl a bouncer! He ended up doing the exact opposite of what the coach wanted and was smacked for a boundary.

'It was ridiculous to see what was going on. All of us were being instructed to look at the coach and his support staff spread out all around the ground. And then just follow the signal system which John had devised. It was natural this wouldn't work and the season would end in disaster,' Ganguly says. He goes on to say, 'I actually felt sorry for Brendon. He was a class act and now that he was captain, he could have done wonders to the team. Instead, he looked lost and had no idea what was going on or what he needed to do. The batting order and team composition was also decided by the coach. In one of the games, Brendon literally came running to me, 20 minutes ahead of the start of play, telling me John wanted him and me to open. We ran back to get ready and go out and bat.'

The more Ganguly opens up about what had happened in South Africa in April 2009, the more it seems to me this is his 'I told you so' moment. He had been humiliated and unceremoniously removed from captaincy and the team management had put a system in place that had no place in cricket. Cricket, unlike football, is not a sport where the captain does not have time to think and marshal his resources. Every ball is followed by a gap of nearly 45 seconds, enough time for the captain to gather his thoughts and execute his plans. By trying to make the captain a mere puppet on the field and control things via an invisible remote control, Buchanan made the same mistake that Chappell had committed two years earlier. He ended up alienating the players and the management; the media, too, was scathing in their reportage of Buchanan's calls once it was clear that KKR's season was going from bad to worse with each passing game.

In an article titled 'Why Knight Riders Coach John Boka-known Must Go', Avijit Ghosh wrote in *The Times Of India* on 28 April 2009: 'The seven deadly sins of Kolkata Knight Riders coach

John Boka-known (*boka* means stupid in Bengali) and why he must go: for floating the four-captain theory; It's surely the dumbest theory in the history of cricket. The last thing that a team, which certainly isn't the strongest on paper, needs is man-made confusion and demotivation. But Boka-known's, oops, Buchanan's theory did exactly that. At a time when the team should have been focusing on strategies to synergise its performance and outsmart its opponent, Buchanan's non-theory ensured that KKR's team spirit had taken a free hit before a ball was bowled . . .'

With KKR finishing the season with the wooden spoon courtesy three wins in 14 games with ten losses and one no-result game, Buchanan's fate was sealed even before the season had ended. A disillusioned management was waiting to wield the axe, which was finally done in August 2009. Buchanan was removed as coach of KKR and, with his ouster, the multiple-captaincy theory, which sought to establish the primacy of the coach over the captain, was shunned. KKR started fresh in 2010 and invested in Gautam Gambhir as captain. Once again, it was back to the conventional way that cricket has been played for centuries. Gambhir led KKR to two titles in the next five years, proving once and for all, that in cricket it is the captain who takes the final call, it is the captain who takes credit for the team's success and it is also the captain who is pulled up for failures. Any deviation from the norm is met with disaster, as had happened with Chappell in 2007 and Buchanan in 2009. While Buchanan expressed surprise at his ouster and claimed Shah Rukh Khan, principal owner of the franchise, had promised him five years at the helm, it was no surprise to anyone that Buchanan had to pay the price for his own obstinacy. Trying to impose radical, utopian thinking on the players when most of them weren't in sync was responsible for his downfall.

When Performance Was Not an Index:
The Kumble–Kohli Saga

Many will argue that the Virat Kohli–Anil Kumble saga was very different from the Ganguly–Chappell or Ganguly–Buchanan clashes. People who think so can be deemed both right and wrong. They're right because the Kohli–Kumble acrimony never played out in public in the manner of the previous two flash points and both men behaved with a modicum of maturity till they eventually parted ways on 20 June 2017. Cricket, despite the brewing tension between captain and coach, hardly suffered and India's record in the 2016–17 home season and the 2017 Champions Trophy is testimony to that.

But then, why am I writing about this most recent captain-coach battle in the same breath as Ganguly–Chappell? Did it actually become that bad in a matter of just 12 months? The answer is an overwhelming 'Yes'.

It was a day after the Champions Trophy final on 18 June 2017 that senior BCCI officials, including secretary Amitabh Chaudhary, CEO Rahul Johri and M.V. Sridhar—the then general manager of cricket operations and who passed away in September 2017—met Kumble and Kohli in a London hotel. Incidentally, they first met Kumble alone followed by Kohli, and then Kohli and Kumble together before a final brief meeting with Kumble again. While Kumble, in his meeting with the BCCI, denied talk of any serious rift, Kohli, according to what members present in the meeting confirmed to me, outlined multiple instances of how the relationship had become unworkable. 'It was not like a slugfest or that the two couldn't stand each other; nothing like that. Instead, there were multiple smaller flash points and a clash of two very different philosophies. They are two very different people,' said one of the men present.

The BCCI officials, still keen to diffuse the situation, suggested a joint meeting to both the concerned gentlemen and they agreed. While the meeting was civil, for the entire 50-minute duration the two did not seem to agree on a single point. 'By the end of it we realized it was unworkable. They weren't fighting or anything, but they just did not seem to agree with each other on anything,' said one of the officials. It was an unfortunate situation and, in the interests of Indian cricket, one had to give in. In the final brief meeting with Kumble, all officials expressed their helplessness at not being able to bring the two of them to a common ground. It was at that point when Kumble, who had by then changed hotels and moved to the Tata Group property on Buckingham Road for the ICC CEC meeting, decided to tender his resignation and not board the flight to the West Indies. That he felt let down was borne out from his social media post that evening, stating his reasons to step down from the position of India's head coach and saying that his relation with Virat was 'untenable'.

Kumble, appointed a year earlier with much fanfare, did have the results to show for himself in his stint as head coach. India had not lost a single series under him and, in normal circumstances, it was rather unusual for the fallout to have happened at a time when the team was playing at its best. In two rather lengthy conversations with individuals governing Indian cricket at the time—one over the phone and the other in person upon his return to Mumbai—Kumble is said to have expressed his grievances over two issues. First, he felt let down owing to the fact that the three members of the 2015-formed Cricket Advisory Committee (CAC), comprising Sourav Ganguly, V.V.S. Laxman and Sachin Tendulkar—all three his former India teammates—did not consult him or bother to hear his side of the story. The second reservation was that the CoA and the BCCI top management looking after Indian cricket affairs under the Supreme Court's directives did not care to find out his side of events.

'What could we have done in this situation? The CAC right through the unfolding of the episode was of the opinion that Kumble should be retained if a patch-up [between him and Kohli] was possible. They had even said so in writing to us and we have a copy of the handwritten letter, hastily penned down when they met at the Landmark Hotel on 17 June,' said one of the officials. In fact, the letter, reproduced on the cover, states clearly that the CAC, after meeting Kohli, still felt that Kumble should continue as head coach and suggested to the BCCI that they should try and resolve their differences for the sake of Indian cricket.

This makes it clear that even if Kumble got a hearing from the men in power, there could only be two different variants of the story. The first variant was that there was no rift between the two individuals, which Kumble claimed in his social media post, but which had already been refuted by Kohli in multiple previous conversations with the BCCI. Second was that he was being treated unfairly, and that the BCCI and the CAC were siding with the captain and not the coach. In a system giving precedence to the captain's opinions ahead of everyone else, as it is in India, this will always be the case, as is evident from the Ganguly–Chappell and Ganguly–Buchanan scenarios. As a result, when the situation had turned unworkable over a period of time, Kumble had to give way.

Could the BCCI have chosen Kumble over Kohli and moved on? The answer, in all fairness, is a no-brainer.

But How Did It All Start to Unravel?

While it is known that things soured between captain and coach over a period of time, it is impossible to pinpoint an exact date when it reached a tipping point. This question can only be definitively answered by two people—Kumble and Kohli, and with both choosing to maintain a dignified silence (and rightly so), I have tried to piece together the sequence of events from speaking to members of the CoA and the senior BCCI management who were all in the know.

The flashpoint—as the multiple interviews I have conducted reveal—was reached at Vizag during the second India–England Test match in November 2016. There had already been a case of difference of opinion between the two at Rajkot in the previous Test, which England had dominated before it ended in a draw. India was the team under the gun going into Vizag and there was talk of England repeating the success of 2012. Alastair Cook's England had beaten India in the previous home series in 2012 and that may have added to the pressure felt by both Kohli and Kumble. While a senior BCCI official tells me that it was over a selection matter that the two had a disagreement, others say it was Kumble's habit of repeatedly sending out instructions to the captain on the field that resulted in the initial heartburn. The moot point here, however, is that there were two alpha males in the dressing room, each of whom had achieved a lot in their cricketing careers, and with neither wanting to back down, things reached a deadlock.

While the storm had started brewing at Vizag, it came to the fore at the end of the tenth edition of the IPL, in May 2017, when the CoA met with Kumble in Hyderabad to talk about a possible pay hike for the players and the coach. 'We had no idea how bad it was till then. We had even asked Kumble if he had the confidence of the players while presenting on their behalf. He said he had discussed the details of what he was presenting with the players and, in all fairness, Sanjay Bangar [former India all-rounder and the team's batting coach] and R. Sridhar [the team's fielding coach], who were also present in the meeting agreed with what he said,' revealed a member of the CoA.

It was only when Kumble mentioned an extension of his contract that the CoA suspected something was amiss. 'His existing contract was till the end of the Champions Trophy and there was no reason for him to feel anxious, given India's performance in the last 12 months. Then why is he pushing for an extension?' the official said. That's when it was decided that Kohli would be consulted and his opinion sought regarding the presentation and what was happening between the captain and the coach. The BCCI CEO, Rahul Johri, it has to be said, was already in the know and others like M.V. Sridhar and secretary Amitabh Chaudhary had also heard of the progressively deteriorating relationship. No one, however, had gauged how deep the problem was. Kohli, when consulted, decided to spill the beans. While he conducted himself with utmost dignity, it was learnt that he did make the point that junior players were finding it difficult to express themselves and that the situation was rapidly escalating. Kohli even went to the extent of suggesting that sending Kumble to England with the team for the Champions Trophy should be relooked at, as confirmed by a CoA member. To anyone who may have followed Indian cricket over the past decade-and-a-half, this episode is likely to come across as a reprise of what had happened with Chappell in January 2007 with Tendulkar suggesting to the then BCCI President Sharad Pawar that Chappell's presence in the Caribbean might end up being counterproductive.

'With the team leaving in just a few days, it wasn't possible to appoint someone overnight. It was also not practical to suggest that Anil Kumble does not travel with the team. For the sake of Indian cricket we had to do something and announcing a new search was the best thing to do under the circumstances. We knew the timing wasn't the best but that was the only solution available,' Vinod Rai, the CoA chairman, confirms.

In the meantime, BCCI officials had informally met with Virender Sehwag and asked him if he would consider coaching the senior national team if an opportunity presented itself. 'We had to do something. The situation wasn't going to improve and we did not want a crisis on our hands overnight. I suggested to Secretary Amitabh Chaudhary that we meet Sehwag, who was in Mumbai for a day, and check with him if he would consider applying for the job if the opportunity ever arose. The secretary agreed and we met Viru for an informal chat,' Sridhar, the then general manager, confirmed.

'Yes, we did meet Sehwag,' reiterates Chaudhary over a cup of coffee at his first floor room at the ITC Sonar on 2 August 2017. Busy transcribing the minutes of the SGM held on 26 July, Chaudhary is very clear about the nature of the conversation. 'As you rightly said it was no more than a casual conversation. I spoke to him again on the subject only during the interview. Rather, I hardly spoke and was a mute spectator during the interview process on 10 July,' he concludes.

It was against this backdrop that the Indian team under captain Kohli and coach Kumble landed in England to defend their Champions Trophy title. The search for a new coach was already on and even before India played its first match against Pakistan at Birmingham on 4 June, the names of a few shortlisted candidates were mentioned in the media. Sehwag, notably, was one of them. Others included Tom Moody, Richard Pybus, Lalchand Rajput and Dodda Ganesh.

'The final call,' Rai says, 'was left to the members of the CAC,' and Kumble, as it transpired was still very much the frontrunner.

For the 100-odd Indian journalists present in England for the Champions Trophy, the captain–coach impasse had become a big story, as important, perhaps, as India's on-field title defence. When the BCCI secretary met the media at Edgbaston in Birmingham a little after noon England time on 2 June, half the questions fired at him, unsurprisingly, was on the captain–coach issue. Chaudhary, to his credit, did not look perturbed and was more brazen than usual in an attempt to side-step the truth. As secretary, there was not much else that he could do. The other option, which was to openly admit the problem, would have opened up a Pandora's box and Chaudhary managed the day with bluster and by pleading ignorance.

However, Chaudhary's rage looked inappropriate and misplaced with CoA member Ramachandra Guha submitting his resignation and making public his reasons for doing so within hours of the Edgbaston press meet. In contrast to what Chaudhary wanted the media to believe, Guha's letter, reproduced in full in the media, cited the poor handling of the Kohli–Kumble issue as one of the reasons for his quitting as member of the CoA. Writing on Kumble, Guha stated (fourth point in his letter addressed to CoA Chief Vinod Rai): 'The way in which the contract of Anil Kumble, the current Head Coach of the senior team, has been handled. The Indian team's record this past season has been excellent; and even if the players garner the bulk of the credit, surely the Head Coach and his support staff also get some. In a system based on justice and merit, the Head Coach's term would have been extended. Instead, Kumble was left hanging, and then told the post would be re-advertised afresh.

'Clearly, the issue has been handled in an extremely insensitive and unprofessional manner by the BCCI CEO and the BCCI office-bearers, with the CoA, by its silence and inaction, unfortunately being complicit in this regard. (Recall that the Court Order of 30 January had expressly mandated us to supervise the management of BCCI.) In case due process had to be followed since Kumble's original appointment was only for one year, why was this not done during April and May, when the IPL was on? If indeed the captain and the Head Coach were not getting along, why was this not attended to as soon as the Australia series was over in late March? Why was it left until the last minute, when a major international tournament was imminent, and when the uncertainty would undermine the morale and ability to focus of the coach, the captain and the team? And surely giving senior players the impression that they may have a veto power over the coach is another example of superstar culture gone berserk? Such a veto power is not permitted to any other top level professional team in any other sport in any other country. Already, in a dismaying departure from international norms, current Indian players enjoy a veto power on who can be the members of the commentary team. If it is to be coaches next, then perhaps the selectors and even office-bearers will follow?'

While the timing of Guha's resignation is questionable and raises very similar questions about him, it is not the subject matter of this book. Guha, a respected historian and intellectual, had dropped his bombshell three days before India's first Champions Trophy match in June. Why he couldn't have waited a couple more weeks is a subject matter of conjecture.

Whatever be his reasons (some say it smacks of regional bias), that he was targeting the Indian captain is beyond doubt. It is public knowledge that Harsha Bhogle was removed from Star Sports' commentary panel because of his differences with specific Indian players and, by suggesting that players now have a veto power on the coach issue, Guha's line of attack was clearly directed at Kohli.

In the Kohli vs Kumble tussle, Kohli, it has to be said, was the softer target of attack. A young, confident, aggressive, multi-tattooed twenty-nine-year-old with a successful film-actor girlfriend, pitted against a forty-seven-year-old legend with a baritone voice and reserved demeanour, and Kohli just did not stand a chance. This was more so after India lost the Champions Trophy final to Pakistan with Kohli making little with the bat. The social media outrage on 20 June, calling Kohli selfish, brash and egotistic, was proof which side the wind was blowing. Unfortunately, none of us knew Kohli's side of the story and assumed he was in the wrong. It was assumed that he had mistreated Kumble and he was the one who was trying to bully one of India's greatest ever match-winners. With the BCCI gag in place, he wasn't in a position to speak out and with Guha taking up the cudgel for Kumble—the duo's Bengaluru connection coming to the fore—Kohli was like a young boxer thrown into the ring with his hands tied.

It may well be that in the Kohli–Kumble tussle, neither was in the wrong. As it often happens in marriages, things go wrong even if neither is at fault. Two different human beings with two different philosophies may not agree with each other. And over a period of time, such a relationship can well become untenable. To single out one person and blame him for all problems is unfair. As captain of the team, Kohli had every right to ask for a coach who understood him and his vision. Ultimately, it is *his* team and he is the one to take flak from the media should India do poorly, like it did in the final of the 2017 Champions Trophy. Even under John Wright, it was always Ganguly's team. Under Gary Kirsten; it was M.S. Dhoni's India. That's how the game is and that's what made the BCCI's choice a foregone conclusion, Guha's rant notwithstanding.

However, serious efforts were made to see if a patch-up was possible. 'One of the reasons for disagreement, which players had mentioned to us, was what happened on the night of the BCCI awards ceremony in Bengaluru. One or two of the players tried calling Kumble to check if there was a dress code for the ceremony. Kumble, they mentioned, was not in his room and did not answer the call. They called Kohli thereafter and asked the same question. Kohli's suggestion was not what Kumble had envisaged and when the players came down to the lobby, Kumble asked them to go and change one more time. Kohli was upset but did not say much,' says one official. 'Again, in the Ranchi Test against Australia, there were far too many times that Kumble sent in instructions, which Kohli did not agree with.'

Treated in isolation, issues like these don't appear irresolvable. Rather, these are more in the nature of minor irritants than anything substantial and that's what prompted the CAC to suggest Kumble should continue provided the differences were resolved.

What appeared to be the final straw in the relationship was Kumble's interaction with certain players at the end of the Champions Trophy final. 'Each and every player was feeling down and perhaps it was not the right time to speak out against Jasprit Bumrah for bowling that no-ball. Everyone knew it was a mistake that had proved costly but to remind someone just as the match had finished was not great timing. It shows an issue with man management skills,' mentions a CoA member.

Kumble, almost every official I have spoken to has confirmed, did give Bumrah a chiding for what turned out to be a fated no-ball against Fakhar Zaman. And Bumrah, they say, wasn't the only one who faced the ire of the coach.

All things combined, on 20 June 2017, Kumble's seemingly tumultuous reign as India's coach came to an end. And in a matter of days, the interest shifted to the succession saga, with India slotted to play some of their toughest cricket yet in the next 24 months.

The Return of Ravi Shastri

Ravi Shastri was first bestowed with the responsibility of the Indian team in 2014, at the end of a dismal Test tour of England. India, under M.S. Dhoni and Duncan Fletcher, had capitulated and plummeted to a 1–3 loss after winning a famous Test at Lord's. By the end of the Test series, however, the team was low on morale and the Lord's win seemed a distant past. It appeared that a repeat of the 2011 tour, when India did not win a single match in England for three months, was on the cards. Shastri, to his credit, turned things around in quick time, and in the ODI series that followed, India won 3–1, ending a miserable run in England. He continued in his position as the Indian team director till the end of the World T20 in April 2016, following which the BCCI announced a fresh search for head coach. Shastri was the leading contender for the job until Kumble decided to throw his hat in the ring and, eventually, after a rather acrimonious fallout with Ganguly, Shastri lost out to Kumble in June 2016. The selection of Kumble over Shastri was not bereft of drama and, till the very end, there was uncertainty over the final appointment. In fact, why Ravi Shastri lost out in 2016 is a question that still remains unanswered. That it was because of the intervention of the BCCI top management into the selection process is a very popular rumour.

Whatever the case was in 2016, Shastri came out of the whole thing badly scarred. And this may have been one of the reasons why he did not apply for the job when it was first advertised in May 2017.

He eventually did, in late June 2017, days after the original deadline was over and the BCCI had extended it to ensure a bigger pool of applicants. The extension, the grapevine has it, was done to accommodate Shastri, an overwhelming favourite of captain Kohli and the team.

'I did not fully comprehend the gravity of the situation. To be honest, I did not know it was as bad. And only when I realised that things were beyond repair [between Kohli and Kumble], did I decide to send in my application,' Shastri says, when I quiz him on the issue.

While much was said at the time, it must be mentioned that from the moment Shastri applied for the job, the decision was a foregone conclusion. Yes there was Sehwag and Moody in the fray, but as a CoA member said to me, 'You don't expect us to choose a greenhorn like Sehwag for the Indian team after all the issues with Kohli and Kumble. Besides, Sehwag may have wanted to get his entire team of support staff and not agreed to an extension to Sanjay Bangar and R. Sridhar, which the captain and the team were very keen on.'

I had met Sehwag in Birmingham during the Champions Trophy and it seemed to me that he had thrown his hat in the ring more because the initial approach had come from the BCCI. It wasn't a make-or-break job for him because the coaching job would make him less than half the money he currently makes in his multiple avatars as commentator, news channel expert, columnist and social media influencer. Finally, and most significantly, he has years left ahead of him to get to coaching and a few years away from the game can only do him good.

For Shastri, however, it was an all-or-nothing gamble. Had he not got the job a second time, it would have been disaster for someone of his stature. All of this meant there was heightened media interest in the process with a lot at stake as far as the future of Indian cricket was concerned.

While the three members of the CAC conducted the process in the most fair and transparent manner, Ganguly's differences with Shastri notwithstanding, it must be said that the Kohli factor forever loomed large in the background. It was impossible to completely ignore the wishes of the captain and the team and Kohli's support eventually played a deciding hand in Shastri's favour.

Among the candidates interviewed on 10 July 2017, Moody and Shastri—those present confirmed—impressed the most, with Sehwag not too far behind. The process, which started around 1 p.m. finished around 4 p.m. or so and the announcement was expected by evening. That's when the first surprise was sprung. I was notified by a BCCI official that Ganguly and Laxman, who were both in Mumbai to conduct the interviews with Tendulkar joining in on Skype from London, were getting ready to address the press and the decision was to defer the announcement by a few days. They wanted to meet Kohli on his return from New York and only then would the announcement be made.

It was odd.

Why would the CAC want to consult Kohli when they had already met him twice in England during the Champions Trophy? And what stopped them from getting him on a conference call and closing the matter?

Ganguly and Laxman did address the press conference at 6 p.m., with Johri and Chaudhury sitting in, and announced that they needed to explain to Kohli that a head coach might want his own space and only when all discussions were concluded would the announcement be made.

The reality, however, was different. While Shastri had emerged as the clear consensus candidate, with Kohli's opinion making the biggest difference, the CAC was still in the process of speaking with

Rahul Dravid and Zaheer Khan as possible consultants alongside Shastri. Shastri, too, as it later transpired, had been spoken to about getting Dravid and Zaheer on board.

Within hours of the press conference, however, things changed. At 9.55 p.m. that night an email was sent by Chaudhury to the three members of the CAC and the head of the CoA, suggesting that the delay was giving the BCCI a bad name and it was in the best interests of everyone concerned that the matter be dealt with as soon as possible. Rai was in Singapore and though he had been consulted on the deferral by Ganguly and Laxman, he agreed to the change in plan late that night. Tendulkar, too, responded in the positive, agreeing to a conference call the following day. Rai thereafter went ahead and instructed the secretary and CEO to make sure that the process was closed by the evening of 11 July 2017.

Ganguly, who was in Mumbai for personal work, had no knowledge of the change in plan and, in fact, questioned it openly in an interview with India Today Television. He had not read the mail trail and it had come as a surprise to him. By early afternoon, however, it was clear that India was sure to have a head coach before the day ended. The announcement would have been made by 6 p.m. that evening had Ganguly not boarded a flight from Mumbai to Kolkata. Shastri was the unanimous choice, thanks to Kohli, and by the time Ganguly landed in Kolkata, the CoA and the BCCI were both restless. Within an hour of him landing, a press release was sent out which mentioned that Shastri was the head coach while Dravid was the batting consultant and Zaheer the bowling consultant of the Indian senior team.

In an interview I conducted with him the following day, Shastri, on his way to Wimbledon, welcomed the appointments of the two consultants and said their experience would be invaluable. Finally, all things seemed to have fallen into place.

Shastri, however, was under the impression that Zaheer and Dravid were consultants and would only be with the team for a few days a year. The CAC, however, had other ideas. While Shastri wanted his full time core group in place, the CAC felt Zaheer and Dravid could do the job. Another flashpoint had been reached. Ganguly even mentioned to the media that Zaheer would be with the team for 150 days a year.

Shastri's choice, however, was Bharat Arun, who had been with him in his two years at the helm between 2014 and 2016. This time around, though, Arun was not in the picture till the night of 13 July, when the BCCI, in a second press release, yet again confirmed the appointments of Dravid and Zaheer. That not all was well was evident when the CAC members shot off a strongly worded letter to Rai complaining that their integrity was being doubted in the media when they had done a job pro bono and with utmost integrity and commitment.

Rai, in an attempt at damage control, thanked them in the release and assured everyone that the CAC had done its job to perfection. Under the surface, however, it was a story of frayed tempers and bruised egos. Ravi Shastri had asked for Arun and was given his preferred bowling coach in a meeting with the BCCI on 15 July. The appointment of Arun meant there was a question mark over the role of Zaheer Khan.

Even when Shastri left with the team for Sri Lanka, on 19 July, with Arun, R. Sridhar and Bangar keeping him company, the CoA was trying its best to ensure there was no further misunderstanding between him and the CAC. This attempt, to an extent, was futile. This was more because Vikram Limaye, the CoA member who had resigned on 14 July, stated in an interview with *The Times Of India*: 'Advisory committee's main task was to pick the head coach. The brief given to them was not to pick the support staff. The rest was their recommendation. Ultimately, it is the head coach who should have a say in who his support staff should be. Whether he needs permanent coaches or additional consultants for specific tours or conditions, the head coach can recommend. The head coach is well within his rights on these matters. You cannot decide arbitrarily who the head coach's team should be without the head coach's involvement in that decision.'

If Limaye is right, the question remains: What prompted the BCCI to mention Dravid and Zaheer as consultants in the press release on 11 July in the first place? Did they not know at the time that these names were 'in the nature of recommendations'? As per the the BCCI release: 'The BCCI announces the appointment of Mr Ravi Shastri as the Head Coach, Mr Zaheer Khan as the Bowling Consultant and Mr Rahul Dravid who will be the Overseas Batting Consultant (Test cricket) for the Indian Cricket Team.' Clearly, there is an element of finality to these appointments. At no point in the release is it mentioned that these appointments could subsequently be relooked at or revisited, making Limaye's claims much more interesting.

Moreover, as mentioned earlier, the BCCI went on to issue a second press release on 13 July. It can be conjectured that 48 hours later the BCCI should have been in a better position to understand the complexities of the situation and take a more reasoned call. The second release states: 'The recommendation for Mr Ravi Shastri was made on the merit of his presentation and the vision that he projected for taking the team to greater heights. After taking the decision on his selection, the CAC consulted him and decided on having batting and bowling consultants on overseas tour-to-tour basis, as per the requirement of the team.'

Again, there is an element of closure in this release. While not contesting the appointment of Arun, one wonders why these two releases would mention the consultants if the appointments were never finalized? One also wonders whether the CAC was ever explicitly told that support staff selection was beyond their brief. It is hard to understand why legends of the stature of Tendulkar, Ganguly and Laxman would knowingly exceed the brief given to them.

As it turned out, the whole process was deemed to be a tussle between Shastri and members of the CAC, especially Ganguly, in the media. Indian cricket did not even feature in this power struggle, making the coach appointment a rather poor advertisement of the way affairs are conducted in the world's richest cricket board. The whole process exemplified lack of transparency and could not have been good for the game except for the fact that the captain and the team finally got what they wanted.

Many, including Ramachandra Guha, have questioned the captain's growing power in coach selection in India. The argument is, if the captain has the final say, then what is the point in having a CAC or, for that matter, any committee in place? And if the captain picks the coach, will he not be all-powerful in the dressing room and will that be good for the team in the long term?

While there is merit in these arguments, the counter points are equally powerful. If the captain and the team don't get along with the coach, as was the case between Kohli and Kumble, the team is bound to lose out. The coach, whether we like it or not, will have to agree to the captain's vision and back him up. At the highest level, it is more about man management in cricket than coaching, and unless you are an excellent man manager, it is virtually impossible for you to succeed. While in difficult overseas conditions the coach has to do far more than just man management, managing international cricketers will always remain a key aspect of the job. Kirsten never needed to teach Tendulkar, Dravid, Ganguly or Laxman how to bat. All he needed to do was manage them in a manner to get the best out of them under a young captain in M.S. Dhoni. While in football we hardly remember who captained Manchester United when Sir Alex Fergusson was boss or who is currently captaining Arsenal under Arsene Wenger or Real Madrid under Zinedine Zidane, in cricket the situation is exactly the opposite. Each time a coach has tried to disrupt this hierarchy he has ended up burning his hands and eventually losing his job. The most successful captain–coach pairings in India over time have been those that have accepted this order of things. Be it Ganguly–Wright or Dhoni–Kirsten or Dhoni–Fleming (for the Chennai Super Kings), it is always the captain who has been at the forefront, with the coach as the backroom player and mentor. That's what worked for Kohli and Shastri during the first few months of collaboration, but only the next 14 months would tell how effective this partnership was for Indian cricket.

PART TWO

CRICKET'S CASH BOX REVOLUTION

1992: Doordarshan demands INR five lakh from the BCCI to telecast cricket matches played on Indian soil.

2012: Star Group pays the BCCI INR 3,851 crore for rights to telecast cricket matches on Indian soil from 2012 to 2018. This breaks down into a fee of INR 32 crore per match between 2012 and 2014, going up to INR 40 crore per match between 2014 and 2018.

2018: Star India buys IPL Telecast rights for five years across all platforms for INR 16,347.50 crore paying 55 crore per match to the BCCI.

In 25 years, cricket has become one of India's most lucrative businesses. This dramatic transformation is recorded here in the voices of the men who've played starring roles in either promoting the cause or standing in its way, through the multiple designations held by them across their careers: Jagmohan Dalmiya (at various points BCCI secretary, ICC president, BCCI president, CAB president); I.S. Bindra (BCCI president, Punjab Cricket Association president, ICC advisor); Mark Mascarenhas (head of WorldTel); Ratikanta Basu (director general of Doordarshan); Lalit Modi (head of BCCI

Marketing Committee, chairman of IPL); N Srinivasan (head of BCCI Marketing Committee, BCCI secretary, BCCI president); Uday Shankar (CEO, Star Group, India); Dr Ali Bacher (president, United Cricket Board of South Africa; chairman, ICC Cricket World Cup 2003 Organizing Committee) and Rahul Johri (BCCI CEO). This oral history is constructed by piecing together excerpts from interviews with these men over the years and from primary documents and letters written by them.

Before I piece the Indian story together, it will help in laying out the context by documenting what was going on in the broadcast realm across the world at the start of the 1990s.

In most mature media markets, a competitive electronic media industry was the general norm by the 1990s. In the US and the UK, India's two common reference points, there were multiple commercial television networks fighting for television rights in an open economy. In the UK, the first license to operate eight radio stations was granted to the British Broadcasting Company (BBC) in 1922. In 1927, the British Broadcasting Corporation replaced the British Broadcasting Company. The Sykes Committee, appointed in the 1920s, considered the overall state control of radio essential in view of its influence in moulding public opinion, but rejected the operation of the medium by the state. Another committee, the Crawford Committee, also recommended that radio remain a public monopoly. Accordingly, BBC was allowed to retain its monopoly till 1954.

In 1954, the British parliament enacted the Television Act, resulting in the formation of the Independent Television Authority (ITA) to provide television-broadcasting services additional to those of the BBC. In 1972, ITA was reconstituted as the Independent Broadcasting Authority, which acquired the powers of direct broadcasting by satellite in 1984. Subsequently, in 1990, the British parliament repealed all government control, thereby bringing in uninterrupted competition or an 'open sky'. Consequently, BBC's monopoly over the telecast of sports events like the Wimbledon (tennis) and the British Open (golf) was exposed to competition from ITV, Channel 4 and Sky TV.

In contrast to the UK, open competition over broadcast rights in the US has been the norm for decades now. Telecast rights of all major US sporting events such as the US Open Tennis, US Open Golf and Major League Baseball are open to free market bidding. As noted by William McPhail, senior vice president, CNN Sports, 'No one broadcaster or group of broadcasters, whether a national broadcaster or cable satellite channel, has any preferred position to act as host broadcasters for an event. The rights owner of an event, such as the Governing Body or Board of Control, owns these rights and exploits them as they see fit. Any company, whether in control of a broadcast channel or private production company, is free to originate coverage on behalf of the rights holders.' In fact, the 1994 FIFA World Cup, which the US hosted, was broadcast by the European Broadcasting Union (EBU). Uplinking was permitted back to Europe and the rest of the world from a central feed point in the American city of Dallas. This feed hub was also controlled by the EBU.

In Australia, China, Malaysia, Indonesia, Singapore and Pakistan, foreign networks were and are allowed to function independently and on a commercial basis. In a global ambience of open competition, and, ironically, against the professed programme of economic liberalization, the government's struggle to retain control over the Indian electronic sky between 1993–95 remains both an anachronism and an absorbing case study.

The story starts in 1992–93 when the BCCI, for the first time in its history, decided to sell telecast rights for cricket matches in India. In the next few pages, I have tried to piece this story together in the words of the many stakeholders who were all closely involved and shaped the predicament of the sport in India. All of the quotes attributed here to the key stakeholders are products of personal interviews with each of them over the years.

Inderjit Singh Bindra (president, Punjab Cricket Association, 2003–04):

> Prior to 1993, Doordarshan (DD) had a monopoly on the telecast of cricket matches in India. For each live telecast, DD demanded sizeable money from the BCCI to meet [the] costs of production. The scenario changed in 1993 when the Board sold television rights for the India–England series to Trans World International (TWI). Doordarshan, in turn, was forced to pay TWI USD 1 million for the right to telecast the matches in India. This agreement, the first of its kind in the Board's history, made it richer by USD 600,000. It allowed the BCCI to tide over the severe financial crisis plaguing Indian cricket between 1987 and 1992.

However, the sale of telecast rights to TWI did not mark the end of Doordarshan's monopoly over the telecast of Indian cricket and the BCCI soon found itself embroiled in a bitter controversy with DD over telecast rights.

Jagmohan Dalmiya (in interviews conducted when he was BCCI president [2001–04] and CAB president [2004–05, 2009-15]):

> Our struggle with DD began on 15 March 1993 when I, as president of the Cricket Association of Bengal (CAB), wrote a letter to the director-general of DD informing him of the six-nation (eventually five-nation, with the withdrawal of Pakistan) international cricket tournament that was to be held in November 1993 as part of our diamond jubilee celebrations.
>
> Our letter asked DD to send a detailed offer for any of the two alternatives: one, that DD would create the host broadcaster signal and also undertake live telecast of all matches in the tournament; or two, any other party may create the host broadcaster signal and DD would only purchase the rights to telecast the matches in India. We emphasised that in either case the foreign television

rights would be retained by the Association. We also asked DD to specify the royalty it was willing to pay for the telecast rights.

On 18 March 1993, the controller of programmes (sports), DD, asked CAB to send in writing the amount it expected as fee for exclusive telecast rights within India. On 19 March, CAB informed DD it was willing to offer DD exclusive rights for India and was agreeable to DD generating its own 'host broadcaster signal' for USD 800,000. CAB, however, declared it would reserve the right to sell the worldwide telecast rights of the Hero Cup [that is, telecast rights excluding India] to foreign broadcasters.

On 31 March 1993, DD sent its bid as 'host broadcaster' in India for a sum of INR one crore. CAB replied on 12 May stating it had decided to sell/allot worldwide TV rights to one party only and asked if DD was interested. A couple of days later, DD faxed a letter to CAB stating it was committed to its bid of INR one crore for exclusive telecast rights for India alone. It also suggested that the speculation over Pakistan's participation in the tournament, which might affect viewership and commercial accruals, might force DD to rethink its bid.

With DD turning a deaf ear, CAB, on 14 June 1993, entered into an agreement with TWI to telecast the Hero Cup. In return, CAB was to receive USD 550,000 as a guaranteed sum. It was also specified that if TWI received any sum in excess of the guaranteed sum, it would be split in a 70:30 ratio in favour of CAB. On 18 June 1993, DD made an announcement in the media that it had decided not to telecast the matches . . . and was determined not to enter into any negotiations with a foreign company to obtain television rights for a tournament being played in India. Soon after the announcement, we wrote to DD to verify the authenticity of the news report. The letter went unanswered.

In the interim, TWI, on 9 September 1993, wrote to VSNL seeking frequency clearance from the department of telecommunications. TWI also informed VSNL that it would be covering the tournament and was formally applying for permission to uplink signals and obtain frequency clearance for the walkie talkies to be used by its crew. On 13 October, the Ministry of Home informed us that it had no objection 'to the filming of the cricket matches at any of the places mentioned in our letter and that the "no objection" pertains to the filming of the matches on cricket grounds only'. The ministry also gave its clearance to the use of walkie talkie sets on the cricket grounds during matches.

On 18 October 1993, we resumed dialogue with DD. In a letter addressed to DD, we emphasized that the offer of Rs one crore was unviable, considering the enormous organisational cost of the tournament. We were looking for a minimum of INR two crore. We also pointed out that the offers we had received, including the one from TWI, were much higher and that payments under these offers would be made in foreign currency. We also pointed out that with DD unwilling to increase its bid, we had been forced to enter into an agreement with TWI. But we were still willing to enter into a dialogue and mentioned in our letter, 'CAB is still willing to negotiate with DD to ensure that millions of cricket lovers in India did not miss out on the action.'

In fact, to ensure DD's participation we had already held a meeting with TWI and convinced them of the delicate necessity of joint production. Following this, we sent a fresh proposal to DD. Its salient features were:

— TWI and Doordarshan would cover nine matches each in the tournament independently.
— TWI would undertake the coverage of these matches with its own equipment, crew and commentators. Similarly, Doordarshan would also have its own crew, equipment and commentators for the matches produced by it.
— Doordarshan would be at liberty to use its own commentators for matches produced by TWI for telecast in India. Similarly, TWI could also use its own commentators if it televised matches produced by Doordarshan through other networks.

— TWI would allow Doordarshan to pick up the signal and telecast live within India, free of charge. Similarly, Doordarshan would allow TWI to access the signal for telecast abroad, also free of charge.

— Doordarshan would not pay access fees to CAB, but allow instead four minutes' advertising time per hour (twenty-eight minutes in seven hours). CAB would be free to give these slots to advertisers and retain the sum earned. We asked DD to respond to these proposals by 21 October 1993.

On 27 October, DD reiterated its decision to not purchase signals from TWI because it was a foreign organisation. This was puzzling because DD had purchased telecast rights from TWI earlier during the India–England series in January 1993. On 29 October, we once again requested DD to reconsider its position, also conceding, purely in deference to DD's apparent sensitivity to taking signals from TWI, that CAB was happy to allow DD to produce its own video for the matches, which DD would directly purchase from CAB, at a mutually agreed price. The very next day DD sent a message stating it would not pay any access fee to CAB to telecast the matches. Rather, for DD to telecast the matches live, CAB would have to pay technical charges/production fee at INR 500,000 per match. CAB would also have to give DD exclusive rights for the signals generated and the parties interested in taking signals would have to negotiate directly with DD.

Following up on DD's letter, CAB, on 4 November, asked for a series of clarifications. Since DD had asked for production fees for the telecast of matches, it was presumed that all revenue generated from advertisements would belong to CAB and that it would have the right to charge access fees from parties abroad. On 5 November, DD rejected these terms.

With the dispute turning ugly, the Information and Broadcasting Ministry stepped in on 5 November and announced, 'According to law, no agency other than that belonging to or appointed by the Government of India has a right to telecast any event live by uplinking signals from Indian soil.' The law being relied upon was the Indian Telegraph Act of 1885.

Jagmohan Dalmiya (from the same set of interviews):

> With no other option, CAB, on 8 November, filed a writ petition in the Calcutta High Court praying that the respondents [the Government of India] should be directed to provide telecast and broadcast rights of all matches as well as make arrangements for the telecast and broadcast of matches by TWI. After hearing the petition, the High Court passed an interim order instructing the Government not to thwart existing arrangements between CAB and TWI.
>
> [T]he film facilities officer of the Information and Broadcasting Ministry informed the Customs department in New Delhi, Mumbai and Kolkata airports that since TWI had not obtained necessary clearances from the Government to cover the tournament, it should not be permitted to remove exposed film outside India till the films had been cleared by government officials. The Customs officials, in fact, went ahead and confiscated all equipment belonging to TWI, causing us huge problems during the tournament.

This alarmed some of the participating teams, evident from a letter written by Ali Bacher of the United Cricket Board of South Africa (UCBSA).

Ali Bacher (12 November 1993):

> The United Cricket Board of South Africa wishes to place on record its extreme disappointment that the Cricket Association of Bengal is unable to ensure that Sunday's historic cricket match between South Africa and West Indies in Bombay [14 November 1993] will not be televised by TWI and therefore not seen by the people of South Africa.
>
> This will come as a great shock to all the people of our country and we trust that you will do everything possible to ensure that the

match will be televised by TWI and thereby seen by the people of South Africa, as has been guaranteed to the UCBSA, South African Television and the sponsors of our national team.

In conclusion I would like you to know that the African National Congress shares these views.

(I have a copy of the letter.)

Jagmohan Dalmiya (same set of interviews):

On 14 November, the high court issued another directive, instructing the Customs authorities to release TWI equipment. The [order] wasn't complied with. TWI, undeterred by Mumbai Customs' continued intransigence over the seized equipment, and having paid us, recorded the West Indies–South Africa match with locally hired equipment.

With the Customs authorities refusing to abide by the orders of the Calcutta High Court, we were compelled to file a writ petition (No. 836) in the Supreme Court on 15 November. Hearing the petition, the court passed an order directing N. Vittal, secretary, Ministry of Communications, to hold a meeting on the same day by 4.30 pm, and communicate the decision by 7.30 pm. It also directed the customs authorities to release the equipment, though prohibiting TWI and CAB from using the equipment till the secretary, Department of Telecommunication, issued us the necessary license. To our disappointment Secretary Vittal issued the following statement later in the day:

'It is true that the Indian Telegraph Act of 1885 enables the government to give licenses to agencies other than Doordarshan or the government departments to telecast. In fact, such permission had been given in January 1993 when the cricket matches were telecast by the same TWI. However, subsequently I am given to understand that the government policy in the Ministry of I&B has been that uplinking directly by private/foreign agencies for the purpose of broadcasting should not be permitted . . .

'Taking into account the facts mentioned above, the only reasonable conclusion I reach is that permission may be given to TWI for telecast overseas through VSNL while Doordarshan will be telecasting within the country. TWI will have to get the signals from Doordarshan for uplinking through VSNL by making mutual arrangements.'

This order was passed around 7.30 pm. We immediately challenged it and to our relief our plea was heard by the Supreme Court later that night itself. Never before in the history of independent India had a Supreme Court division bench sat in judgment at 11.30 pm on a government holiday. In a landmark judgment, the court overruled Vittal and directed that TWI could generate its own signals by focusing their cameras on the ground where the matches were being played. It also ordered the customs authorities to release the confiscated equipment forthwith.

The text of the order passed by Justices J.S. Verma and P.B. Sawant went as follows:

The order passed by Shri N. Vittal, Secretary DoT on 15-11-93 is stayed to the extent that it imposes the condition that TWI will have to get the signals from Doordarshan for uplinking through VSNL by making mutual arrangements. TWI can generate their own signal by focusing their cameras only on the ground where the cricket matches are being played, as directed by the Home Ministry, they will take care not to focus their cameras anywhere else.

The learned counsel appearing for Doordarshan states that Mr Basu, the Director General of Doordarshan informed her at 5.30 p.m. today over telephone that the Custom Authorities are releasing the equipment as directed by the Court. Shri [Kapil] Sibal appearing for the petitioners informs us that the equipment has not been released by the Customs Authorities. The learned counsel further informs after taking instructions from his junior that a copy of the Court's order was served on Mr Devendra Singh, Under Secretary, Ministry of Finance who was present before

Mr Vittal at the time of this hearing. In case the Customs Authorities have not yet released the equipment, they are once again directed to release the equipment forthwith.

The order was passed by Justices J.S. Verma and P.B. Sawant. The deadlock, however, persisted even after the Supreme Court order. In fact, a fresh issue arose over the first choice of camera positions at the venues. It had resonance in the international broadcast arena and with administrators the world over. This was evident when Ali Bacher and the head of WorldTel, Mark Mascarenhas, who had bought the telecast rights for the 1996 World Cup, expressed serious disappointment at the turn of events in India.

Frustrated with what was going on, Ali Bacher threatened that South Africa would withdraw support for the subcontinent's bid to host the 1996 World Cup unless the wrangle over telecast rights was sorted out immediately. He also warned that he would take the issue up with the ICC. Bacher, upset that South African viewers had not been able to watch their team playing in the Hero Cup, said South Africans did not want the World Cup to be staged in a country where problems over telecast rights thwarted the successful organization of an international tournament. In a personal letter to Dalmiya, Robin Kempthorne, production director, South African Broadcasting Corporation (SABC), wrote: 'In light of the developments I am going to have to recommend to the SABC that our participation in the negotiations for the broadcast rights for the 1996 World Cup should be reconsidered.'

Mark Mascarenhas (in a letter faxed to the BCCI, 16 November 1993):

I am writing to you on the utmost urgent basis to express my shock and concern over the implications for the 1996 World Cup of the Indian government's decision to ban TWI from producing the South Africa versus Zimbabwe and the upcoming South Africa versus West Indies [matches] . . . I'm sure you are aware of this, since reports here [in the US] are that the matter has become an international political issue, with Mr Nelson Mandela of the ANC attempting to reach the Indian Prime Minister on the matter.

However, I want to emphasize the significance of the matter in terms of its negative implications with international broadcasters around the world. We understand that TV networks that have paid huge money for the five nation tournament will not be receiving their television signal and word of this has spread rapidly. When combined with reports that TWI's equipment was actually confiscated, the blow to the credibility of major sporting events held in India is staggering.

As you know, it was a premise of our agreement regarding the world cup that the event will be produced by WorldTel, with internationally recognized television production and the event will be offered to broadcasters on this basis. Based on the TWI situation, I have already received a letter from the Director of Sports Programming at the SABC in South Africa advising that the circumstances lead him to recommend that his organization withdraws from negotiations for the World Cup. Other TV networks from around the world have called me this morning expressing similar sentiments.

In my opinion irreversible damage has already been done. We look to the Board to take all steps necessary to rectify the situation before it jeopardizes the 1996 world cup and the investments of all involved, and does lasting harm to India as a sponsor of major sporting events.

(I have a copy of the letter.)

Earlier that year, Mascarenhas had written a letter to the joint organizing committee of the World Cup, which said: 'We are interested in the worldwide television rights for the 1996 World Cup and would like to submit the following proposal for your consideration: USD 9.5 million minimum guarantee for exclusive worldwide television rights to the competition, with a 75-25 split in favour of the World Cup committee on additional revenues. Or USD 10.5 million for the outright purchase of the exclusive worldwide television rights to all matches in the competition.'

I.S. Bindra (same set of interviews):

> How many times and for how long can we [the BCCI] go to court? We can, at most, go on appealing. But if the government has taken a decision, we have to know where to stop. Now it's only a matter of time before WorldTel demands [its money back] from the joint management committee. If there is no worldwide television coverage, it [organizing the World Cup] will cost the management nothing less than INR eighty to ninety crore. That's not feasible. The BCCI will go bankrupt.

On 2 June 1994, Andrew Wildblood, international vice president, TWI, in a letter to the director general, Doordarshan, wrote:

> It is our hope that a satisfactory agreement can be reached regarding co-production and rights fees. As you have told me that a rights fee of USD 100,000 per day for a minimum of 27 days of international cricket per year plus a contribution to production will not be possible, I would ask you to make a counter proposal to us of a figure that would be possible in view of our mutual desire to progress with matters.

On 13 June 1994, he reiterated his interest in entering into an arrangement with DD:

> The BCCI is extremely keen to fully explore the potential of arriving at a mutually acceptable arrangement regarding production and broadcast of Indian cricket, both international and domestic, with Doordarshan . . . The BCCI's position remains that they are optimistic that an agreement with your esteemed organization can be reached. TWI, for its part, very much wishes to pursue co-production arrangement between our two organizations.

I.S. Bindra:

> Finally, on 17 June 1994, I wrote to the director general, DD, saying, 'I'd like to reiterate on behalf of the Board of Control for Cricket in India our desire and commitment to fully explore the potential of arriving at a mutually acceptable agreement regarding the production and broadcast of Indian cricket, both international and domestic, with your esteemed organization. Such an agreement can encompass a suitable arrangement between TWI and DD for co-production of an internationally acceptable signal.

Hopes of a solution were rekindled when a group of ministers, headed by the home minister, S.B. Chavan, decided on 23 August 1994 to allow the setting up of private radio and TV stations in the country. Within days, the BCCI requested the director of Sports, Ministry of Human Resource Development, Department of Youth Affairs and Sports, to grant permission to the cricket authorities or TWI/ESPN to telecast the India–West Indies series. However, in a letter dated 30 August to the secretary, Department of Sports, the Information and Broadcasting Ministry opposed the grant of uplinking facilities to any foreign agency.

Doordarshan continued to be obdurate.

Ratikanta Basu (director general of DD, on 20 September 1994):

> As a matter of principle the Board should have explained the nature of the cricket matches this season and negotiated with us directly. It's not that Doordarshan is new to sports. Who created Sunil Gavaskar or Kapil Dev in India? Doordarshan has been in the forefront of telecasting cricket Tests and one day internationals. Until last year, it was Doordarshan that telecast the home series and also a few other series played abroad. They [Bindra and Dalmiya] have not even met us on the issue. Why should Doordarshan talk to intermediaries like Trans World International? There is a case between us [TWI and Doordarshan] in the Supreme Court . . . I told TWI that Doordarshan would be keen to talk only if it [TWI] withdrew the case.

Basu even defended DD's decision to pay less:

> Well, there are solutions to this provided people and organizers keep personal considerations aside and put the viewers' interest ahead of everything. We got the rights, through the Asia Pacific Broadcasting Union (ABU) for the Atlanta Olympics at the cost of Star TV, which had bid for the rights for India alone at USD 5 million. We had bid for the rights through ABU at USD 1,10,000. Finally we agreed to pay USD 500,000, which is one-tenth of the Star TV bid. Keeping in mind the larger audience that Doordarshan commands, the IOC opted for Doordarshan. If the IOC had gone by the highest bidder pattern, Star TV would have got it.
>
> Doordarshan paid the All India Tennis Association (AITA) INR 20 lakhs for the India–Australia tie at Chandigarh, INR 25 lakhs for the India–US match played at Delhi and for the India–South Africa rubber at Jaipur, Doordarshan would pay INR 10 lakhs. Doordarshan and AITA will also share the revenue from advertising. All sports federations inform us of the championships and come to the negotiating table. But not the cricket body.

The BCCI appealed to the Supreme Court once again on 3 October 1994. Responding to the Board's petition, the court passed the following order:

> Pending the final disposal of the matters by this interim order confined to telecast the international cricket matches to be played in India from October 1994 to December 1994, we direct Respondents 1 & 6 to 9 [representing the government of India] in Writ Petition No. 836 of 1993 to grant forthwith necessary permission/sanctions and uplinking facilities for production, transmission and telecasting of the said matches.
>
> We also direct Respondents 2, 3 and 4 in Writ Petition No. 836 [also representing the government of India] and all other government agencies not to obstruct/restrict in any manner whatsoever production, transmission and telecasting of the said matches for the said period by the petitioner applicant only on

the ground where the cricket matches would be played and the
signals are generated under the direct supervision of the VSNL
personnel. So far as the production, transmission and telecasting
of these matches in India is concerned, Doordarshan shall have the
exclusive rights in all respects for the purpose, and the petitioner
applicant shall not prevent Doordarshan from doing so, and in
particular shall afford all facilities for Doordarshan to do so.

So far as the placement of cameras are concerned both
petitioner applicant as well as Doordarshan shall have equal rights.
This shall be ensured by Shri Sunil Gavaskar in consultation with
such technical experts as he may deem necessary to consult.

As far as the revenue generated by the advertisement by
Doordarshan is concerned, Doordarshan will deposit the said
amount in a separate account and preferably in a nationalized
bank. Doordarshan will have the exclusive right to advertisement.

Noting that this interim order had failed to calm the storm, India's
apex court passed another order on October 18:

The BCCI will ensure that all Cricket Associations and staging
centres shall extend every facility to the personnel authorized by
Doordarshan to enter into the cricket ground for production,
transmission and telecasting of the matches without any let or
hindrance.

The BCCI will also ensure that all Cricket Associations
staging the matches will make available every facility and render
such assistance as may be necessary and sought by Doordarshan
for effective telecasting of the matches at the respective grounds
and stadia.

The BCCI shall not permit ESPN to enter into any contract
either with ATN or any other agency for telecasting in any manner
all over India, whether through the satellite footprints or otherwise,
cricket matches which are being telecast in India by Doordarshan.
If ESPN has entered into any such contract either with ATN or
any other agency, that contract should be cancelled forthwith.

> The BCCI and Doordarshan will mutually solve the problem
> of the control room and storage room facilities needed by
> Doordarshan, preferably in one meeting in Bombay on 20-10-1994.

Responding to the BCCI plea that telecast of matches by its chosen broadcaster was part of the fundamental right of freedom of speech and expression, the Court declared that from the standpoint of Article 19(1)(a) (freedom of speech and expression), what is paramount is the right of the listeners and viewers and not the right of the broadcaster—whether the broadcaster is the state, public corporation or a private individual or body. A monopoly over broadcasting, whether by government or by anybody else, it was argued, 'is inconsistent with free speech right of the citizens. State control really means governmental control, which in turn means control of the political party or parties in power for the time being. Such control is bound to colour the views, information and opinions conveyed by the media. The free speech right of the citizens is better served in keeping the broadcasting media under the control of the public.'

The problem was finally resolved in February 1995, when the Supreme Court upheld the BCCI plea that telecast of matches by its chosen broadcaster was part of the fundamental right to freedom of speech and expression. The order was passed by a division bench consisting of Justices P.B. Sawant, B.P. Jeevan Reddy and S. Mohan.

In the words of the Supreme Court order: 'The airwaves or frequencies are public property. Their use has to be controlled and regulated by a public authority in the interests of the public and to prevent the invasion of their rights. The right to impart and receive information is a species of the right to freedom of speech and expression guaranteed by Article 19(1)(a) of the Constitution. A citizen has a fundamental right to use the best means of imparting and receiving information and as such to have access to telecasting for the purpose.'

Having won the battle against Doordarshan, the BCCI finally started making big money on cricket rights from the turn of the millennium, selling the rights to Doordarshan for four years (2000–04) for USD 54 million.

Jagmohan Dalmiya (same set of interviews):

> Indian cricket was now a robust property. We were glad that Doordarshan agreed to pay approximately INR 240 crore for rights for the years 2000–04.

Between 2000 and 2004, the rights multiplied manifold in value and when Dalmiya once again tried selling the rights in 2004, he got a bid of USD 308 million from Zee Telefilms. ESPN's was the second-highest bid at close to USD 300 million. However, the rights weren't awarded to Zee on technical grounds and the matter went to court, with both parties alleging foul play. The rights were finally awarded to Nimbus by the new BCCI dispensation under Sharad Pawar, with Lalit Modi driving the deal in 2006 for USD 612 million, subsequently renegotiated to USD 549 million (INR 2,400 crore at 2006 rates).

Lalit Modi (on the Nimbus deal, 18 February 2006):

> Indian cricket had been undervalued. Now we are beginning to see the real value of the property.

The Nimbus contract was extended for another four years in 2009. This time round, Nimbus agreed to pay INR 31.25 crore per match. Once again Lalit Modi was at the forefront of negotiations. The deal was finally scrapped in 2011 with the BCCI pulling up Nimbus for non-payment of dues, and the contract was finally awarded to the Star group for six years from 2012 to 2018 for INR 3,851 crore.

Uday Shankar (CEO of Star Group, 4 April 2012, on Star's vision):

For us it is a long-term strategy. We believe in the brand power of cricket and have invested in the brand long term. There's no doubt cricket will continue to be the driver of the sports business realm going ahead.

In collaboration with our partner ESPN, we will do a commendable job. We have already got three channels which have a lot of credibility and we will showcase cricket in this bouquet of channels.

[*On the importance of cricket in India*]

I think as far as Indian identity is concerned, cricket overtakes even Bollywood. While Bollywood is a big source of entertainment, its conscious articulation as an Indian medium by the common people is not so pronounced. But cricket is perhaps the most conscious nationalistic activity Indians indulge in. To that extent, there is no cricket minus India. Every time you watch cricket, you are reminded, consciously or subconsciously, of the Indian identity . . . in terms of importance, cricket has now left Bollywood far behind. It is next only to big political stories and really big economic stories . . . And very often, it overtakes political and economic stories as well.

For an average Indian cricket lover, a player doing something that costs India the match is the closest thing to treason . . . The kind of interventions we make in other activities like politics, civic and municipal administration, and economics, we have now started making in cricket. In the same way that I look at who is responsible for misery during the Bombay floods, who is responsible for this goof-up in administration, we look at who is the culprit of the match.

Shankar argues that under Star, the next major innovation will happen in the domestic cricket broadcast space.

The next round of innovation [pause], though it is too early for me to say this, will have to come in the domestic cricket broadcast space. The domestic cricket experience in India continues to be poor. The number of cameras used is far fewer, the best analysts are not used and overall the experience has not been marketed well. There is no difference, in essence, between the Indian Premier League and the Ranji Trophy, for example. Both are domestic competitions run by the BCCI and there is no reason why we can't make the domestic cricket broadcast experience something to look forward to for the passionate Indian cricket fan.

In fact, in domestic cricket, the connect is greater because all the cricketers are from a particular Indian state or region and are not hired arsenal who will be there just for six weeks. Yes, I agree that in a match between Bengal and Delhi, for example, there will be no connect in Tamil Nadu, but in the two competing states, there will be a lot of passion. We have to tap this passion and make domestic cricket an important property. That's where the next round of innovation is waiting to happen.

N. Srinivasan (at a press conference in Chennai on 2 April 2012):

The BCCI is very happy with the deal. Now the media rights have been fully evaluated and fully priced with Star coming out with such a deal.

2017: The Process Is Complete

On 3 September 2017 the suspense was finally over—INR 16,347.50 crore was the magic figure that won Star India the IPL rights for the next five years. '16347' was trending on Twitter the moment it was made public and curious fans started asking if they would have to shell more to watch IPL telecast based on the huge amount that Star bid.

Is pay-per-view where India will soon move to? Can this humongous amount of money be recovered or is it a rather ambitious bid? What does this mean for Star's other properties like the rights for international cricket in India, EPL, Pro Kabaddi League, and all else that supplies content for its coveted bouquet of 12 sports channels? What does this mean for other market leaders like Sony Pictures Network India, who were used to having the market share of viewership in April–May for the last decade? Finally, what does this mean for the franchises and, most importantly, the players?

Let's dwell upon the franchises and players first. With 40 per cent of the income decidedly going to the franchises, it means they stand to gain an additional INR 800 crore over five years. A whopping INR 160 crore of added revenue per year, the valuation of each of the eight franchises is all set to sky-rocket. Each one of them will now be valued at over INR 1,000 crore and any interested buyer will have to pay that much more to acquire an IPL team, or even a majority stake. Also, it is certain that a significant portion of the added revenue will be passed on to the players. Unless that happens Virat Kohli's annual salary of INR 17 crore in comparison to the BCCI's income of INR 16,500 crore appears miniscule. To expect Kohli to earn the same amount of money he had been earning so far while the IPL's income pool has gone up five times is naive and unfair.

Close to 200 other cricketers also stand to benefit from this influx of money. Some of them who are skilled domestic cricketers will also profit from the extra funds that teams are now in a position to spend on them.

Fans, however, may find it difficult going forward, with the broadcaster passing on some of the monies they have spent to the fans. Recovery is only possible if Star maximizes income from advertisements and subscription monies and that may well result in a pocket pinch for viewers in the near future.

Also, does the bid signify a decisive win for franchise cricket over international cricket? That's also another real challenge for the BCCI. While the Board did well to fetch a massive amount from IPL rights, it was always well known that IPL was the jewel in the BCCI's crown. Will the Board get an amount close to INR 60 crore per game for an India match in 2018 or will Indian international cricket be the big loser in the future?

For the BCCI, much maligned in the Supreme Court for non-implementation of the Lodha Committee reforms, this was a huge fillip of sorts. Even with brand Indian cricket at its lowest, the BCCI managed to fetch massive monies for a domestic Indian property, which is now in sync with the world's premier sports properties. For a league emanating from the global south and one which is only a decade old, this was a massive development.

Just hours before the bids were opened, Lalit Modi had tweeted USD 5 billion for *five* years is what he wished to see. Ambitious as with all-things-Modi, the BCCI may well target such an amount or more come 2022, when the rights will be up for grabs yet again.

Rahul Johri (CEO, BCCI, during an interview on 3 September 2017):

> It shows the potential of the game in India and is proof Indian cricket is on the right track. Investors continue to look at cricket as a favoured investment opportunity and that's a big takeaway for us. We also expect serious market demand when the India rights come up for renewal in 2018.
>
> Two things stand out in the bidding process. First is the entry of Facebook, a strictly American company with no background in cricket, with an INR 3,900 crore bid for the IPL's digital rights. This bid is proof of the growing strength of the Indian diaspora across the world. With more and more Indians making the US, UK and Europe home, takers for the IPL across these consumer markets has consistently risen. The IPL for many of these non-resident Indians is the only connect to things Indian. In a world dominated by information and capital flows and where technology has broken spatial and time barriers, the IPL helps nurture an Indian collective of consumers who continue to celebrate Indianness through the prism of this uniquely Indian export. Star could conceive of a global bid largely on the strength of this highly

influential community. Finally, it justifies the BCCI's decision to segregate the rights across regions in an attempt to maximize revenue from the sale.

Second is the steady growth of the Indian broadcast market. Sony's bid of INR 11,000 crore for the Indian TV market is more than double of what they paid earlier this year to telecast the IPL. It is proof that India, a late entrant in the sports media rights game in the 1990s, has caught up with the leagues of the West. The three bids in 2017—Star for IPL media rights, Oppo for the national team sponsorship and Vivo for the IPL's title rights (INR 16,347.5, 1,079, 2,199 crore respectively) has earned the BCCI more money than it has cumulatively earned in its eighty-nine-year-old history.

From shelling out INR five lakh per match in 1992 to earning INR 40 crore a game in 20 years and 55 crore for every IPL match in 25 years, this is nothing less than a revolution.

Is there a lesson to be learned in this? The answer is overwhelmingly affirmative!

Did the Bombay Parsis, who played the game in the 1870s and the founders of the Bombay Pentangular in the early twentieth century, ever think what could happen a century later? That a pastime could become a multi-billion-dollar industry?

Cricket already had political and commercial currency in the 1920s and 1930s and that's what best explains the early history of the game in India. Since inception, it was steeped in nationalist rhetoric and was imbued with mass appeal, a mesh that made it attractive for the princely aristocracy and upwardly mobile middle-class, who pulled at it from multiple courses giving it direction in the colonial context.

SOAPS, SERIALS AND POLITICS
CRICKET AND TELEVISION IN CONTEMPORARY INDIA

Once the skies had opened up it was only a matter of time before cricket and the evolving satellite television industry started feeding off each other. While the culmination of this process was the launch of the IPL, stray efforts had started from the turn of the century. The marriage was at two levels. Cricket, it was soon evident, was consumed and appropriated by the television business in varied ways, best explained by the coverage of the CAB elections across vernacular television channels in July 2006. At another level, cricket tournaments, or rather tournaments aimed at producing television content, were planned and executed by the BCCI, a process that found its perfect bedfellow in the IPL in April 2008.

The Story of the Cricket Association of Bengal Elections

Tele-visual hype generated for a regional cricket body election in July 2006 in West Bengal, especially by the multiple 24-hour Bengali news channels, draws attention to the emerging relationship between big-money television and even-bigger-money sport.

Most say that the run-up to the CAB elections began on 25 May 2006 when former Bengal players and some well-known Jagmohan Dalmiya baiters met at the local Calcutta Club to garner support in favour of Sourav Ganguly and protest against the unfair treatment being meted out to him by the BCCI. The common refrain in this meeting was that Dalmiya was responsible for dropping Ganguly from the Indian team and that he had used him as a pawn to further his ambitions within the BCCI. While this meeting was the start of the formal run-up, the real beginning goes back to 30 November 2005, when Dalmiya lost his stranglehold in the BCCI to the Sharad Pawar-led alliance. Soon after beating Dalmiya at the Taj Bengal hotel in Calcutta, I.S. Bindra, one of the most powerful figures in Indian cricket at the time, had declared in private quarters, 'Jaggu is half-finished. We will complete the process next year when we oust him from the CAB.'

It is this realization that spurred Dalmiya to convince his colleagues at the CAB to put in the extra bit to ensure that Bengal cricket was on firm ground. That he was closely monitoring the situation was evident when Bengal played Railways in the Ranji Trophy semi-final at Eden Gardens in February 2006. When Bengal chased down a mammoth total to reach the finals of the Ranji Trophy after a gap of eight years, Dalmiya personally cheered the team on from the boundary line and was prompt in declaring a cash award of INR 1.5 lakhs for the victorious side under Deep Dasgupta. The bottom-line of this episode was: Dalmiya was preparing his team for a tumultuous election for over six months, knowing well that he was about to face one of the toughest challenges of his life.

Confronted by allegations of financial irregularities, Dalmiya had little option but to fall back on the CAB. In an interview in March 2006, he made clear his intention of fighting back and not succumbing to unfair political pressure. His confidence received a boost when the Bombay High Court gave him a reprieve on 9 April, condemning the BCCI's actions in no uncertain terms in the case over PILCOM (Pakistan–India–Lanka Committee) accounts relating to the 1996 World Cup. Announcement of suspension by the BCCI on 10 April for further charges relating to PILCOM failed to eat into the impact of this emphatic legal win. He won another major victory when the Supreme Court, too, condemned the actions of the BCCI and the Maharashtra government in May 2005, after which there was no further opposition against his anticipatory bail, which was sought to counter the FIR filed against him in Mumbai on 16 March 2006 for reasons of financial mismanagement.

The opposition, too, was hardly sitting idle. Soon after Ganguly was dropped from the Indian team was it said that Dalmiya had sacrificed his protégé to further his ambitions. Ignored was the fact that Ganguly was brought back into the Indian Test team in the last selection committee meeting in November 2005 when the Dalmiya-backed regime was in power.

The initial plan for the CAB elections was to pit a well-known industrialist against Dalmiya. However, the plan was soon changed and the equation was simple: It was upon the chief minister of West Bengal to convince Prasun Mukherjee, the police commissioner of Kolkata, to contest. Mukherjee, a man with considerable clout and fan following, it was thought, would be a perfect candidate to take on the mighty Dalmiya.

Another major opposition coup was to garner the support of the Ganguly family, once considered closest to Dalmiya. However, this wasn't difficult as relations between the two families had gradually soured since December 2005, with the Gangulys tending to believe the rumour that Sourav had been used by Dalmiya for personal gain. Finally on 25 May 2006, it was confirmed that Mukherjee would contest Dalmiya for the post of CAB president. That the Communist Part of India (Marxist) (CPI[M]) party machinery would be used was evident when the Urban Development Minister Ashok

Bhattacharya, known to be close to the chief minister, demanded Dalmiya's resignation for his role in the Ganguly issue. Assured of government support, Mukherjee announced his formal candidature on 18 June, a decision that met with mixed reactions from the political fraternity of the state. While former chief minister, Jyoti Basu questioned the prudence of Mukherjee contesting, Ashok Bhattacharya, Mayor Bikash Bhattacharya and IT minister Manab Mukherjee welcomed the decision. But the big election bomb was dropped on 19 June when Buddhadeb Bhattacharjee, fresh from a landslide win in the West Bengal parliamentary polls, declared that he wanted Dalmiya to quit the CAB and not contest the polls. He asked his sports minister, Subhash Chakraborty, to convince Dalmiya not to contest. No sooner than Buddhadeb had come out in open support of Mukherjee than the anti-Dalmiya camp organized a convention at the Aryan Club to gather support for their panel. However, with only a dozen or so clubs attending, the gathering was a flop. It was, in fact, a boost for the Dalmiya lobby to see that the clubs were still with them in the local politics of the Calcutta maidan.

With the chief minister openly canvassing for Mukherjee, it was inevitable that the CAB elections would be appropriated by television channels and made into a major media event. And with the West Bengal news-channel turf becoming more competitive with the addition of two new 24-hour-news-channels in March 2006, it was only a matter of time before the election was converted into a television spectacle. From the last week of June, with still a month to go for the polls, each of the four Bengali 24-hour news channels had special segments allotted to the CAB elections. Further, each of these segments had special names assigned to them. While Star Ananda (now renamed ABP Ananda) called it 'Crossbat', 24 Ghanta called theirs CAB *Singhashan Kar?* (Whose is the CAB throne?). Kolkata TV, in its bid to outdo the other channels, did a special show on the West Bengal sports minister, who was openly supporting Dalmiya against the wishes of the chief minister, and titled the programme *Banda Ye Bindaas Hai* (He is a jolly good fellow). The trailer portrayed Chakraborty in a felt hat waving at his supporters in an open jeep and soon after cut back to the studio where Chakraborty was interviewed for an hour by two of the channel's resident experts on the issue of the CAB election. As the election approached, the Star Ananda segment, Crossbat, started with the tagline *Ebare are frontfoot e noy, back foot eo noy, ebare larai cross bat e* (Not on the front foot, not on the back foot; now on crossbat). And while the tagline was being aired, the two incumbents, Dalmiya and Mukherjee, were shown riding on horses, wearing full military armour and carrying swords, which crossed paths.

Once the sports minister conveyed the chief minister's wish to Dalmiya formally on 21 June, the television war intensified. Things soon got divided into camps. While Star Ananda, a channel owned partly by the Anandabazar Patrika (ABP) group adopted a pro-Dalmiya stance, 24 Ghanta and Kolkata TV, known to be owned by proprietors close to the chief minister, adopted a pro-Mukherjee stance.

After the chief minister's wish had been made known to him, Dalmiya was left with little option but consult his colleagues to judge the level of support he could still garner inside the CAB. He was delighted to see Chakraborty and Kshiti Goswami, two powerful ministers in Buddhadeb Bhattacharjee's cabinet, come out in his support. And this open fissure within the Left Front, an unprecedented happening in West Bengal, was too enticing for the media to let go. The news segments on the elections soon followed a set pattern. Inevitably, a Chakraborty statement in favour of Dalmiya would be followed by one from a heavyweight of the Mukherjee camp and vice versa. Reporters who covered the legislative assembly were given strict instructions to ask each MLA they met about their loyalties in the election and any radical revelation was broadcast as 'Breaking News'. For example, when Subrata Mukherjee, former mayor, rubbished Bhattacharjee's intervention on the grounds that a sports-body election should be allowed to remain autonomous, it was the first headline on the primetime 9 p.m. news.

And when the BCCI decided to add salt to Dalmiya's wounds by announcing its decision to withhold all subsidies and payments to the CAB for reasons of irregularities over the PILCOM account, it was flashed as a major breakthrough for the anti-Dalmiya combine. Dalmiya's condemnation of the decision as nothing but a stunt was also given adequate coverage. And when Dalmiya summoned an emergency general meeting of the CAB on 2 July, on the pretext of conveying to the affiliate members the chief minister's wish, it was the first ever occasion when multiple OB vans were present at the CAB to cover the meeting live. Every time a major heavyweight from either camp entered the CAB, the anchors from the newsroom cut across live to the CAB to find out the latest update. On occasion, channels had more than one reporter at the CAB, each with a brief to cover one particular camp. When it was known that 116 out of 121 affiliated units attended the meeting, Dalmiya was once again hailed by sections of the media as a true master of realpolitik—the huge presence being perceived as a marker of his popularity. While this was predominantly the version broadcast by Star Ananda, which was followed by an exclusive interview with Dalmiya, the rival channels followed a radically opposite line. As the emergent general meeting was abandoned in quick time, they declared that Dalmiya's reign was to end soon and went on to interview Snehashish Ganguly and Samar Pal, candidates from the Mukherjee faction in the elections.

That the opposition was not taking any chances was mentioned in the media much before Samar Pal, secretary candidate of the opposition combine, moved court demanding the appointment of an independent observer for the CAB polls. This was followed by what was arguably the biggest electoral blunder of the opposition combine—they made public a private email from Ganguly in which he vents his anger against the corrupt functioning of the CAB, alleging that Dalmiya and his colleagues had leaked Greg Chappell's email in September 2005, which had hurt Ganguly considerably. It was this email, perceived as an election masterstroke, which caused the ruin of the Mukherjee faction. The email was revealed to the media in a quickly put together press conference, which was broadcast live by all the channels. And the photograph of Snehasish Ganguly holding up Sourav Ganguly's email before the media was picked up not only by the regional channels, but also by each and every 24-hour news channel in the country. The picture also made its way to almost all the newspapers the following day.

Snehasish Ganguly holding up Sourav Ganguly's email before the media

Ganguly's iconic status, which has no parallel in Bengal, took a huge beating after the email was made public and he was openly condemned for being ungrateful. In fact, each of the four television channels ran SMS polls on whether Ganguly was a traitor.

*Ganguly portrayed as Aurangzeb
on one of the TV channels*

On the other hand, this email went a long way in converting Dalmiya into a martyr, which was well appropriated and also projected by the media.

The shaded area in red at the very top is a statement by Dalmiya, which mentions that loyalties change with time. That was the line adopted by Anandabazar Patrika.

Another major electoral disaster on the part of the opposition was the use of official might. The television channels played a leading role in projecting the use of state power as a coercive act. All the channels reported how the state diktat over not allowing the district sports officials to come and vote had provoked mini rebellions across West Bengal. That some of the university representatives were disgusted at the pressure being put on them was also made public, placing the opposition in an extremely precarious position. In fact, that in the ultimate analysis the opposition failed to garner more than 15 of the 26 votes in the districts and the universities was largely a handiwork of the media.

With the elections drawing closer, Dalmiya could fathom that he was in with a chance to carve out a miraculous win. It was confidence, inspired in part by the media, that urged him to agree to have an independent court appointed observer, another move that caught the opposition unawares. While they were banking on garnering public sympathy on the observer issue, the Dalmiya faction's agreeing to the appointment caught them napping. In fact, they were forced to welcome this move saying that it was what they had wanted from the start.

And when on 26 July, the urban development minister Ashok Bhattacharya met Indian Football Association secretary, Subrata Dutta, at 11 p.m. and literally pleaded with him to support, it was surreptitiously recorded by cameramen from *10 Minuter Khel* (A game of ten minutes), a popular sports show broadcast on Akash Bangla, another Bengali infotainment channel. The public disclosure of this meeting allowed Dutta to continue with his neutral stand, something that was falsely perceived as support for Mukherjee. The opposition was so confident that they even demonstrated the audacity of ignoring a confidential report submitted by the Intelligence Branch on the eve of the election, which suggested that the election was far closer than originally envisaged. As this report expressed apprehension over Mukherjee's chances, the Calcutta Police thought best to ignore it.

Perhaps the only event that the channels missed during the whole election saga was the meeting between the Rashtriya Janta Dal leader Lalu Yadav and Dalmiya on the eve of the election. During this meeting, Dalmiya managed to confirm the support of the RJD leader, a move that was looked upon as almost inconceivable given the nature of past relations between them. With the three Railway votes in his kitty—Eastern Railway, South Eastern Railway and Bengal Nagpur Railway, each having one vote at the CAB—and with sports minister Chakraborty's support, Dalmiya spent the election eve looking at pictures of Mukherjee meeting his voters on television.

The final nail in the opposition's coffin was drilled in by the rumour, once again, spread by visual media, that Dalmiya would have his voters shifted to hideouts. While the opposition spent hours trying to find out where the hideout was, Dalmiya went on with his business of last-minute calculations. The plan was simple: When the opposition finally gave up and retired contented that voters weren't being moved and the whole thing was a false media build-up, the final plunge would be taken. On the morning of 30 July, Dalmiya loyalists all assembled at the Eden Gardens by 11 a.m. in the morning. And by early afternoon, most of Dalmiya's committed voters were in the safe haven of the Club House at Eden Gardens. The opposition had little clue as to what was going on and by the time they came to know, the battle was beyond them.

Television coverage climaxed on the day of the election when all regional channels, as well as some national broadcasters, dropped all other news and began showcasing the event of the day. Analysts were present in studios from early morning to discuss the election threadbare and dissect each group's strengths and weaknesses. It was more like a general election, not an insignificant election of a state cricket body. And once the results were disclosed and Dalmiya declared winner, the media went berserk. While the counting was on, minute-by-minute updates were being shown on some channels. For example, Kolkata TV and 24 Ghanta were intermittently flashing that Dalmiya was ahead by five to eight votes. That such flashes were, in fact, rubbish was revealed when I was told that the counting was going on in a closed room where only the two rival presidential candidates and the court-appointed observer was present. But such was the charm of the elections that sensationalism, which had no basis in fact, was given a pass. On election day, each channel had two, or at times three, reporters covering the event. As soon as a voter came out after casting his vote, the media hounded him for quotes and ask what the mood in the election hall was like. Multiple SMS polls were conducted with viewers asked to SMS the name of the candidate of their choice and give reasons for their answers.

Even after the results were announced, poll analysis went on like general polls with discussion-based programming that follow the conclusion of a thrilling cricket match. Except, the graphics had changed, adding fuel to the fire. The Star Ananda graphic, which showed the two contestants locked in crossbat, now went a step further and showcased Dalmiya knocking Mukherjee down from his horse with his sword. Another graphic on Kolkata TV had Dalmiya dwarfing the chief minister. That all of this had an impact was evident the following day when Buddhadeb Bhattacharjee, fresh from signing an MOU with the Salem Group for promoting industry in the state, declared in disgust that the victory of Dalmiya was the victory of evil over good. 'If you want to call it a *jihad*, go ahead and write it,' the chief minister thundered, caring little for any probable dressing down from the party headquarters at Alimuddin Street later. 'It is a victory of evil over good, over right-thinking people. This happens at times in history when growth is reversed.'

And even though the party secretariat came down hard on the chief minister and censured him for his comments, television channels had a field day. Star Ananda did a special programme titled *Ball e*

Budhha, Bat e Jyoti (Buddha with the ball and Jyoti with the bat), in which they interviewed former mayor, Subrata Mukherjee and RSP leader and minister, Nandagopal Bhattacharya. The main aim of the programme was to bring to the open the hostility within the upper echelons of the CPI(M). It was a phone-in programme and viewers from as far as the Andaman and Nicobar Islands called in to say that they had lost respect for the progressive and upright Budhhadeb Bhattacharjee.

The DLF Cup: 12–24 September 2006, Kuala Lumpur, Malaysia

Even the most ardent of cricket fans will admit that the tournament played at Kuala Lumpur in September 2006 was not conceived to boost cricket in Malaysia. In fact, a sample survey conducted weeks before the start of the tournament pointed out that only three among 100 people in Kuala Lumpur knew that such a tournament involving the world's three leading teams was to start in a matter of days in the Malaysian capital. In Australia, the tournament had hardly evoked any murmur. Perhaps the only time people referred to it was because Glenn McGrath and Matthew Hayden had made it back to the ODI team and when Adam Gilchrist had announced his unavailability citing possible burnout.

Blatantly put, Australia hardly took it seriously. As the Australian selector Andrew Hilditch stated on the issue of Gilchrist's selection: 'Gilchrist is a vital member of the Australian Test and one-day side and performs an extremely demanding role . . . The best way to prepare him physically and mentally for the upcoming summer of cricket is to allow him to continue his training program at home. We consider this to be an ideal preparation for Adam before the ICC Champions Trophy, the Ashes and the 2007 World Cup.' Even Mahinda Vallipuram, vice-president of the Malaysia Cricket Association had stated in an interview: 'We would certainly like to make it an annual tri-series event, making Malaysia a neutral venue for other teams to come and play . . . We don't just have the grounds but we have the infrastructure, hotels, an airline hub and a well placed time zone to back us.' Interestingly, not once did he mention in the course of the interview that the tournament would help boost local cricket in Malaysia.

The question that crops up is, why was the BCCI desperate to send the Indian team to play before a paltry crowd of 7,000 Indian expatriates? Even with temporary stands, erected specially for the purposes of the DLF cup, the Kinrara Oval in Puchong, Kuala Lumpur, could only house a little over 7,000 spectators. Moreover, why did the BCCI spend USD 4 million to install floodlights at the venue when any stadium in the Indian heartland or in any of India's north-eastern states would have been far better off with such an installation? Was it simply to help the 7,000-odd spectators to view their cricket better? Finally, was such a huge expenditure for such a small audience justified? Or was there yet another ulterior motive that went far beyond the politically correct argument of trying to boost cricket in Malaysia and thus furthering the timeless objective of trying to globalize cricket?

The truth is, the DLF Cup in Malaysia was a satellite TV bonanza. It was nothing more than attractive programming organized for the Indian satellite television market by the BCCI. Just like the soaps and the serials that dominated evening television in India, the DLF Cup helped provide yet another alternative to these in the two weeks between 12–24 September 2006. It was an attractive package for the television industry, not only for the broadcaster, which had the rights to beam the games live, but also for the news channels, each of which was invested in cricket programming. Indian journalist and social scientist, Nalin Mehta, puts it well: 'Unlike any other country in the world, the Indian television industry has consciously ridden on cricket's shoulders to such an extent that by 2006, cricket-oriented programming accounted for the greatest expenditure in news-gathering across most news channels. So dependent is news television on cricket, for revenues and for viewers; so prominent is cricket in news programming, that it would be fair to call this process the "cricketization" of Indian television.'

It was for these channels that the floodlights were installed; it was for them that Kuala Lumpur was picked ahead of Toronto. Had it been the latter, matches would have started at 7 p.m. India time and continued till the wee hours of dawn. And if played under floodlights, they would have consumed the entire night. In contrast, matches at Kuala Lumpur started at midday in India and ended by 9 p.m. in the evening. Television programming around the games easily continued till midnight, allowing the broadcasters the opportunity to reap real dividends.

This is not to say, however, that the entire agenda was driven by economic imperatives. While the monetary certainly overshadowed everything else, the political, too, sneaked its way in. It was top-down cricket imperialism at play—host a tournament at a neutral South-east Asian venue, provide them with the necessary funds to build infrastructure, contribute somewhat to promoting cricket in uncharted territories and build on votes of these Associate Member countries within the International Cricket Council as well as the Asian Cricket Council. It was a form of neo politico-economic imperialism, where the Americanization model of globalization is turned on its head.

This was borne out when on 1 May 2006, the subcontinent, led by India, outwitted Australia and New Zealand in what turned out to be a rather one-sided battle for the rights to host the 2011 World Cup. Aside from the usual exhilaration a successful bid brings forth, the late subcontinental entry culminating in an euphoric triumph in the face of stiff Western resistance drew attention to certain defining truths centering the future of India's most loved passion. The World Cup bid, more persuasively than ever, brought to the fore the political and economic might of Asian cricket, a might acquired largely on the strength of the booming satellite television market.

When the subcontinental delegation, led by the BCCI and the Pakistan Cricket Board (PCB), landed in Dubai for the ICC meeting to decide the hosts of the 2011 World Cup, they had the necessary financial muscle to take on, and overpower the West. The subcontinental financial might was such that it could easily buy out the West Indians, as was alleged in the media, with a promise to help them monetarily before the 2007 edition of the World Cup. And in their bank balance, the BCCI-led Asian delegation had elements of aggression that is historically so typical of the West.

As mentioned earlier, satellite television played a central role in this role reversal because of its unique relationship with Indian cricket. Why are they such good bedfellows despite the high costs of international cricket coverage? Simply because had television not generated the money it does for cricket, the organization of these tournaments would not be feasible. On the other hand, these tournaments worked well for the television industry for wooing prospective advertisers. The strategy was to convert a cricket series that would otherwise have been covered as part of the regular sports news into a mega news event like the general elections or the annual Union Budget to tap into the unique Indian passion for cricket.

Given the structure of satellite television in India, in which there is an extreme reliance on advertising in the absence of proper monitoring of households with access to cable, cricket is like the Pied Piper's magic flute, which has a lasting charm on advertisers. According to a study, a single game of cricket affords 127 different ways to advertise a product on television. In 2001, for instance, as many as 473 brands advertised on cricket for 16,400 advertising spots on television. For television in general, cricket is a predictable news event, for which advertising can be bought and sold well in advance. For news television, in particular, cricket's centrality to notions of Indian identity offers an opportunity to capture audiences and advertising.

This is why every match is dissected across many channels in great detail, with the media alternating between baying for a player's blood and deifying him. This media hype explains the large scale convergence of politicians around the cricket field. A simple math is enough to explain the politician's interest in cricket: As agriculture minister in 2006, Sharad Pawar was on television not more than once every fortnight. As BCCI president, he was on television more than twice a day.

It was this ground reality that raised key questions on the future link between cricket and television. Would this be limited to being a money-spinner for both the BCCI and the television industry or could it have a deeper significance for the nation, both at home and in the diaspora?

Whether India won at Kuala Lumpur or not was irrelevant, the BCCI and the Indian television industry had already won their matches. The wedding could only become more colourful with an Indian victory. And it eventually did with the IPL in 2008, when irrespective of who played, India always won. An Indian domestic league backed by Bollywood and big corporates for Indian satellite television for the Indian sports and entertainment audience—it was a formula waiting to be cracked. And it was the enigmatic Lalit Modi who cracked the code in the most dramatic fashion. But before he did so, he had already started to flex Indian muscles, pushing world cricket to the brink of a divide in early 2008.

The world knows this crisis as 'Monkeygate'.

MONKEYGATE

It was the first morning of the Sydney Test in January 2008 and the fairly large contingent of Indian journalists covering the series weren't in their best mood following the news of Zaheer Khan's return to India with a heel injury. Zaheer, the spearhead of the Indian attack, had bowled with good rhythm in the first Test in Melbourne but was now out of the entire series with a recurring heel problem. With Zaheer unavailable, the onus was now on young Ishant Sharma to step up and show nous. Beaten in Melbourne by 337 runs inside four days, the Indian batting, too, needed to make amends and redeem itself in Sydney.

The first two sessions on day one could not have gone better for India. Despite an umpiring howler at the stroke of lunch, the first of many in the match, when Ricky Ponting had clearly edged a delivery to the wicketkeeper, India had reduced Australia to a score of 134/6 and was firmly on the ascendancy. Andrew Symonds, the last of the recognized batsmen, was out in the middle facing up to Ishant. That's when one of the most talked-about incidents in the history of the game occurred. Symonds, batting on 29 (and Australia still precarious at 183/6), edged a delivery to the keeper and the sound of the edge was heard by most in the stands! It was a regulation edge and he was out caught behind. Or so we thought in the press box till the action turned to umpire Steve Bucknor. To everyone's dismay, Bucknor was unmoved. The Indian players, who at first couldn't believe what was going on, clearly lost their mojo in the aftermath of this decision and Symonds went on to score an unbeaten 162, taking Australia to a very healthy total of 463 in the first innings. The fact that Symonds had stood his ground despite the regulation edge was starting to add to the already tense atmosphere surrounding the Test match. India needed to bat well to stay afloat in the series.

V.V.S. Laxman and Sachin Tendulkar batted with authority, and much to the delight of the Indian fans and journalists, India was on course to go past Australia. Laxman scored his customary 100 in Australia and Tendulkar continued his love affair with the Sydney Cricket Ground (SCG). Playing with elegance and flair, the duo gave the middle- and lower middle-order a solid foundation to build on. Thereafter, a handy knock of 63 from Harbhajan Singh, who came in at number nine, made a significant difference to the batting effort. And that's what irked the Australians. When Anil Kumble was out and India was at 345/7, Australia felt it was only a matter of time before the tail would fold. Harbhajan, with the bat, wasn't considered much of a threat in Australian conditions and soon frustration started to creep in among the hosts. Watching it from a distance, all we—those in the press box—could sense was that things weren't going too well. There was a lot of talk among the players and the game was frequently getting interrupted as a result. What the talk was about, however, we had little knowledge of and it was only after the day's play had ended did it come to light that Australia had complained to match referee Mike Procter against Harbhajan, alleging he had racially abused Symonds and called him a 'monkey'.

As the story started to unfold in all its hues, sources within the Australian team revealed that during the side's visit to India in October 2007, Harbhajan had once called Symonds a 'monkey'. Symonds, understandably, had taken serious offence to the remark. That's when it was agreed between skipper Ponting and the Indians that if the comment was ever repeated in future the Australians would straightaway complain to the match referee and not wait for any further dialogue.

The Indian camp, on the other hand, vehemently denied the charge and was utterly disappointed with Australia, blowing what they called 'routine banter' out of proportion. They were upset that a rather regular on-field spat, common in India–Australia cricket, was being made a huge issue of and that Harbhajan was being targeted unnecessarily. The sense of disappointment turned into rage when the match referee charged Harbhajan with a level three offence, which could result in anything between a two to four-Test ban. This was unacceptable to the Indians and clearly impacted their focus. India challenged the ban and the hearing was fixed for the end of the Test match. The Australian complaint meant the spirit of camaraderie, which was visible in Melbourne, had given way to a feeling of animosity between players of the two teams. They weren't talking to each other, and frayed tempers defined the last two days of the Test. What made matters worse was the poor standard of umpiring. A host of umpiring decisions went against India and both umpires, Mark Benson and Bucknor, had the worst game of their careers. Trying to save the match on the last and final day, India lost the wicket of Sourav Ganguly to a catch that was grassed but umpire Benson gave Ganguly out with the Australians claiming the catch. Television replays, however, made it clear that the ball had touched the ground before it was caught by Michael Clarke at slip. Dravid was also given out caught behind when his bat was far away from the ball and these two crucial wickets snuffed out the Indian resistance on day five. Australia won with just minutes to spare, and even the end of the match was marred by an ugly spat. The Australians claimed that none of the Indians had congratulated them after the victory and that did not go down well with the Indian team who were all miffed with what they called 'a long-drawn and ugly celebration'.

The media, too, was not left untouched and there was a clear India-versus-Australia divide in the press box. Very rarely does such a thing happen and the animosity was further fuelled when Kumble declared in the post-match press conference, 'Only one team was playing in the spirit of the game.' It was a throwback to the famous 1932 Bodyline comment of Australian captain Bill Woodful ('There are two teams out there. One is playing cricket and the other is not.') and the statement was met by rapturous applause from the Indian media covering the tour. There were verbal altercations between Indian and Australian journalists immediately after the press meet had ended and it is fair to say it was extraordinary what was happening around us. G. Rajaraman, a senior Indian journalist, had an argument with Malcolm Conn, currently a senior official with Cricket New South Wales, and objectivity and political correctness gave way to nationalist jingoism in Sydney.

All this took place even before the Harbhajan hearing had even started.

The BCCI, it soon came to light, asked the ICC to stand down umpire Bucknor for the third Test match at Perth, terming him as 'incompetent', and it was in no mood for a compromise. It was also rumoured that the BCCI was arranging for a chartered aircraft and, in case the hearing did not go as per plan, it would airlift the players back to India and abandon the tour. With Lalit Modi in power in the BCCI, everything was possible.

Moments after the press conference was over the hearing started. Not one journalist had left the stadium and all of us hoped it was just a matter of time before the hearing got over. We could see from a distance that players were going in and out and no one really had a sense of how long it would go on for. India were represented by captain Kumble, Tendulkar, Harbhajan, manager Chetan Chauhan and media manager Dr M.V. Sridhar, whereas Australia sent Matthew Hayden, Adam Gilchrist, captain Ponting, Clarke and, of course, Symonds. Umpire Bucknor was also present. During the hearing conducted by Procter, and as narrated to me by two of the people present, rival sides were asked for their respective versions of the incident and Bucknor was also asked if he had heard Harbhajan say the word 'monkey'. He said he hadn't and only got into the picture when Harbhajan and Symonds were seen arguing. Considering match footage did not reveal anything extraordinary, it was apparent that it was turning out to be one side's word against the other's.

Most journalists were initially seated in the stand closest to where the hearing was going on. By the time it ended, we had all walked around the whole stadium in an attempt to overcome the growing anxiety. Every attempt at news gathering was tried out but nothing seemed to work. No SMS sent to Indian players and members of the management inside was reciprocated and all we were left with was conjecture. News organizations kept calling their reporters at the SCG every few minutes and soon a sense of frustration started to creep in. There was nothing to sustain the breaking news machinery back home and all that was being put out was conjecture.

Anyone who has been to the SCG will agree there aren't many eateries around and when it turned dark, each of us started to wonder what to do for dinner. Most had not eaten the whole day given the manic nature of the action and around 11 p.m., a journalist colleague managed to get two packets of chips from somewhere for the entire collective. Each of us had a chip each and thanked him profusely for the generosity! The players, too, did not eat anything surviving on food that was left behind in the dressing room at the end of the game. Finally, around 1.30 a.m., the hearing ended. The players and the media did not leave immediately thereafter, with Procter wanting to deliberate and then announce his decision. The Indians looked exhausted and deflated. It was another hour before all of them were called in again and the decision to ban Harbhajan was announced. 'We protested right there and said we will challenge the ban. We said this was an unfair decision as there was no proof to back the claim and the umpires, too, had not substantiated the claim made by Symonds. The match referee was giving out an arbitrary decision and it wasn't good for the game,' said a senior member of the Indian management who attended the hearing. The match referee had supposedly said to them that while they were very much within their rights to challenge the ban, his decision was full and final.

Eyes red with exhaustion at the end of what was a 20-hour working day, the players were finding it difficult to walk back to their cars to go back to the team hotel.

Clueless as to how things were supposed to unfold from thereon, fatigue was fast giving way to anxiety. Each of us had a job to do and had started feeling the pressure. I had hardly slept when my phone started ringing. It was 4.30 a.m. and I saw my phone buzzing with a call from Dr Sridhar, who resigned from his post of BCCI's general manager of cricket operations in September 2017, and passed away soon after. 'As you know, Harbhajan has been banned for three Test matches for allegedly making a racist comment and we are going to challenge the ban. Please inform your colleagues that we are doing a press conference soon,' he said before disconnecting the phone. I still couldn't believe what I had heard. A press conference in Australia in the wee hours of the morning was unheard of!

We had our 'Breaking News' and all of a sudden Sydney was *the* place to be in.

The conference room was packed when it was announced that the Indian team would not back down and were firmly behind Harbhajan in this injustice. The crisis, clearly, hadn't ended with the hearing. Rather, the story had just begun to get complicated.

Print journalists hurriedly sent copies for the late edition newspapers in India, each trying to be as up-to-date as possible. Television crews were all recording their pieces, knowing the country would wake up at 6 a.m. and start following the developments.

This was the perfect news story for the Indian media. A white match referee backing the statements made by white Australians against the virtuous Tendulkar and the rustic but lovable Harbhajan Singh. Indian sensibilities had been hurt and a new India, aggressive and cosmopolitan, had to retaliate. How could the BCCI, the new arbiter of world cricket and the financial powerhouse, be snubbed and not respond? A backlash was imminent and CA, if rumours were to be merited, feared the worst.

What was to transpire subsequently would largely be a question of who blinked first.

The Indian team was due to leave for Canberra in the morning for a two-day practice game and the team bus was stationed outside the Hyatt Hotel from 7 a.m. onwards. The players were starting to come down and load their gear in the bus. Most had not slept and looked tired and fatigued. There was an unwritten media ban in place and no one was really saying what had gone on in the last two hours. Ganguly, my closest friend in the team at that point, came down at around 8 a.m. with his wife and I immediately asked him for an interview. Reluctant at first, he eventually gave in. 'Don't speak to me in public,' he said and asked me to join him for breakfast in some time. Ganguly, disappointed and frustrated at being given out the way he had been, was straightforward in saying the Australians had wrongly claimed the catch and the ball had touched the ground. The interview, played out in India within minutes, spread like wildfire and the headline understandably caused ripples: 'Ganguly Alleges Australians of Cheating.'

The BCCI, which had already upped the ante, spoke to senior players like Tendulkar and Kumble and it was unanimously agreed that Harbhajan would be given every possible form of legal help to contest the ban. Sharad Pawar, the then president, thereafter entrusted legal luminary and future BCCI and ICC president Shashank Manohar with the task and the case was handed over to Manohar's father V.R. Manohar, one of India's foremost lawyers at the time.

The level of aggression was being escalated with every passing minute.

Under specific instructions from the BCCI, the Indian team cancelled the trip to Canberra and the two-day game was abandoned. The bus stood there till midday and was soon being seen as a mark of Indian defiance. Finally, the whole group, in a public show of team-bonding, travelled to Bondi beach to play a game of volleyball. Harbhajan was the cynosure of all attention and credit must be given to him for having retained his composure amidst all the talk surrounding his victimhood. Tendulkar jokingly started calling Harbhajan 'Bhajji Jackson' (inspired by Michael Jackson) given the tremendous media interest in the sardar. It was clear to everyone present that the Indians would not travel further without a resolution to the crisis, a fact that was driven home by this statement issued by the BCCI: 'The Indian board realizes the game of cricket is paramount but so, too, is the honour of the Indian team and for that matter every Indian. To vindicate its position the board will fight the blatantly false and unfair slur on an Indian player.'

What further fanned the fire was a scathing indictment on Ponting by the venerable cricket writer and commentator Peter Roebuck. Roebuck, in his column, demanded an immediate sacking of Ponting and declared, 'If Cricket Australia cares a fig for the tattered reputation of our national team in our national sport, it will not for a moment longer tolerate the sort of arrogant and abrasive conduct seen from the captain and his senior players in the past few days. It was the ugliest performance by an Australian side for 20 years. The only surprising part of it is that the Indians have not already packed and gone home.'

While opinion was divided on Roebuck's column, it was indeed a shot in the arm for the Indians. Many looked at it as a vindication of Kumble's comment in the post-match press conference and Ponting, despite having won a record 16th consecutive Test match, could hardly savour the achievement.

Both sides had an opportunity to end the controversy when Kumble called Ponting just days after the Test match had ended. It was a well-meaning gesture and the Indian captain is reportedly said to have asked his Australian counterpart to withdraw the charge and move on. Some excellent cricket was being played and it was in the larger interest of the game that the issue be dealt with maturity and prudence. Ponting refused and insisted that the Australians wouldn't relent until some form of punishment was handed out to Harbhajan.

'Monkeygate', the name given to the impasse, could only turn murkier thereafter.

I had to fly back to Melbourne for a day to meet the ICC chief executive Malcolm Speed. The meeting was about a possible history of the ICC that Speed was keen on commissioning and when I met him at the Cricket Australia Headquarters on Jolimont Street, his first words were, 'It seems we are currently in the middle of a 15-round boxing match with India and it is still round five.' Speed, it was evident from his slouched posture, was visibly worried at the turn of events and was keen to restore normalcy as quickly as possible. The first real step in this direction was the summoning of Ranjan Madugalle to Perth to calm the nerves of both sides. India had lost faith in Procter and the only way the Indians could be made to travel to Perth for the third Test was if the ICC asked someone to step in who was acceptable to both teams. Madugalle, the former Sri Lanka middle-order batsman and a highly respected ICC match referee, was asked to fly to Australia immediately and take control of the situation. The Indian pressure had worked and it was round one to India.

Madugalle's arrival helped cool the Indians' frustration to an extent and the team finally travelled to Perth to play what was easily one of the most anticipated Test matches of recent times. A section of the Australian media added to the growing Indian determination by suggesting that the inclusion of Shaun Tait was enough to send a chill down the Indian spine. Tait, bowling at 160 kmph, was expected to blow the Indians away at the WACA in Perth and help Australia set the world record of 17th straight Test wins.

On the eve of the Test, Madugalle got Kumble and Ponting to shake hands for the cameras but it was apparent to everyone present that the brewing animosity was still very much alive.

The touring Indian media, which by now was an extension of the team, had the worst possible start to the Test match. There were roughly 35 journalists from India and we were given 12 seats to accommodate ourselves at the WACA. It was humiliating and deliberate. And when we complained to Daniel Davini, the head of media at Perth, the complaint was hardly given importance. Soon there was news of a scuffle between an Indian cameramen and an organizer, with the cameramen being shoved aside and abused. This pushed the situation to a boil. The entire Indian media was united and demanded better treatment and, finally, at the intervention of Australian media manager Philip Pope, whom I knew since his Cambridge days, the matter was resolved. We were given decent seats and the focus returned to the Test at hand. Deep down, all we wanted was the Indians to play the match of their lives. We wanted them to stand up to the challenge at the WACA and demonstrate that Sydney was indeed an unfortunate blip in the history of Test cricket. And, may I say, we weren't disappointed. Virender Sehwag, who was returning to the team after a year, started well and a 50-run opening partnership set the tone for the match. India, it was clear, were there to fight. We were cheering every run and were more fans than journalists. Sheer brilliance from Dravid and Tendulkar meant Tait was rendered ineffective and India's first-innings total of 330 was more than competitive. With R.P. Singh, Irfan Pathan and the young Ishant Sharma bowling with intensity, Australia was never allowed to bat with freedom. The real moment for India, however, came when captain Kumble got Symonds to edge to Dravid at slips picking up his 600th Test wicket. Kumble's reaction said it all. With arms flayed in celebration, it was evident that he was a deeply satisfied captain and bowler. He was anxious for the one extra second that umpire Asad Rauf took to declare Symonds out and just as the finger started going up did the celebrations start. Even after Symonds had walked back, Kumble continued soaking in the applause. He asked the umpire for the ball and showed it to the crowd, savouring the moment. Adam Gilchrist, the non-striker, walked up and congratulated Kumble and it was good to see the players exhibiting a semblance of civility in the middle. Kumble had conducted himself with great maturity in the aftermath of Sydney and it was a befitting culmination to the whole act. Deep down, he must have been smarting and had chosen the 22-yard WACA strip to deliver a telling blow.

With R.P. Singh picking up four wickets and all the other bowlers bagging two wickets apiece, Australia were bundled out for 212 handing India a commanding 118-run lead. Subsequently, when the Indians were bowled out for 294 in the second innings, thanks to a gritty 79 from Laxman, Australia had a mammoth 400-plus score to chase down to win the match. It was a challenge even for the likes of Ponting and Michael Hussey and the Test was set for a classic finish. With two Australian wickets down at the end of the third day, India had the advantage going into day four. But there was Ponting. And Hussey. And Symonds. And, finally, the ghost of Monkeygate.

Ponting and Hussey did put together a partnership and it took one of the best spells of fast bowling from an Indian speedster to break it. Ishant, playing only his fourth Test, breathed fire every time he came on to bowl and it was a treat for the eyes of every Indian supporter present in the stadium to see the very best in Ponting struggling to counter the young bowler. He could have been out at least six times to Ishant but, credit to him, Ponting survived. Just when it seemed that Ishant, hair all over and running in with steam and purpose, had come to the end of his spell, Sehwag ran up to Kumble to have a word. Despite having gone through an eight-over spell, Ishant was given one additional over. Sehwag, who had seen Ishant come up the ranks in Delhi and knew of his ability to bowl longer spells had urged Kumble to give him another over, which went on to change the course of the match. Ponting, uncomfortable right through, eventually edged Ishant to Dravid at slip and the Indians were ecstatic, having gone past the Australian captain. Ishant had missed out in Sydney despite having got the edge and the cricket gods could not be as cruel as to deny him again in Perth. Wickets fell regularly thereafter and despite a late resistance from Mitchell Johnson, an Indian win was only a matter of time. Finally, it was R.P. Singh who bowled Tait in giving India one of the best Test victories of all time. Delighted and relieved, the players let their guard down and the Indian dressing room was a sight to behold. Irfan Pathan, making a comeback to the team, was named Man of the Match for his all-round performance and, to the delight of everyone in the media, he walked across to us with a bottle of champagne to celebrate the award. Beating Australia in Australia was in itself a rarity and to do so at the WACA, the fortress of Australian domination, was an extraordinary achievement. Coming at the back of the Monkeygate scandal, the Test match was more than a cricket victory and was considered a statement of intent from India for the injustice meted out to Harbhajan.

Monkeygate and the unfairness of Mike Procter had been partly avenged.

India went on to compete hard in the fourth Test in Adelaide, which ended in a draw. Even though the series ended 2–1 in Australia's favour, most Indians considered it a moral victory for Kumble's team. Despite the fierceness displayed through the competitiveness of the on-field action, the attention soon turned to the Harbhajan hearing—which was scheduled for the end of the series—even before the Adelaide Test was over.

Harbhajan, who had been slapped with a three-match ban for committing a level three offence by Procter, was the player in focus in every sense. A day after he had been declared guilty of using a racially abusive term, Harbhajan had picked up Australian captain Ponting with his very first delivery and the celebration was a hugely exaggerated one. He literally ran across half the ground and finished off with twin somersaults, rubbing it into Ponting. A lovable, expressive young man, Harbhajan has courted multiple controversies in his career thereafter. His volatile, expressive nature, over-the-top celebrations and overtly passionate persona has often made him the primary target of the opposition. Having known him well over the years, one is forced to appreciate his resilience and determination and innate ability to hold his own in the face of adversity. Leading up to the hearing, he held multiple telephonic meetings with his lawyer V.R. Manohar to prepare his defence. 'We spoke to him several times to understand exactly what had happened and what had resulted in him losing his cool. We asked him not to leave out a single detail when he was speaking to us,' Shashank Manohar recounts while speaking of the trial.

What changed the entire scenario was the BCCI's decision to send senior cricket administrator Inderjit Singh Bindra to Australia. Bindra, a former BCCI president, had held every conceivable post in world cricket and was by far the best man for the job. The Indians were in Adelaide when Bindra arrived, and in the next 48 hours, a series of meetings took place between the lawyers of both sides.

With the case having turned into a judicial enquiry, it wasn't possible for the BCCI and the CA to reach an out-of-court settlement and bury the hatchet. The hearing had to continue, and in such circumstances, the best thing to do was to agree not to escalate the situation further.

'Cricket Australia blinked,' said one of the members involved. 'In Mr Bindra's presence, we signed a declaration two days before the hearing that the Australians would reduce the level of the charge and it was a sign of things to come. Both sides, it was agreed, would sign the declaration. The Australian players weren't present at the meeting and we were later informed that they were somewhere in the outskirts of Adelaide giving Adam Gilchrist a farewell for he had just announced his retirement from Test cricket. The lawyers went to meet them at midnight and got them to sign the declaration.'

The Australian players, who had little knowledge of the backroom deliberations, were understandably miffed and felt let down. Some of them vent their frustrations in court and also said a few unpleasant things about their home board.

What further helped Harbhajan was the leak of Procter's confidential report to the media just days before the judicial trial. The report, which made it evident that Procter had relied on the Australians' words against the Indians', had the effect of weakening the intensity of the charge. The leaked transcript from Procter's report read as follows:

> I have heard evidence from Andrew Symonds, Michael Clarke and Matthew Hayden that he [Harbhajan] did say these words. Harbhajan Singh denies saying these words. Both umpires did not hear nor did Ricky Ponting or Sachin Tendulkar. I am satisfied and sure beyond reasonable doubt that Harbhajan Singh did say these words . . . I am satisfied that the words were said and that the complaint to the umpires, which forms this charge, would not

have been put forward falsely, I dismiss any suggestion of motive
or malice.

Harbhajan continued to deny the charge and with the BCCI making
the matter a test of national prestige and a trial of Indian clout at the
ICC, CA was forced to back down. The charge was downgraded to
a level two offence (use of obscene language, and not a racial slur)
by mutual consent even before the hearing on 29 January. Eventually,
Harbhajan was let off with a fine. The ban, to the relief of Harbhajan
and the BCCI, was overturned.

Australian players felt further let down because Harbhajan
was only fined 50 per cent of his match fee, which Justice Hansen
concluded later, was a mistake.

'I need to add something about the penalty I imposed. In imposing
that penalty, I took into account Mr Singh's previous transgressions
as advised to me by the counsel assisting Mr Jordan. I was told
that Mr Singh had one infraction in April 2003 for what was the
equivalent to a 2.8 offence under the present Code. That was for
an abusive comment made to the umpire when he was fined 50 per
cent of his match fee. That was the only infraction that Mr Jordan
had been advised of by the ICC. After the penalty was announced,
I was made aware that in fact there were three further matters I had
not been informed of. Overnight I have given earnest consideration
to the Code of Conduct to see if it empowers me to reopen the
sentencing process. Regrettably, I have concluded that I cannot do so
and the penalty imposed by me must stand. At the end of the day,
Mr Singh can feel himself fortunate that he has reaped the benefit
of these database and human errors. But judicial experience shows
that these are problems that arise from time to time,' said Judge
Hansen.

He also went on to say, 'In the course of submissions I raised
directly with counsel for Cricket Australia, Mr Ward, what was the

level of offence that Mr Symonds took from what was said to him. He confirmed that Mr Symonds took the language to be offensive and seriously insulting but did not consider it fell under the requirements of 3.3 [of the ICC Code of Conduct]. Given that is the view of the complainant, it is hard to see how the requisite elements of 3.3 could be satisfied.'

The verdict was looked upon as a victory of Indian financial muscle as this piece in the *Sydney Morning Herald*, by Australian journalists Chloe Saltau and Alex Brown bear testimony to: 'World cricket authorities have caved in to the game's financial superpower, India, and Cricket Australia has incurred the wrath of its own Test players by pressuring them to drop a racial slur charge against Harbhajan Singh. Cricket Australia was anxious to have the charge dropped because it feared its board would be sued for a figure understood to be about $60 million if India quit the tour. India's broadcast partner, ESPN, owns the lucrative contract to beam cricket from Australia into the subcontinent. If ESPN sued successfully, it could take 10 years to recoup the losses, Cricket Australia told the players.

'But the Australian cricketers were understood to be furious last night after the International Cricket Council lifted the ban and instead fined the controversial spinner half his match fee.

'It is understood the Australians had expected Harbhajan would be hit with a one-match ban and were dismayed to hear he had avoided any meaningful punishment.

'One Australian player, who refused to be named, told the *Herald* last night: "The thing that pisses us off is that it shows how much power India has. The Aussie guys aren't going to make it up. The players are frustrated because this shows how much influence India has, because of the wealth they generate. Money talks."'

While the controversy formally came to an end on 29 January 2008, with the verdict going in favour of Harbhajan and India, several questions continued to remain unanswered in the aftermath of the verdict. First and foremost: Did Harbhajan Singh say the word 'monkey' or did he not? If he did not call Symonds a 'monkey' what exactly had he said? Under what provocation was he forced to do so and what all had Symonds said to him? Had Symonds and Ponting blundered by taking the matter to the match referee without consulting Kumble and the Indians? Finally, will we ever know the real truth about 'Monkeygate'?

In a private conversation at the end of the series, a senior Australian team official on condition of anonymity confessed to me that the Australians, in hindsight, believed they had overdone it. While there was little doubt in their mind Harbhajan was guilty of calling Symonds a monkey, the matter, he felt, could have been dealt with differently. To lose face and cause a rift with the CA was never the intention and few had envisaged the damage the issue ended up causing. Most importantly, it scarred Symonds deep down and he never recovered from it fully, going steadily downhill as a player ever since.

On 13 March 2017, Michael Clarke, one of the witnesses in the controversy and Sourav Ganguly, a key player at the time, were in conversation with me on the issue while launching Clarke's autobiography at the Fanattic Sports Museum in Kolkata. Both were relaxed and said it was water under the bridge. Clarke, who had testified in favour of Symonds, agreed that the issue was not handled well by Symonds and the Australians. While he never directly answered if Harbhajan did say 'monkey', he did not deny it either. All he said was, 'I was very close to Andrew [Symonds] at the time. I asked him if he was racially vilified. It wasn't only about being racially abused for Andrew but a lot of other things as well. Now it's not the right time to discuss those things. But I didn't

think he [Symonds] should have continued with that [incident]. It should have ended right there.'

Clarke, not the seniormost in the Australian team at the time, could do little because Ponting, Hayden and others wanted to go official with the complaint and see an end to the situation. 'It did not help Australian cricket in the end,' Clarke asserted.

Ganguly, too, tried to diffuse the issue saying, 'Only a sardar will know what Harbhajan tried to say. No one can paint a fully accurate picture of it ever. You can call it "Monkeygate", you can call it "Hanumangate" and whatever gate you want. Unless I was standing next to Harbhajan Singh and I know exactly what he meant, it is impossible to state the real fact.' Ganguly went on to add, 'Nonetheless, that incident was a bit more than "Monkeygate". The next morning, everyone was angry and there were calls going on with the board on whether or not to go back and abandon the tour. It was a very intense but also a wonderfully fought-out series.'

Harbhajan, who was at the receiving end for the next few months in Australia and was forever under intense media scrutiny, did well to come out of the controversy without feeling scarred. To have one camera exclusively monitor your movements during a cricket match has very rarely happened and that's what happened to Harbhajan in the Commonwealth Bank one-day series that followed. Each time he fielded at the boundary, he would incur the wrath of the local fans who continued to call him names. That he was feeling the pressure and wanted to prove a point was borne out when, in the second final of the tri-nation series, he managed to trap Andrew Symonds leg before wicket. It was a huge wicket in the context of the game and was as much important to India as the two gems from Tendulkar in the two finals. India, after 22 years, beat Australia in Australia in an ODI competition and, in hindsight, it must be said that 'Monkeygate' helped the team bond better and play cricket at a level very few teams have been able to accomplish in Australia.

'I never wanted to win a cricket match as much as I wanted to win the Commonwealth Bank series final. It is not pleasant to be targeted. It was as if I was a criminal and had done something seriously grievous. Even after the verdict had come in my favour, the matter wasn't really over. And that's why winning the two finals had given me so much satisfaction,' recollects Harbhajan.

While we will never know the real truth on 'Monkeygate', it can be said with certainty that such a thing will never happen again in the annals of world cricket. With franchise cricket having taken over and with players from all countries spending a lot more time with each other than ever before, cultural differences and inter-personal relationships have seen a sea change over the last decade. What was once considered impossible is no longer unimaginable. Harbhajan and Symonds playing for the Mumbai Indians was one such thing. And the duo, for the world at least, did bury the hatchet while playing on the same team in the IPL. They even appeared as experts on India Today Television during the 2015 World Cup, getting along fairly well during the month-long extravaganza.

Symonds, however, will never forget the hurt of 'Monkeygate', an incident that ended up derailing his career.

Opening up in a candid chat at the end of the India Today cricket conclave on 13 March 2015, 'Symmo' put it rather poignantly: 'What you don't expect to see as cricketers is people hiding the truth. That's why we call it the "gentleman's game". That's why we play it. Unfortunately, that's what happened in Sydney in 2008. Our captain ended up looking arrogant and unreasonable and that should never have been the outcome. The issue ended up being politicized, going against the very essence of what the game stands for.'

Does he still feel victimized and believes it was Indian money that won the day? Can he ever erase 'Monkeygate' from memory and move on? Does he still relive the Sydney memories from time to time?

I must say I asked him all of these questions. All I got was a wry smile. It was as if Symmo was telling me, 'Interpret it as you like. I am over and done with what you guys have labelled to this day as "Monkeygate".

IPL: THE BILLION DOLLAR BABY

I had interviewed him a few times before, but this one was different. It was the height of 'Lalitgate' and Lalit Modi—fallen sports czar exiled in London, fugitive to many and persona non-grata for the IPL, which he once lorded over—was driving the Indian media industry 24x7 and enjoying the action. Every tweet of his was lapped up by the Indian news media and every statement monitored, reported and distorted. Here was a banished baron soaking in every bit of the media energy from London. Like most other Indian journalists, I, too, had asked Modi for an interview. A disclosure of what really happened when he was handed out a suspension by the BCCI on 25 April 2010. How could world cricket's most powerful man get pushed out from his own kingdom, treated with disdain and disrespect? How could he be forced to leave the country and labelled a 'fugitive'? Had the IPL, masterminded by him, consumed him in the end? Or was it the end at all? Did the IPL close in on him and force him to make mistakes? When did the noose tighten and did Lalit not realize what was happening around him? Most importantly, could he ever make a comeback to run the world's most-watched franchise cricket league? Did he even want to?

He had promised me a tell-all, showing me papers and not hiding anything.

That's as Lalit Modi as he could ever be.

As I started out from my brother-in-law's apartment in West Hamstead to the Bulgari Hotel next to Harrods, Modi's base for the evening, I was busy rehearsing the questions in my mind. I was in no hurry and wanted answers to most of them. The puzzle had to be solved and the story completed.

When I was about halfway there, Modi called. 'When are you coming?' he asked. It seemed he was in a good mood and I was in luck—or so I thought. The next statement was characteristic of Modi. 'Come, and let's have some great Lebanese food together. I will show you everything, but no interview.' With Modi, it was safe to assume that everything was possible. He could change his mind in minutes, rather seconds, and it was useless to try and persuade him on the phone. So what if I had mentioned to my channel back home that I would get him on camera? Why should it matter to him if I was left embarrassed? Or maybe it did. With him you never really knew. The best course of action was to just go and not turn back midway. Meet him at least. Speak to him and understand his side of the story. And then try one final time to convince him to speak on camera. As I said, with Modi everything was possible.

When I reached the hotel in 30 minutes' time, each minute agonizing and painfully slow in passing by, I was surprised to see Modi sitting at one end of the lobby with multiple lawyers sitting around him. Papers were neatly arranged on the table and people busy taking notes on multiple laptops. He had set up a mini office in the hotel lobby. Wearing his trademark suit, with a fluorescent scarf sticking out from the pocket, he looked like he had lost weight since I had last seen him. When I entered, he did not even bother to look at me—a very Modi-like thing to do again. I knew it could be awkward with him. Mostly was. Finally, when I made a rumbling noise did he look up. 'Boriaaaaa,' he said. It was good that I was able to rouse some interest. Or so I thought to placate myself. Having asked me to sit, he had once again gone back to his Blackberry. He was busy typing tweets, 140-character torpedoes that on a daily basis, rather hourly, was running India's media industry. These were his words, not mine. He may have lost weight but he did not seem the least bit scared or uneasy. Certainly not edgy as some, who had met him earlier, had mentioned. He was every bit the Lalit Modi you'd expect him to be—confident and indifferent at the same time, with an attention span of no more than five seconds.

'No interview, Boria,' he repeated again. 'My lawyers have asked me not to speak on camera,' he said with a chuckle. Maybe they did, but the way he said it, it was clear he did not take the warning seriously. It was his call (like it always was!) For some reason unknown to the rest of the world, he wasn't in the mood to do an interview. I had just reached the hotel and it was too early to press the panic button. He immediately ordered a Lebanese platter and went about explaining to me how good the food was. The honest truth, though, was that I wasn't remotely interested in this topic. 'Yes, I will show you all the papers,' he said and flipped open a notepad. 'Do you know how I got the bidders in early 2008? No one was willing to come forward. Why should they? No one, including me, really knew how the IPL would turn out. Whether it would fly or bomb. Was India ready for it? I personally had to convince each and every one of them.'

As he was speaking, he was also scribbling some numbers on the notepad. Perhaps, they made sense to him, for I couldn't find meaning in the exercise. Very Modi again. This is how he used to do deals when he was the IPL boss. Within seconds, contracts were done. If he thought the numbers were right, you had a deal. No sounding out the governing council or the BCCI working committee. They were there to rubber-stamp it. He was the boss. To his credit, he did create the league. It was he who got the bidders and convinced them to put in money. It was he who got the movers and shakers of the country to back the concept. It was he who made a success story of it from nothing. It was he who got his relatives to pick up stake as a show of intent. It was make-or-break for Lalit Modi and make he did. Shashank Manohar, the man who suspended Modi in April 2010 for unethical conduct, agrees Modi had done the hard work. 'You have to agree Lalit worked day and night to make it work. He had spoken to people and got them on board. Very few people were willing to come forward at the time because no one really knew what was in store,' Manohar, as straight-talking a man as ever, says. 'We, in the BCCI, never expected the IPL to become what it has, and credit must be given where it is due,' notes the current ICC chairman. IPL was Modi's baby through and through. But what happened in the subsequent run of events that he lost it all? What necessitated him to be unceremoniously pushed out of the BCCI overnight? What caused him to be hounded and questioned, to be pulled up for corruption and suspended for life?

Just as he was about to get back to his Blackberry, did I ask him *the* question. 'Are you scared?' Honestly, it was something I asked rather instinctively. Any person hounded by the Enforcement Directorate (ED), the Central Bureau of Investigation (CBI) and the political big wigs in Delhi ought to be. It was normal, at least for people like us. I hadn't anticipated the reaction the rather innocuous question could evoke. Modi, all charged up, looked at me straight in the eye. The smile didn't leave his lips when he said, 'Scared? For what?' Thereafter, he asked me to follow him through the lobby straight out on to Kensington High Street. I did as asked. As we were on the road, he said to me rather mockingly, 'If I put my hand up here, armed security will surround us in no time. Trained for armed combat . . . my personal security is. I am not scared. People in India ought to be. I have done nothing wrong,' he thundered. 'So why don't you say this on camera and tell me why the BCCI went after you in the first place,' I said, in a manner of making conversation. 'Do you have a camera? Tell them to set up in the park across,' he ordered and just walked back to the hotel lobby, leaving me stranded.

Again, very Modi.

I couldn't help but wonder to myself, *Had he really changed his mind and was he really going to do the interview?* I still wasn't sure, and wanted to check with him one more time before I asked my colleague Loveena Tandon to set up. As I had made it back to the lobby, one of his lawyers walked up to me and said, 'Ask whatever you want on cricket. He will answer. In fact, I would say ask him all the tough questions for it is important for people to know his side of the story.' That left me to get things set up before he changed his mind again. Once we were ready and I went in to call Modi, he had a changed look. He had buttoned-up his shirt and combed his hair. Just as we stepped out to walk across the park, a few Indians walked up to him and shook his hand. They congratulated him for what he had done for Indian cricket and asked him to keep fighting and not give up. He loved it. Here he was exiled in London but every bit the celebrity he was in India. Or so he thought. 'People keep walking up to me,' he said. 'They know I am innocent. They know I have given Indian cricket the biggest success story of all time. You can never take that away from me,' he mumbled as we walked up to where Loveena had set up.

Just as we were getting miked-up for the interview, his phone buzzed again. I was irritated to see him take the call. As he left us, I heard him say, 'No, no, don't worry.' While there was no way of knowing who had called, my best assumption was that it was an Indian politician. I did not, obviously, ask Modi and showed no curiosity. He walked back to where we were within minutes and gave me a knowing smile, which was both self-assured and cocky. It was obvious he was guarding secrets. He knew much more than he would ever say and many in the Indian political hierarchy were in touch with him.

Modi's Money-Spinning Monster

The IPL has resulted in an unprecedented windfall for the BCCI and for franchise owners of the eight competing teams, a number that had gone up to ten in 2011. Contrary to initial fears, the board earned INR 350 crore from the inaugural edition itself, much more than its entire profit of INR 235 crore in 2007 from overall operations. Even before the semi-finals were played, 99 million viewers had tuned in to watch the IPL matches. Several franchise owners like Shah Rukh Khan had recovered a major part of their investment in year one itself. It is this unprecedented success of the IPL, repeated for ten straight years between 2008–17, that has helped consolidate India's position as world cricket's centre of gravity and completed the process of Indian cricket's financial takeover of the global game.

Apprehensions

Lalit's decision to put iconic cricketers under the commercial hammer in February 2008 met with vociferous opposition from more than one quarter. Moralists and politicians throughout India were up in arms against this public auctioning of the country's biggest stars, even threatening to raise the issue in Parliament. Gurudas Dasgupta of the Communist Party of India (CPI) claimed that the auction had sounded the 'death knell' of the gentleman's game. In Mumbai, Shiv Sena supremo Bal Thackeray castigated the then BCCI president Sharad Pawar for turning cricketers into 'commodities'.

Modi, however, was unfazed. He believed in the spectacle and, in Pawar, he had an ally who was willing to travel the distance with him. So what if you *bought* Sachin Tendulkar? Could you imagine the thrill of seeing M.S. Dhoni being *sold*? How titillating was the prospect of possessing the man who had won India the World Cup or a legend who is deemed the god of the sport! You could now *buy* them in an auction. The very thought was enough to rouse fan passion and, more importantly, investor interest. Modi knew it and did his best to ignite appeal among these stakeholders.

There were, however, a host of key questions that confronted him before the start of the IPL: Would the benefits of monetization of the players filter down to the grassroots and contribute to improving the domestic cricket superstructure? Would fans come out to spend their hard-earned money and watch games in the oppressive heat of April and May?

The question of fan participation was pertinent because, in India, fans generally only ever attend international cricket contests, where countries are pitted against each other. Nationalism, in other words, has been at the core of cricket-watching in India. Meanwhile, Indian domestic contests such as the Ranji Trophy or the Duleep Trophy, even when major Indian stars like Rahul Dravid or Sourav Ganguly are playing, hardly attract more than 1,000 spectators per match.

It was also conjectured that faced with teams made up of random conglomerations of players, the draw for most spectators was less the game and more the entertainment on offer. But would fans really want to be merely 'entertained' for seven straight weeks? Even in terms of television viewership, the IPL—pitted against soaps and reality-television shows—faced stiff competition. Finally, it was hotly debated if the benefits of the new league could ultimately serve as a supply line for future national stars?

Did any of these questions matter to Modi, I asked him. Was he ever apprehensive that the concept might not take off and result in a serious loss of face for him? Was it a risk worth taking when he had already added much to BCCI's revenues by getting TV rights for cricket matches in India sold for an unprecedented USD 612 million?

Modi, whether or not you like it, has never been averse to risk-taking. From pleading guilty for possession of cocaine as a student to marrying his mother's friend 20 years his senior, he has been a maverick in the real sense of the term. 'Cricket's potential had hardly been exploited,' he said. 'Players were earning pittance when they could easily earn amounts equal to or more than the English Premier League stars,' he declared. Here was a man who believed every bit in what he was doing and was willing to be ruthless in chasing his dream. Enemies would be made on the way, he knew. Egos shattered. People in power rubbed the wrong way. Nothing mattered, though. The success of the IPL, he knew, would silence all detractors and contribute to his stock in India. Nothing succeeds like success and no one knew it better than Lalit Modi.

A Success Story Like No Other

When the legendary Arthur Morris, key member of Don Bradman's invincible team of the 1940s, was asked what he got out of playing cricket, his answer was startling. Morris negotiated the question with a single-word retort: 'poverty'. With the onset of a cricketing revolution courtesy the IPL, contemporary cricketers are likely to have a radically different answer to a similar question. Most of them, it could be conjectured, will suggest with a welcome smile, 'We became millionaires.'

A billion dollars in TV rights for a ten-year period; 12,700 advertisement slots on Sony Entertainment Television Pvt. Ltd (the host broadcaster) for the 59 games between 18 April and 1 June 2008, all sold; hitherto unthinkable players earnings; USD 3 million in prize money; USD 5 million for title-sponsorship rights for five years, unprecedented television ratings and capacity crowds in practically all the games in its first year of existence, the IPL had unequivocally driven home the reality that the shift of the nerve centre of cricket to the subcontinent was complete.

There's little doubt that 18 April 2008 will go down in cricket history as the date when the game changed forever. Modelled on Major League Baseball and the National Football League, the IPL had come at a time when the Indian economy had opened itself to global riches and big corporates were trying to make India home and were in search of lucrative investment platforms across the country. IPL, for many, was the answer. At one go, it had given them a foothold in a market of a billion-plus and generated eyeballs that millions of dollars spent on advertisements wouldn't garner.

Add to this the fact that, for a billion-plus cricket fans, filling stadiums was hardly difficult with proper marketing and hype. With celebrity owners like Shah Rukh Khan and Preity Zinta—leading Bollywood stars doing their bit in earnest—fans had more than cricket on offer for a few hundred rupees—a great evening out at a reasonable price. In addition, with fans thronging the grounds or picking their seat in front of the TV set, sponsors queued up and paid millions for ten-second slots on Set Max, on in-stadia hoardings and team apparel.

The IPL Impact

With each of the first three seasons hugely successful, most matches selling out and with national cricket boards seemingly making room for it already, Modi was at an all-time high. He was on magazine covers the world over, dressed in his trademark style and flashing a smile. He was world cricket's most powerful man. The more he bulldozed the media, the more they loved him. A Lalit Modi interview was one of the most keenly sought-after conversations in the industry. And he knew that the ICC would not dare to react. The one time the ICC clashed with innovative private entrepreneurship in the 1970s, it was humiliated at the hands of Australian media tycoon Kerry Packer, an episode described best by journalist Gideon Haigh in his book *The Cricket War*. Says Gideon,

> Once the game had a price put on it, it became a commodity ripe for commercial exploitation. The only question was whether it could remain more than that. Perhaps the only surprise is that privateers have not revisited it with similarly grandiose visions. But perhaps

that emphasizes how audacious Packer's scheme was. Packer came at a moment when it could hardly have been more unthinkable to the authorities, off the back of the Centenary Test, when cricket was hugging itself with glee. But I also think that World Series Cricket evolved. When Packer first recruited players, he was not so piratical. He simply wanted players for what were not much more than made-for-TV exhibition matches, to compensate for having been denied the broadcast rights he had sought in 1976. It was the action of the authorities in trying to impose bans on players, restrict access to venues etc that intensified the roll-out.

If the IPL, too, humiliated it, control of the game's most lucrative version may well slip from the ICC's hands because the IPL is that unique tournament that inspired English players to revolt against their own board and, for which, Australian cricketers contemplated giving up the coveted baggy green cap.

Interestingly, even when the league moved to South Africa in 2009, at short notice, because of its clash with India's general elections, its popularity hardly waned. Half-full grounds or less than animated spectators in Durban or Cape Town could be perceived as blips only when IPL season two was compared to the packed stands and wild spectators back home in its inaugural edition.

For South Africa, the tournament was a success. Anyone with any knowledge of South African sport will agree that the IPL—a foreign import—did much to present the country as a perfect sporting destination before the FIFA World Cup in 2010. Social integration, still far from complete in mainstream South Africa, received a significant boost thanks to the IPL. And, sports organizers, fearing a Western backlash citing under-preparedness for the FIFA event, had their hands hugely strengthened.

IPL season two was also a successful experiment with globalization. It was India's first truly global sporting export and helped create the country's first international sporting brand. Considering most sports are still controlled and dominated by the West, the IPL was the best case study of 'atypical' globalization, where the West has to look to the East. It led to the possibility wherein Indian administrators could justify the claim that in cricket, at least, an Indian hegemony was about to commence. Unifying the global cricket world under its aegis, India was successfully consolidating its commercial hold atop cricket's global hierarchy. With leading exponents of the game like Shane Warne, Chris Gayle and others urging the ICC to create a window for the IPL, it was expected that this 'grip' over world cricket would grow stronger in years to come.

Also, the lasting gain from IPL's second edition was evident once the tournament returned to India in March 2010. The IPL came back to its home base having established itself as a leading global sports brand with multiple global enclaves and constituencies, carefully created and nurtured in the course of the second edition of the tournament.

At a time when the irresponsible actions of some global sports administrators like the Australian Tennis Federation tried to identify India as an unsafe sports destination (the Australian Davis Cup team refused to tour India in May 2009 citing security concerns, which was a strange decision because the Australian cricket team toured India for a seven-match one-day series in October–November 2009), the IPL was India's best bet in reversing this unfortunate trend. Having received rave reviews in South Africa and having done much to woo the world's best, IPL 2010 continued to bring together the most impressive assemblage of the world's leading cricketers. And with resolute government support coming to its aid in 2010, it did much to strengthen India's claim to being a safe sporting destination months before the New Delhi Commonwealth Games in October 2010.

King Without a Kingdom

Unprecedented success meant Modi was the universal talking point of world cricket. And Modi, as journalists would agree, made good copy. He was temperamental and would give you quotes which made headlines. He wasn't ever politically correct and, with him, there was always an element of unpredictability. He could ask a senior politician to go buy tickets and not ask for freebies; he could put up a personal message sent to him on social media, and could turn ruthless if he had to. Brutal even, as was witnessed in 2010; stretched thin only to soon become a pariah.

Having read the minutes of all of the IPL governing council meetings since its formation, it is evident that Modi was firmly in control of proceedings before he was questioned by Manohar, the BCCI president, on the amount of money being paid to International Management Group (IMG), the global sports management company, in mid-2009. IMG, it is recorded in the minutes, was to be paid 10 per cent of the gross revenue generated from the IPL for their services rendered in conducting the tournament. Manohar, who had met IMG officials in London separately, decreed this agreement untenable and suggested a fixed sum to be paid to IMG. Take it or leave it, the message from the president was clear. Modi, reluctant to accept the proposition, had to eventually give in because Manohar controlled the numbers in the governing council and could override any decision in his capacity as BCCI president. The chairman, all powerful for a period, now had a stronger opponent to deal with.

'I felt the money being offered to IMG was not justified. It was much more than what was fair and I couldn't allow it to be paid. I was agreeable to paying a fixed sum and suggested the same to members of the IPL Governing Council. If IMG did not agree, we would be forced to cancel the contract. What was improper would not be done when I was BCCI president,' says Manohar.

This had been more a skirmish than a battle. Modi, after a point, had given in and focussed his energies on adding two new teams to the world's fastest growing sports league. Valued at billions already, the base price for the two new teams was fixed by him at USD 225 million, double of what the highest bidder had paid in 2008. The base price, however, wasn't the problem.

In February 2010, Modi added two further clauses for prospective bidders. They had to have a net worth of a billion dollars and would have to furnish a USD 100-million bank guarantee. Neither of these two clauses was part of the 2008 tender and meant a number of prospective bidders were rendered ineligible to apply. Further, these two clauses had been added without clearance from the governing council and without informing the BCCI in any form of written communication.

Irked by the inclusion of these additional clauses and based on complaints he had received from the Indian team's sponsor Sahara India Pariwar and the Jagran group, Manohar was upset with the way Modi was conducting the tender process. That the president was livid is evident from the minutes of the IPL governing council meeting of 7 March 2010.

> The President, BCCI . . . went on to explain to the members that the conditions laid in the tender is unreasonable and reprimanded the Chairman for fixing unreasonable conditions for the eligibility. He explained that these preconditions were not part of the 2008 tender. The President further explained that he had further received complaints from GC members in regard to these conditions and Sahara who are sponsors of the Indian Cricket team and pay the BCCI 500 crores per annum have deliberately been kept out of the tendering process due to some of the conditions and they have written to him saying if they are good enough to pay 500 crores to BCCI how can they not be worthy enough to pay 150 crores a year [30 million dollars] even if they were to have bid 300 million dollars. Similarly other companies like Jagran group have also expressed the same concern that it is a deliberate attempt to keep most companies out . . .

The minutes go on to state that the president, for issues of probity and transparency, demanded that the tender process be cancelled and a fresh tender issued. The BCCI, he argued, was a public body and could not be seen to be indulging in unethical practice.

Modi, it is recorded, did speak to the president on the phone before adding the new clauses but Manohar had not seen the final document nor had he received complaints from prospective bidders at the time. The house unanimously sided with Manohar, and Modi, all of a sudden, was alone. He had to agree to cancel the process and reissue a fresh tender to be opened in two weeks' time.

Modi, the all-powerful voice in the IPL governing council, was fast losing ground.

The downslide had clearly begun.

Did he, however, not try to stem the tide and mount an opposition? Or was the match rather one-sided? With Modi around, was a one-sided contest even conceivable?

Modi did try saying that it was the president and the secretary who had cancelled the tender and dropped enough hints to say he was only trying to protect the BCCI's interests in the long term. Sadly for him, though, there were no takers for this argument.

The final act in the drama was played out when the Sahara group and the Rendezvous Sports World (a consortium of five companies) won the bids for the two new teams—Pune and Kochi—on 21 March 2010. Modi, grapevine has it, had not anticipated this. While he had no issues with Sahara, for a few weeks after the tender process was over, he refused to sign the Kochi franchise agreement on the ground that their share holding pattern was improper. Modi had doubts about Rendezvous' ability to honour the franchise agreement and also questioned the ethicality of the consortium.

Manohar, who by now was getting regular calls from people at Rendezvous and other interested parties, flew into Mumbai without informing Modi to check what was going on. 'I parked myself in the

BCCI office for four straight days and scrutinised all the papers. I found it fishy that Lalit was not signing the Kochi franchise document and told him he had to do so because they had won the bid fair and square. That's when he suggested we make public the share-holding pattern of the franchise. We had not made public the share-holding patterns of the existing eight franchises, so why [make] an exception in the case of Kochi? I did not allow him to do so.'

A frustrated Modi resorted to Twitter, and many of us know what ensued thereafter, including the resignation of Shashi Tharoor, from his post of minister of state for external affairs.

What Manohar had found—something that continues to be unresolved even now—is that Modi had also cancelled the television contract the BCCI had entered into with Sony in 2008 on the night of 14 March 2009, and parked the rights with World Sport Group (Mauritius) Ltd (WSG) for a facilitation fee of USD 80 million. On 17 March, within 48 hours of the cancellation, Sony won the rights back but only after paying WSG the INR 435 crore facilitation fee.

According to a letter from the BCCI to WSG, published in the media on 28 June 2010, this deal was a case of 'fraud'. 'The BCCI has very recently noticed that the said agreement [IPL Media Rights Agreement . . . for the Indian subcontinent] purportedly executed by Mr Lalit Modi, is in fact, a document which is totally vitiated by fraud perpetrated by you [WSG, India] in conspiracy with WSG, (Mauritius) Limited and Mr Lalit Modi. The agreement is, on the face of it, vitiated by fraud.'

The letter further said that this was done 'with your [WSG, India] connivance to defraud the BCCI of monies which ought to have been legally received by the BCCI . . . There was no bargain/ understanding between the BCCI and you [WSG, India] for these terms. We strongly believe that the agreement was signed by you [WSG, India] and Mr Lalit Modi to defraud the BCCI of the amount of at least USD 80 million.'

Modi had lost the platform he had used to build the IPL. Was he bigger than the institution and could he counter the charges levelled against him? He still claims he has done no wrong and, each time he says so, he backs it up with multiple tweets and posts on social media. Are these legally tenable and are his claims backed by facts? The jury is clearly out on this one. Manohar, on the other hand, had covered his tracks while issuing the chargesheet which accused Modi of serious wrongdoing. The chairman was losing allies and it was finally over for him on the night of the final of the third season (25 April 2010), when, within minutes of the match getting over, he was handed a suspension notice.

'Everything was ready by 20 April,' Manohar says. 'We did not want the tournament to suffer in the final few days and did not want to take a chance. We were waiting for the final to get over before we suspended Lalit and wrest control.'

Did Modi know about his impending suspension? The answer is an overwhelming 'Yes'. The lord of the IPL knew that his time had run out and that he would be stripped of all powers despite his attempts to counter the humiliation. But then, this was Modi—chairman and impresario. How could he bow out with a whimper? How could he go out disgraced and without making noise? So what if he was cornered and accused of corruption?

Modi still flew into the stadium in a helicopter with a smile on his face, looking radiant and confident. The battle wasn't over yet. In a speech full of sentiment, he went on to say: 'As the Bhagavad Gita says, "Fear not what is not real, never was and never will be. What is real, always was and cannot be destroyed." All I wanted is to leave a small footprint in the glorious history of the game, I thank my family, my children who have stood by me through the trying times all these years and continuously stay with me; I take my strength from them. My final thank you is to you, the fans all over the world. We missed you last year in India and it's wonderful to be back home.

It's your passion and this is the reason we built the IPL; it's your passion that sustains us, your passion that enriches us, this is not the Indian Premier League, it's the Indian People League. I humbly dedicate my dream to all the people in this country. Thank you.'

The Modi who took the stage that evening was very different to the one the world had come to know—a Modi who knew he was saying a final thank you but wasn't willingly doing so. He never would. In his mind, he had done no wrong. He was philosophical and sarcastic, belligerent and passionate. He had created India's only global sports brand and no one could take it away from him—a fact mentioned rather eloquently in his most recent letter to BCCI CEO Rahul Johri in mid-2017, saying he was leaving cricket administration. 'When I joined the system way back in 2005, Indian cricket was healthy but had still not achieved its true potential. Then as we set about course correcting, we unlocked the real potential regarding the commercial value of the game in India. When I came into the BCCI, the revenues were languishing at about INR 260 crore and when I left in 2010, the reserves were more than INR 47,600 crore. A game that would sell for a paltry INR 40–50 lakhs today sells for INR 100 crore. Today India is at the pinnacle of the world cricketing economy . . . Special mention here for one Mr Sharad Pawar—who shared the vision and encouraged me in our quest to launch and run one of the world's most viable cricket products of all time—the Indian Premier League. In 2010, it was valued at USD 11 billion and today the value of IPL has fallen to USD 4 billion due to lack of innovation. That has still increased the value of cricket in India by nearly eight times. Columbia and Stanford University have done case studies on how I built the league and sustained it.'

Modi is no longer there in the system; rather, he was pushed out of it, if we make no bones about being politically incorrect. However, during the process, he made a few things clear in the most inimitable manner—that the IPL was his creation, and will forever be. He was chairman and boss. The only czar.

To the world, however, he will always be the fallen one. Discredited and exiled.

As for me, I have my own little story on Modi's suspension. Just as the final had started at Dr DY Patil Sports Stadium Navi Mumbai, I got a call from a very senior sports administrator, who is no longer connected with cricket. He informed me Modi would be suspended soon after the final had finished. He read out the suspension notice and said firmly that he wouldn't take any further calls for the rest of the evening. I was free to do the story if I wanted to.

What if the information turned out to be wrong? It was Modi, after all, and with him, there were always repercussions. I called on the editor of Times Now, the English news channel I was working with at the time, and we decided to break the story at 9 p.m. IST, convinced that this was the bigger news headline of the day. Whoever won the IPL was a secondary headline to Modi losing the battle for his survival.

We were on the story for a straight two hours between 9 p.m. and 11 p.m. and it was only then that doubts started creeping in. What if my source turned out to be wrong? What if the notice wasn't given that night itself? And what could Modi do if I did get it wrong? Could there be a backlash of sorts?

Finally, at 11.30 p.m., other networks started following the story, but with a question mark. They weren't sure yet but it was too big a story to ignore. It was only around midnight that the story turned out to be correct with Modi being handed the suspension letter.

The IPL Rolls On

With or without Modi, the IPL rolled on. With celebrity owners and India's leading business magnates backing the league, its success continues uninhibited. So much so that the telecast rights for the tournament for the five years between 2018 and 2022 has fetched the BCCI a whopping INR 16,347 crores, an unprecedented increase in value.

In the course of the 11 years since the inception of the IPL, I have spent time with multiple teams and owners and have been amazed at the kind of passion the league generates. For example, the entire senior management of one of the teams used to leave the hotel together around 2 p.m. on match days to offer pujas for the team. They would never be a minute late, and the kind of discipline shown in performing this ritual was unbelievable! That the team did not have the greatest results is a different matter altogether.

Team owners, men and women who run big corporations, are not as tense in their business meetings as during IPL games. One team owner clutches a worn-out picture of his family deity for the whole time a match is on, and every wicket falling or boundary scored is greeted by a *pranaam*. Surrounded by friends and family, an IPL owner's box best defines the complex Indian modernity of today. Most people in this box wear expensive clothes and watches, carry fancy phones with powerful cameras and drive to the stadium in luxury cars. But when it comes to the game itself, they turn into devout god-fearing Indians who pray for the success of their teams. So what if they are not playing or have themselves never played the game? Prayers, many feel, are enough to win cricket games. *Prashad* (devotional offering made to god, usually referring to food) is passed on to the team members hours before the game and everything from vaastu to feng shui is tried out. Team names and jersey colours have been altered to align better with the stars, and it is fandom of a different nature that makes the IPL a very different beast in comparison to international cricket.

Tendulkar has alluded to the fascinating behavioural patterns of IPL owners in the book *Playing It My Way*. Owners in the IPL, he says, have their own superstitions, which are then passed on to the team. In one of the teams, it is always the team owners' priest who decides when the players should leave their hotel rooms on match days. It can be at any time during the day and on this issue there are no arguments. Whatever state the players are in, they will have to leave the room when the priest orders them to do so. 'I have seen players wandering in the corridors in towels or forced to go down for brunch even if they aren't hungry because they have been forced to vacate their rooms,' he says.

Another team owner believes in vaastu and their dressing room is always organized in a particular manner with mirrors set at specific angles. To go back to Tendulkar, 'It once happened that in a match against us [Mumbai Indians] in Mumbai, this team had even gone ahead and changed our dressing room at the Wankhede, putting in mirrors like the way they usually did at their home venue. Because it was our home game, this arrangement was changed late in the night and all mirrors were covered with towels to ensure the opposition was thrown out of their comfort zone.'

Things often turn funny as a result of these superstitions. On one particular occasion, the Mumbai Indians players were told not to use a washroom in the dressing room and a signboard was placed outside declaring, 'Bathroom out of order'. Seeing this practice being repeated a few times, one of the players went into the bathroom just as a matter of curiosity and it was soon discovered that it was in perfect working condition. 'Eventually,' Sachin recounts, 'the entire team decided on using this particular bathroom and that didn't stop us from winning that particular game.'

When it comes to performance, however, the owners turn ruthless. Reputations don't matter and it becomes a case of winner-takes-all. This was best borne out when Rising Pune Supergiant (RPS), owned by Sanjeev Goenka, removed Dhoni from captaincy and appointed Steven Smith as leader in their second and final season after a dismal seventh place showing in the inaugural season. There was much talk whether Goenka was justified in removing Dhoni, arguably India's best white-ball captain of all time and whether the choice of Smith, an Australian, was a rational one considering it was the *Indian* Premier League.

Goenka, it must be said, faced a serious backlash in the media for this decision and was even trolled on social media. Here was a business magnate removing one of India's all-time favourite icon from his perch! Goenka, however, was steadfast. The fact that RPS made the final of season ten losing out a last-ball thriller to the Mumbai Indians by a solitary run vindicated Goenka's decision and proved that in franchise cricket there are no holy cows; never was and never will be. Consider the case of Ganguly. Arguably one of the most popular Bengalis of all time, it was considered inconceivable that Ganguly would not be a part of KKR. When Shah Rukh Khan's franchise parted ways with him in 2011, there was a huge backlash in Kolkata. Some predicted that KKR was about to lose its fan base and that KKR's matches would be played to near-empty stands at Eden Gardens. Others went on to suggest that Gautam Gambhir will find it impossible to fill Ganguly's shoes as captain given Dada's god-like status in the state.

Yes, it started badly for KKR. A couple of games did see poor attendance. However, soon after the team started doing well, the fans returned to fill the stands. Furthermore, once Gambhir led them to the title in 2012 and again in 2014, the bitter Ganguly saga was all but forgotten. Nothing succeeds like success was the mantra and the franchise has since moved a long way forward.

This is what the IPL is all about. A commercially driven, ruthlessly competitive business proposition with a dedicated base of followers globally. It has little place for emotionalism. There can never be any debate on Dhoni's place in India's cricket pantheon. A true legend of the game, he will forever be perched atop the pedestal. But for Goenka, who had won the franchise for a period of two years only, it was now or never. Dhoni's past success was no satisfaction, for, under the Pune banner, Dhoni had the poorest of his IPL seasons in 2016. Goenka needed instant success and felt Smith was better suited to ensure that.

Virender Sehwag moving out of Delhi or Rahul Dravid moving to Rajasthan are other instances of marquee players shifting base from their state teams that come to mind. While Dhoni fans felt upset and let down, a few wins under Smith and the issue was soon water under the bridge.

Conclusion

It was around 11 p.m. and KKR had just won the IPL for the first time in 2012. It was a Sunday night; it wasn't supposed to take me more than 15 minutes to get to the television studio from my house. That's what I had assumed but I was totally wrong. Central Kolkata that night was a sight to behold—people on motorbikes and in cars with KKR flags, running havoc all over the city. It was no less than India winning the World Cup and was an eye-opener of sorts. I was stunned. As the words '*Korbo, Lorbo, Jeetbo Re*' (the team's theme song) reverberated through the air, it was borne out to me that the IPL, a domestic cricket tournament, had indeed captured the fan's imagination in a manner never seen before. Seeing me stand in front of a camera, fans jumped off their cars and bikes and started hugging and singing in front of the camera. While at one level, it is deeply frustrating to see fans do so and interrupt the show's flow, on another, it makes the show. They make for great television. Five thousand people on Park Street celebrating at midnight because KKR had won the final in Chennai was inconceivable, and that's what was happening in front of me. Modi stood vindicated—exiled or not. And the BCCI stood vindicated. But more significantly, with or without Modi, the IPL had not lost any of its charm. Indian cricket stood vindicated, for here was a model that was now the toast of the nation and was soon to be emulated the world over.

When the KKR players returned the next day, 60,000 people greeted them at the Eden Gardens with the chief minister felicitating the victors. The IPL had been appropriated. It was a spectacle that fans loved to consume. Playing the IPL was fast becoming an ambition in itself and questions were no longer asked about the viability of the league. It was past that stage. It had given cricket a very different kind of financial stability and, in doing so, had opened itself up to the unholy lot: bookies, middlemen and fixers. Players were relatively easy prey and soon the IPL would be in news for very different reasons. Yet again, it would end up transforming Indian cricket forever.

SKY-FALL

Not one of the 25,000 people present at the Wankhede Stadium on the night of 15 May 2013 to watch the encounter between Mumbai Indians and Rajasthan Royals could predict what was to unfold within six hours of the completion of the match. Mumbai had edged out Rajasthan by 14 runs and it had been a perfect night out for the home fans. For the Royals, on track to make the playoffs, the defeat was one to take in their stride and move on.

At least, that seemed like the plan.

'We were staying at The Oberoi and I got a call at 5.30 a.m. from the duty manager of the hotel. My wife picked up the call and passed it to me in a jiffy. The duty manager was saying to me that several policemen, including an assistant commissioner from the Mumbai Police, were waiting downstairs and I was to go down as soon as possible. We had a sponsor shoot with Cyrus Broacha [a television anchor and video jockey] the previous day and my first thought was this was a prank. I was being made a *bakra*. I even said so and tried to laugh it off. That's when I was told it wasn't a prank and that I was being summoned,' recounted Raghu Iyer (Rajasthan Royals CEO), still somewhat apprehensive about what to make of

the events on that fateful May morning that changed the course of
Indian cricket forever.

The Royals CEO went down within minutes and was met by
a team from the Delhi Police, led by an Assistant Commissioner
of Police (ACP) in a safari suit. The cops had done due diligence
and were there to arrest three of the Royals players on charges of
spot-fixing. Iyer had literally been pulled out of bed and was now
being told of the arrests. He was helpless, and found it hard to
comprehend—as would anyone in his position. All he managed to
ask was if the cops had a warrant. They did, and for the next hour,
they explained to Iyer all the evidence they had against the three
players in question. It was incontrovertible proof; something rotten
was going on.

'They were in no hurry and only after explaining to me in detail
did they tell me that they were going to Ankeet Chavan's room to
pick him up,' said Iyer. There was very little for him to do but feel
gutted and apprehensive. The two others, S. Sreesanth and Ajit
Chandila, had already been nabbed and were waiting in a police van
outside. For Iyer, the happenings seemed more reel life than real, but
the truth was he was one of the central characters of the drama. He
was caught in the middle of the biggest crisis the IPL had ever seen,
and as chief executive, he was expected to take charge of a situation
that was on a downward spiral. The misty morning, very typical
of Mumbai, best described Iyer's state of mind. To see three of his
players being arrested and hauled away on charges of corruption was
the worst a chief executive could ever anticipate.

The Royals owners, away in London, weren't available then (it
was 2 a.m. London time) and Iyer was counting down the clock. He
needed to inform Rahul Dravid and Paddy Upton, the captain and
coach of the team, and figure a way out before the media caught
wind of the story.

It was the lull before the storm and Iyer had 120 minutes to prepare himself for the media tornado that was to unleash itself upon the franchise.

'I informed Rahul at 8 a.m. and he was distraught. He had his hands on his head and just couldn't speak. To see a player of his calibre and stature having to go through this was painful. None of us really knew what to do except to go ahead and support the investigation. I informed Sundar [Raman], the IPL CEO, and my owners in London. It was decided that we would immediately issue a press release and not try to hide anything.'

It was around 9 a.m. in the morning when I got a call from the assignment desk of Times Now, the news channel I had a consultancy with at the time. I was busy working on an op-ed on the IPL, arguing that the brand was trying to free itself of taint and controversy and had been successful in doing so. Rocked by a number of scandals since its inception in April 2008, the IPL authorities were keen that the tournament, in its home stretch for the year, ended without controversy. The call, I must concede, came as a complete shock and turned things upside down. 'Sir, we need you live. Three players of the Rajasthan Royals team—S. Sreesanth, Ankeet Chavan and Ajit Chandila—have been arrested for spot-fixing,' the caller said before hanging up. He was in a hurry to put the news out and I immediately knew that all I had written so far was a waste. The IPL, the arrests meant, was faced with its worst crisis yet. As we went live on the story, news started to trickle in that the BCCI management was stunned by the sudden turn of events. It also transpired that the special cell of the Delhi Police, which had made the arrests, had been tracking the three players for a while and had enough evidence to indict them on charges of spot-fixing.

The first person I called was Iyer. I knew him well and was sure he would take my call. He did. His voice was low and he seemed depressed and lost. Not that I was surprised. On condition that all talk was off-the-record, Iyer narrated to me what had happened and said he would keep me posted. I wished him luck, for I knew he needed a lot of it to stay afloat. The police and the media were closing in on the Royals and even Dravid would find it hard to protect them.

Within moments of the news becoming public, the media went berserk. Rumours of other players also being involved started to do the rounds and critics began questioning the credibility of the tournament at large. All of a sudden, every match of the IPL played in 2013 was under the scanner for suspected corruption, sending the BCCI into a tizzy. They needed to start a process of damage control. The Royals management, shaken and stirred, issued a statement saying they would do everything to help with the investigation. The statement read:

> We have been informed that three of our players have been called in for investigation on spot-fixing in matches. We are completely taken by surprise. We do not have the full facts at this point and are unable to confirm anything. We are in touch with the BCCI on this matter. We will fully cooperate with the authorities to ensure a thorough investigation. The management at Rajasthan Royals has a zero-tolerance approach to anything that is against the spirit of the game.

This was a dull PR exercise and did little to calm people down. Legitimate questions, like why the officials had failed to stop the players from indulging in corrupt practice, started doing the rounds. Did they not know anything or were they trying to hide things? The questions hurled at them by the media were endless.

Iyer's statement, having gone viral in minutes, wasn't going to buy him time; he needed to put a plan into place as soon as possible. This statement from the Royals was followed by a release from the BCCI secretary Sanjay Jagdale, declaring the BCCI's commitment to stamp out every form of corruption and take serious action against the guilty. 'As of now, the three players—Ankeet Chavan,

Ajit Chandila and S. Sreesanth—stand suspended pending enquiry. All information required to bring the persons involved to book will be collected and strictest action will be taken, if found guilty. The BCCI is shocked and saddened at the recent developments. The BCCI has zero tolerance to corruption. We will offer all cooperation to the Delhi Police and all other authorities in their investigations in this matter. The IPL governing council has met and decided that the cricketers found involved will be dealt with severely.'

Jagdale, an upright cricket administrator, sounded distraught when I called him to understand the details. 'I really don't know what to say. We will, of course, take serious action. But I have no idea why people do things like these,' Jagdale said, trailing off.

The 24x7 news media industry jumped on the story. Cricket sells on television and this was a story which combined cricket and crime, two of contemporary India's most ardent obsessions. Reporters were instructed to get more on the story and correspondents were deputed across the country to figure out if there were other cases of fixing that could be brought to light.

Live pictures of Sreesanth, a double World Cup winner, being paraded like a criminal by the Delhi Police became a rage in India and everyone was keen to know what lay in store for the tainted trio. But what did the arrests mean for the tournament at large? Would it be stopped or would it carry on? Would the fans give up on the IPL and stay away from the knockout stages of the tournament? Were the arrests only the tip of the iceberg, with the possibility that more instances of cricketers' corrupt behaviour could unravel in the days ahead?

Even as the questions kept multiplying by the minute, the Royals, due to play in Hyderabad next, decided to carry on with their plans with the CEO staying behind in Mumbai. Dravid, everyone agreed, would meet the press in Hyderabad and do his best to stem the tide.

'It helped to have Rahul as captain. He is one the world listened to and believed that the team as a whole really had no idea about what was going on,' Iyer said.

What was of interest was that Sreesanth, picked up late that night by the police, was in Mumbai on personal work and was not part of the playing XI against the Mumbai Indians. He, Iyer confirmed, was desperate to play but was not included by Dravid and Upton. Sreesanth was displeased with the decision and did not want to be with the team if he was not included in the playing XI. The team management, based on inputs from Upton, had agreed. He could be a negative influence if he was around, had been Upton's argument.

It is a matter of conjecture what Sreesanth might have done had he played the match against the Mumbai Indians and if his displeasure stemmed from the fact that a deal had turned sour.

Things moved fast, with the BCCI ordering a probe into alleged spot-fixing under its anti-corruption chief Ravi Sawani and the Royals filing an FIR against the tainted trio. BCCI chief N. Srinivasan termed the three as 'three rotten eggs' and stated that the tournament as a whole could never be stained by a few bad elements.

Already under intense public scrutiny and pressure, the Royals lost the game against Hyderabad despite bowling the opposition out cheaply.

'Things had impacted the team,' said Iyer. 'There was a lot of mistrust floating around with players starting to look at each other with suspicion.' This was especially true of the foreigners who had started to look at the Indians, except Dravid, with very different eyes. Former Australia fast bowler Shaun Tait, too, Iyer confirmed, was suddenly the subject of scrutiny. 'It was rubbish, you know. All of a sudden we were told that Shaun was bowling wides and no balls. I was not sure where all this was coming from and Tait was concerned with these rumours.'

Trying to get a hand on the situation, the Royals cancelled a trip to Delhi and flew back to the team home base in Jaipur. This could give them some respite from the media and also allow them to regroup. 'Paddy Upton led a team-bonding exercise for well over five hours and it really helped. Not everything and everyone was corrupt and we were still a team that stood united was the message,' Iyer concluded.

To their credit, they won the next match in Delhi and travelled to Kolkata to play the qualifiers in a slightly better mental space.

Just when it seemed that the Royals and the BCCI had managed to get a hold on the crisis, the Mumbai Police made a second major arrest, which escalated the calamity to a very different level. The arrest of Vindoo Dara Singh, son of Dara Singh, the legendary wrestler, actor and politician, and himself a small-time actor, for his alleged association with bookies, seemed to open up a very different trail of investigation which went far beyond the BCCI's 'three rotten eggs theory'. On 23 May, the Mumbai Police called the Chennai Super Kings (CSK) boss Gurunath Meiyappan—who is also the son-in-law of BCCI chief N. Srinivasan—for questioning. This meant the BCCI itself was now in the corruption radar. Srinivasan, despite his many attempts, could not distance himself from his son-in-law and when Meiyappan was arrested by the Mumbai Police late on 24 May, the crisis turned into a catastrophe of humongous proportions.

CSK, as a franchise, made a gigantic blunder on 24 May in trying to distance itself from Meiyappan, stating that he was neither the owner nor team principal. Within minutes of the declaration, his photograph wearing the owners' badge started doing the rounds on Facebook and Twitter, adding to the embarrassment of the franchise, the BCCI and its supremo, Srinivasan.

Srinivasan, who wielded enormous power in Indian cricketing circles at the time, rejected all calls for his resignation on moral grounds and blamed the media for hounding him. That he was feeling the heat, however, was clear. Prior to a press conference which Srinivasan was supposed to preside over only hours before the IPL final in Kolkata on 26 May, he is said to have called his friend and advisor-of-sorts Shashank Manohar for guidance. Manohar, a former BCCI chief and one known for his no-nonsense stance, allegedly advised Srinivasan to step down pending inquiry. This conversation was the start of a bitter fallout between two of Indian cricket's most powerful figures, a spat that continues to influence major cricketing decisions at the time of writing. Srinivasan wasn't keen on giving up his BCCI post and differed from Manohar and his resignation theory. Manohar, on the other hand, believed that the only way Srinivasan could protect the BCCI and keep his own dignity intact was by resigning and distancing himself from the inquiry.

The press conference in Kolkata on 26 May was one of the worst in the history of the BCCI. By terming Meiyappan a mere 'enthusiast', Srinivasan allowed the media to take pot-shots at the BCCI and label it a body that lacked transparency and probity. Fans started lampooning him on social media, saying they, too, wanted to be a mere enthusiast and rub shoulders with the likes of Dhoni and Suresh Raina. Srinivasan also announced the setting up of a three-member inquiry commission, which included secretary Jagdale, and stated that Meiyappan had been provisionally suspended pending inquiry.

Srinivasan's stand was dealt a major blow when Jagdale declared his unwillingness to be a part of the inquiry commission and resigned from his position. Resignations from Jagdale and treasurer Ajay Shirke on moral grounds added to the pressure on Srinivasan and his position, it seemed, was fast becoming untenable. These resignations, which happened in real time on primetime national news television, added to the theatre and meant that the IPL, for all the wrong reasons, was the most important news story in the country. On 30 May, I got calls from a senior BCCI official, asking me to get in touch with the secretary and the treasurer. I was also told that both of them were ready to resign on moral grounds. It turned out to be true when Jagdale confirmed the news on live television around 8.45 p.m. in the evening. 'I have resigned from the post of the secretary of the BCCI because I am deeply hurt with the recent developments in Indian cricket. Let some new faces come and take the responsibility,' he said to me on a live television broadcast when asked if the news of his stepping down was accurate.

Shirke followed suit and was considerably more aggressive and critical. '[Under the current dispensation], the BCCI has called for innumerable emergency meetings to deal with even minor things. The same president called for many emergency meetings to resolve crises involving Deccan Chargers, Sahara Pune Warriors and even over bank guarantees. A meeting was called when three Rajasthan Royals players were arrested too. Why can't an emergency meeting be called now when there's such a serious situation at hand? I don't know about other board officials, but I do believe that if they care for their reputation, they'll also think the way I am doing [he had resigned by then]. Otherwise, go through the trial by the media,' Shirke declared in an interview with *The Times Of India*.

Under fire from all quarters, the BCCI was finally forced to convene an emergency meeting on 2 June 2013. This came at the back of the resignation of IPL chairman Rajiv Shukla the previous day. The meeting, many within the BCCI revealed, was called to decide on the future course of action and the fate of N. Srinivasan whose position, a large number of the members believed, had turned untenable. It was also suggested that Manohar, who was held in high esteem for his tough handling of situations, had the backing of political heavyweights in Delhi who wielded considerable clout in the BCCI, and would be the person to take over. Manohar, however, was adamant that Srinivasan would have to step down, not step aside. There was no provision of stepping aside in the BCCI's constitution and Manohar, it was suggested, would not take over unless things were done in a constitutionally correct manner. Srinivasan, however, was determined not to step down and was, at best, willing to step aside pending inquiry. It had turned into a battle of huge egos with Manohar eventually refusing to throw his hat in the ring. In a compromise formula, which was aimed at diffusing the crisis, it was agreed that Srinivasan would step aside till the inquiry process was complete and veteran administrator Jagmohan Dalmiya would be brought back as interim president of the BCCI. For Dalmiya, who had been suspended and thrown out of the BCCI on corruption charges in February 2006 (none of these were ever proven, though), this was a massive vindication of sorts. Arguably India's most decorated sports administrator, Dalmiya was back at the helm at a very critical time and was entrusted with the responsibility of taking some tough calls and restoring faith in the game.

At a time of serious tumult for the BCCI off the field, it was expected that the IPL, in its final stretch, would also suffer a fan backlash. A number of Mumbai Indians players who were in Kolkata for a playoff encounter against Rajasthan on 24 May confessed to me that they could hardly sleep that night and were glued to their television sets following the unsavoury Meiyappan saga. Two of them even suggested that the players were in no mood to celebrate the win against the Royals given what was going on in the country. They were apprehensive that the final against Chennai could turn out to be a damp squib with fans boycotting the game. To everyone's surprise, though, Eden Gardens was packed to capacity on 26 May, with 61,000-plus fans attending the match. Off the field events, it was evident, had little impact on the game itself and the IPL still had takers. While Srinivasan was booed by the crowd when he stepped on to the podium to hand over the IPL trophy, a loud cheer was reserved for the Mumbai Indians and Sachin Tendulkar.

Within days of the IPL final, the Indian team was scheduled to depart for England to play the ICC Champions Trophy. In the customary pre-departure captain's press conference, it was inevitable that Dhoni would be asked questions on the IPL spot-fixing scandal and Meiyappan. As captain of CSK, Dhoni had known and spent time with Meiyappan and the media was very much within its rights to ask the captain of the national team the tough questions. It was, however, somewhat surprising and disappointing to see Dhoni refuse to answer any of these questions and just sit through the whole exercise with a wry smile on his face. The media manager, Dr R.N. Baba, in trying to police the questions and stopping journalists from asking what the country wanted asked, cut a rather sorry figure. It was apparent that Baba was under instructions to avoid uncomfortable questions relating to the probity and transparency of the IPL or the Board, and in doing so, he ended up reducing the press conference to a charade. To see an India captain sit through a media interaction without answering the most obvious questions that came his way wasn't the most pleasing experience. Frankly, it wasn't befitting of an India skipper to do so.

While Dhoni and his boys played some creditable cricket in England and won the Champions Trophy against all odds, the on-field achievements did not mean that the off field scandals had gone away. While the country celebrated India's wins against South Africa, the West Indies, Pakistan and finally England, the IPL brand, many suspected had taken a serious hit and was in need of immediate correctives to be put in place.

There's no doubt that Dhoni and his team deserved much credit for keeping focus on the task at hand and winning cricket's second-most important tournament after the World Cup. However, I have never understood how and why fans would want to use this achievement to gloss over other ills. Shikhar Dhawan had a fabulous tournament as did Rohit Sharma and the spinners. Just as we heap lavish praise on Dhoni for his captaincy in England, it must also be acknowledged that his conduct as captain of India in the pre-departure press conference was disappointing. That he did not stand up for issues of probity, transparency and ethical behaviour will always be one of the criticisms levelled against India's best white-ball captain of all time.

While the team was away playing the Champions Trophy, the BCCI went ahead with its commission of inquiry under two former judges of the Madras high court, Justice T. Jayaram Chouta and Justice R. Balasubramanian. This commission, appointed by the BCCI itself, eventually cleared 'Super Kings owner India Cements, Royals co-owner Raj Kundra and Royals parent company Jaipur IPL Cricket Pvt. Ltd of "wrongdoing".' This was revealed to the media in Kolkata by Niranjan Shah, one of the five vice presidents of the BCCI and long-standing Board member from Saurashtra. For some of the BCCI members, the matter had ended with the commission's report and it was time to move on. However shocking it might appear, the majority of the members felt the hullabaloo around the spot-fixing scandal was all a media creation.

Within 48 hours, however, proceedings took a dramatic turn. The Bombay High Court set aside the BCCI-appointed commission's inquiry report and ordered a fresh probe into the scandal. Responding to a petition filed by the Cricket Association of Bihar secretary Aditya Verma, the Bombay High Court contended that the commission had been constituted wrongly and its formation was not according to the rules enshrined in the BCCI's constitution.

With the court saying that the entire incident needed to be reinvestigated, it was apparent that one had not seen the last of the issue. With every passing day and growing media reportage on the matter, the BCCI's image was taking a beating. Was it serious about putting its zero-tolerance approach against corruption into practice? What was the process followed in giving a clean chit to Meiyappan and Kundra? Who were the people interviewed, and will the transcripts ever be made public? Was Srinivasan questioned on the matter and will his deposition ever be made a public document?

That not all was well with the BCCI was evident in its working committee meeting in Kolkata. The meeting was also attended by Arun Jaitley, then a BCCI heavyweight and one of the most respected ministers of the current central cabinet. It must be stated here that had Arun Jaitley not taken up a central government portfolio, he was in line to take over as the president of the BCCI after Srinivasan. Jaitley, a legal luminary, was a voice that most listened to in the BCCI without hesitation and it was important to try and understand what he made of the situation. Soon after the meeting was over, Lokendra Pratap Sahi, one of the seniormost sports journalists in the country and I took the service lift in the Taj Bengal Hotel in the absence of a key card to go up to Jaitley's room to seek an audience with him. As always, Jaitley was composure personified. Seeing us both at the door, he welcomed us in and explained the situation to us in detail. While I am not in a position to write more about the conversation because it wasn't recorded, suffice to say he was not happy with the goings-on in Indian cricket.

Things turned dire for the Board when Verma, the petitioner in the case in the Bombay High Court, moved the Supreme Court of India, praying that a new commission of inquiry be put in place to look into the spot-fixing scandal and investigate the role of Meiyappan and Srinivasan. The BCCI, too, moved the Supreme Court challenging the decision of the Bombay High Court.

After hearing the counsels from both sides—Harish Salve, representing the Cricket Association of Bihar and C. Aryama Sundaram, representing the BCCI—Justices A.K. Patnaik and J.S. Khehar declared on 27 September: 'In case Srinivasan is elected as President, he will not take charge until further orders . . . Why he is in charge [as the BCCI president] if his son-in-law has been charge sheeted? Why are you [Srinivasan] so keen to be elected? When the Supreme Court of India is hearing the matter then why are you so keen? What about your son-in-law? Hold the election, but don't take charge till we decide it.'

The matter was clearly not over and, more importantly, no attempt at trying to side-step it would work any more, with the Supreme Court taking up the case with utmost seriousness.

Srinivasan, who was elected unopposed on 29 September, was eventually allowed to take charge by the Supreme Court on 7 October, at a subsequent hearing. However, more importantly, the court appointed a three-member committee headed by Justice Mukul Mudgal, former chief justice of the Punjab and Haryana High Court, senior counsel and Additional Solicitor General L. Nageshwar Rao (currently a sitting judge of the Supreme Court of India) and senior advocate Niloy Dutta to investigate the case. For the first time, the spot-fixing investigation, it was clear, had been taken out of the BCCI's hands and entrusted to a panel of independent legal luminaries with impeccable reputation and credentials. The all-clear granted to Meiyappan and others had been set aside and Indian cricket, forever a closed institution, was finally being opened up by an outside force—in this case, the force of judicial intervention under the aegis of India's apex court.

'Justice Patnaik called and asked me on the evening of 6 October if I was agreeable to take charge of the case. He said he had suggested my name and had asked the two parties if they had any objection. I had been a keen follower of the game for ages and was also a keen amateur cricket player, which Justice Patnaik was aware of,' says Justice Mudgal with a chuckle. 'That may have prompted him to give me the responsibility.'

The Mudgal Committee, as it came to be called, was given four months to submit its report and there was little doubt Indian cricket was entering a very different phase. Justice Mudgal and his team could not be won over by the riches of the BCCI and the truth, it was apparent, would come out at the end of the investigation, however dire and unpleasant it might be. For a body that was refusing to reform itself from within, this was the top-down intervention that it had always tried to resist. But now it was different. It was an order of the Supreme Court of India, which was binding and all-pervasive.

In a matter of weeks, Indian cricket was about to change. And change radically. For years the BCCI stood for dictatorship. There was one strand of opinion and everyone else fell in line. Meetings were routine, difference of opinion was crushed and the dissenter brutally punished. It was a show of power, plain and simple. In an institution full of people with huge egos, there was never a difference of opinion. It seemed unreal but it was true.

Judicial intervention was about to change all of this. The ordinary cricket fan, neglected and dismissed for the longest time, was finally finding a voice. The media played a critical role in this transformation, drawing support from the growing sense of public outrage. The media was the catalyst, certainly, but the real power was that of unified public opinion.

For some years, we—all stakeholders in the game outside of the BCCI office-bearers and those residing in the political corridors— were all helpless. Every cricket fan felt frustrated when told about the debauchery in post-match IPL parties. Fans hated the strategic timeouts instituted to rake in the fast buck. These helped bookies fix sessions and corrupt the edifice of Indian cricket. We were shocked to note that the second season of the IPL, run by Modi, did not even have an anti-corruption unit monitoring the matches. Gross illegalities were considered par for the course. Now, all of a sudden, reform was the buzzword.

Pushed to the brink, the BCCI knew it had to reform itself and its biggest money-spinner—the IPL. The spot-fixing scandal helped in bringing about Indian cricket's first mass movement and the impregnable BCCI could no longer stay immune from it. Its bastions had been breached, and this resulted in resignations of the secretary, the treasurer and the IPL chairman, unheard of in the eighty-five-year-old history of the institution.

In Chennai, on 2 June, the media did not get the headlines they were waiting for. Srinivasan wasn't forced to resign but was allowed an honourable exit. However, for all practical purposes, that working committee meeting was a step forward. Issues of morality and propriety, neglected for the longest time, took centre stage, and even the India captain wasn't able to immunize himself from the hard questions. Sooner or later, Dhoni would have to speak up; depose himself before the Mudgal Committee. Staying quiet was no longer an option.

Against the backdrop of the Mudgal Committee appointment, several questions came up: Would the BCCI clam up and fall back to practising the worst form of feudalism in the future? Would the cushy club of 30 finally start looking beyond their own ambitions? Would there be tangible reform, or would the bosses try to placate the outraged cricket fan by bringing in some cosmetic changes? What added to the discomfort of the BCCI was that every action of the Board was being monitored by an aggressive and vigilant media, working on behalf of India's billion-plus cricket fans.

Back to Action on the Field of Play

Just when it seemed that Indian cricket was all about spot-fixing, corruption and judicial intervention, and the Champions Trophy win in England was a fast-fading memory, attention turned to on-field action on 10 October 2013 when arguably India's greatest cricketer of all time, Sachin Tendulkar, decided to call it a day after playing the game at the highest level for an unbelievable 24 years.

Immediately, the action moved again. Spot-fixing, for the time being, was not front-page news. It had not gone away (just like it hadn't totally disappeared in June when Dhoni's boys won cricket's second biggest prize), but Tendulkar and on-field action had started to occupy centre stage.

This mesh between the cricketing dynamics that play out on

and off the field of play, which I have repeatedly alluded to in the book, is what explains the story of Indian cricket in its entirety. Tendulkar's retirement, it can be argued, had given the BCCI a breather, a respite from the probing media and the ever-aggressive Indian cricket fan, who had started to lose faith. All of a sudden, it was no longer about Sreesanth and Meiyappan but about a sixteen-year-old who had successfully played the likes of Wasim Akram and Waqar Younis in Pakistan in 1989 and had over the next 24 years scored a staggering 100 international centuries for India. He stood for the faith that the BCCI was fast losing. He could carry a billion dreams on his shoulders and was a player unparalleled. Clearly, it could not be a retirement like any other.

GOD-BYE

Between 27 September and 9 October 2013, most newspapers in the country carried details of the spot-fixing investigation as front-page news. This was the main cricket story of the time. Not so after 10 October. On 11 October, the day after Sachin Tendulkar announced his retirement, every newspaper had multiple pages dedicated to him and, for the next few days, it was Tendulkar all around. Television channels did the same. Every Tendulkar milestone was written about and televised and every person connected to Tendulkar was interviewed. *The Times of India* launched a countdown clock with a different piece every day right up to retirement day in mid-November. Close to 35 pieces were published overall by *The Times of India* alone to commemorate the momentous occasion.

It is significant to note that the two events were occurring simultaneously. First, Tendulkar, an embodiment of nationalism and a successful brand of 'Indian-ness' for his countrymen, was winning over anti-nationalism mirrored in the spot-fixing investigation. A form of aggressive nationalism, perhaps the most powerful and potent force in contemporary India, was once again coming through the ranks, pushing everything else to the background. Spot-fixing and corruption was anti-national and the exact antithesis of what Tendulkar personified. Clearly, it stood no chance with Tendulkar as opponent.

The second trend was that the moment Tendulkar announced his decision to retire, his critics, who had been calling for him to leave for a year and more, for good or bad, disappeared overnight. Yet again, it was a play between good and bad or, rather, between national and anti-national. Tendulkar's retirement was fast turning into a massive national celebration and anything critical was unacceptable—in fact, unwarranted. That his last international appearance would be his 200th Test—a first ever in cricket—added to the drama and enriched the spectacle.

Full editions of newspapers and magazines were dedicated to Tendulkar and day-long conclaves were organized. One man literally brought the country to a standstill by his decision to stop playing cricket.

This was a repeat of what had happened in June 2013, when M.S. Dhoni's India won the Champions Trophy in England, beating the hosts in a rain-truncated final. The sight of more than 5,000 Indians forming a human chain around the Edgbaston Stadium ground, singing 'Hum honge kamyaab' at 10 p.m. BST was surreal, and any critical voice that dared raise questions about Dhoni's involvement in the spot-fixing scandal was drowned out in this wave of mass euphoria. Fandom, it has to be acknowledged, is a far more powerful energy than critical commentary, and once the force of fandom comes to the fore, the media has no option but to consume and appropriate it. This isn't a moral judgement of sorts, but a true testimony to the fan's role in Indian cricket.

While much has been written about Tendulkar's retirement, and we have documented it from his perspective in *Playing It My Way*, the backstage narrative of what was going on is no less significant.

I remember working in my office at my residence at 2.30 p.m. or

so when the icon of 'private number calling' started to flash on my
phone. I was half-expecting Tendulkar to call because I had asked him
for an interview before he started the home season. Maybe he was
calling to confirm the time. What he said, however, was significantly
different from what I had anticipated: 'It is a decision taken from
the heart. It has nothing to do with my body or mind.' This was
Tendulkar's first statement on the phone once he had taken the
hardest decision of his life. 'What? What? *What*?' I could still not
fully comprehend what he meant to convey. 'The two Tests against
the West Indies will be my last,' he clarified.

It must have been an emotional churn for Tendulkar but he
sounded calm and composed. He even chuckled when asked if the
impact of the decision had sunk in yet. 'Anjali [his wife] and Ajit
[his elder brother] are both very emotional, but I am okay,' he said.
'Let's talk about something else. I don't want to start leading a retired
life even before I have retired.'

The last statement summed up Tendulkar perfectly. He still had
two Tests to play, and he was determined to treat them with the same
seriousness that marked his preparation for the 198 he had played
so far. As he uttered those words, one could sense the unassuming
persona masking the fierce pride that made him the champion he is. It
was clear that he was determined to give his best in his last two Tests
bringing down the curtains on a career that defied comprehension.

Tendulkar was the perfect representation of the quintessentially
modern India: Wearing a mask to hide any form of emotion that may
be perceived as weakness; standing straight in the face of adversity;
yet appearing calm and in control. Was he actually calm and if he
indeed was, how could he do it all the time? I quizzed him in detail
when I was writing *Playing It My Way* and the guard was hardly ever
let down. Tendulkar, it was an unwritten national rule, could have no
weakness. If he was weak and vulnerable, how would his fans react?
He could not afford to let down millions of men and women whose

sense of self-belief and 'Indian-ness' had been shaped by him. Most importantly, he wasn't part of fiction, nor did he belong to the reel existence of celluloid. He did not score his runs away from public glare and then get projected on screen. He was there for the fans to see and feel, for them to experience and be a part of; shape and consume. He was Indian nationalism in its confident and assertive avatar—proud and engaged in an ever-ending quest for perfection.

It is this narrative that shaped Tendulkar's retirement discourse. At least, on the face of it. Behind the scenes, however, was another India. Traditional, conservative and affectionate—this was the inner domain that has forever overlapped with the more visible public self of modern contemporary India. And this, if I may say so, was as important in the making of Tendulkar as Sachin himself.

With the work on the autobiography going full steam ahead, I asked him for time when he came to Kolkata for his 199th Test match. I wanted to record his emotions raw and fresh rather than wait for the West Indies series to come to a close. And when I did meet him at the Taj Bengal Hotel the night he arrived, I asked him a question I had put forth a few times before. 'What defined your life and his legacy?' I asked. 'Playing for India,' he said within microseconds of the question being asked. He had said the same each time I had asked him this question. Somehow, when he said it, I knew it was not just a platitude but a heartfelt truth.

This truth, which Tendulkar embodied, was far more powerful than the disillusionment over spot-fixing. We were used to corruption in India for the longest time. We were used to the narrative of poverty and discrimination, of things not being there and being beyond our means. We were used to missing out. We were used to not winning medals at Olympics. We were used to our only individual Olympic gold medal winner being called Avinash, and not Abhinav, by the head of the Indian Olympic Association days after he had won the gold medal in Beijing. The Tendulkar narrative was different. It was a narrative of dominance and assertion, of winning and achievement. It was positive rather than negative, overtly national as opposed to the covertly anti-national.

Was retirement on his mind? Was he speaking about it to his near and dear ones? Did the media reports about his retirement bother him? Was he pushed to the decision? I asked him all of these questions and he has answered them all in *Playing It My Way*. It is his book and he reserves the right to do it the way he wanted to.

What I did not tell him when I met him in Kolkata was that I had spoken to Anjali behind his back and convinced her to come and watch him play at Eden Gardens. And Anjali, superstitious when it comes to Tendulkar, had finally agreed on the condition that Tendulkar would have no idea of what was being planned.

This is the very unique Indian complexity I was referring to earlier. A superstitious, traditional, conservative yet confident wife backing her husband before and during his final hurrah—like she had always done. From backstage, away from the public glare.

That anything else would not stand a chance against this potent combination is easily understandable.

To the BCCI, the retirement was a godsend. Under intense scrutiny, it finally offered them a breather they badly needed at the time. Focusing on making the Tendulkar retirement special was a priority and all else could take a backseat. By allocating Tendulkar's last and 200th Test to Mumbai, the beleaguered BCCI boss N. Srinivasan regained some lost ground, for fulfilling god's wish meant other sins could be temporarily forgotten.

But did the BCCI have a hand in the retirement? Did the selectors push Tendulkar to take the call and did the management want him to go?

The truth is, Tendulkar's decision was entirely his own and had come from the heart. He did not think that after the 200th Test he would enjoy playing the game as much as he had always done—and that was it. He had never given an iota less than 100 per cent for India every time he took the field. And he would not in future. It was time to leave. Over the years, Tendulkar defied time, constantly reinventing himself to stay one step ahead of a sportsman's greatest enemy. Once he realized that it was becoming difficult to do so, he declared his innings closed.

What does one say about Tendulkar's career that has not already been said or written? Perhaps the only thing to say is that it is a testimony to commitment that can never be challenged by even the most ardent critic. Cricket has always celebrated Sir Jack Hobbs for scoring 100 first-class hundreds; Tendulkar got 51 Test match hundreds. The difference between first-class and Test cricket is like chalk and cheese. Scoring 100 hundreds in international cricket is a feat that has, once and for all, set Tendulkar apart from his predecessors, contemporaries and probably even generations of future greats to come.

It would be no exaggeration to say that Tendulkar's landmarks put him among the very top echelon of sportspersons across diverse fields. His achievements rank alongside those of Usain Bolt, Babe Ruth, Mark Spitz, Michael Phelps and Roger Federer. The only batsman against whom Tendulkar can truly be benchmarked is Sir Don Bradman. But Bradman never played with the pressure of the hopes of a billion-plus people on his shoulders; he never had to deal with a situation where a loss was similar to a criminal conviction, with the world's second-most populous country presiding over collective judgement. Bradman played a sport. Tendulkar was the presiding deity of a nationally-unifying religion called cricket.

So how did he deal with the pressure of nationalism? Here's what the man himself has to say: 'The most important thing in trying to deal with pressure is to evolve your own mechanism to cope with the situation. I have been fortunate that crowds, both at home and away, have given me a rousing reception every time I have stepped out to bat. There has been a build-up right through my career. At times, however, the crowd was so loud that it added to my nervous tension at the start of the innings. Finding it difficult to concentrate, I had to devise my own technique of trying to control the crowd. Whenever I found the crowd too loud, I decided to walk down the pitch and tap it for a while, giving myself an extra 15 to 20 seconds to adjust. I'd be hoping that in this extra time the crowd would mellow a little and settle down.'

He had to try out this ritual in two more Tests.

In Mumbai, during his 200th and last Test, the crowd just refused to quieten down. When the host broadcaster showed his mother, wife, brother, son and daughter on the giant screen while Tendulkar was batting in the last few minutes of day one, the applause at Wankhede was deafening. It was just the thing to do as far as the host broadcaster was concerned. They had to make the most of Tendulkar's last batting effort. These pictures, forever immortal, stand tall in Indian cricket's archive. One man, all of five-feet-five, a resplendent symbol of the resurgent Indian nationalism that unites a billion and more. For Tendulkar, however, it wasn't easy. Seeing the pictures flashing one after the other, he was bound to get emotional, feel even more pressure if that was possible. But, as always, he wasn't allowed, to show it. He could not afford to lose his nerve and get out due to the immensity of the occasion. He had to battle it out and stay unbeaten overnight for the ritual to enact itself one final time the next morning. The applause that attended his last walk to and from the pitch will forever reverberate in the cricket world.

Tendulkar, it must be said, has made peace with the fact that there is life after cricket. But millions of worshippers are still consumed by a feeling of hollowness as they try to come to terms with cricket without Tendulkar. While some seek solace in Kohli, the true heir, others have found their own ways and means. Sudhir Gautam, Indian cricket's very public symbol of nationalist fandom—a brand that has now found corporate support—wears it on his chest all the time: 'We miss you, Tendulkar.'

The Uncomfortable Reality

While no less than 60 per cent space was dedicated to Tendulkar and Tendulkar alone in every Bengali newspaper published in Kolkata during his 199th Test match at Eden Gardens, and the queue of outside broadcast vans at the Wankhede was a mile long during his 200th, it is a sad reflection on Indian cricket's existing state of affairs that neither Eden Gardens nor the Wankhede was full. Even when Tendulkar batted at the two stadia in his final two games, there were empty pockets in the galleries at both venues.

This stands out in stark contrast to the 61,000-plus people present at Eden Gardens for the IPL final only days after the spot-fixing scandal had come to light.

Was Tendulkar a lesser brand than the IPL and did he not have a legion of fans in Kolkata? That these questions are baseless have been proved time and again whenever Tendulkar has come to the City of Joy in the last few years. Thousands gather in no time when Tendulkar is around and the chants 'Sachinnnnn, Sachinnnnn' fill the air each time he sets foot on Kolkata soil. When he made a very personal visit to my house for my daughter's rice-eating ritual in December 2014, 5,000 people had gathered in front of the house bringing traffic to a complete standstill. It was only after he gave a very public *darshan* from the terrace that the crowd dispersed and the police were able to take control of the situation.

Yet Eden Gardens and the Wankhede remained empty in part.

While ordinary cricket fans couldn't take part, every VIP from every sphere of life made it to Kolkata and Mumbai. Tendulkar's farewell series had turned into a page three party and to be present for the occasion was a status symbol of sorts. With these men and women making a beeline for tickets and often wasting them, the ordinary cricket fans, as happens more often than not, missed out. To make it clear, I refuse to believe that cricket fans in either Mumbai or Kolkata would not have wanted to go and watch Tendulkar play for one final time. It is a no-brainer that the ordinary cricket fan would love to do so. It is unfortunate that they continue to miss out. In Mumbai, for example two-thirds of the tickets are given out free to members and associations while the ordinary fan, desperately craving for a ticket, is forced to consume the spectacle on television.

The IPL is different. An out-an-out commercial property, franchises and not association bosses are in charge of IPL tickets; association members have no entitlement. This means almost every ticket is sold and done so at a premium. Fans, who pay hard-earned money to buy the tickets, inevitably make it to the stadium, unlike in Test matches, including Tendulkar's retirement series.

Empty pockets at Eden Gardens and the Wankhede, I will argue, were a poor advertisement for Test cricket in India. Had any of these matches been played at Lord's or the MCG, we would have had a full house. Indian expats would have come in droves to celebrate the greatest batsman of our era and taken back a piece of Tendulkar with them.

India won the twin Tests against the West Indies but the results were of little or no consequence. The series, after all, was all about Tendulkar's farewell. What mattered to the fans was the experience of seeing him out there, appropriating him, consuming him, being with him and, most importantly, being a part of the same imagined community for one final time. We were all part of Tendulkar's India created and nurtured over a 24-year-long era between 1989 and 2013.

For Tendulkar, though, after a point, it was business as usual. He was still an active player and was focused on doing well for India. But for millions of Tendulkar fans worldwide it was time for one final bonding—an occasion to celebrate being an Indian, resident or non-resident, and a Tendulkar fan. Unlike the nation-state allegiance drawing on Benedict Anderson, this imagined community of Tendulkar followers had one central commonality between them: fandom.

Fans are the only constant loyalty in human life. In this age of capital and information flow, where space and time turn irrelevant, one starts to become a sports fan at the age of five or six and turns into a committed follower even before touching double digits. For the next 70 to 80 years of his or her life, this is the only loyalty that stays on. You can have multiple affairs, a broken marriage, changing tastes of food and clothing, evolving views on politics and economy but a Tendulkar fan at five will remain a Tendulkar fan even at 80. So much so, that 50 years down the line, he or she won't take a backseat in arguing that Tendulkar, come what may, remains the greatest. For the seventies generation in India, Sunil Gavaskar continues to be the greatest Indian batsman ever and Maradona the best ever to have played the beautiful game. However much Messi and Ronaldo and Neymar earn in millions, El Diego comes only second to god. One could differ on whether brand IPL has taken a hit as a result of the spot-fixing scandal but there is never any divergence when it is a question of allegiance to Tendulkar.

As he started the last walk of his life to the pavilion, having been dismissed for a well-made 74, time came to a standstill for many of us. For nearly all of us, the runs scored were of little consequence; 74 or 54, Tendulkar was already the declared champion, and each and every one of us across the country wanted to hold on to the memories he had left us with. Each time he climbed one more step on his way to disappearing inside the safe haven of the Wankhede dressing room, a lump formed in a million throats worldwide. This was again the case when he was out there in the middle of his farewell speech. The address was all Tendulkar because it was heartfelt—and spontaneous. From making eye contact with Anjali and thanking her for her support, to thanking everyone who had played a part in his career, the greatest batsman of his time had all his fans' eyes on him. From being a great champion to being decreed immortal, to finally being labelled the greatest—every accolade possible was shared by all of us on social media.

This is one loyalty that will never be taken away from us. More powerful than nationalism, this is what makes modern sport the global marketer's dream. Brand Tendulkar, despite the failure to score 100 in his last innings, was at its most powerful. The final 74 had, in fact, added a tinge of mortality to his immortality. He, too, could fail. He was human. Bradman had scored a duck in his last innings. Maradona finished second best to Germany with Andreas Brehme netting the penalty in 1994 and Federer and Phelps have both lost on occasion. Bolt, too, finished third in the final individual race of his life. And Tendulkar scored 74. But just like the others mentioned here, he, too, will go down in history as the greatest. At least, we, his legion of fans worldwide, will say so. And this community will forever remain a constant.

All good things necessarily come to an end. As Tendulkar's farewell party at the Waterstones club in Mumbai was on in full swing and a few of us were enjoying the stunning food on offer, someone asked me if he had invited N. Srinivasan. It was a bolt from the blue and I really did not know the answer to it. Did Tendulkar invite the BCCI president? The answer was, 'I don't know.' The person who asked me the question went on to say with a chuckle, 'Knowing you, you'd have asked him about Gurunath [Meiyappan] and spot-fixing!' I certainly wouldn't, but the Mudgal Committee certainly would in a few days' time. One-and-a-half of the four months given to the Mudgal Committee had gone by and they had a task at hand. Planning for the 2014 IPL would soon be underway and it would be of interest to see if Chennai Super Kings and the Rajasthan Royals were a part of it.

Exactly 15 days after Tendulkar's farewell bash, the BCCI issued the following press release: 'The Committee on 5th December, 2013 interacted with Mr Mehmood Abdi, constituted attorney for Mr Lalit Modi, assisted by Mr Abhishek Singh, advocate and Mr Sandeep Singh Hora, advocate. The Committee also interacted with players Ajit Chandila and Siddharth Trivedi.'

The Tendulkar interlude had passed. And it was time to talk about the not-so-pleasant elements of cricket yet again.

WHAT DO THEY KNOW OF CRICKET?

Exactly four months after being asked to take charge of the investigation in October 2013, the Mudgal Committee was ready to submit its report on the IPL spot-fixing scandal on 9 February 2014. Besides all else, three central questions needed answering by the Committee: Was Gurunath Meiyappan the team principal or owner of the Chennai Super Kings (CSK) and had there been an attempted cover-up by the BCCI and its president N. Srinivasan? Did Raj Kundra, owner of the Rajasthan Royals, guilty of betting, bring disrepute to the game? Finally, what was to happen to these two franchises with the 2014 IPL less than six months away?

It was around 10 p.m. on 8 February that I got a call from someone closely associated with the Committee. My wife was eight months pregnant and it hadn't been a great health day in the family. I remember telling her to try and get some sleep as I attended the call. 'There are two reports, not one,' the caller said. 'The reports will be submitted to the Supreme Court tomorrow morning at 10.30 a.m.,' he concluded and disconnected the line.

Now, this was big news. Why should a three-member committee submit two reports and what did this mean? Would this impact the credibility of the work done by them and how would the apex court deal with it?

'Advocate Niloy Dutta wanted to submit a separate report and both Nageshwar Rao and I felt he was within his rights to do so,' Justice Mudgal mentions.

Despite the two reports, however, the central point of contention had been unanimously agreed upon. Meiyappan, the Committee contended, was CSK's principal/owner/official and had defamed the game. In arriving at this conclusion, they had spoken to a cross-section of people including players and administrators. Legends of the game like Sachin Tendulkar and M.S. Dhoni were also spoken to and Dhoni, the report declared, held the view that Meiyappan was a mere enthusiast who had little to do with the franchise.

'Representatives of India Cements, who appeared before the Committee, contended that Mr Meiyappan had no share holding in India Cements and hence cannot be considered as an owner of CSK. Further, Mr M.S. Dhoni, Mr N. Srinivasan and officials of India Cements took the stand that Mr Meiyappan had nothing to do with the cricketing affairs of Chennai Super Kings and was a mere cricket enthusiast supporting CSK.'

This testimony, interestingly, was rejected and the Committee concluded that 'Mr Gurunath Meiyappan formed an integral part of Chennai Super Kings and most persons viewed him as the face of the team. Though the de-jure ownership vests in India Cements, the Committee finds that Mr Meiyappan was, in fact, acting as a team official, if not the de-facto owner of CSK.'

While there has been much talk in the Supreme Court over Dhoni's testimony with senior advocates Harish Salve and C. Aryama Sundaram, arguing over it at length, suffice to say the Committee had found Dhoni not forthcoming when they questioned him on the role of Meiyappan in the day-to-day running of the franchise.

It was only when he was asked how an auction scenario worked did he explain in detail that the franchise held sessions prior to the bidding, where it was decided how much to bid for a particular player. When a Committee member asked how the franchise reacted if the bid amount went beyond what had been initially decided, Dhoni said that it was decided on the table by Meiyappan, among others.

Why would Dhoni do this and did it not bother him? Should it have bothered him in the first place? Can we label this an ethical issue and judge him by the same standards of ethics that applies to us all? Or is it unfair on our part to expect that he would say things against Meiyappan when he was/is an employee of India Cements and captain of CSK? Finally, do moral questions like these impact his legacy in the long term? While Dhoni is certainly one of the greatest Indian captains of all time, the question remains that when it came to the spot-fixing scandal did India's best white-ball finisher lack the courage of conviction?

Frankly, I don't have definitive answers to these questions. Maybe Dhoni had his compulsions. Maybe not. He has chosen to remain silent on the matter and he is within his rights to do so. But cricket, the gentleman's sport, is poorer as a result. Did Dhoni need CSK that much more to say what he did to the Committee? Could he not have stepped beyond the loyalty to money and more and stood up for Indian cricket? I leave that for the readers to decide.

In my colleague Rajdeep Sardesai's *Democracy's XI: The Great Indian Cricket Story*, Dhoni, however, has refuted all such accusations levelled against him. Sardesai writes: 'Dhoni was accused of not revealing the true extent of his involvement in the team before a Supreme Court-appointed panel that was investigating the betting and spot-fixing scandal. "Let me tell you, it is an absolute lie that I told a probe panel that Meiyappan was only a cricket enthusiast, all I said is he had nothing to do with the team's on-field cricketing decisions. I can't even pronounce the word 'enthusiast,'" he says with a touch of sarcasm.'

For the Committee, however, Meiyappan was culpable in spite of what was said by Dhoni and Srinivasan.

The report also included serious observations on Raj Kundra and asked for further investigation on the matter. 'The Committee is thus of the view that if the allegations of betting against Mr Raj Kundra and Ms Shetty, who are part owners of Rajasthan Royals, stand proved, the same would constitute a serious infraction of Sections 2.2.1 and 2.14 of the IPL Operational Rules for bringing the game in disrepute, Articles 2.2.1, 2.2.2 and 2.2.3 of the IPL Anti Corruption Code for acts of betting and Articles 2.4.4 of the IPL Code of Conduct for Players and Team Officials, for bring [sic] disrepute to the game of cricket. Thus the Committee is of the view that after a thorough investigation, if the allegations of betting and/or spot fixing/match fixing can be proved, appropriate action should be taken against Mr Kundra and Ms Shetty as well as the franchise.'

Finally, having come across multiple allegations of sporting fraud in the course of the investigation, all of which were in the nature of allegations with no conclusive proof, it was suggested that further investigation was needed on the role of 13 individuals, names that were submitted before the Supreme Court in a sealed cover.

The suggestion for further investigation was debated in threadbare fashion in the Supreme Court and while it decided to allow the Royals and CSK to participate in the 2014 IPL, it asked Srinivasan to step aside on 27 March 2014, appointing Sunil Gavaskar and Shivlal Yadav as interim bosses of the BCCI. Srinivasan's was one of the names in the sealed cover and it was deemed unethical and improper for him to remain in office when he was being investigated for corruption.

In a subsequent hearing, the Supreme Court asked the BCCI to come up with possible names for a three-member committee that could continue the investigation on the lines suggested by the Mudgal

Committee, a suggestion that prompted the BCCI to convene an emergent working committee meeting in Mumbai on 20 April.

This meeting, it must be said, was forced upon the interim boss Yadav, with as many as ten associations writing in, demanding it. Shashank Manohar, by then Srinivasan's primary adversary and one who had started taking an active interest in the BCCI again, was planning to attend the meeting and stage a coup to upstage Srinivasan. He was working in close proximity with Jagmohan Dalmiya, another former president and the Manohar–Dalmiya combine, many expected, would win the day, with the wind blowing in favour of reform.

But this was the BCCI. A body that has forever resisted change and one that turns inward every time there is an external threat. The Supreme Court intervention was one such. Manohar and Dalmiya were hopelessly outnumbered in the meeting and, to Srinivasan's credit, the members, who were in constant touch with him from inside the venue, mooted the names of Ravi Shastri, former Justice Jai Narayan Patel and former CBI Director R.K. Raghavan, as three possible members of the new committee. Each of these, the grapevine had it, were Srinivasan's choices. In a game of numbers, he still had an overwhelming majority within the BCCI's boardrooms despite having side-stepped as a result of the Supreme Court order.

The Court, however, rejected the BCCI's suggestion and asked the Mudgal Committee to carry the investigation forward, in what was considered a blow to the Board. The Mudgal Committee meant business, and based on its earlier findings, it was clear that it could not be compromised with or influenced upon and this neutrality was something Indian cricket badly needed at the time.

When I asked Justice Mudgal if there were attempts at outside interference, he was cautious with his response. 'I wouldn't say so,' were his exact words. 'They knew we would do our work with integrity and honesty and it was better they stayed away,' he emphasized.

Unlike in October 2013, when the main question was whether Meiyappan was team principal, this time around the real interest centred around the 13 names handed to the court in a sealed cover, including that of Srinivasan. The other issue of consequence was the committee's take on the future of the two teams, CSK and Royals, and, in a way, the very future of the IPL was now under the scanner.

The 13 names submitted remain concealed and away from public knowledge to this day under Supreme Court orders. While Srinivasan and former IPL CEO Sundar Raman were investigated and cleared of any personal wrongdoing, one wonders why the yardstick is different for players? Why should Srinivasan have to go through intense media and public scrutiny while some players, mentioned in the sealed cover report, continue to get away without being investigated?

While I am in no position to conjecture on some of the names mentioned—and will not, because it is a Supreme Court mandate—I must say that all the sources interviewed for the book point out that one of the names indicted for corruption is a World Cup-winning icon with a massive fan following. He was investigated at length by former CBI official B.B. Misra (who had been added to the Committee) and was eventually pitted face to face against a bookie who spilled the beans. It so happened that the interrogation took place in rooms adjacent to each other, one of which had the bookie and the other the player in question. While the player continued to deny involvement in betting and fixing, eventually he was brought face to face with the bookie and that's when his guard collapsed. Those in the know say he ended up pleading with the investigators to care for his reputation and let things be. Former BCCI president Inderjit Singh Bindra, who had testified before the Committee, is said to have mentioned this player at length and how he had to intervene to foil an attempt at wrongdoing in a ODI match at Mohali against Sri Lanka. Could it be that in case the names are ever made public, he is the one cricketer whose reputation will be in tatters? Again, it remains a matter of conjecture.

If this cricketer is indeed corrupt and has indulged in wrongdoing, he should be pulled up for doing so. He should be stripped of his medals and his national awards should be snatched. If a dope cheat can be pulled up by the IOC years after a competition is over, why should we protect cricketers who have cheated the nation? Just because they are icons, do they deserve special treatment? Shouldn't icons adhere to stricter norms of ethics and morality? More, if Sreesanth, who is also a double World Cup-winner, could be paraded like a criminal by the Delhi Police, why should others guilty of similar crimes get judicial protection? Why should the Supreme Court of India not make the names of the corrupt public? And if there are no names that are corrupt, there is all the more reason that the contents of the sealed envelope be made public and the matter closed. If the end ambition is to cleanse the system, it should not be done in a half-baked fashion that is restricted only to administrators. With the cricketers being the most important stakeholders in the game, they need to be the cleanest for the reputation of the game to remain intact going forward.

In its final report submitted in November 2014, the Mudgal Committee found Meiyappan and Kundra guilty, and it was clear that the two teams (CSK and the Royals) now found themselves facing serious penalties moving ahead. Much to the relief of the BCCI, Srinivasan was absolved of any personal wrongdoing and immediately demanded that he be reinstated as president.

This demand, which found support from within the BCCI, was symptomatic of all ills that had come to define the body over the years. While he wasn't guilty of betting or fixing, he was still closely associated with India Cements and CSK, which was firmly in the line of fire in the Mudgal Committee recommendations. With his son-in-law guilty of betting, how could Srinivasan continue to preside over a body that could have a hand in doling out punishment to a team, which was his very own? Much to everyone's chagrin, the BCCI failed to see reason in this line of argument. For the BCCI members, it was all a botched media trial that was unfairly targeting Srinivasan. In fact, had it not been for the Supreme Court of India, things in the BCCI would have forever remained the same with India's cricket establishment turning a blind eye to every form of unfair practice.

In the aftermath of the submission of the Mudgal Committee report, all eyes were on the Supreme Court yet again. Would the apex court suspend CSK and the Royals, and would it chart the road ahead for the BCCI, or would it appoint a fresh committee to do so? Could the BCCI, with all its financial might, resist any further or would it now be ground down to submission? These were questions doing the rounds in India's cricket circles as the team travelled to Australia to play a four-match Test series to be followed by the 2015 World Cup in Australia and New Zealand.

It is a matter of conjecture which was of greater interest to members of the BCCI: Srinivasan's future in cricket administration or how India fared in Australia under new skipper Virat Kohli, with Dhoni, all of a sudden, deciding to stop playing Tests in the middle of a series. Could Srinivasan keep his iron grip intact even when he wasn't president and could Kohli, in sublime form and scoring centuries in every Test, mark a new beginning for Indian Test cricket?

While Kohli's India was competitive and almost scripted a fairy-tale win chasing a mammoth score in Adelaide, with the captain leading with a brilliant century, that the Supreme Court was in no mood to relent was evident when it handed the spot-fixing investigation over to the able hands of three former judges of the Supreme Court—Justice Rajendra Mal Lodha, a former Chief Justice of India, Justice Ashok Bhan and Justice Raju Varadarajulu Raveendran. Men of impeccable credentials, they were asked to decide on the quantum of punishment for the two teams, CSK and the Royals, and also chart out a detailed plan for the reform of the

BCCI, an institution that had fundamentally remained unaltered in its 80 years of existence.

In going about the task assigned to them, the first veiled message that the Lodha Committee decided to send out was that it wasn't going to be affected by what I call the 'fanboy syndrome'. With Indian cricketers being the countries' foremost national icons, most people who come in contact with them turn fans for a brief period of time. Taking selfies and trying to enjoy the moment is natural, but in doing so, particular ground is ceded. Not so with the Lodha Committee. Men of legal eminence, they discussed this issue in one of their early meetings and put it into practice in one of the first encounters with the management of the Royals. Unlike the Chennai team, which was represented by a battery of lawyers, the Rajasthan team had sent Rahul Dravid, among others, to put forward their case before Justice Lodha and his team. 'It was interesting to see the two very different strategies being adopted by the two franchises. While Chennai was going the legal route, Rajasthan had Rahul Dravid with them for the very first meeting. Dravid had no role and it was clear this was an attempt to make an impression on the committee,' said a source working closely with the three former judges. 'It was of great interest to see how the Committee members dealt with Dravid. Would it turn out to be their fanboy moment of sorts or would they just talk to him as just another individual? This, in a way would define the direction the committee would take,' he concluded.

Justice Lodha, he went on to confirm, was very polite but clear with Dravid. He wasn't needed in the meeting was the message that was conveyed to Dravid reasonably early and was respectfully told that they would call on him as and when required. It was an indication that this Committee, unlike others before it, was going to do its job as three former Supreme Court judges and would not be influenced by who was sitting in front of them.

Taking help from a few journalists associated with the game for decades and lawyers who had worked on sports law, the Committee went about working out a 82-part questionnaire, which was first sent to the BCCI president and secretary to be distributed to the office-bearers and heads of state associations. A study of the questionnaire makes it evident which direction the Committee was planning to take.

In the early months, the Committee encountered periodic non-cooperation from the BCCI. 'We would have to ask for everything because nothing would be voluntarily sent to us. The BCCI had a young lawyer working for them at a time, Rohan Bhammar, and he and I used to be in touch from time to time. He was very good and sent us all the documentation we needed,' said Gopal Sankaranarayanan, secretary to the Committee.

More than the non-cooperation, what disappointed the Committee most was the disrespect shown by the BCCI. 'We had sent prior missives to the BCCI and only then did we fix dates for a meeting in Mumbai with the president and secretary in May 2015. But to our surprise neither turned up. The secretary, Anurag Thakur, was never directly in touch and was using his office to tell us about his non-availability. Eventually we had to tick him off on this,' said Sankaranarayanan.

It was gradually turning into an ego battle of sorts. On one side was the BCCI, one of India's traditional bastions of power controlled by politicians, corporates and men of eminence, and on the other was a committee of three former SC judges appointed by the apex judiciary. Neither wanted to cede an inch and the loser, it must be said, was Indian cricket.

Even when the Indian team under Dhoni was dishing out some quality performances in the 2015 World Cup, eventually losing to Australia in the semi-final, most BCCI mandarins were more concerned with its elections on 2 March 2015. With Srinivasan ineligible, Jagmohan Dalmiya returned to the helm unopposed for his final innings in cricket administration. And Thakur, a Bharatiya Janata Party (BJP) MP from Hamirpur, beat the Srinivasan nominee by a solitary vote 15–14 to become secretary. All the other positions, including that of the treasurer and the five vice presidents were won by men from the Srinivasan camp.

This was now a Board that wanted to reform but did not have the numbers from within to do so. The president and secretary were keen to make a difference but at times were in a minority within their own working committee. Everyone, from office-bearers to the media manager officiating in Australia, was cagey. Dr R.N. Baba, media manager of the team during the World Cup and perhaps the worst ever candidate for the job, went to the extent of telling a journalist that he would confiscate his accreditation for congratulating Dhoni on the birth of his daughter. Touring journalists weren't allowed to say hello to players and the relationship between the team and the media was at its lowest. I had my own run-ins with Baba and had to politely tell him on a number of occasions that we were both doing our jobs and any overreaction on his part may not lead to the best outcome. Journalists deserved basic courtesy, which Baba was lacking. That he lost his job at the end of the World Cup was somewhat expected, with the media-savvy Thakur having taken over as the new secretary.

I remember meeting Thakur at the Melbourne Airport on my way back from the World Cup and the entire talk was about the BCCI and the way forward. Thakur, who has done much for cricket in Dharamsala, appeared committed and keen. Even if he was anxious, he managed to mask it well, trying to give the impression that the Lodha Committee wasn't preying on his mind. Dalmiya, too, was finding the going hard. In a conversation from Australia, he had given me the impression that he was not in the best health and this was working against him in trying to accomplish all that he wanted to.

Things reached a crescendo in July, when in a packed press conference at the India International Centre in Delhi, Justice Lodha announced that the two teams, CSK and the Royals, were suspended for two years with Meiyappan and Kundra banned from cricket administration for life.

This was supposed to be a routine press conference. And it wasn't being conducted by a celebrity in the conventional sense of the term. A 65-plus retired Supreme Court judge and two of his mates of similar age did not qualify as celebrities in any broad understanding. Yet there was not a single media outlet in India that wasn't present at the press conference. Every journalist present wanted a piece of Justice Lodha and even when he was the chief justice of the Supreme Court, he might not have encountered a similar situation. Here he was, the presiding deity over India's mass religion, and was about to deliver a verdict that controlled the fate of this religion going forward. As Kushan Sarkar, senior journalist with the PTI and one with a real nose for news said to me, 'On Lodha's words, literally, depended the future of Indian cricket and it was no surprise that he was the newsmaker of the day across every single media platform in the country.'

While CSK and the Royals had avoided permanent termination, some like Raghu Iyer, still continuing as CEO of the latter, considered the punishment harsh. 'We felt it was a tad harsh because the players and the professional management was being asked to pay the price for a folly we had not committed or even remotely knew,' said Iyer.

He is wrong on this one. His players and owner had committed the act and it was only natural that team Royals would have to pay.

'The press conference was final indication that we meant business; that we couldn't be influenced and wouldn't spare the high and mighty. The Supreme Court of India had given us a job to do and we would do it the best we could,' says one of the members of the Committee.

He was right. The judgement had sent a chill down the BCCI's spine and no one was considered safe any longer. From the president, secretary and office-bearers down to state association officials, everyone had started to wonder what was next. What would the ambit of reform suggested by the Lodha Committee be and how deep would the three judges go? Would they suggest sweeping changes that fundamentally altered the nature of India's cricketscape or would they hold back a little? If the questionnaire was proof, the Committee was trying to do something seriously ambitious, something that had never been attempted in Indian sport ever before.

What complicated matters further was the sudden demise of the incumbent Board president, Jagmohan Dalmiya, in September 2015. He was succeeded by Manohar and, soon after taking over, Manohar commissioned Deloitte to submit a detailed report on the workings of the various state associations to try and understand the urgency for reform. This report, which revealed rampant corruption in some associations, further had the effect of pegging the BCCI back in its tussle with the Court-appointed Committee.

Manohar, who was one of the few to have created an impression on Justice Lodha, did start to implement a slew of reforms since taking over, a number of which were on the lines the Committee would later go on to suggest. Whether this was a pre-emptive measure or a sign of desperation in trying to save a sinking ship will forever remain a matter of conjecture.

Also of interest was the fact that the Vasant Kunj office, in Delhi, of the secretary to the Committee was twice broken into in the second half of 2015. On both occasions, Sankaranarayanan filed FIRs with the Delhi Police citing the seriousness of the issue. 'While I had everything in soft copy, it was worrying to note that we were being pried upon,' said he. While there was no direct case of trying to meddle into the affairs of the Committee, the break-ins, I would argue, were similar in nature. Here was a high-profile Committee entrusted with reforming a high-profile institution and was constantly dealing with high-profile celebrities. That the papers would be of a sensitive nature was anyone's guess and to see burglars target these papers not once but twice couldn't have been a coincidence. Moreover, it is hard to believe thieves in Delhi were overnight interested in papers on Indian cricket and its functioning! 'More than anything, it was a feeling of intrusion into your privacy. It was as if you were being watched all the time,' argues Sankaranarayanan.

What further added to the Committee's discomfort was the sudden appearance of media reports suggesting five selectors were key to the welfare of Indian cricket or that the old guard had actually done great work or that a one-state-one-vote formula was unworkable. Anyone reading them would find such reports innocuous but for the Committee, which was about to suggest the reduction of selectors from five to three, and the implementation of the one-state-one-vote formula, this was the old guard trying to get back at them through the most clandestine of ways. 'We couldn't trust anyone. With each passing day, we were becoming more and more careful about stopping any possible leaks from our end,' says one of the members.

Here was a Committee asked to reform Indian cricket, not perform some covert military intelligence work. Yet the nature of the beast was such, and the stakes involved were so high, that anything was possible. Men in power at the BCCI would do everything to hold on to power and a backlash from the old guard was only par for the course.

The veil of suspense was finally lifted in January 2016 when the Committee submitted its final report to the Supreme Court asking for fundamental changes in the manner in which Indian cricket was run and governed. The changes, if implemented, would completely overhaul the BCCI and it was only natural that the reforms proposed were met with resistance and cynicism from within the echelons of Indian cricket's corridors of power. The months between January and July 2016 saw growing acrimony between the Committee and the BCCI office-bearers, with both sides taking pot shots at each other in the court and outside. The media was having a ball with stories planted almost daily, trying to influence public opinion.

The moot question debated in the court was whether these recommendations were binding and practicable. The BCCI believed they were not. The Lodha Committee, on the other hand, argued that all of the recommendations made were to be implemented if total cleansing was the ambition.

Turning to the recommendations, it must be said that most of them followed the principles of good governance and had drawn upon practices from the International Olympic Committee charter. Age, term and tenure were prime examples and were a welcome suggestion. To see people heading state cricket associations for decades was the worst practice of all. It eroded accountability and often turned an association into an unholy cartel. And there were many such associations within the BCCI which had been headed by the same people for more than two decades.

That the Committee suggested no uniformity in central subsidy for state associations was another serious recommendation. There were some associations in which there was no accountability on how crores of rupees were spent. Goa, for example, still does not have a stadium and, to go with that, has a bank balance that is pitiable. Question, therefore, remains as to what happened to the hundreds of crores of subsidy that was paid to the association over the last ten years? The same question could be asked of many other state bodies.

Where the Lodha Committee might have gone a little beyond its remit was with reference to two sets of recommendations. First, it recommended the one-state-one-vote principle, which, sources close to the Committee mention, was first mooted by former BCCI secretary and Maharashtra Cricket Association (MACA) president Ajay Shirke. Shirke, a source close to the Committee confirmed to *The Times of India*, had done so when he was president of MACA and had not taken over as secretary of BCCI, following Manohar's move to the ICC as its first elected chairman. Shirke, they said, was of the belief that one vote per state would mean Maharashtra, the state, would get the nod ahead of Mumbai. The same would be true of Gujarat. That the right to vote could be based on rotation was not something he had taken into account. Shirke, however, denied the charge.

While on paper it is understandable why the Committee had recommended the one-state-one-vote formula, the structure of Indian cricket is such that it is impossible to implement this position without impacting the very foundation of the game in the country. According to this recommendation, the three existing institutions in Maharashtra—Mumbai, the Cricket Club of India (CCI) and Maharashtra would have one vote by rotation. Contrast this with the suggestion that the north-east, which has little or no cricket but many small states, will all have a vote each. If every state is a Full Member and has one vote, the north-east will end up having six votes while Western India—the hotbed of cricket, will end up with two votes—Maharashtra and Gujarat. It might create for a situation where states with no cricket background whatsoever start to have a vote and start controlling Indian cricket's purse by virtue of their voting power.

More than the one-state-one-vote principle, the recommendation that was practically unworkable was the one concerning broadcast. The Committee suggested doing away with commercial breaks in-between overs, arguing it impacted viewing experience. This recommendation, if implemented, could curtail BCCI's revenue by a drastic 70–75 per cent. What several legal luminaries whom I spoke to pointed out was that the BCCI sells the telecast rights of the games to the broadcaster and no more. It sells the action and not the breaks. In other words, the advertisement breaks are not owned by the BCCI. The commercial time during the lunch or tea breaks are not the BCCI's property that they can decide on how to monetize them. They are the broadcaster's property and not the Board's. If the broadcaster is not permitted to monetize these breaks, the very cost of the broadcast involving 20-plus cameras will be a cost that will have to be borne by the BCCI. It will then be a throwback to the 1980s, when the BCCI would pay money to Doordarshan to telecast Indian cricket. Broadcasters like Star and Sony, which spend enormous amounts in cricket telecast, were seriously concerned by this and wanted to renegotiate their existing contracts in case this recommendation was implemented.

Given the practical problems in implementing some of the changes proposed, the best way forward was amicable dialogue. But growing mistrust between the BCCI and the Lodha Committee prevented dialogue and it was all back to where it started—the Supreme Court.

What went against the BCCI in court was their continued inaction on the issue. While the recommendations were made public on 3 January, the BCCI convened a Special General Meeting (SGM) on 19 February. Had it done so earlier, there would have been no reason to doubt its intent. That it was dealing with a Supreme Court-appointed Committee was often forgotten and the final order on 18 July 2016, while giving some relief to the BCCI, largely upheld the views of the Committee. The broadcast regulation was done away with and was the only big takeaway for the Board.

Defiance

The BCCI-versus-Lodha-Committee battle, however unequal it may seem, was still continuing a year after the court had passed its order on 18 July 2016. It's true that the BCCI lost its president and the secretary in January 2017, ousted for failing to implement the order. But defiance, both at the BCCI and also at the state-association level, continued.

Clearly, this case is a first of its kind in India. Contrary to all expectations, an institution was in open defiance of a judicial order passed by the highest court of the land and literally forced the hand of a Supreme Court-appointed committee of administrators.

Two questions came up repeatedly as a result: Could the BCCI eventually manage to get away by not implementing what was a binding judicial order? Also, what precedent would the case set going forward?

What had started out as a case against corruption, trying to rescue Indian cricket from the growing threat of spot- and match-fixing, ended up being an ego tussle between the world's richest cricket board and the Supreme Court-appointed Lodha Committee, and subsequently, the CoA. In the process, the game itself was often placed on the sacrificial altar. Nothing else explains BCCI secretary Shirke writing to the English cricket establishment in November 2016 stating that the BCCI was not in a position to sign the MOU with the England and Wales Cricket Board and hence, it could not pay for hotel and travel bills of the touring England cricket team. In what was no more than posturing—this action of the BCCI was, at best, an ineffective form of blackmail. No one could take Shirke seriously for a cancellation of the series would have meant the BCCI would have to pay the host broadcaster hundreds of millions of dollars, a few hundred times more than the cost of hotels and domestic air travel. However, what this statement did was indicate to the ordinary cricket fan that the game, which should be above all else, was being treated as a pawn in the battle for power. And the moment the Supreme Court allowed the BCCI to spend the meagre sum of INR 58.66 lakh per Test match, the threat ceased to have any relevance. For the record, the MOU was not signed until the middle of the series and yet, the series went on uninterrupted.

By suggesting that the series could be in jeopardy, the BCCI was trying to reach out to the ordinary cricket fan and evoke sympathy. It tried to demonstrate that the Committee's lack of cooperation was forcing Indian cricket to a standstill. The Lodha Committee, on the other hand, blamed it on the BCCI president and the secretary, saying they were the ones responsible for putting a question mark on the series by not complying with the Supreme Court's order.

One of the final acts of defiance occurred on 26 July 2017, when, in another SGM convened to discuss implementation, the BCCI informed the apex court that it was back to where it was on 1 October 2016. The stand was simple: Let the Supreme Court force the BCCI's hand if it wants to.

Incredible as it may sound, this was the truth.

On the face of it, the BCCI said that it opposed *only* five key points of the Lodha recommendations. These were the proposed membership structure, constitution of the apex council, distribution of powers to office-bearers and professionals, age and tenure, and number of selectors. A cursory look at the objections would make it clear that the BCCI rejected every tangible reform outright. By retaining the existing membership structure, they said no to the entry of new members and, by saying they opposed the age and tenure norms prescribed, it was suggested that every member above 70 years of age continued to be eligible!

Was the BCCI trying to suggest that the entire exercise conducted by the Supreme Court of India, the body that is the highest law-making authority in this country, a farce? For three years—between 2015 and 2017—the Court had been deliberating on this case. Only in 2016, after much consideration, did it pass an order that, under normal circumstances, is binding. Not so, however, for the BCCI.

Finally, on 26 July 2017 the BCCI openly suggested that the entire reforms process was a charade. It was, in essence, telling the SC: 'We are not going to change come what may and we stand united against every grain of reform proposed to us.' It was defiance of a very obstinate nature: Brazen and outright.

In doing what it did the BCCI continued to frustrate the CoA—a body appointed by the Court in January 2017 to ensure the implementation of the reforms. A body headed by the former Comptroller and Auditor General of India, Vinod Rai, the CoA looked powerless pitted against all the politicking. Left frustrated, all the CoA could do was hope the Court empowered its own body to carry the reforms process forward.

As for the Supreme Court, it had passed an order which continued to be violated. It appointed a committee to implement that order, which was humiliated and insulted. It repeatedly suggested that certain members be kept away from the BCCI but by saying no to the age and tenure restrictions, the BCCI's retort was that these members were every bit welcome!

The case, which dragged on for four years and more, ended up being about civil society and the rule of law. Are we a society governed by a set of laws and rules framed more often than not by the Supreme Court of India? Can a body, however strong and rich it may be, openly defy a legally binding order of the Supreme Court and win? What message did it send to the common citizen and to other Indian sports bodies, which, too, are in crying need of reform?

To conclude, readers must know the level to which certain BCCI mandarins, supposed custodians of the gentlemen's game, can stoop to hold on to their chairs. Knowing that the Supreme Court can ask for the audio recording of the SGM to find out who the dissenters were, the first 30 minutes of the two-hour SGM on 26 July 2017 was spent quibbling about whether the proceedings should be recorded. For the record, all BCCI general body meetings from 2003 onwards have been recorded. Yet, here were four members, the audio tapes reveal, who were opposing recording the meeting in a desperate act to hold on to power. Representatives of Tamil Nadu, Himachal Pradesh, Haryana and Kerala were finally overruled by the secretary and discussion resumed after half-an-hour had elapsed.

I can do little here but fall back on C.L.R. James: 'What do they know of cricket who only cricket know?'

MISPLACED AMBITION FOR
WORLD DOMINATION
THE BIG THREE CARTEL AND THE ICC

Former ICC president Ehsan Mani's baritone voice made for a nice sound effect on an unusually chilly January morning in Kolkata. 'Boria, *aap log aisa kyun kar rahe ho*? [Boria, why are you all doing this?] The game will lose out, don't you realize?' '*Aap log*' [You all], understandably, wasn't directed at me personally. He meant India or rather specifically the BCCI. The pleasant effect had given way to a sense of apprehension and uncertainty. Ehsan Mani was not one to call and waste time. That he was on the phone, sounding unmistakably concerned, meant something serious was happening.

'The BCCI, with Australia and England, are trying to divide world cricket and make it into a monopoly,' Mani said. 'See if you can help. Everyone in the media should speak out and I am happy to talk to you if you think that might work,' he concluded.

Clearly, I needed to know more. All I was aware of was that something was going on behind the scenes for some months now.

The first person to give me details of what was going on was Mahendra Mapagunaratne, a lawyer based in Canada, who had already spoken to a few former cricketers on the issue. He was even planning a signature campaign to create consensus once the ICC had made its plans public.

On 9 January 2014, the ICC revealed that it was working on a fundamental structural overhaul of world cricket, which, if effected, would cede ultimate control of the game and its finances to the 'Big Three'—India, Australia and England.

The overhaul, a brainchild of former BCCI president N. Srinivasan, who was also the BCCI's nominee in the ICC, was based on a simple premise: Considering India contributes the bulk of the revenue to world cricket, it was only fair that India ran the game and its finances.

Concerns such as whether India could run it alone, or what long-term effects the structural overhaul could have on the game and its health were not something the powers that be were concerned with at the time.

The 'Big Three' formula, given its timing and context, worked well in diverting attention from the spot-fixing investigation at home and keeping the flock together in the BCCI. Under this new arrangement, drafted by a working group of the ICC's financial and commercial affairs committee, India, Australia and England were all set to have overwhelming control over world cricket's finances and, in turn, stood to earn hundreds of millions of dollars more from the ICC's central revenue pool. This meant the BCCI would subsequently be in a position to pass on more to the state associations—issues of transparency and accountability notwithstanding—and Indian cricket's finances would be robust going forward. Srinivasan, the architect, had to be backed to see the transformation through and every attempt was made to protect him from the Supreme Court, and by extension, the Mudgal Committee.

The document also detailed Test match promotion and relegation and suggested exceptions for the Big Three in contravention of all

democratic principles. Finally, it suggested that the position of the
ICC chairman would change annually and rotate among nominees
of the Big Three.

Exactly two decades earlier, on 2 February 1993, India had taken
the lead to end the Australian and English veto at the ICC. Twenty
years later, it was India yet again taking the lead in trying to reinstate
the veto and hand it back to the English and the Australians. The
only difference this time around was that India, too, was a beneficiary
of this oligarchy that was being proposed within world cricket's
governing body.

The oligarchy, Mani argued, would force cricket's support base
to shrink in the long term. South Africa, Pakistan, New Zealand,
Sri Lanka and the other cricket playing nations would lose out
significantly as a result of the cartelization being proposed by the
Big Three formula. While benefitting cricket's most powerful troika
in the short term and resulting in some good matches, the sport
itself would be the loser going forward. 'It is a short-sighted measure
mooted by administrators who are hardly concerned with what will
happen to the sport a decade from now, when they, men who are
in power at the moment, will no longer be in positions of control,'
lamented Mani.

The most disturbing clause in the proposal was the one concerning
relegation. The Big Three, it suggested, could never be relegated. So,
if India, Australia and England were ever at numbers six, seven or
eight in the rankings, cricket would be in a serious fix! The underlying
assumption was that such a situation would never arise, which, in
turn, implied that Pakistan, Sri Lanka, New Zealand, South Africa
and the West Indies could never ever upstage the Big Three.

The proposals, as Mani pointed out, smelled of arrogance and
was initially met with resistance from Pakistan, Sri Lanka and South
Africa.

South Africa was the first country to come out in criticism and called the whole plan fundamentally flawed. In a position paper submitted to the ICC, Cricket South Africa (CSA) invoked Nelson Mandela and declared, 'Our people have the right to hope, the right to a future, the right to life itself. No power on this earth can destroy the thirst for human dignity. Our land cries out for peace. We will only achieve it through adherence to democratic principles and respect for the rights of all.'

Knowing that the Big Three needed the South African vote to get the proposals passed, CSA went on to demand that they be given a permanent position in the revamped ICC Executive Board alongside India, England and Australia. This is what the paper stated:

> CSA believes that the role of EXCO is going to be very important within the ICC and therefore its composition should be increased from the proposed five to six members. Furthermore, CSA strongly believes that, apart from being a Founding Member of the ICC, it is also a major cricket nation and deserves status on the ICC EXCO and F&CA committees during this transitional period.'
>
> The conclusion of the paper was no less dramatic: 'To put it mildly, the original Proposal was extremely disappointing and indeed hurtful when originating from three great cricketing nations, and three great democracies from which South Africa [and our Past President Nelson Mandela] learnt many wonderful lessons. The groundswell and global rejection of the proposals that followed cannot be ignored and we, as the current guardians of the game, will be judged by history.

From submitting the position paper to jumping the fence and voting in favour of the proposals was a really long distance travelled by CSA. The question, however, was why did CSA do so and what did they get in return?

Till the night before the meeting in Singapore, in early February 2014, CSA, Sri Lanka Cricket (SLC) and the PCB were speaking in one voice. But things changed after CSA president Chris Nenzani met Srinivasan, his Indian counterpart, in Singapore. Soon after this meeting, the CSA decided to change sides, going against the very grain of the position paper they had presented.

In a press statement, Nenzani tried to justify the changed stance. 'Nothing in life is perfect,' he said. 'All countries, including the so-called Big Three, have had to rethink and make concessions and the final terms that were approved today include significant changes from the original proposals presented in January.'

While changes had been made to the original draft, there was no doubt that several decisions went against the paper that South Africa had claimed they stood for.

This was evident from the ICC press release issued after the meeting, which made it clear that CSA's demand for a six-member Executive wasn't met and nor were they given a permanent position in the newly formed Executive. Yet, CSA decided to vote in favour of the proposals. Theirs was the crucial vote that clinched the deal for the BCCI, CA and the ECB. The question thus arises as to why CSA agreed to vote in favour when most of its demands weren't met? Had they been promised more tours in return for their support? Why did they decide to leave PCB and SLC in the lurch and walk away and, by doing so, did they end up opposing the principles that Mandela stood for?

This was turning out to be a classic case of commercialism emerging triumphant over the principles of ethics and good governance. Principles were thus sacrificed at the altar of commerce.

Could, however, world cricket benefit as a result?

As is the case with most governance matters at the ICC, things did not move at the pace originally envisaged by Srinivasan and his cohorts. In due course of time, Srinivasan lost support within the BCCI and was removed as the BCCI's nominee to the ICC in November 2015. The position, subsequently, was awarded to Shashank Manohar, with questions being asked on the feasibility of the formula.

Manohar, who had taken over as ICC Chairman by virtue of being the BCCI nominee, was an ardent critic of the model from day one of taking charge. However, considering he was the BCCI's nominee, the question was if he could go ahead and press for a radical overturn of the formula, something that was adding substantially to the BCCI's share of ICC revenue.

The question was debated in multiple BCCI meetings with a section opposing Manohar and arguing that an overturn would cost the BCCI many thousands of crores, which, in the light of the Lodha recommendations, was money the BCCI couldn't do without.

This was Manohar's first real test since taking over as president in November2015.

Manohar eventually won the day in a SGM, in February 2016, with none of the office-bearers, other than the treasurer Anirudh Chowdhury, saying anything critical about the restructuring. In fact, Bharat Raman, representing Tamil Nadu Cricket Association (Srinivasan's home association), was also silent on the matter though the state board's secretary Kashi Vishwanathan had sent a letter to the BCCI president questioning his rationale behind the overturn.

Such a reaction, very symptomatic of the BCCI, points to two things. First, it was clear that Manohar had an overwhelming majority and the opposition voices had been reduced to a poor minority. Second, Manohar, with his penchant for reform, had managed to win over some supporters. His decision to restore the democratic governance model in the ICC, welcomed by many from across the sporting world, was finding takers within his own Board.

Those opposing Manohar had cited the United States example within the International Olympic Committee (IOC). It is true that the United States Olympic Committee, for the longest time, enjoyed a larger share of the IOC's revenue because the National Broadcasting Company (NBC) and the US broadcasting fraternity contributed the maximum monies to the IOC's telecast rights. As a result, it was deemed logical that the US should receive preferential treatment and get a larger corpus of the largesse.

However, from the very beginning, this was a matter of serious trouble within the IOC. While they did get the money, the Americans stood alienated as a result and if IOC insiders are to be believed, it did not help the Americans in many aspects of decision-making. A number of smaller nations opposed the US in matters of governance just because they felt discriminated and side-lined. Richard Pound, one of the most influential members of the IOC and former president of the World Anti Doping Agency, alluded to the complications the differential revenue structure had created in the IOC and also outlined the way in which the IOC ultimately went ahead in solving the problem.

The international sports federations, which depend on the IOC for a significant amount of their revenue, were the other firm advocates of the differential revenue model. In the words of Pound: 'Distribution formulae regarding television revenues led to increasing pressures from International Federations, which believed that the number of spectators was an important factor in the determination of each IF's share of those revenues . . . One management technique that the IOC discovered early in the process of allocating television revenues among IFs was to fix the global amount available to the IFs collectively, but to require the IFs to agree amongst themselves as to how the money would be divided. There was no upside, and all downside, were the IOC to assume the responsibility of ranking the sports. It was far better to have the collective of IFs pleased with the increasing amounts directed at the IFs by the IOC, and to let them fight amongst themselves for the appropriate shares.'

Such a thing was not being done by the ICC. Rather, it was the Big Three that decided on everything and handed down the decisions to the others. That most of the others accepted what was thrust upon them by the three nations was down to the fear of India bullying them into submission. They were also scared because any opposition could result in the Indian team deciding against touring the dissenting nations.

Manohar knew the situation was not ideal. Scaring people into submission was hardly a model of good governance that can be sustained over a period of time. As the new nerve-centre of world cricket, India needed to act with far greater social responsibility than was being exhibited, and in the long term, it could only end up shrinking the size of the world cricket market. A cartel running a global sport was not the best solution and the sooner the BCCI recognized it, the better it was for them. Rather than focusing on short-term revenues, the BCCI, as cricket's most powerful national apex body, should refocus its energies on how to make Test cricket viable. To see only 3,000 people in 30,000-plus stadia across the world was the worst advertisement for cricket and that, more than anything, needed the BCCI's attention. To address this issue, the BCCI needed supporters at the ICC, something Manohar's radical overturn of the Big Three monopoly helped him garner.

However, the battle was far from over. Once Manohar had taken over as the first elected chairman of the ICC and had given up his position in the BCCI, things turned again. Dissenting voices grew louder and, in early 2017, just weeks before a very crucial ICC meeting on the matter, a section of the BCCI upped the ante and mooted the threat of India's pull-out from the ICC Champions Trophy in June.

Manohar, however, had done his homework. He had overwhelming support within the ICC, and a failed Indian coup in South Africa in October 2016 to overthrow him had further strengthened his position. BCCI officials had tried to reach out to world cricket bosses to throw Manohar out and failed spectacularly in doing so with heads of CSA, CA, the West Indies Cricket Board and ECB all siding with Manohar. As a result, to stop Manohar from going ahead with his model of financial redistribution, the BCCI had to do something spectacular ahead of the meeting. They needed to show the ICC that they continued to wield clout much more than a normal member and were willing to escalate the confrontation to the next level.

Announcing the sale of IPL telecast rights for five years instead of ten was one such attempt. On the face of it, it was part of the BCCI's effort to maximize revenue in the short term. But the bigger picture was fundamentally different. It was a show of strength and a veiled warning to the ICC. The ICC telecast rights would come up for renewal in 2023, just months before the IPL rights came up for sale again in 2022–23. And it is anyone's guess which is a more lucrative proposition. The IPL, the BCCI was telling the world, is a bigger brand than all ICC events combined and it was willing to take the ICC head on. If the IPL brand value generates more revenue than multiple World Cups combined, it doesn't leave an iota of doubt who wields the most power in world cricket.

Having said that, was this enough in stopping the ICC from going ahead with the financial redistribution plan? Could the statements made by some of the disqualified BCCI officials that the ICC could still be made to eat humble pie hold any ground? Could India realistically use the bait of not playing the Champions Trophy to try and protect BCCI's financial interests?

The answer, gleaned from the many conversations conducted while writing this book, was an overwhelming 'No'. The ordinary cricket fan did not care if the BCCI made USD 500 million less than what it might have earned under the Big Three formula. For the fan on the street, the BCCI was already in prime financial health and all that mattered to them is the game on the field. To be told that the Board, for money, was planning to stop Kohli and his team from playing the Champions Trophy was simply ridiculous. Fans paid to watch Kohli and his boys play, and it was the action on the field that made the BCCI what it was, not the other way around. To even think that the BCCI could get away by refusing to play the Champions Trophy and blackmailing the ICC by using the threat of not playing, was to live in an alien universe where reason and logic do not exist. Manohar, more than anyone, knew this and was in no mood to give in to blackmail in the meeting on 25 April in Dubai.

That's where the sale of the telecast rights became a little more relevant than it was hitherto. This was a real threat to the ICC and a declaration of war that could unnerve the apex body in the long run. If the BCCI was able to generate more money with a domestic cricket tournament, the ICC would clearly look poor. It could turn out to be an assertion of Indian hegemony and give the BCCI pole position in world cricket; a position that had otherwise been in doubt because of its obstinacy.

The numbers, however, were firmly stacked against the BCCI. It was soon clear that, by trying to flex its muscle in the ICC meeting on 25 April, the BCCI stood to lose more. Rather, it was important to sit across the table with Manohar and the stakeholders and push its points across to get more money allocated to India. Dialogue rather than defiance was the way forward.

The BCCI, however, hedged its bets on playing hardball and, in a first in the history of the ICC, was defeated 13–1 in the Board meeting. Unwilling to see the writing on the wall, they raised the Champions Trophy pull-out threat again. It was difficult to understand how by withdrawing from the Champions Trophy the BCCI was expecting India to get back all its control at the ICC. Was such a thing possible at a time when the ICC was united against the BCCI and had already voted in favour of the new financial model? Were they expected to eat humble pie and take back their own decision because India threatened a pull-out?

For once it is necessary to move away from the politics of the BCCI and the ICC and start with the players. For me, the biggest stakeholders of Indian cricket have always been the players. They have made the game what it is and they are the icons fans follow and worship. The BCCI today is what it is because of Tendulkar, Ganguly, Laxman, Dravid, Dhoni, Sehwag, Kumble and now Kohli, Ashwin, Rahane and the like. The team had just won a tough home series against Australia and made India the world's number one Test side. They were the ones who won the Champions Trophy in 2013 and did their best by finishing second in their title defence in 2017. By threatening non-participation in the event, was the BCCI being fair to the players? Were the players in sync with such a call? Could a few administrators, to satisfy their own egos, decide on whether India will play the Champions Trophy? Did they have the mandate to take such a call in the first place?

If one were to gauge the prudence of the decision and its ramifications, a number of questions begged to be answered. First, could India really afford such a call and would it have any impact on the ICC? Objectively speaking, the Champions Trophy could indeed turn into half the tournament if India decided to stay away. But what about the backlash? Would the other boards not feel let down and would they not want to take action? Could India afford to alienate every other board and then want to rule world cricket? If the rumours within the ICC boardrooms were to be believed, certain members had even threatened the BCCI with dire action. Unbelievable as it may sound, false bravado was not going to work for the BCCI this time around. Knowing that a few BCCI members might want to use the Champions Trophy to protect their egos, the ICC was prepared well to deal with them. India's withdrawal, ICC sources revealed, would have immediately prompted boards like Australia and England to rethink their bilateral calendar with India, and some boards could even mull on withdrawing players from the IPL in 2018. Without international players, the IPL would turn out to be one-tenth of what it is now.

Most importantly, world cricket couldn't afford such a standoff. And the BCCI, too, for its own interest and the interests of world cricket, couldn't afford to walk the path alone. It needed England, Australia and South Africa as much as they needed the Indian Board.

As for the reason behind India's snub at the ICC, there was more to the story than met the eye. Manohar, it had come to light, had offered the Indians USD 100 million more as a compromise formula. He confirmed this to me just moments after the ICC Board voted in favour of the proposal. 'Look, let me make it clear. ICC recognizes the contribution of the BCCI and hence I am still willing to go up to 390 million dollars for the BCCI. This is USD 100 million more than the current allotment. And let me give you the real picture. Out of the ICC's net revenue of USD 1,800 million, this amounts to 21.5 per cent. England, which gets the second largest share, gets 7 per cent. So India in effect gets INR 1,500 crore more than England. Now that's a sizeable sum, isn't it? While we recognize India's contribution, any distribution will have to be based on the principles of equity and good governance,' argued Manohar. When I pushed him saying this sum was still much less than the USD 570 million promised earlier, he came back with a sharp retort. 'It is not true. The Big Three formula was never implemented. It was never a reality. It was supposed to be implemented in 2016, and when I took over, many boards were opposed to it. This is why a working group was constituted to relook at the model. To say India's share was 570 million, etc. is all hypothetical talk. These things have no basis in fact and everyone needs to know the real truth,' he declared.

Manohar also made it clear that dialogue was the only way forward. 'India needs to come forward and accept the proposal. We want India to get the best possible and move on. We have done the best we can. But now it is upon the BCCI to decide. As I told you, as chairman I will have to ensure all distribution is based on equity and good conscience.'

And when I asked him about the Champions Trophy threat, he was statesmanlike and philosophical. 'This was raised at the meeting and the members don't think this was right. World cricket needs to be together and that's what will benefit India.'

Was he willing to negotiate further with India? Manohar did keep the window open for the BCCI. 'I am always available to sit down and talk, and as I said, I have always recognized India's contribution as ICC chairman. That will never change. But the model is based on principles of good governance, and that will not change either. As chairman, I will always uphold the principles I stand for.'

Using his words cautiously, he was also trying to send out a veiled message. Indian cricket was more than the egos of a few administrators. It was about Kohli getting an opportunity to hold the Champions Trophy aloft at the Oval on 18 June 2017. That's what the fans wanted to see, not some officials quibbling in an ICC boardroom threatening a pull-out.

In the debate over withdrawal, there was one constituency which was surprisingly silent; rather, absent. It was the most important constituency: The players. No one had spoken about the players. Did the players want to play or withdraw? How did Kohli or Dhoni feel about the matter? By suggesting withdrawal from all ICC events between 2017 and 2023, the BCCI office-bearers could end up ensuring Kohli never played another World Cup.

Did the BCCI have the moral right to decide on behalf of the players? Rather, cut short careers and rob them of the opportunity of playing World Cups and World T20 competitions? After all, was it not the players who have made the BCCI what it was and earned them their money? How was it that they didn't have a say in the entire process and were being treated as a herd?

This issue also made it evident that a players' association in India was a dire need. In Australia, for example, the players were engaged in an eight-month long dispute with CA over a fair share of pay.

For the entire period, they rejected CA's offer of a certain percentage and were speaking in one voice. Eventually, the unified stand paid off, with both parties coming to the negotiating table and reaching a compromise. In India, however, there is no such association; no group to take up the cudgels for Kohli and the other players and deliberate with the office-bearers. Perhaps it is time someone takes the lead in forming a players' association. Imagine a situation where Tendulkar, Ganguly, Dravid, Sehwag, Dhoni and the others did not get to play the World Cups or the Champions Trophy tournaments. Would they have become the kind of legends they are without their World Cup exploits? Tendulkar, it is known, considers the 2011 World Cup triumph his finest hour. And to be told that Kohli may not have an opportunity to have a crack at the title in 2019 or 2023 sounds unfortunate and naive.

Finally, in May 2017, under instructions from the CoA, the BCCI confirmed Indian participation in the Champions Trophy and, eventually, in the ICC meeting in June 2017, the matter was resolved, with the BCCI getting its share increased to USD 405 million. The BCCI had finally started to see reason and was coming to terms with the writing on the wall. Take it or leave it was the message, and they showed prudence in accepting the offer and ending the standoff.

While this temporary standoff has come to an end, the BCCI does need to realize and accept one cardinal lesson: That Indian cricket, first and foremost, is about the players and the office-bearers are, at best, the support cast.

INDIAN CRICKET
A PHOTOGRAPHIC HISTORY

H.H. The Jam of Jamnagar

to encourage the game, among the natives has been the only motive. Whether I might as well leave it alone or not, you are perhaps a better judge than

Yours, dear Sir,

A WOULD-BE-CRICKETER.

Sylhet, March 3, 1845.

LIGHT COMPANY—*1st Innings.*

Captain Powell, 0, bd Ross,	0
Lieut. Sneyd, 1, bd Salmon,	1
Sepoys Sungum Opudeale, 11216, bd Salmon,	11
,, Soophu, 1, bd Ross,	1
,, Goordut, 111, ct Costley, bd Salmon,	3
,, Swsahai, 1, bd Ross,	1
,, Dabie 1st, 1, run out,	1
,, Roostum, 21, bd Salmon,	3
,, Merwan Sing, 211, bd Ross,	3
,, Davie. 21111, not out,	1
,, Rambit, 1, ct Ross bd Salmon,	6
Byes, 11211,	6
Total	**37**

THE OTHER COMPANIES—*1st Innings.*

Lieut. Lyssght, 213, bd Sneyd,	6
Ens. Costley, 0, bd Powell,	0
,, Ross 1123, stumped, Sneyd	7
,, Salmon, 21, ct Ramhit, bd Powell,	3
Sepoys Buldee, 2, bd Sneyd,	3
,, Bendoo, 151, bd Sneyd,	7
,, Uckball, 312, ct Roostum, bd Powell,	6
,, Sewpersand, 12132, bd Soophul,	9
,, Dwan Sing, 112, not out,	4
,, Mattabux, 1, run out,	1
,, Pattondeen, 211, ct Roostum, bd Sneyd,	4
Byes, 1111111111,	10
Total	**59**

LIGHT COMPANY—*2nd Innings.*

Capt. Powell, 0, ct Uckball, bd Salmon,	0
Lieut. Sneyd, 1521, stumped Ross,	9
Sepoys Sungum Opudeah, 4111, bd Ross	7
,, Soophul, 112, bd Ross,	4
,, Goordut, 31, tipped himself out,	4
,, Sewsahai, 2, ct Ross, bd Salmon,	2
,, Dabie 1st, 112, bd Ross,	4
,, Roostum, 422222, bd Ross,	14
,, Dabie 2nd, 0, ct Costley, bd Ross,	0
,, Merwan, 0, bd Sneyd,	0
,, Rambit, 0, not out,	0
Byes, 12112,	7
Total	**51**

THE OTHER COMPANIES—*2nd Innings.*

	3
Lieut. Lyssght, 3, bd Soophul,	14
Ensign Costley, 211122311, bd Powell,	12
,, Ross, 2145, ct Sungum,	14
,, Salmon, 11133122, bd Soophul,	8
Sepoys Buldee, 12221, bd Sneyd,	6
,, Bendoo, 0, bd Sneyd,	0
,, Uckball, 121111, not out,	4
,, Sewpersaud, 4, ct Sneyd, bd Powell,	0
,, Dewan Sing, 0, bd Powell,	0
,, Mattabux, 0, bd Powell,	2
,, Pattandeen, 2, bd Sneyd,	10
Byes, 111112111,	
Total	**73**

It affords us most particular gratification to have been made the medium of the first record of a native Cricket match,—not merely for the novelty of the event, but for its *precursive* character as a leader of the way, and an example, to the introduction of so noble a game among the Sepoys, many of whom we are sure in every corps will delight to be instructed in it by their European officers. Jack Sepoy is in many respects an athletist, and has no objection at all to the robust foot-sports of England; as we can ourselves alleged upon our own experience, for we have often (with other officers of a most happy regiment) had a tussle with them in leaping, running and even at "fives" though Jack was rather awkward at the last named amusement, which, to our thinking requires as much skill and activity as "rackets." We hope to find Cricket taking its place as a regular native regimental game; and, if so, we think that as the Government build fives, courts, &c. for the recreation of the European soldiery, they would also supply all native corps ready and willing to use them,—and this not only for the sake of encouraging manly recreation, but for the new bond that it will form between the men and their officers.—ED.

CRICKET MATCH.

Light Bobs 28th Regt N. I. v. the Flat Foots.

TO THE EDITOR OF THE ENGLISHMAN.

Dear Sir,—I have much pleasure in sending you the following account of a return match, that came off at [this station on Thursday the 20th instant. The score of the former match has been mislaid, or I would have sent it also ; however, it is but fair to mention that the Flat Foots were, on that occasion victorious, beating the Voltigeurs in one innings. The result of the return match was very different to what had been expected by them of the flat understanding, and they have I hear challenged the Light Bobs to another Bout. The play on both sides was in my opinion very fair, and where all did their duty it is difficult, &c. &c. (refer to the winding up yarn of any action for the rest) but it certainly was a caution, as Sam Slick says, to watch the skilful play and activity of the Lieute-

Natore Team, 1906

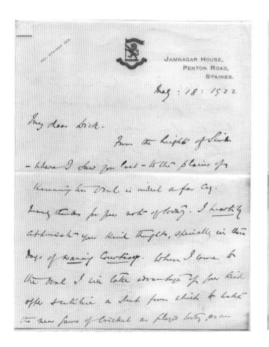
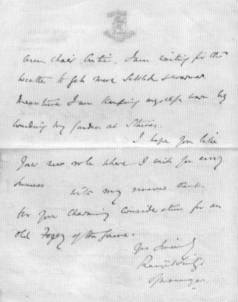

Letter of Ranjitsinhji, 1922

THE JUBILEE BOOK

OF

CRICKET

BY

K. S. RANJITSINHJI

WILLIAM BLACKWOOD AND SONS
EDINBURGH AND LONDON
MDCCCXCVII

All Rights reserved

Ranji stamps   The Jubilee Book of Cricket

C.K. Nayudu and other team members, 1932, London

England vs All India Scorecard, June 1932

The Board of Control for Cricket in India, 1932

Douglas Jardine playing a stroke at Lord's, 1932

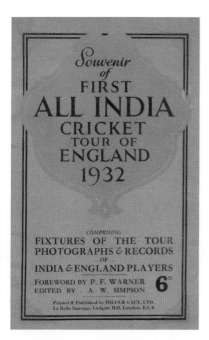

Souvenir of First All India Cricket
Tour of England 1932

C.K. Nayudu and Wazir Ali, 1933-1934

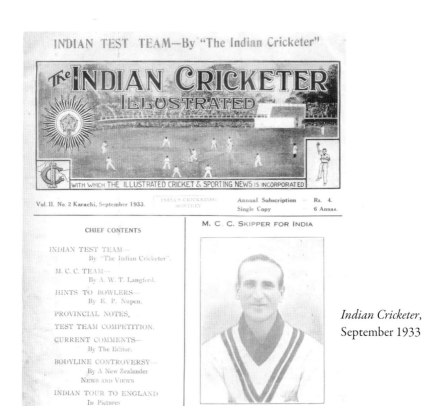

Indian Cricketer,
September 1933

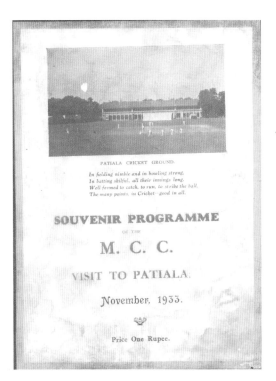

PATIALA CRICKET GROUND.

In fielding nimble and in bowling strong,
In batting skilful, all their innings long,
Well formed to catch, to run, to strike the ball,
The many points, in Cricket—good in all.

SOUVENIR PROGRAMME

OF THE

M. C. C.

VISIT TO PATIALA.

November, 1933.

Price One Rupee.

TWO FAST BOWLERS

Apply stating :—

1. Laming capacity
2. Number of opponents compelled to retire hurt.
3. Number of opponents made to go to hospital injured

with copies of photographs and testimonials which will not be returned to :—

RAI BAHADUR BUTA RAM,
PATIALA.

*Note.—*Messrs. Larwood and Clark not to apply.

MOTIBAGH PALACE (PATIALA)

Souvenir Programme 1,
MCC visit to Patiala, 1933

Souvenir Programme 2, MCC
visit to Patiala, 1933

MCC Calcutta Visit Souvenir,
1933-1934

Quadrangular Cricket Tournament 1934, *Official Programme*

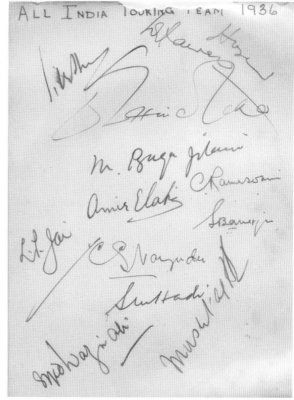

All India touring team 1936, autograph sheet

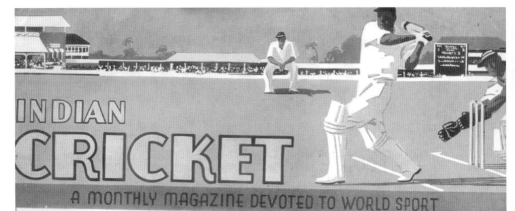

IN DIAN
CRICKET
A MONTHLY MAGAZINE DEVOTED TO WORLD SPORT

1st MARCH 1938.　　　　　　　Price 8 annas.　　　　　　　Vol. 4. No. 5.

Indian Cricket, 1938

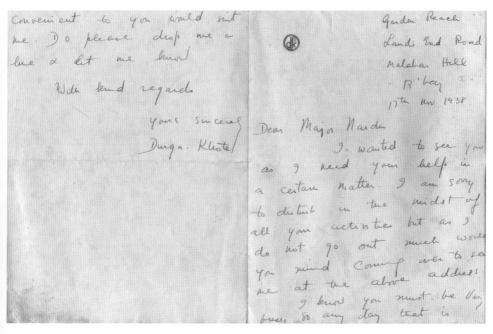

Letter of Durga Khote to C.K. Nayudu, 1938

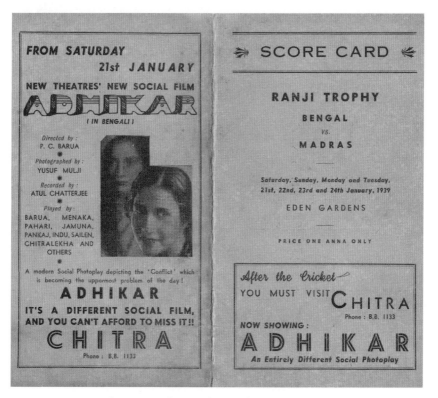

Ranji Trophy Scorecard, Bengal vs Madras at Eden Gardens, 1939

BENGAL	1ST INNINGS	2ND INNINGS	MADRAS	1ST INNINGS	2ND INNINGS
1. P. I. Van der Gucht	b. Rangachari 4		A. V. Krishnaswamy	R. 11. 2	
2. S. W. Behrend	c. Ramaswamy b. Do 20		A. W. Stansfeld	R. 11. B.4 15	
3. P. N. Miller	c. b. Parthasarathy 83		A. G. Ram Singh	R. W. B.4 5	
4. K. Bose	Run out 50		B. F. Bhadradri	R. 9. 52	
5. A. Jabbar	c Gopalan b Spiteler 46		C. Ramaswamy, Capt.	R. 9.c.1. 00	
6. N. Chatterjee	c. Nailer b. Gopalan 9		R. Nailer	R. 9.c.1. 00	
7. B. W. Malcolm	Not out 191		M. J. Gopalan	R. 10. 22	
8. T. C. Longfield, Capt.	Run out 8		G. Parthasarathy	R. 9.c.1. 15	
9. J. N. Banerjee	c Bhadra b P. Sarathy 3		T. M. Duraiswamy	R. 11. 0	
10. K. Bhattacharjee	L.B.W. not out R. 9.19		C. R. Rangachari	R. 11. 0	
11. T. Bhattacharjee	B. 8.		R. Spiteler	not out	
* Captain † Wicket Keeper	Extras b.9, n b 8, l.b. 7 Total 8 Wkts 515		* Captain † Wicket Keeper	Extras Total 114	

Fall of Wkts: 1 for 15, 2 for 81, 3
for 108, 4 for 188, 5 for 209, 6 for 283,
7 for 309, 8 for 322. 9 for 400.

Fall of Wkts: ... 26.

UMPIRES: Messrs. J. W. Hitch and M. Dutt-Roy. Scorers: Messrs. K. Hinton and I. Surita. Lunch Time 1p.m. to 1.45p.m. Tea Time 3.45p.m. to 4p.m.

ANALYSIS OF BOWLING	O.	M.	R.	W.	O.	M.	R.	W.	ANALYSIS OF BOWLING	O.	M.	R.	W.	O.	M.	R.	W.
C. R. Rangachari	29	2	76	2													
M. J. Gopalan	27	9	64	4													
R. Spiteler	11	2	43	1													
G. Parthasarathy	21	3	91	2													
A. G. Ram Singh	22	1	86	0													

Tara Nett.
J. Banerjee
Longfield
Behrend

BENGAL WON TOSS

Morning Score Card   **Sunday 22nd January, 1939**

Ranji Trophy Scorecard, Bengal vs Madras at Eden Gardens, 1939

Maharajkumar of
Vizianagram

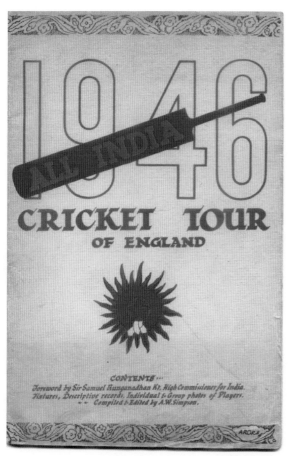

All India Cricket Tour of England, 1946

Indian team 1946, autograph sheet

Indians in Australia, 1947-1948

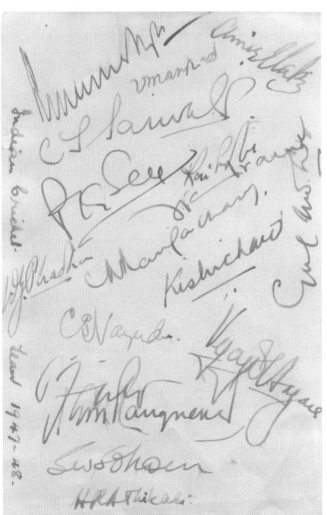

Indian team 1947-1948,
autograph sheet

Lala Amarnath batting in Australia, 1947-1948

Donald Bradman during India's tour of Australia, 1948

C.S. Nayudu caught in the slips, Australia 1948

Vijay Hazare seen picking out a stump, Australia 1948

Indian players returning to the dressing room after an innings, Australia 1948

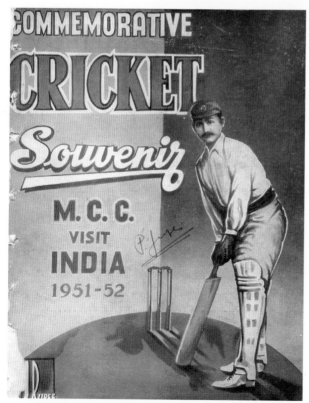

Commemorative Cricket Souvenir, MCC Visit India, 1951-1952

MCC vs India, Official
Souvenir of MCC Tour
in India, 1951-1952

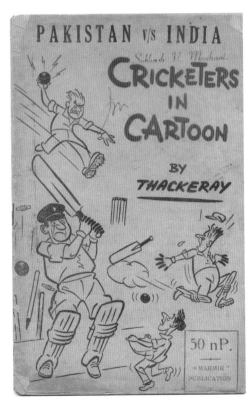

Cricketers in cartoon, 1951-1952

Scorecard 1, Pakistan vs India, 1952

Scorecard 2, Pakistan vs India, 1952

Scorecard 3, Pakistan vs India, 1952

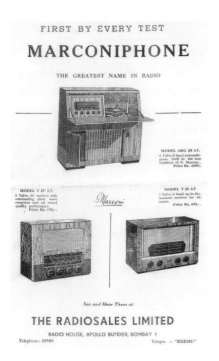

Scorecard 4, Pakistan vs India, 1952

Scorecard 1, New Zealand vs India, 1955

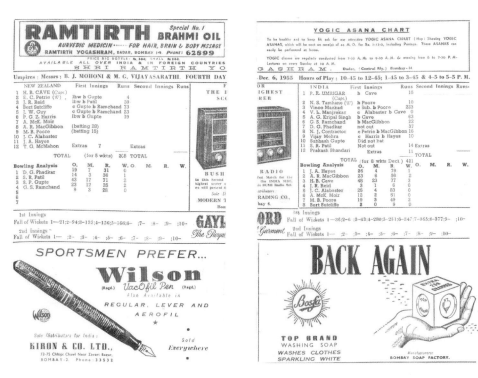

Scorecard 2, New Zealand vs India, 1955   Scorecard 3, New Zealand vs India, 1955

Dinner to the Indian Cricket Team, 1959

India vs New Zealand Scorecard, 1965

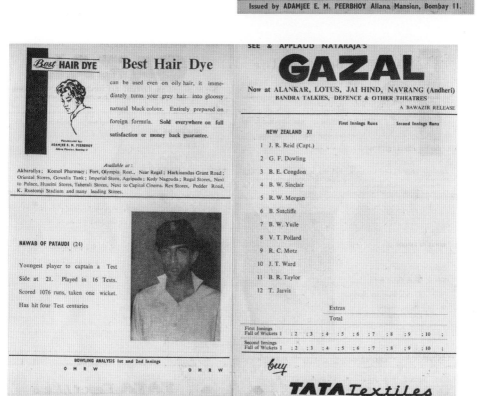

India vs New Zealand Scorecard, 1965

India vs New Zealand Scorecard, 1965

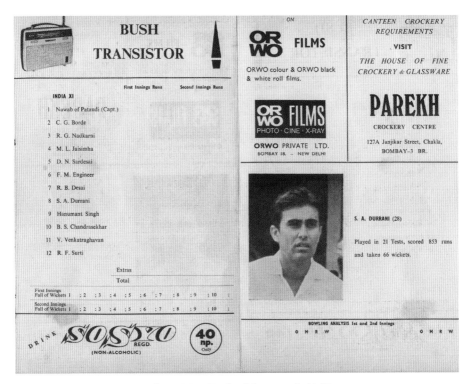

INDIA XI	First Innings Runs	Second Innings Runs
1 Nawab of Pataudi (Capt.)		
2 C. G. Borde		
3 R. G. Nadkarni		
4 M. L. Jaisimha		
5 D. N. Sardesai		
6 F. M. Engineer		
7 R. B. Desai		
8 S. A. Durrani		
9 Hanumant Singh		
10 B. S. Chandrasekhar		
11 V. Venkatraghavan		
12 R. F. Surti		
Extras		
Total		

First Innings
Fall of Wickets 1 : 2 : 3 : 4 : 5 : 6 : 7 : 8 : 9 : 10 :
Second Innings
Fall of Wickets 1 : 2 : 3 : 4 : 5 : 6 : 7 : 8 : 9 : 10 :

BOWLING ANALYSIS 1st and 2nd Innings
O M R W   O M R W

India vs New Zealand Scorecard, 1965

OFFICIAL
SOUVENIR

WEST INDIES

VERSUS

NDIA

1966-1967

Rs. 2-50

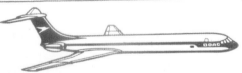
Official Souvenir, West Indies vs India, 1966-1967

CAB Official Souvenir,
Australia vs India, 1969

Official Souvenir, Australia vs India, 1969

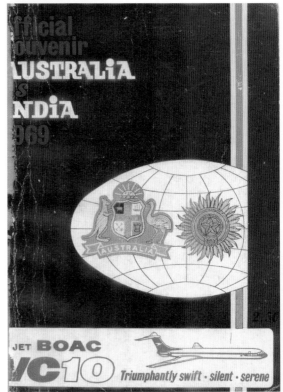

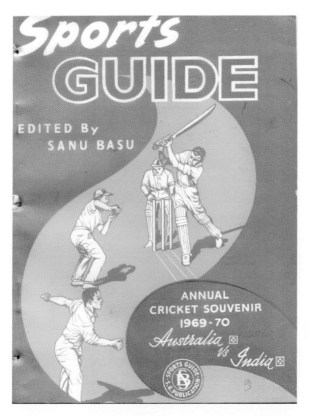

Annual Cricket Souvenir, Australia vs India, 1969-1970

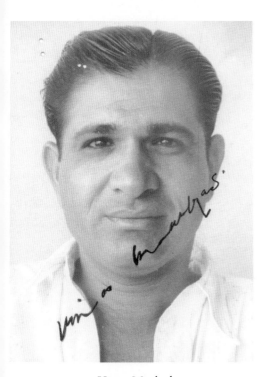

Vinoo Mankad

Vijay Merchant

This card does not necessarily include the fall of the last wicket

(5p) LORD'S (M) GROUND (5p)

ENGLAND v. INDIA

Thurs., Fri., Sat., Mon. & Tues., July 22, 23, 24, 26 & 27, 1971 (5-day Match)

ENGLAND		First Innings		Second Innings
1 G. Boycott	Yorkshire	c Engineer b Abid Ali	3	
2 B. W. Luckhurst	Kent	c Solkar b Chandra	30	
3 J. H. Edrich	Surrey	c Venkat b Bedi	18	
4 D. L. Amiss	Warwickshire	c Engineer b Bedi	9	
5 B. L. D'Oliveira	Worcestershire	c Solkar b Chandra	4	
*6 A. P. E. Knott	Kent	c Wadekar b Venkat	67	
†7 R. Illingworth	Leicestershire	c Engineer b Bedi	33	
8 R. A. Hutton	Yorkshire	b Venkataraghavan	20	
9 J. A. Snow	Sussex	c Abid Ali b Chandra	73	
10 N. Gifford	Worcestershire	b Bedi	17	
11 J. S. E. Price	Middlesex	not out	5	
		B 8, l-b 12, w , n-b 5,	25	B , l-b , w , n-b ,
		Total	304	Total

FALL OF THE WICKETS

1—18	2—46	3—56	4—61	5—71	6—161	7—183	8—223	9—294	10—304
1—	2—	3—	4—	5—	6—	7—	8—	9—	10—

ANALYSIS OF BOWLING 1st Innings

Name	O.	M.	R.	W.	Wd.	N-b	O.	M.	R.	W.	Wd.	N-b
Abid Ali	15	3	38	1	...	5	...	...	...	...	...	...
Solkar	8	3	17	0	...		...	...	...	...	...	...
Venkataraghavan	28	8	44	2	...		...	...	...	...	...	...
Chandrasekhar	49	10	110	3	...		...	...	...	...	...	...
Bedi	39.3	18	70	4	...		...	...	...	...	...	...

INDIA		First Innings		Second Innings
1 S. M. Gavaskar	Bombay	c Amiss b Price	4	
2 A. V. Mankad	Bombay	c Gifford b Snow	1	
†3 A. L. Wadekar	Bombay	c Illingworth b Gifford	85	
4 D. N. Sardesai	Bombay	c Illingworth b Gifford	25	
5 G. R. Vishwanath	Mysore	C KNOTT B HUTTON	68	
*6 F. M. Engineer	Bombay	c Illingworth b Hutton	28	
7 E. D. Solkar	Bombay	C KNOTT B GIFFORD	67	
8 Abid Ali	Hyderabad	LUCKHURST B SNOW	6	
9 S. Venkataraghavan	Tamilnadu	CHUTTON B PRICE	11	
10 B. S. Bedi	Delhi	C PRICE B GIFFORD	0	
11 B. S. Chandrasekhar	Mysore	NOT OUT	0	
		B 7, l-b 9 , w , n-b 2,	18	B , l-b , w , n-b ,
		Total	313	Total

FALL OF THE WICKETS

1—1	2—29	3—108	4—125	5—175	6—267	7—279	8—302	9—311	10—
1—	2—	3—	4—	5—	6—	7—	8—	9—	10—

ANALYSIS OF BOWLING 1st Innings

Name	O.	M.	R.	W.	Wd.	N-b	O.	M.	R.	W.	Wd.	N-b
Price	15	4	46	2	...		...	...	...	...	...	...
Snow	31	9	64	2	...		...	...	...	...	...	...
Hutton	24	8	38	2	...		...	...	...	...	...	...
Gifford	45.3	14	84	4	...		...	...	...	...	...	...
Illingworth	15	7	43	0	...		...	...	...	...	...	...

Umpires—D. J. Constant & C. S. Elliott   Scorers—E. Solomon & R. V. Kapadia
† Captain   * Wicket-keeper
Play begins 1st, 2nd, 3rd & 4th days at 11.30 5th day at 11
Stumps drawn 1st, 2nd, 3rd & 4th days at 6.30 5th day at 5.30 or 6
Luncheon Interval 1.30 p.m.—2.10 p.m.
Tea Interval 4.15 p.m.—4.35 p.m. (may be varied according to state of game)
England won the toss

England vs India Scorecard,
Lord's Cricket Ground, 1971

Ajit Wadekar returns from the U.K., April 1971

MCC tour of India, 1972-1973

Bedi and Chandra accepting the salutations of the crowd after beating the West Indies, 1975

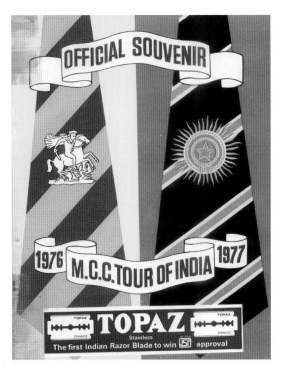

MCC tour of India, 1976-77

Scorecard 1, MCC vs India, 1977

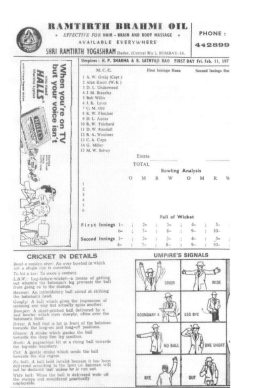

Scorecard 2, MCC vs India, 1977

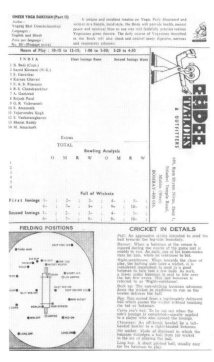

Scorecard 3, MCC vs India, 1977

Scorecard 4, MCC vs India, 1977

India vs West Indies Scorecard, Prudential Cup Final, 1983

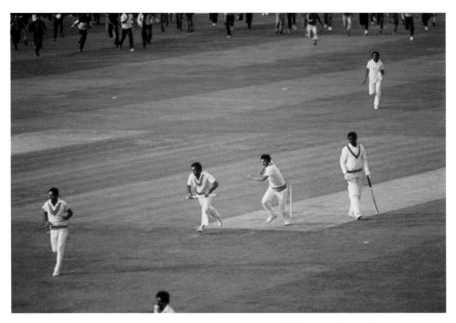

The historic moment when India won the 1983 Cricket World Cup

Kapil Dev holding the 1983 Cricket World Cup

LORD'S (MC) GROUND 20p 20p

CORNHILL INSURANCE TEST SERIES
ENGLAND v. INDIA

THURS., FRI., SAT., MON. & TUES., JUNE 5, 6, 7, 9 & 10, 1986   (5-day Match)

ENGLAND	First Innings		Second Innings	
1 G. A. Gooch ....Essex	b Sharma....................	114	l b w b Kapil Dev.........	8
2 R. T. Robinson..Nottinghamshire	c Az'roddin b Maninder	35	c Amarnath b Kapil Dev	11
†3 D. I. Gower ....Leicestershire	c More b Sharma	18	l b w b Kapil Dev.........	8
4 M. W. Gatting ....Middlesex	b Sharma....................	0	b Sharma	40
5 A. J. Lamb ...Northamptonshire	c Srikkanth b Sharma..	6	c More b Shastri	39
6 D. R. Pringle.................Essex	b Binny....................	63	c More b Kapil Dev	6
7 J. E. Emburey..........Middlesex	c Amarnath b Kapil Dev	7	c and b Maninder.........	1
*8 P. R. Downton..........Middlesex	l b w b Sharma	5	c Shastri b Maninder ...	29
9 R. M. Ellison ....Kent	c Kapil Dev b Binny	12	c More b Binny	19
10 G. R. Dilley ....Kent	c More b Binny	4	not out	2
11 P. H. Edmonds ....Middlesex	not out	7	c Binny b Maninder.....	7
	B , l-b 15, w 1, n-b 7,	23	B , l-b 6, w 1, n-b 3,	10
	Total	294	Total	180

FALL OF THE WICKETS
1—66   2—92   3—92   4—98   5—245   6—264   7—269   8—271   9—287   10—294
1—18   2—23   3—35   4—108   5—113   6—121   7—164   8—170   9—170   10—180

ANALYSIS OF BOWLING	1st Innings						2nd Innings				
Name	O.	M.	R.	W.	Wd.	N-b	O.	M.	R.	W.	Wd. N-b
Kapil Dev	31	8	67	1	...	...	22	7	52	4	... ...
Binny	18.2	4	55	3	...	...	15	3	44	1	1 1
Sharma	32	10	64	5	1	5	17	4	48	1	... 2
Maninder	30	15	45	1	...	...	20.4	12	9	3	... ...
Amarnath	7	1	18	0	...	2	2	2	0	0	... ...
Shastri	10	3	30	0	...	...	20	8	21	1	... ...

INDIA	First Innings		Second Innings	
1 S. M. Gavaskar ....Bombay	c Emburey b Dilley.....	34	c Downton b Dilley	22
2 K. Srikkanth............Tamil Nadu	c Gatting b Dilley	20	c Gooch b Dilley	6
3 M. B. Amarnath..........Baroda	c Pringle b Edmonds ...	69	l b w b Pringle	8
4 D. B. Vengsarkar........Bombay	not out	126	b Edmonds	33
5 M. Azharuddin ......Hyderabad	c and b Edmonds	33	run out	14
6 R. J. Shastri..............Bombay	c Edmonds b Dilley.....	1	not out	20
7 R. M. H. Binny ....Karnataka	l b w b Pringle	9	....	
†8 Kapil Dev ....Haryana	c Lamb b Ellison	1	not out	23
9 C. J. Sharma ....Haryana	b Pringle	2	....	
*10 K. S. More ....Baroda	l b w b Pringle	25	....	
11 Maninder Singh ....Delhi	c Lamb b Emburey	6	....	
	B , l-b 5, w 1, n-b 9,	15	B , l-b 9, w 1, n-b 5,	16
	Total	341	Total	136

FALL OF THE WICKETS
1—31   2—90   3—161   4—232   5—238   6—252   7—253   8—264   9—303   10—341
1—10   2—31   3—76   4—78   5—110   6—   7—   8—   9—   10—

ANALYSIS OF BOWLING	1st Innings						2nd Innings				
Name	O.	M.	R.	W.	Wd.	N-b	O.	M.	R.	W.	Wd. N-b
Dilley	34	7	146	4	...	7	10	3	28	2	... 4
Ellison	29	11	63	1	1	...	6	0	17	0	1 ...
Emburey	27	13	26	1	...	...	...	...	...	...	... ...
Edmonds	22	7	41	1	...	1	11	2	51	1	... ...
Pringle	25	7	58	3	...	...	15	5	30	1	... ...
	...	...	...	...	...	...	...	...	...	...	... ...

Umpires—K. E. Palmer & D. R. Shepherd   Scorers—E. Solomon & Yashvant Chad

† Captain   * Wicket-keeper

Play begins each day at 11.00
Luncheon Interval 1.00—1.40
Tea Interval 3.40—4.00 (may be varied according to state of game)

Stumps drawn at 6.00, or after 90 overs have been bowled, whichever is the later. (In the event of play being suspended for any reason for one hour or more in aggregate on any of the first four days, play may be extended to 7.00 on that day). The captains may agree to stop play at 5.30 on the 5th day if there is no prospect of a result.

India won the toss and elected to field

India won by 5 wickets

Cornhill Insurance Test Series,
England vs India Scorecard, 1986

Sourav Ganguly with Greg Chappell

Sourav Ganguly with John Buchanan

Monkeygate

Australia cricket tour, SCG 2008

Lalit Modi

Virat Kohli with Anil Kumble during the ICC Champions Trophy, 2017

PART THREE

RENAISSANCE AT MIDNIGHT

Never before had India won a Test match against the West Indies. And in what was a fateful tour to the Caribbean in 1962, India almost lost its captain Nari Contractor forever to a vicious Charlie Griffith bouncer. While Contractor survived the threat, his cricket career was over. Shaken by the incident, a 0–5 defeat against the likes of Sir Wes Hall and Griffith wasn't a surprise. With a new captain in Mansur Ali Khan Pataudi forced to take charge and no one wanting to open the batting in the aftermath of what happened to Contractor, the tour ended up a poor misadventure for the touring Indian team. Given the reputation of lethal fast bowlers operating on surfaces conducive to pace with no limit on the number of bouncers, coupled with the relentless earful doled out by the hostile crowds, touring the West Indies was considered the ultimate test for a cricketer in the 1960s and 1970s. While it is true that the 1971 team that faced India did not have fast bowlers of the quality of Hall and Griffith, it was still a West Indies team led by Sir Garfield Sobers and included batsman like Clive Lloyd, Rohan Kanhai, Roy Fredericks and Sobers himself. To even suggest that it was a series win of modest significance is to miss the point altogether.

The build-up in India had already started in September–October 1970, with the team selection fixed for mid-December. Unlike the current system, in 1970–71, the BCCI selection committee met twice. The first meeting was to select a manager, who, it was considered had a key role in managing the team, doubling up as coach on occasion and a second to select the captain and the rest of the squad.

M.A.K. Pataudi, captain of the winning team in New Zealand in 1968, was all set to be reappointed skipper till things underwent a dramatic transformation in the last two months leading to the selection meeting. At the centre of it all was the role played by M. Dutta Ray, alias Bechu Datta Ray. Datta Ray, a veteran administrator who had lost favour in the BCCI, was voted out of the selection committee in September 1970. However, not one to give up, he worked with the president, A.N. Ghosh, and managed a temporary comeback on 30 September. The deal which was struck allowed Datta Ray to be back as selector for two months and in lieu of the favour done to him, he handed the president a resignation dated 60 days from the time of reappointment. The deal was a face saver, an honourable exit for the veteran.

But this was Datta Ray the BCCI was dealing with. A shrewd master of realpolitik, Datta Ray knew the backstage well. Once back as selector, he had no intentions of honouring the resignation he had submitted. And he was a firm backer of Pataudi and the deciding third vote. Had Datta Ray continued as selector, Pataudi, it was clear, would lead the Indian team to the Caribbean and have another opportunity at redeeming the ignominy of 1962.

In end November, however, the BCCI struck back. 11 out of a total of 27 voting members wrote to the president objecting to Datta Ray continuing as selector. His two months in office had come to an end on 30 November and the BCCI argued that he had no right to attend the selection committee meeting fixed for early December. Unless the president was firm with Datta Ray, the members would move court to settle the issue. Not one to buckle under pressure, Datta Ray, in complete disregard of the clamour for his resignation, backed the appointment of Keki Tarapore as manager against the wishes of the bulk of the BCCI members. This was intransigence. He was taking the BCCI head on and there were bound to be consequences. Having successfully backed the appointment of Tarapore, Datta Ray was lobbying hard for Pataudi. Livid to see him hold on to power, members all but made up their minds to go to court with a copy of the resignation he had submitted in September. Datta Ray, pushed to a corner, had little option but to back off.

His departure cleared the deck for Ajit Wadekar and closed the doors on Pataudi. In the selection committee meeting on 8 December 1970, the four selectors who attended the assembly were divided into two groups with two each on either side. Vijay Merchant, the chairman, closed the issue in favour of Wadekar with his casting vote. While there was some talk of Datta Ray voting in absentia, the BCCI constitution had no such provision and the selection committee drama finally came to an end. To add to the confusion, Pataudi informed the selectors on the day of the meeting that he was unavailable to tour the West Indies and was contesting the Lok Sabha elections instead. Whether this decision was taken because he was no longer captain is not known.

The rather acrimonious removal of Pataudi resulted in a media backlash. However, it did not deter Merchant from declaring in an interview that he was right in using the casting vote in favour of Wadekar. He also criticized Pataudi for the timing of his withdrawal and stated that had the Nawab sent the cable a couple of days in advance, the bitterness could have been avoided.

The other key selection conundrum was over Farokh Engineer. There was little doubt Engineer would walk into the Indian team based on form and potential. But with the BCCI issuing a mandate that men who had sought residence away from India would not qualify for selection, the doors had closed on Engineer. This, it was unanimously agreed, was a blow to the touring Indian team and wasn't a policy that helped Indian cricket. Merchant, however, was not bothered. He refused to comment on the prudence of the policy and despite having met Engineer in Bombay on the eve of the selection committee meeting, refused to put any pressure on the Board to pick the enigmatic Engineer. In the absence of quality fast bowlers, the emphasis was on spin and with a young Sunil Gavaskar to back up the experience of Dilip Sardesai, Wadekar and Eknath Solkar, the batting was considered strong for the slow West Indian wickets. Sardesai, as his son Rajdeep has written in his book *Democracy's XI*, was longing for this opportunity and, thanks to Wadekar, was the last man chosen on the side against the wishes of Vijay Merchant.

In a piece for *ESPNcricinfo*, Wadekar describes the surprise at being appointed captain. 'I certainly hadn't thought I'd be the captain. I reckoned the captaincy race was between Tiger Pataudi and Chandu Borde. In fact, before the tour, I had gone up to Tiger and asked him to ensure that I was there in his team. Tiger replied that there were no doubts about my selection and instead asked me to ensure his place if I was asked to lead. His reply stunned me as I had never dreamt that I was in contention for the captaincy. The day the captain was named, I had gone out with my wife Rekha to buy curtains for our new home in the State Bank of India officers' quarters. When I returned around 8 p.m., I saw a large crowd waiting outside our building with garlands. My first thought was that some guy in the building may have been promoted. Little did I realize that it was me!'

To his credit, Wadekar marshalled his resources brilliantly in the Caribbean despite his own poor form, and with Sardesai and Gavaskar both having the series of their lives, India was competitive right through the five-match contest. Off the field, too, Wadekar had his moments. Sipping tea in his apartment in Worli, he has a smile on his face while describing the build-up to the second Test at Port of Spain, a match that transformed India's status in world cricket. 'We knew the wicket would aid spin and were concerned what impact Lance Gibbs might have on the match. He was a quality performer and had the ability to run through a side. Keeping this in mind, we approached the match against the Board President's XI with a well thought-out strategy. Jack Noriega was playing in that match and we deliberately gave him a few wickets to make sure the selectors found it impossible to replace him for the Test match. It was certain they would pick one off-spinner and we wanted it to be Noriega and not Gibbs. The plan worked and Noriega was included in the team ahead of Gibbs,' Wadekar says.

The other thing that worked for India was losing the toss. The pitch, Wadekar mentioned, looked on the dry side and he was glad to lose the toss. Sobers was almost compelled to bat first and the match started in the most dramatic fashion with the first delivery from Syed Abid Ali turning out to be a shooter and uprooting Roy Fredericks' stumps. India had drawn first blood and won the first exchange. From being reduced to 75/5 in the first Test at Jamaica and staging a miraculous comeback piggy-backing on a spectacular Sardesai double-hundred, India were gradually starting to take control of the series at Port of Spain. This had never happened in the past and to go back to Wadekar, was 'a sign of things to come and had given the team a renewed sense of belief'. With Prasanna and Bedi bowling extremely well, the rest of the West Indies line-up were not able to get away, setting it up for Gavaskar and Sardesai. Sardesai followed up the double-century with another hundred, and the mirage—beating the West Indies in the West Indies—was gradually starting to seem real. A good bowling effort in the second innings and India could win the contest. Centre stage Salim Durani. The mercurial Durani, a man not given his due in Indian cricket, made the real difference in the second innings, picking up the wickets of

Lloyd and Sobers, exploiting the rough created by the West Indian fast bowlers. I met Salim *bhai* in Mumbai at the CCI in November 2016, and while it was painful to see him finding it difficult to walk, the conversation was fascinating. When I asked him about his spell in Port of Spain, he had a delightful smile on his face. It was evident he was enjoying the jog back to 45 years ago. 'I had promised the team I will get Lloyd and Sobers out. They were the two crucial wickets and could easily take control of the game. I asked Wadekar to give me a spell, and I can honestly tell you, I was very confident of doing the job for him. The plan worked. First it was Sobers and then Lloyd. West Indies could not stage a comeback and it was on our batsmen to close out the game,' he said with a glint in his eye. My friend Vikram Dayal and I were gulping down every word being said.

It was now Gavaskar's turn. C.K. Nayudu notwithstanding, he was Indian cricket's first global superstar. Solid, dependable and all poise, an unbeaten 67 from Gavaskar had given Wadekar and India a 1–0 series lead and their first ever Test victory against the West Indies. Gavaskar, on debut, had scored 65 and 67 and also scored the winning runs, something that gave him a lot of joy. It could not have been a better initiation to international cricket. He went on to score hundreds and double-hundreds ending with a mammoth 774 runs in the series, immediately escalating himself to the status of a would-be great. Comparisons to the best ever had started and with Sardesai, he was India's Batsman of the Series.

For Wadekar, things couldn't have been better. From fearing that he wouldn't be picked to being named captain and to now winning the first ever Test against the West Indies, Wadekar was living a dream spell.

Forced to follow on in the first Test and beaten in the second, Sobers, it was expected, would mount a strong rally to get back in the series. In trying to do so, the Caribbean think tank had even recalled Sir Wes Hall for the Board President's XI match against India in Barbados ahead of the fourth Test in an attempt to exert pressure on the Indians. Hall had had a psychological hold on the Indians during the 1962 tour and his return was expected to be a grim reminder of things to follow. However, with no Griffith, and Hall ten years older and on his last leg, the strategy was unsuccessful. In fact, it turned out to be the last first-class game of Hall's career.

Even in the final Test of the series in Port of Spain, the Indians held the aces on the final day. Despite trailing in the first innings, they staged a remarkable comeback in the second, banking on Gavaskar's sparkling 220 and managed to set the West Indies a challenging 250-plus chase in the fourth innings. The match ended with the hosts at 165/8 in 40 overs, staring at a second defeat in the series.

To the Indians it did not matter. A second victory was welcome but what really mattered was the series win. The embarrassment of 1962 had been avenged and giant strides had been taken in establishing themselves as an evolving power in world cricket. Gavaskar was hailed the world over as a new phenomenon and Wadekar's support of Sardesai stood vindicated. This was proof what a captain's faith could do to a player's confidence. Sardesai, who had made it to the team based on Wadekar's confidence in his ability, played the best he ever had in his career. For the Goa-born Sardesai, who had never played on turf wickets till he was 17, to star in India's first-ever series win in the Caribbean was a fairy tale.

K.N. Prabhu, one of India's most well-respected cricket writers, who covered the tour for *The Times of India*, summed up the victory in the following words: 'The 1971 tour of the West Indies will be remembered for three distinct achievements. These are: India's first victory in the Caribbean, our players' team spirit through the series and the emergence of a young batsman who can lay claim to a place in cricket's hall of fame.'

This is how he described the performance of Sunil Gavaskar:

'Gavaskar's performance in this series could well serve as a theme for a cricket historian. He should serve as a model to all aspiring cricketers. He learnt as he went along, cutting out his faults and perfecting his strokes. Unspoilt by success, he accepted all the praise showered upon him as the day's routine.'

That this victory had struck a chord with fans back home was evident when thousands turned up at the Santa Cruz airport in Bombay to welcome the players back. This was also a sign of things to come when we note that television had not yet become a mass medium of communication in India and all that the fans could rely on was radio commentary and newspaper reports which were a day old because of the time difference.

Yet they were there, and in huge numbers, drawing attention to the growing popularity of the game in India. The victory meant a lot to them and the iconicity that we attribute to contemporary Indian cricketers was, in many ways, born in 1971, in the wake of the victory in the Caribbean.

Fans everywhere wanted a piece of the players and there were multiple felicitations organized in the next few weeks. Prime Minister Indira Gandhi met Wadekar, Bishan Bedi and Gavaskar in Delhi and Indian cricket was at an all-time high. With hockey on the decline—India had not won an Olympic medal in field hockey since the Tokyo Games of 1964—cricket was fast emerging as India's foremost sporting passion, displacing hockey from its pedestal.

There was, however, a section that remained unconvinced. West Indies, it was argued, was no England and Wadekar's real Test would come two months later when the Indians toured the UK. England, fresh from an Ashes victory under Ray Illingworth and a comeback victory against Pakistan after being behind, was widely accepted as the best team in the world and most did not give the Indians a chance. India's poor away record in England: Lost 0–5 in 1958 and 0–3 in 1967, was repeatedly cited in the media to keep a lid on people's expectations. A drawn series, it was felt, was as good as a win in English conditions. Former India players, too, while praising the team for winning the away rubber in the West Indies for the very first time, were circumspect of India's chances in England. In the absence of a good crop of fast bowlers and a stable middle-order, India were always going to struggle against the likes of Snow, Underwood, Boycott and Illingworth.

Team selection was delayed because the Datta Ray issue was still unsolved. Even though Wadekar's appointment was a formality in the follow-up to the West Indies success, Pataudi and Engineer's inclusion posed serious questions for the selectors. Engineer, with his experience of English conditions and his versatility, was essential to the team's success and it came as welcome news to see the BCCI lift the ban on his selection. Engineer would add muscle to the middle-order and was someone Wadekar could turn to at times of crises. Pataudi, yet again, made himself unavailable, a decision that soured relations between him and Wadekar. Wadekar, by his own admission, deemed Pataudi's experience invaluable and felt let down by the decision.

The other major selection highlight was the inclusion of Bhagwat Chandrasekhar. Out for four years, his comeback was a welcome sign for Indian cricket. England was suspect against wrist spin and Chandra's record against England in 1967 went in his favour. The question that dominated the selection meet was how Chandra could be best used. A section of the committee believed he had been over-bowled by Pataudi in 1967 and that had also resulted in aggravating his injury. Wadekar, it was emphasized, had to use him sparingly to get the best out of his ace leg-spinner.

In the British media, the series was built as a contest between England batsmen and Indian spinners. Most argued that England was the overwhelming favourite and Illingworth, in an interview, declared that his team was ready to take on the famed Indian spin quartet consisting of Bishan Bedi, Bhagwat Chandrasekhar, Erapalli Prasanna and S. Venkataraghavan.

That the Indians were worthy opponents was evident when they won five of the first seven games they played in England, losing only to Essex going into the first Test at Lord's. The quality of the spin-bowling unit was borne out yet again when Prasanna had to be left out of the team to accommodate Venkat, who was a better batsman and fielder. Prasanna, one of the stars of the West Indies series win, who had picked 125 wickets from just 24 matches, was a match winner in his own right and could walk into any team at the time. Yet he did not find a place in the final XI in any of the three Test matches in England.

While the Indians missed out at Lord's and got lucky at Manchester because of the rain, it all boiled down to the third and final Test match at The Oval in London. With a record of 15 defeats in 19 Tests at the ground going into the match, Wadekar's team needed something extraordinary to happen to change their poor track record at The Oval. This was more so after England had managed a 71-run first-innings lead and looked in firm control of the contest. With two days still to play, India's breakthrough summer was gradually starting to get out of control.

And then came the Bhagwat Chandrasekhar show.

In his own words: 'A few people may have been surprised when I was included in the 1971 squad for England (it had been three-and-a-half years since I had left the Australian tour injured, and I had missed 19 Test matches since). I was confident of doing well, though the hiatus was preying on my mind. I was realistic enough to know that if I failed, my Test career would probably be over.

'My bowling in the first innings at The Oval was nothing special, though I did get the wickets of Basil D'Oliveira and Ray Illingworth. The second innings . . . well, that was just one of those days. I had never been a bowler who planned things. Most of the time, I bowled whatever I liked, without giving much importance to the conditions or who I was bowling to. I always believed that if I bowled well, I could trouble most batsmen because I could get extra bounce from a placid pitch and get some nip off it. That afternoon everything just fell into place.

'We won the match, if I'm not wrong, on Chaturthi day— someone had even brought an elephant to the ground. But it was only when we arrived back in India that we realized the enormity of our achievement. They took us from the airport to the Brabourne Stadium in open cars and some of those cheers still echo inside my head even today.'

To Wadekar's credit, he attacked from the outset in England's second innings. The deficit of 71 runs wasn't something that had influenced his tactics, and the aggression fetched him immediate dividends with England reduced to 24/3 against the guile of Chandrasekhar. Chandra had picked two wickets off the last two balls before lunch in five minutes of intense drama. His first scalp was John Edrich, bowled by a quicker delivery. He had changed his mind in the middle of his run-up and darted a quicker one which had beaten Edrich and got India the much-needed breakthrough. The very next delivery got Keith Fletcher caught superbly by Eknath Solkar at short leg.

As the Indians walked back for lunch, the first thoughts of a miracle started to form in the skipper's mind. A superstitious man, as most cricketers are, Wadekar must have felt delighted seeing that an elephant had been brought to The Oval by a group of Indian supporters from the nearby Chessington Zoo.

That you could actually parade an elephant into a cricket ground in London seems unreal in modern-day circumstances. It was clearly a very different age and time and all things were permissible. In fact, to try and loan an elephant from a London zoo and bring it to a cricket ground in the middle of a Test match seems outrageous in 2018. But to Wadekar's amusement, it did happen in 1971 and seemed a good omen for India on the occasion of Ganesh Chaturthi.

India kept up the pressure post lunch and with Venkataraghavan and Solkar backing up Chandra with excellent close-in fielding and catching, England was bowled out for 101, their lowest total against the Indians in 50 years since India's Test debut at Lord's in 1932.

Dicky Rutnagur, writing for *Wisden*, aptly summed up Chandra's impact at The Oval. 'Batting again, they [England] were put to flight in a matter of only two-and-a-half hours. The havoc was wrought by Bhagwat Subramaniam Chandrasekhar who, in a spell of 18.1 overs, captured six wickets for only 38 runs. Chandrasekhar's match-winning effort at The Oval was the climax of a highly successful tour performance. He took 50 wickets in all first-class matches, 13 of them in the Tests. Although such figures were no novelty to Chandrasekhar, his success on this trip will have for him special significance, for he had spent the four previous years in the backwoods.'

The job, however, wasn't done yet. India still had to score 172 runs for victory and the pressure of a first ever series win against England *in* England could not be ignored. The nerves only multiplied when John Snow got Gavaskar out lbw for a duck early in India's second innings. With India's best batsman out, the captain had to play one of the most important knocks of his career to set up the run chase. Wadekar, to his credit, was well up to the task. Losing Ashok Mankad had also not deterred him and, with Sardesai, he lent the innings stability and finished the day at a total of 76/2 with less than 100 required for history to be scripted.

'I was convinced we would get the runs,' recounts Wadekar. 'This was our best opportunity and every member of the team was up to the task. It was a defining moment in our cricket and there was no looking back.'

Though he was run out at the start of the fifth day, his conviction didn't waver and he immediately went to sleep in the dressing room.

Only when India had won was he awakened by Ken Barrington with the news that the Indian summer was a reality. Wadekar had successfully beaten the West Indies in the West Indies and England in England in a matter of four months, and, in doing so, had turned a new leaf for the game in India. Abid Ali had scored the winning runs but more important was Engineer's contribution of 28 not out in 50 minutes off 59 balls. Engineer, dropped and humiliated by the BCCI three months earlier, had turned things around in style in England and redeemed himself in the process. His inclusion, which had been a subject of intense debate ahead of the tour, was an important call taken by the selection committee and the BCCI's policy of not including players who lived away from India was to be abandoned forever.

The significance of the victory is best understood from the media reaction back home. Sports magazine *Sportsweek* published a special issue celebrating the victory priced at INR 2; its subscription had seen a steady upswing right through the series. From 35,000 a few months earlier, its print order had reached 61,000 by the time of the third and final Test match at The Oval—an indication of how cricket was being increasingly consumed by the upwardly mobile Indian.

The victory against England against all odds in 1971 was the best ever in the history of Indian cricket. It was a full-strength England team playing at home and unlike Nigel Howard's second-string team in 1952 or Ted Dexter's team in 1961–62, this was a team widely acknowledged as the best in the world. The Indians had exceeded expectations under Wadekar, giving the game a serious shot in the arm in India. For an erstwhile colony, which had appropriated the British game at the close of the nineteenth century and made it their own by the early twentieth, 1971 marked the completion of the turnaround. Indians were no longer exotic imports from the Orient to be represented in Punch cartoons and written about as subjects of curiosity in the mainstream media. Their cricketing ability was more important than the number of languages they spoke or their widely varying food habits. Their primary identity was that of a quality cricketing side that could compete on even terms with Illingworth and his team.

The 1971 cricket triumph was in every way comparable to India's victory over England in hockey at the London Olympics in 1948 within a year of independence in August 1947. For a newly independent India, the London Olympic Games of 1948 was more than a mere sporting event. The event offered an opportunity for assertion and was a stage for a young nation to cement for itself a place in the world parliament of successful sporting nations. It was also a platform for an infant Indian nation-state to compete with its former master and give vent to years of frustration and discontent. When the Indian hockey team won gold at the London Olympics in 1948, defeating the English 4–0 in the final, much more than an Olympic victory was scripted. It was a newly independent nation's declaration against the forces of colonialism, retribution for the humiliation meted out by the English for almost 200 years and, finally, a statement to the world about the significance of 'sport' in an era of decolonization. Hockey, the victory demonstrated, held the promise of being the new opiate of the masses.

Cricket did something very similar in 1971. Also, at the time when Indians were contesting for honours at The Oval, the nation's borders were being set alight by a third war with neighbouring Pakistan, the 'unfinished agenda' of Partition which had led to a war in 1965 and continual tension since. In the months immediately after The Oval win, the Indians back home were firmly focused on the political crisis at hand and, in that sense, the victory was a salve for a troubled nation.

On their return to India, a red-carpet welcome was given to the 1948 hockey team. The victory celebrations continued for several days and climaxed in Delhi where President Rajendra Prasad and Prime Minister Jawaharlal Nehru attended an exhibition match involving the team in a packed National Stadium. The victorious team of 1952 was to receive a similar welcome but, in terms of its significance, the London hockey victory finally got a worthy rival when real national hysteria overtook India in the aftermath of Wadekar's team beating England in England in 1971.

This is how Dicky Rutnagur summed up the scenes in *Wisden*: 'In Bombay, the birthplace of Indian cricket, unprecedented scenes were witnessed on the night of August 24, the day India beat England in the third Test match at The Oval. There was dancing in the streets. Revellers stopped and boarded buses to convey the news to commuters. In the homes, children garlanded wireless sets over which the cheery voice of Brian Johnston had proclaimed the glad tidings of India's first Test victory in England, a victory which also gave them the rubber.'

These scenes were next matched and, in fact, overtaken when India, under Kapil Dev, conquered Lord's on 25 June 1983 and lorded over world cricket, winning the Prudential World Cup, beating the West Indies in the final. To this rather unexpected Indian summer of lore we now turn.

To conclude, it should also be said that Pataudi remains, perhaps, India's most iconic captain ever, credited with giving Indian cricket the steel to take on the best in the world without backing down. In many ways, he remains the forerunner to the Sourav Gangulys and Virat Kohlis of the world. If Datta Ray had his way, he would have been captain in the West Indies and in England, not Wadekar. Who knows how things would have panned out then. Maybe India would still have won. Maybe not. But nothing succeeds like success, and Wadekar brought India unprecedented success. And it all began with one of the most acrimonious phases in the BCCI's history.

CRICKET'S TRYST WITH DESTINY
LORDING IT AT LORD'S

I was seven years old when India won the Prudential Cup at Lord's on 25 June 1983. I must confess I did not see Mohinder Amarnath picking up the final West Indian wicket and run the fastest he ever has in his life to escape the invasion of Indian fans who made Lord's their own that day. Yes, I have watched it a million times since— on television and elsewhere—and each time I've enjoyed it more than ever. Not watching the final moments of a World Cup-win is something I have in common with Sachin Tendulkar. He did not watch M.S. Dhoni hit the final six at the Wankhede in 2011 and, as his biographer, how could I have watched the final moments of the 1983 thriller at Lord's? Jokes aside, I was crestfallen when the Indians were bowled out for 183 and literally wept myself to sleep. For seven-year-old me, the match was over with the West Indians having the likes of Gordon Greenidge, Desmond Haynes, Sir Viv Richards and Clive Lloyd in their ranks. It was one of the best batting line-ups ever and the West Indies was chasing a record third World Cup title. My dejection, I would still argue, was legitimate. My mother—she reminds me as I write this—did try her best to wake me up when the West Indies were eight down. All of India was watching Kapil Dev and his team turn over a new leaf. I finally woke up to a new dawn in Indian cricket and was told we were 'world champions'. We had beaten the mighty West Indies by 43 runs and Indian cricket had changed overnight. There were millions like me all over the country who shared this joy, and it was the highest point in the history of the game in India. Interestingly enough, it was achieved on the same day that India had debuted at Lord's a little over half-a-century earlier in 1932.

My second encounter with the 1983 World Cup took place 25 years later, in June 2008. I was at the Lord's library for research, when the trophy was all of a sudden brought out to be cleaned. It was kept a foot away from where I was sitting when the staff started working on it to get it back to full glory for the 1983 Indian team's visit to mark the 25th anniversary of their World Cup glory. I have known Adam Chadwick, the curator of the Lord's collections, for years, and could not resist the temptation to go and ask if he would allow me to hold the trophy once. Chadwick found the request amusing and, with a smile on his face, permitted me to do so. My imagination knew no bounds and I wanted to do what most in India would give an arm and a leg for: Take the trophy to the Lord's balcony and hold it aloft a la Kapil Dev in 1983. It was my fanboy moment and, in many ways, a connect to the past, to the tournament that shaped my understanding of the game and ignited a passion that still drives me to watch every game India plays the world over.

Seeing a thirty-two-year-old academic behave like a kid, Chadwick had little option but to agree to my request. The only caveat was one of his staff would accompany me to the balcony to ensure I don't do anything stupid! As I repeated what Kapil had done 25 years ago, something that was re-enacted by him and his team later that afternoon, the enormity of the achievement dawned on me yet again. For a team that had lost the inaugural match of the 1975 World Cup by a margin of 202 runs, scoring 136/3 in 60 overs, in response to England's 334/4, and had lost all their matches in the 1979 edition of the tournament, to win the competition in 1983 was more than a miracle. Limited-overs cricket had not yet established itself in India and the performances in the preceding editions were a fair reflection of this ground reality. In fact, India had never won a limited-overs tournament hitherto. Hence, the prospect of defeating teams like the West Indies, England and Australia, in English conditions, was considered impossible.

Yet, they conquered the impossible, and in real style. Beating the world's best limited-overs team in a dramatic final at cricket's Mecca, Kapil and his men had transformed the game for all times to come.

It is pertinent to say that it wasn't me alone who behaved like a kid seeing the Prudential World Cup 25 years later. Men, who had accomplished the feat a quarter of a century earlier, did the same in 2008 and evidently enjoyed doing so. While reminiscing about every little detail of what happened on that incredible 1983 afternoon, signing autographs and posing for photographs with the very few present, every member of the team had transported themselves a few years back in time.

The Cult of Kapil's Classics

For Kapil, who was then only five years into international cricket, it was nothing short of a dream come true. The victory was a second wonder that occurred after his 175 not-out against Zimbabwe at Tunbridge Wells, where India were staring at a World Cup exit after having slumped to 17/5. To be extraordinarily talented is one thing, but to be able to bring that talent out in most trying circumstances is a feat not many achieve in their careers. Ivan Lendl at Wimbledon is an example that readily crosses one's mind in this regard. Best in the world in the mid-1980s, Lendl never managed to conquer the grass at Wimbledon. But Kapil, carrying no baggage as he left for

England, managed to do so at Tunbridge Wells and subsequently at Lord's.

This is how Syed Kirmani, India's best wicketkeeper-batsman before M.S. Dhoni, describes the innings against Zimbabwe: 'The final turning point for us in the tournament was the match at Tunbridge Wells. Unfortunately, there is no video available for this game. The BBC had gone on a strike probably because both India and Zimbabwe were minnows and they were not interested in televising that game. But this game was critical for us to qualify for the knockouts. We had lost to Australia and West Indies in our last two games and this was a must-win encounter. We were batting first and because I batted low down, I was relaxing in the dressing room, preparing for a nice shower and breakfast. Suddenly I heard someone scream from the outside, "Hey, Kiri, pad up quickly!" I stuffed my toast in my mouth and peeked through the window to see the scoreboard. 17 for 5! The next thing I remember is walking in to bat at 140 for 8 in 30-odd overs. We were still struggling and Kapil said to me, "Kiri *bhai*, we have to bat 60 overs."

'I replied, "Kaps, don't worry, we will play the full 60 overs. I will give you maximum strike and you have to hit every ball. You are the best hitter in the team." We did play the full number of overs; Kapil was unbeaten on 175 and I was on 24. From there on, we were on a roll.'

Ranked 66–1 outsiders with the bookmakers at the start of the tournament, India's journey is a case study of what all is possible in sport. Reputations and past achievements mean little and, on a given day, the underdog can easily take out the best and make history.

For Madan Lal Sharma—who had bowled the first ball in World Cup history in 1975 and had suffered the humiliation of the English clobbering more than 300—to come back eight years later at the same venue and pick up Vivian Richards in the final was the ultimate cricketing moment. 'I can't really tell you what I had felt or what was going through my mind. It is impossible to recollect because it is all a blur. In moments of extreme happiness you tend to let your guard down and this was one such moment. Vivian Richards was batting beautifully and we knew that if he stayed on for ten more overs, the match could be beyond us. And when he hit that shot, my first reaction was to see who was under the ball. Seeing it was Kapil, I was confident something was about to happen. Those three or four seconds were perhaps the longest three or four seconds of my life. Once Kapil had taken the catch, we knew we were onto something special that day,' Madan Lal says as he silently strolls out to the Lord's turf 25 years later.

'I did not play a single game but was there, out in the middle, in spirit every ball right through the tournament. For those few weeks in England, the squad just had one purpose and that was to play our best cricket,' says Sunil Valson, the only cricketer in history to have won a World Cup without playing a single international match.

Kapil has repeatedly emphasized on the importance of the process. To try and be perfect on an imperfect day like the final and do the best possible was the mission he had set out for his team. Without a coach to guide the players, seniors assumed mentoring roles and each of the 15 men backed each other in scripting Mission Impossible. India had beaten the West Indies in Berbice in the Caribbean going into the World Cup and had again beaten them at the start of the tournament. These victories, Kapil argued, had given the team the necessary self-belief. That every team could be beaten was the deep-seated conviction drilled into each of the players and even after the Indians had been bowled out for 183 in the final, the spirit had not waned.

'West Indies had to get the 183 we had scored and we were determined to make every run count. Balwinder Sandhu bowled the delivery of the competition to Gordon Greenidge and it had a massive impact on every player,' says Krishnamachari Srikkanth, one of the architects of the victory and the top scorer in the final. Greenidge shouldering arms to Sandhu to see his stumps knocked off at the start of the West Indies innings acted as a huge psychological lift for the Indians. 183 wasn't a daunting target, but the match wasn't over yet.

For me, a personal postcard moment remains Srikkanth half-sitting on one knee and dispatching Andy Roberts to the square boundary. This stroke, C.L.R. James would have argued, was the closest the batting could get to art. With multiple fielders behind the stumps and a fearsome fast bowler bowling at full tilt, this was one stroke Srikkanth could forever be proud of. Timing, power, grace and position, everything was impeccable about the shot and it gave India some much-needed momentum.

Pressing Concerns: From Vitriol to Validation

While the final transformed Indian and world cricket forever, the other match of immense significance was the victory over England in the semi-final. This was more because of the derisive reportage in the British press from the start of the tournament, a pattern of sneering that climaxed when it was known that England was pitted against India for a place in the final. English writers were sure of England winning and, as John Thickness declared in *The Standard*, a semi-final against India had given England a virtual passport to the final. Similarly, for Mathew Engel of *The Guardian,* there was no rational explanation for India's triumph over Australia and entry into the knockouts of the tournament. The worst, however, was David Frith. Ahead of the tournament, Frith had urged the Indians to withdraw from the competition, a suggestion that provoked serious outrage from Man Singh, the erstwhile Prince of Jaipur, who was then a resident of the United States of America. Writing after the Indians had won the tournament, Man Singh stated, 'I try to keep up with all the cricket news and scores by reading British journals and papers. I used to subscribe to another leading journal but since its writers were too biased, I decided to change to *Wisden*. I find now your journal is guilty of the same sin. I like to read about cricket from a writer who is fair in his reporting, not one-sided. I refer to David Frith's preview of the World Cup in the June WCM. He really berates the Indian team and suggests that they should withdraw from this tournament. I don't know how far back he goes but I go back quite a way, and back in 1948, when [Don] Bradman's Australians—with Lindwall and Miller—were demolishing England with scores as low as 52 in Tests, no one suggested England should withdraw from Test cricket.'

And then, in true celebratory mode, he goes on to suggest, 'I saw this year's semi-final against England, and what a demolishing England got from India, the same team he wants to withdraw from the tourney . . . I am enclosing the cutting from my copy of WCM with the remarks that have so inflamed me. In all fairness to good journalism and sportsmanship, Mr Frith should eat this, be a good sport and swallow the lousy paragraph he wrote.'

Much has been written on the final in the last two decades. That the achievement had not been digested overnight in India is evident from the rather tame match reports following the stunning victory. It was only a day later that the reality dawned and the Press Trust of India reported: 'Jubilant Indian players and their supporters celebrated India's sensational win in the World Cup with champagne and *bhangra* till the early hours of yesterday morning.' Even Pakistani stalwarts like Abdul Qadir and Sarfraz Nawaz joined the Indians, and the huge bottle of champagne that Amarnath had earned as Man of the Match, was emptied in no time. 'Indian supporters, many carrying the tricolour, would not leave the Lord's cricket ground hours after India's victory as they waited for Kapil and his team to come out from a reception hosted by the MCC. Later, they went to the hotel to cheer their heroes.'

The headlines in the English papers summed it up perfectly. *The Times* declared, 'Kapil's men turn world upside down: Cannon fodder turned cannon.' *The Sunday Express* reported that India's victory was the biggest upset in cricketing history. Finally, Tony Lewis wrote in *The Sunday Telegraph* that India had performed one of the 'most mystical acts in her long cricket history.'

The Adroitness of Amarnath

The one cricketer who capped the best phase of his cricket career with match-winning performances in the semi-final and the final was Mohinder Amarnath. Having started his career as a slow medium-pace bowler, much like his father in the 1930s, Amarnath gradually turned himself into the mainstay of India's middle order in the early 1980s. Fearless against lethal fast bowling and with a penchant for playing the hook shot, Amarnath was outstanding against Imran Khan in Pakistan in 1982–83 and followed it up with a superb series in the Caribbean against Malcolm Marshall and the Caribbean pace battery. Hit on the head a few times in his career, telling blows that could have damaged him forever, Amarnath had turned fearless by the time he went to Pakistan and subsequently to the West Indies.

'The experience of playing quality fast bowling for close to six months leading into the World Cup helped us a great deal. I was batting well and carried the good form into the tournament. What made it more satisfying was we beat Australia, England and the West Indies in the last three games we played,' he remembers with fondness.

As the vice-captain and one of the seniors in the team, Amarnath had the added responsibility of mentoring Kapil in times of crisis, and he did so with aplomb, scoring a valuable 46 against England and 26 against the West Indies, while coupling his returns with the bat in the final with impressive figures of 3/12 with the ball. Rarely has one individual had such impact in a World Cup semi-final and final.

The West Indian Perspective

The one question I posed to almost every past West Indian great while researching for this book was about how they looked back at 1983. Was it something they have deliberately tried to distance themselves from? A bad dream, not to be spoken about? Or was it something they had anticipated, something which wasn't a miracle after all? Among the many West Indians interviewed, it was most fascinating to hear Clive Lloyd and Jeffery Dujon speak on the subject.

For Dujon, it was just a bizarre day. He was insistent that 25 June 1983 was different, a day when he had a feeling that something uncanny would happen. In fact, while returning to the pavilion after having bowled India out for a paltry 183, the West Indians hardly rejoiced. Rather, Dujon remembers mentioning to Andy Roberts that he was convinced they would struggle to overhaul the relatively small target. 'I am not a superstitious person in that sense. But I had this strange premonition that day was different. I knew we would struggle, and Andy agreed with me. Even the way I got out was destined. I had struggled hard to bring the match back in our favour and at 119 we just needed 65 more runs to win. Another 30 minutes of batting and it could have swung our way,' said Dujon.

It wasn't to be. 'It wasn't an unplayable delivery by any means but I could not help but edge that ball on to my stumps. The gods were with India. The cricket world was destined to change,' he concluded.

For Lloyd, 1983 remains a melancholic memory that he has relived many times since. While the wound has healed with time, the scar remains. The first time I discussed the 1983 World Cup at length with Lloyd was in Oxford, in 2009, during the ICC Centenary Conference, which I had the pleasure of organizing. Lloyd had come for two days and stayed at St John's College's Alumni Guest Accommodations in the very next room to mine. And in each of the days he was there, we would end up chatting till 2 or 3 a.m. in the morning. Lloyd in a good mood is one of the best storytellers of the modern game. A real great, he has seen the game transform into a commercially successful spectacle and has presided over the transformation. Chasing a record third consecutive World Cup title as captain, Lloyd was emphatic in declaring there was no question of complacency. The West Indians had lost to India in the opening round of the tournament and knew what Kapil and his men were capable of. India was not a team to be taken lightly. 'They had beaten Australia and England on their way to the final and had some excellent all-round cricketers in the team,' Lloyd says.

It was just that the final was a bad day, a day when nothing worked for the West Indies when they came out to bat. 'Bowling India out for 183 was a very good effort, and on most days, we would easily chase this score down,' he laments. 'But for cricket, however, it was a great result. It helped Indian cricket turn into something fundamentally different and world cricket, too, benefitted from this turnaround. Finally, the notion that the West Indies could be beaten had seeped in and it had the effect of breaking the West Indian monopoly. 'Even when we beat the Indians convincingly in the winter of 1983, we knew that it was only a matter of time before they became a cricketing superpower. The self-belief the World Cup victory had given Indian cricket had little parallel. It was great for your cricket,' says the greatest ever West Indian captain.

'I don't want to go into what went wrong for us. We did not bat well is the very simple answer. We needed one batsman to stay on for a big score but that didn't happen. Indians bowled and caught well and never really allowed us to get into groove, which is so very essential in a big final,' Lloyd concludes.

Prior to 25 June 1983, India's victories were hardly accorded the recognition they merited. News of English county games were reported in equal measure and the sports pages of newspapers covered news of other sports, be it local football, hockey, tennis or badminton, as well. Cricket was one of the many sports India played and watched. Mohammed Shahid was as big a star as Kapil Dev. Post 1983, however, it all changed. The genesis of the modern cricket page in newspapers began there. What followed the World Cup triumph was a media revolution that has now made cricket in India a secular religion. From 1990, cricket has regularly made it to the front pages of newspapers and has been treated as mainstream news. Playing for India became a national aspiration of sorts overnight. Gauging the changes in trends, Ganguly puts it beautifully, 'It made me want to be a cricketer that much more. And it made Indian cricket what it is today.'

The victory paved the way for corporate investment and offered the media an event to build up hype about. In the next few years, the epicentre of the game gradually moved to the subcontinent. It was a tortuous process. The machinations of the 'Western' lobby make the story most interesting, though, bringing to light the fissures and tensions that plagued the cricket world then and continue to do so even now. This shift, I would argue, is the telling legacy of the 1983 World Cup win.

The World Cup Moves to India

On 26 June 1983, a day after India won the Prudential Cup, *The Telegraph* published the following report: 'West Bengal Congress (I) MLA, Mr Rajesh Khaitan has urged the Indian Cricket Control Board President Mr N.K.P. Salve to press for holding the next World Cup cricket tournament in the country. In a statement here, Mr Khaitan said Mr Salve's initial response to the suggestion was "favourable" and he had agreed to "positively take up the matter".'

Reflecting on this dream, Raj Singh Dungarpur, one of the country's foremost cricket administrators, wrote in his foreword to N.K.P. Salve's *The Story of the Reliance Cup*, 'It was like a cricket utopia at the time. The concept was well beyond the Western world's imagination that India and Pakistan could jointly hold the World Cup. The ICC was no exception.'

The organization of the 1987 tournament was the first indication that the subcontinent was no longer content playing second fiddle to either England or Australia. India and Pakistan, in a rare show of unity, out-voted England 16–12 at the ICC general body meeting on 19 July 1984, successfully moving the 1987 World Cup to the subcontinent. This was a big moment, evident from the following comment by Salve: '[This] would virtually threaten more-than-a-century-old era of England's supremacy in the administration of international cricket. The Mecca of cricket all these long years had been Lord's. If the finals of the World Cup, the most coveted international cricket event, were played at any other place, it would shake the very foundation on which the super edifice of international cricket administration was built.'

Soon after the euphoria of India's Prudential Cup triumph had subsided, Indian and Pakistani cricket administrators started working on a bid considerably better than England's proposal for the 1987 tournament. The bid was drafted by Jagmohan Dalmiya, then treasurer of the BCCI, in consultation with other Board members. Its highlights were:

> A minimum guarantee of £200,000 was offered to the seven participating Full Members and £175,000 to the qualifying associate member. By contrast, England offered £53,900 plus inflation (between the 1983 World Cup and the date of payment) for Full Members and £30,200 for the qualifier.
>
> India and Pakistan offered £20,000 to each Associate Member while England set aside only £ 11,666.
>
> The aggregate prize money offered was £99,500. England came up with only £53,000.

Though the financial package offered by India and Pakistan was significantly better, the English, with support from Australia, tried their best to thwart the Asian bid. Invoking rule 4(C) of the ICC's rulebook—'Recommendations to member countries are to be made by a majority of Full Members present and voting and one of which in such a majority should be a Foundation Member'—the Test and County Cricket Board argued that the Indo-Pakistani bid should be rejected because it did not have the support of either Foundation Member, that is, England or Australia. However, the ICC Chairman, under considerable pressure from India and Pakistan and also the Associates, announced that a simple majority was enough. Eventually, as Salve writes: 'The matter was put to vote—16 in favour of India and Pakistan, 12 in favour of England. ICC had decided to shift the World Cup from England to India and Pakistan. It was a miracle, which created history in international cricket. Perhaps for the first time, a battle had been successfully fought in ICC . . . India and Pakistan and her friends had shown England and her allies that they were no longer supreme in the matters of cricket administration, their power of veto notwithstanding. I must mention here that the voting was not based on the pattern of whites or non-whites because countries voting for India included Holland and Canada.'

However, England, Australia and New Zealand were yet to come to terms with the subcontinent's ascendancy. At the ICC meeting in June 1987, they turned down an Indian proposal to participate in a match between the Champions and the Rest a couple of days after the World Cup final at Eden Gardens in Kolkata. Though the Australians changed their minds in September and agreed to play the match if they won the tournament, in a letter dated 5 October 1987, D.L. Richards, representing the Australian Board, conveyed their unwillingness to play even if they won the 1987 World Cup.

The Western lobby also had its way when the rights to host the 1992 World Cup was awarded to Australia. The Pakistani proposal for another joint bid with India fell through and even the Indian request to play the 1992 World Cup in January–February, instead of February–March, was not acceded to. This is striking because in 1987 the Indians and Pakistanis had readily accepted a similar Australian proposal in relation to timing and scheduled the World Cup for October–November. The struggle for equality was still on. It is in this context that one needs to read India's spearheading of the move to bring South Africa back to international cricket in 1991.

Uniting the World

Though the Indian Board had agreed in principle to support the motion for South Africa's re-entry, that the Indians would move the motion at the ICC was a last-minute decision. Supported by then BCCI president, Madhavrao Scindia, Dalmiya moved the proposition for South Africa's re-admission at the ICC annual meeting in June 1991. However, even when the Indian delegation championed the South African cause, thoughts of a friendship series between the two countries was a distant dream. It was Pakistan's cancellation of a proposed tour of India that created room for the historic tour in November 1991, marking South Africa's re-entry into the international cricketing fold. The tour was the culmination of a dramatic 48 hours of planning in Kolkata. As Geoff Dakin, president of the United Cricket Board of South Africa (UCBSA), was to recall: 'We were in Calcutta on a goodwill visit when Jagmohan Dalmiya proposed this tour. We were, to put it mildly, thrilled. It was a long-cherished dream to tour the country of Mahatma Gandhi. We will never forget the reception we were accorded in Calcutta and at the Eden Gardens. It was special.'

Having thus earned the friendship of another Full Member of the ICC, the Indians pressed for the rights to stage the 1996 World Cup. By making it a collaborative venture with Pakistan and Sri Lanka, the united face of Asian cricket was once again put on display. If the 1987 World Cup had been the initial step, the 1996 World Cup was the big leap; instrumental in making the subcontinent a major player at the ICC and in global cricket.

The 1996 World Cup

At the BCCI working committee meeting on 10–11 August 1990 in Mumbai, Board president Scindia suggested the BCCI should start work in earnest and formulate a bid for the 1996 World Cup. Accordingly, a sub-committee comprising Scindia, I.S. Bindra, A.W. Kanmadikar and Dalmiya was asked to submit a report before the Board's working committee by the end of October 1990. At the next Board meeting on 23 October, the secretary was asked to inform the ICC that India was preparing its bid. The Board's working committee was unanimous that the bid 'be sent well in advance of the due date . . . This would enable India to keep the question alive for discussion.'

Finally, on 25 September 1992, the chairman informed the members of the working committee that the Board had decided to submit a joint bid for the 1996 World Cup, along with Pakistan and Sri Lanka. Dalmiya was appointed coordinator to work out the modalities and was advised to meet his counterparts from Pakistan and Sri Lanka before submitting the bid on 1 December 1992.

Eventually, the bids of both England and the India–Pakistan–Sri Lanka combine were to the tune of £5 million. However, the subcontinental bid offered more money to Associate Members and for the qualifying ICC Trophy. This money was expected to aid the development of cricket in these nations. Also, while the English bid reserved the right on wearing of logos by the players, the joint bid reserved the right on only one logo out of a permissible three. In other words, it allowed Full Members to get their team sponsored independently and earn extra money. Sponsorship from logos was expected to earn each Full Member a minimum of £100,000. Given these advantages, it was not unnatural that 16 of the 19 Associate Members, particularly the countries from Asia and Africa, pledged overwhelming support for the three-nation bid. The mood of the times can be gauged from the following observations of the BCCI working committee, recorded on 23 December 1992: 'Unnerved at the prospect of losing out to the joint bid, UK is likely to use their veto power and in their efforts are likely to be assisted by Australia. In 1984, when the fourth World Cup was allotted to India and Pakistan, the same was decided by a simple majority. Similarly, the fifth World Cup held in Australia was also allotted on the basis of a simple majority and England or Australia had never wanted to use their veto power to decide the venue of the world cup.'

Apprehensions were also cast on the ICC's neutrality. Accordingly, the Board resolved to mobilize Associate Members to ensure a substantial majority during voting. Having observed that some Associate Members stayed away from ICC meetings for want of funds and often asked their English representatives to attend the meeting on their behalf, the BCCI and Board of Control for Cricket in Pakistan (BCCP) agreed to share the expenses to allow Associate Members to travel to London. It was also resolved that till such time as the Pakistan–India–Lanka Joint Management Committee (PILJMC) was able to sustain itself, the Boards would spend the money, pending future reimbursement by PILJMC.

At the ICC meeting of 2 February 1993, convened to decide the host(s) of the 1996 World Cup, the PILJMC was represented by Scindia, Dalmiya, Bindra and Amrit Mathur from India; Shahid Rafi, Ehsan Mani and Imran Khan from Pakistan; and Tyronne Fernando and Neil Perera from Sri Lanka. The meeting is thus described in the records of the BCCI: 'The meeting on February 2 was a gruelling one, lasting nearly thirteen-and-a-half hours. It was a battle of wits with the ICC solicitors being dragged into the meeting. The ICC solicitors argued in favour of a "special majority" to decide on the venue of the World Cup, but the representatives of the subcontinent countered such arguments effectively . . . Members of all countries present in the meeting appreciated the logic and rationality of the arguments of the joint bidders. The joint bidders found support from Full Members of the ICC, apart from overwhelming support from the Associate Members. Finally the ICC had no other option but to allot the 1996 World Cup to India, Pakistan and Sri Lanka.'

Soon after the allotment of the World Cup, the joint organizing committee received a fax message from G.I. Dowling, chief executive of the New Zealand Cricket Board. It suggested that the World Cup be moved to October–November 1995 from February–March 1996 as the scheduled dates would greatly upset New Zealand's domestic programme. The letter ended with the threat that if the request was not met, the New Zealand Board would demand substantial compensation from PILJMC. The BCCI was no longer in a mood to relent. Minutes of the working committee meeting of 3 June 1993 make this clear: 'I.S. Bindra drew the attention of the members that a decision was taken at the Special ICC meeting held on February 2, 1993 that the 6th World Cup competition will be held between the end of January and the beginning of March 1996 and since this was a binding decision [on every cricket playing country], New Zealand will have to adjust their domestic programme in such a way that the period of the World Cup competition does not clash. So where does the question of payment of compensation arise?'

The success of the 1996 World Cup was a big boost for the subcontinent. Even before the tournament ended, a decision was taken by the BCCI, with support from Pakistan and Sri Lanka, to propose Dalmiya as the next chairman of the ICC. The issue was first discussed during the World Cup final in Lahore when it was observed that Dalmiya, with an overwhelming support of ICC Associate Members, was suitable for the post. However, Dalmiya's election to the top job at the ICC wasn't smooth and it was over this issue that the next round between the Asian countries and the West was fought.

The First Indian ICC Chief

Soon after Dalmiya's candidacy for the ICC presidency was mooted by the BCCI, a complicated legal drama began to unfold. It was decided that 'the election of the Chairman was a Binding Resolution as per the ICC rules and that it would require a special majority of the Full Members'. Nevertheless Dalmiya was fielded by India for the election of the ICC chairman-elect at the ICC annual conference in June 1996. Krish Mackerdhuj of South Africa and Malcolm Gray of Australia were the others in the fray.

None of the candidates was willing to step down and a vote seemed inevitable. As per the ICC's rules, while each Full Member had two votes, each Associate Member had only one. In the first round, Dalmiya secured 16 votes (three Full Members and ten Associate Members), Gray 15 votes (four Full Members and seven Associate Members) and Mackerdhuj nine votes (two Full Members and five Associate Members). Realizing he had little chance of winning, Mackerdhuj withdrew.

In the second round, Dalmiya polled 25 votes (four Full Members and 17 Associate Members). Gray could muster only 13 votes (four Full Members and five Associate Members). Even though Dalmiya had won by an overwhelming majority, the ICC chairman did not declare him the winner. His argument was that, besides the simple majority of all members, a two-thirds majority of Full Members was necessary. The BCCI sought legal opinion from Sir Michael Beloff, Queen's Counsel, and Justice R.S. Pathak, former chief justice of India. Both agreed that the ICC's rules did not permit the elections to be governed by a special majority of Full Members. At this stage, BCCI president Bindra informed the working committee that he had been approached by the Australian Cricket Board (ACB) and told that had he been fielded as a candidate from India instead of Dalmiya, a unanimous election may have been possible. At this, Dungarpur warned that the ACB was trying to divide and rule. He also praised the Indian delegation 'for taking the right decision and not falling prey to their bait'.

Dalmiya was not declared ICC chairman in 1996–97 and the

BCCI had to once again nominate him for the post at the ICC annual conference in June 1997. Prior to the conference, an informal meeting and a special general meeting of the ICC took place at Kuala Lumpur on 22–23 March 1997. Here ICC officials were insistent that, as per the recommendations of the Rules Review Committee, an executive board be formed to run the ICC. The executive board would comprise a chairman and representatives of all Full Members. The position of the ICC president, it was suggested, would be that of a figurehead and separate from that of the chairman. It was also suggested that the tenure of the ICC president should be two years instead of three. India, Pakistan, Sri Lanka and Zimbabwe strongly criticized the recommendations of the Rules Review Committee and the meeting ended in a stalemate. Thereafter, a select committee was formed—with John Anderson of New Zealand, Ali Bacher of South Africa, Raj Singh Dungarpur of India and Ehsan Mani of Pakistan—to find a solution. The select committee was unanimous that the position of the ICC president should not be projected as a figurehead since this would 'weaken the very fabric of the world cricket body'. It also felt that the position of the ICC president would be diluted by the creation of the position of a separate chairman for the executive board. However, it conceded that since the position had already been created, the ICC president should also function as the chairman of the executive board.

At the special general meeting of the ICC on 23 March the solutions forwarded by the select committee were unanimously accepted. It was decided that the ICC president would have the same powers as the ICC chairman and that the president would himself be chairman of the executive board. The term of the president would be three years. Finally, members unanimously accepted Dalmiya's nomination as the first ICC president. His term commenced after the ICC annual conference in June 1997.

Cricket's great power shift moved another step in two years with the 1999 World Cup being held primarily in England, with some games being played in Scotland, Ireland, Wales and the Netherlands. Even though India was eliminated from the competition at the Super-Six stage, the overwhelming support of the Asian community in the British Isles made the tournament a financial success. That the subcontinent was central to this was largely acknowledged.

A process that had started with an Indian win in England in the 1983 World Cup reached culmination in the same country 16 years later. India was the new powerhouse of world cricket, a process that gathered further momentum in the next few years. With its billion-plus cricket fans and growing corporate muscle, India offered world cricket the best mesh of passion and commerce, as was evident when the 2011 World Cup was staged in the subcontinent.

ELEVEN GODS AND A
BILLION INDIANS

In England in 1983, it was Kapil's team that won the World Cup. In 2011, Indian cricket won the World Cup on home soil. For 28 years Indian cricket had readied itself for the moment. And in television terms, this was the Mount Everest. No other event, political stop press events included, even remotely came close.

—Vikrant Gupta,
senior journalist and sports editor, *AajTak*

2 April 2011 had just turned to 3 April 2011. However, it was a midnight like no other. All of India had bid sleep a temporary farewell. It was party time. It was a haphazardly progressing passage of temporal sequences, when every by-lane in every Indian city, irrespective of its geographical location, was engulfed in unimaginable euphoria, commemorating the actualization of world dominance. Delhi, Mumbai, Kolkata and Bengaluru were all partying. Guwahati was partying, and so was Bhubaneshwar. After a prolonged 28 years of agony, the World Cup had been won.

It was just past midnight when the players finally made it back up to the sixth floor of the Taj Mahal Hotel in Mumbai. A journey that normally takes 20 minutes, had taken close to three hours. However, it hardly mattered. No one seemed to be in a hurry and every player was trying to soak in as much of what was going on as possible. Videos were being made and photographs taken almost every second. The moment had to be frozen for posterity. Eleven gods had given a billion Indians a night to remember and, subsequently, turned immortal. The Taj Mahal Hotel, a centre of public attention some two-and-a-half years earlier for very different reasons, was back in all its glory—a symbol of a resurgent India, scarred, yet potent enough to come back stronger and far more appealing. In many ways it was very similar to the Indian cricket team. There were as many television cameras focused on it as there were on that fateful night of 26 November 2008, when highly trained assailants attacked the Taj in one of the deadliest terrorist attacks in our country's history. Only this time, no one feared for their lives and no commandos had to be readied. It was a battle won, but with weapons of a different kind, by an army possessing a different avatar—a troop of spirited achievers, wielding willow and chasing leather, helmed by M.S. Dhoni. And yes, Pakistan had been beaten in the process. Gautam Gambhir, an ardent admirer of the armed forces—he wanted to be part the artillery arm of the Indian army before his cricketing dream took flight—had made the *jawans* proud with his valiant 97 and, for once, didn't object to being called a hero. The Taj Mahal Hotel, full of fans from the world over, was once again a cosmopolitan melting pot, pulsating with life and all set for another sleepless night, albeit a very different one.

As the players were starting to unwind, a message was relayed to each of the rooms that the party would begin around 3 a.m. That is when it dawned on Virender Sehwag, Yuvraj Singh and Virat Kohli that none of them had eaten much. Sehwag blurted out something along the lines of, '*Arre bahut ho gaya, ab toh kuchh khaya jaaye*

(Enough is enough, it's time to eat something).' Sehwag ordered
biryani. As the clay pot turned up in 15 minutes, full of aroma and
succulent flavours, all of us assembled in Yuvraj's room and made a
dash for it. Yuvraj, very kindly, had invited me over and it was one
invite no Indian cricket follower would ever refuse. Nishant Arora,
a friend and fellow journalist, was also there and, in a way, it was
another of our fan boy moments. How often do you get to have
biryani with the World Cup by your side? Not often, right? Yuvraj,
Man of the Tournament, was in a daze and still a bit teary-eyed.
He literally pinched himself a couple of times to see if it was all
real. Yuvraj had no idea then he had cancer; with the body hurting
and a lot to prove, he had delivered. Just as Tendulkar had said to
him at the start of the tournament, he had mattered when India
needed him the most. It was the second time he had won Man of
the Tournament in a World Cup, an achievement almost impossible
to emulate. Kohli, still the youngster in the team but one who was
taking giant strides towards super-stardom, was trying to see how
heavy the trophy really was. He even passed it on to me and it turned
out to be far heavier than I had imagined. It was better if Sehwag
and I concentrated on the biryani, I realized. Celebrating the World
Cup win with the architects of the victory, while devouring some
of my favourite food, ranks among the best memories of my life as
a sports scholar and journalist.

I had covered the World Cup from start to finish: Watched each
India game as closely as possible, discussed the proceedings on and
off the field with the players, seen fans celebrate every win and sink
into despair with every loss, heard people oscillate between abuse
and praise more randomly than a lunatic could ever imagine. I had
tried my best in understanding the minds of the players. Were they
feeling the pressure of playing at home or was it something they
had mastered already? Answers to these questions were valuable
research. But nothing could better place the World Cup in context

than a discussion with Gary Kirsten in Mohali the morning after India had beaten Pakistan and made the final.

India had just won what Tendulkar calls the 'most tense' match of his career. With a television rating of 35.2, the Mohali encounter had broken all viewership records. And having managed the Indian team quite adeptly, Kirsten deserved a fair share of the credit. But this was Gary Kirsten we are talking about—perfect backroom man with little desire for the limelight. So far in his stint as India's coach, he had not done a single television interview. That wasn't part of the deal. It did not matter to him what people said or thought. He was doing a job and doing it to the best of his ability. So when I met him at breakfast the morning after the victory, it wasn't a surprise to see him enjoying his breakfast alone. Paddy Upton soon joined him. Being alone was quintessential Kirsten: Less talk and more work, meticulous planning but no leaks to the media. It was still fairly early in Mohali and the roads to the hotel were all deserted with people sleeping in after partying all night. The war had been won and the enemy vanquished. The final against Sri Lanka was more of an after-party. Not so, however, for Kirsten. Him being a South African, I did not expect Kirsten to comprehend what an India–Pakistan World Cup semi-final meant to us all. Unless you are an Indian or a Pakistani, you can't. Each time I have passed through Rajabazar, barely 15 minutes from my house near Manicktala, and seen a Pakistani flag during an India–Pakistan contest, I have felt a sense of outrage. This has been a feature in all my growing-up years in Kolkata. It was as if people were deliberately failing the nation, something that wasn't acceptable even in a liberal, secular India. Sedition or not—that's a separate debate. I am no legal luminary to give my opinion on it. But all I can say is it did not stir a positive feeling in me, seeing Pakistani flags a stone's throw away from a very traditional north Kolkata neighbourhood. That Kirsten could never see Rajabazar with the same eyes as I did was perhaps best for him and the team. He was a professional coach and, for him, the job was only partly done. The final was still to be won and he wasn't one to stop short.

'The team is looking great,' I said trying to make conversation. I knew he wouldn't talk on record, and an interview was out of the question in the middle of the tournament, given that the final was still to be played. But because he knew me and we had interacted a fair deal in the lead-up to the World Cup, he looked up and smiled. 'The sense of camaraderie and bonding is great to see,' I said. That's when he stopped, put his fork down and said calmly with a smile, 'You think all of the players are friends? To be honest, it doesn't matter to me if they are. All I want is when the last catch goes up and whoever is under the ball the rest of the 14 should pray he takes the catch for India.'

That one sentence made all the difference. They were prophetic words. In one sweeping statement, Kirsten had unravelled the essence of team sport. Here were 11 super-achievers with mammoth fan-followings and mountain-sized egos. Each bigger than the other. Each a superior icon. Some of them arguably the biggest brands India has ever produced. Some of the others, the biggest brands in the making. How could they all be friends? It wasn't humanly possible and it wasn't necessary either. Did Sehwag, the man who transformed Test cricket forever, ever nurture an ambition to be captain? The answer is, yes. Anyone in his position would. And were he and Dhoni best buddies? Could they be? But both, as Kirsten articulately implied, were playing for India. Winning games for India—doing their jobs to perfection. Did they ever clash? Did they ever have disagreements or differences of opinion? It is absurd to expect they didn't. Anyone who was there at Sehwag's press conference in Australia in January 2012 when he had taken a blinder at slip will see merit in what I am saying. Dhoni, the captain, had made a point about rotating senior players because they weren't the most agile on the field. Sehwag, it was known, was one of them. Having taken a blinder, all Sehwag said was, 'Did you see my catch?' when asked what he made of Dhoni's comment. Sehwag followed it up with a very 'Viru' smile. Sehwag, for the record, had scored the first hundred of the World Cup against Bangladesh in Dhaka, a century that had helped exorcize the ghastly memories of the 2007 misadventure. Dhoni, on his part, played a blinder in the final against Sri Lanka, having promoted himself up the order in the most important match of his life.

This is why Kirsten was spot on.

You didn't need to be friends to be successful teammates. All you needed was zeal to excel. Raise the bar and pursue a dream. And this Indian team had that fire in them. That's why they were world champions after 28 years. It was Indian cricket's second tryst with destiny. More importantly, on home soil, with a billion Indians praying for their victory.

Once the biryani was polished off, it dawned on me that in another 45 minutes the players would all disappear for the team party. The Man of the Tournament was in front of me and I hadn't interviewed him yet. Yuvraj sportingly agreed to do the interview. When I asked him at the end of it what lay next for him to achieve, he gave me the best possible answer: 'The team party and you are keeping me from going to it!'

It was all one big party, indeed. Beating Australia, Pakistan and Sri Lanka in one week, Indian cricket had never seen it better. Australia was the defending champions, Pakistan the arch-enemy and Sri Lanka the opposition that had knocked India out of the 2007 edition of the tournament in the Caribbean. Each was a special victory and a story in itself. Knockout games always have an additional degree of significance to themselves and this was the biggest stage of them all. While much has been written about the World Cup and about India's triumph, each game had multiple side stories, which are no less fascinating.

Sample this from Gary Kirsten on the India–Pakistan encounter at Mohali: 'If I remember [correctly], the Pakistani premier was here in India for the 2011 Mohali semi-final. And I remember a lot of Indian dignitaries were also present. On the morning of the match, I went down for breakfast fairly early and, to my shock, I was told that there was no breakfast available. I said my boys were soon to be coming down for breakfast and it was a team event. But the hotel staff would hear none of it. The Pakistan premier and his team was coming down and the entire breakfast area had been cordoned off. So my boys could not eat anything in the morning before they left for the ground. And the story doesn't end there. Even at the ground, lunch was not served on time. We were told that the food truck was stuck behind a whole bunch of cars and it was not until 2 p.m., just about 30 minutes before the game started, that the truck finally reached the venue. However, none of it mattered in the end because we won what was a historic semi-final.'

All I said to Gary was, had he told me this story earlier, the headline next morning would have read 'Pakistani premier deprives Indian players of breakfast and lunch!'

If this could happen to the players, imagine what was in store for the media and the fans. Having finished my television broadcast leading up to the game, I remember navigating through a sea of humanity on my way into the stadium. And it was only when Umar Gul was about to bowl to Sehwag did I finally find my spot in the media box.

We journalists were fighting our own war of deadlines and TRP ratings—for better or worse.

Watching an India–Pakistan semi-final and studying fan behaviour is an exercise in itself. Every boundary hit by Sehwag and Sachin was followed by a sustained roar from a crowd that was all Indian. Or nearly so. The hype and nationalist passion was such that the most important thing for Kirsten and the team was to keep the players insulated from this fervour. You can't play an emotion, and it was essential for the players, many aged 25 years and less, to shut out the fact that premiers of the two countries were watching them play, with millions uttering silent prayers for them while watching the game on television. My media pass did not grant me access to the galleries. *Jugaad*—that typical Indian way of learning to work one's way around—did. I told the cops I was a journalist and it was essential for me to interview a few of the fans for my piece the following day. One of the cops looked convinced and let me into the gallery. For those who had bought tickets for absurd sums, nothing but an Indian victory would suffice. They were happily abusing every Pakistani cricketer they could name. And when Tendulkar was dropped, the decibel of abuse went up a few notches. 'Here was a Pakistani *behen***** who had sold himself! How could he take the catch?' sneered the bunch of Indian teenagers I was sitting with. I controlled my anger. And when a young man in his early twenties said 'well bowled' at Wahab Riaz having knocked over Yuvraj, he got a solid tap on the back of his head from one of the many seated right behind him. Secularism was passé, India was playing Pakistan and one had to offer jingoistic support. For once, I was glad I had not reacted. A few punches from people half my age wouldn't have been pleasant. I was sure to fail the Indian version of the Tebbit Test and could easily get a few taps on either side of my cheeks. This was no '*aman ki asha*' being enacted out in the middle. It was proxy war and the crowd wouldn't brook any failure from Dhoni and his boys.

One of the stars for India in this game, following up on his quarter-final heroics against Australia, was Suresh Raina. Suresh, 25 at the time, was not in the team for the initial few games and in his words, 'was doing everything I can to attract attention that I was the best option at number six. I would spend maximum time doing fielding practice and was determined to make a case to Gary and Dhoni for my inclusion. Playing the World Cup at home was a dream and playing Australia and Pakistan were two of the biggest occasions for any player playing the sport.'

He did get an opportunity in India's last group encounter against the West Indies in Chennai but that was because Sehwag was sitting out with an injury. With Sehwag back in the playing XI against Australia, it was a toss-up between Raina and Yusuf Pathan. And this is where one has to give Dhoni his due. While it is all well to say Dhoni is India's best white-ball captain ever, there have come occasions when his captaincy has been under serious scrutiny. This was one such. Should it be Raina or Pathan? It was one decision that could impact India's progress in the World Cup and Dhoni had to get it right. And he did. Raina, sitting next to Tendulkar in the dressing room, must have had a thousand ideas flooding his mind when Tendulkar said to him at the Motera dressing room, 'Look at this as an opportunity. A World Cup quarter-final with 78 runs left and you have a chance to win it for the country. It is your day, go win it for India.' Raina, a Tendulkar fan since childhood, was lost for a second or two. 'It was Sachin *paaji* who was speaking to me. He had waited for six World Cups to win the trophy. And here he was urging me to do it for him and India. With Dhoni out and 75 runs still to get, I could not have asked for a better opportunity to make a mark. All I told him was, "*Paaji aaj jita ke aayeenge* [Will win it for India tonight, elder brother]"' recounts Raina. To keep him company in the middle, he had a well-set Yuvraj Singh. Raina made a 28-ball 34 during his unbeaten knock on the night. These weren't many runs when you consider the asking rate towards the close of the innings. But that near-one-hour stint he pulled off in the middle, batting with Yuvraj, was perhaps the most invigorating one hour for each of us in the stands. Starting with three dot balls, he soon asserted himself with a pull shot off Brett Lee and followed it up with regular singles and another four and a six to seal it for India. 'I remember telling Yuvi *paaji*, "*Mujhe mera natural game khelne do. Aaj hum log jeet ke hi jayenge.* [You must let me stick to my natural style. We will be the victors tonight].'''

How does a twenty-five-year-old react to shouldering a billion dreams? Did Raina think of the crowd when he was batting out there for himself and India? Did it matter that one false note could lead to bowing out of the World Cup at home and miss out on an opportunity to play Pakistan in a historic semi-final?

'All Yuvi *paaji* and I were seeing was Brett Lee, Mitchell Johnson and the others. To tell you the truth, even when I hit those boundaries or sixes, I did not feel any sense of elation. The job was still not finished. All I was thinking was, I had got this opportunity after a lot of effort and I couldn't let it go.'

Innocent words from a twenty-five-year-old, but in doing what he was, he was elevating Indian cricket to a very different pedestal. Making sure that Australia, world champions for 12 years, was soon going to be champions in the past tense and the media market in India had a new note to mint. With each run scored, cricket was consolidating itself as India's most reliable blue-chip investment, which had no parallel in India's sports universe. And Raina, thanks to his priceless 34, was now a certainty at number six for the rest of the tournament—the semi-final and final.

'Wahab was bowling really well in the semi-final and getting the ball to reverse,' Raina said. 'At 205/6 in 42 overs, and with Dhoni out, we weren't safe. I walked up to Bhajji pa, who came to the crease and told him we needed to get 60 runs more to make it our game. We had to forge a partnership and there was no need to try and hurry things up.'

Did he not panic seeing Tendulkar and Dhoni get out before him? It was India playing Pakistan, a match that we just couldn't afford to lose! Did that not play on his mind as he was giving sane advice to an older and more experienced Harbhajan Singh? What is it with high-performance sportsmen at that level that they can keep poise in the face of humongous pressure?

It is time to pause for a moment and dwell on a hypothesis. If Pakistan had indeed won the Mohali clash, they would have played the final in Mumbai, a bastion of the Hindu right. Hindu fundamentalists had dug up pitches in the past in 1999 and vandalized the BCCI office more recently to stop Pakistan from playing in India. And here was a possibility of Pakistan playing in Mumbai having beaten India in a World Cup semi-final. Talk of rubbing it in. Chasing 261, Pakistan did have a chance but, as has often been the case with the side in recent times, they disintegrated after a reasonably good start.

Did Raina ever think of the possibility of Pakistan playing in Mumbai in the final? Did Tendulkar, himself a Mumbaikar to the core, ever contemplate this? Would the match have taken place uninterrupted and what would the BCCI have done to stave off political interference?

Counter history always ends up throwing countless possibilities but the good thing is they aren't ever real and the real world never has to deal with them.

The real world was all about India. About Gambhir—rightly or wrongly—saying he dedicated the win to the victims of the 26/11 terror attacks and about a billion people getting their best chance to accord a World Cup farewell to their biggest home-grown cricketing superhero. For Tendulkar it was his last chance. It was now or never.

'Right through the tournament, we used to listen to Sachin *paaji*. There was something about him this tournament. First he was playing some great cricket himself; he scored two hundreds already. And when he said our fans wanted us to win, you could see a very different confidence in his eyes. He was calm but confident and each of us drew inspiration from him,' Raina said.

Raina ended up getting 36 off 39 deliveries against Pakistan, but as Tendulkar says, 'It was an innings as important as any in the context of the match. 260 was a competitive total and Raina had a major part to play in it.'

In the end India won by 29 runs, just a few less than what Raina had scored. He had redeemed himself, and in doing so, had made sure Tendulkar had an opportunity of fulfilling his lifelong dream—win the World Cup for India in front of his home crowd. His journey had completed a full circle.

A confession is in order here. When I was co-writing *Playing It My Way*, one of the things I was very keen on knowing was what emotion Tendulkar felt when Dhoni hit the winning six at the Wankhede. From the time the ball had left his bat to being dispatched over the ropes, three or four seconds at best had elapsed. What was Sachin thinking as he tracked the ball back from the 22 yards strip to over the boundary? To my disappointment, he had not watched Dhoni hit the winning runs.

'I was in the dressing room with Virender Sehwag and had even forbidden Viru from going out to the balcony. I have seen the shot a million times on television thereafter but no, I did not see Dhoni hitting it,' Tendulkar admits. And that's when I told him that I had not either. I had already taken my position outside the Wankhede for the live post-match broadcast and had missed the last few balls of the Indian innings. Not me alone, every television journalist covering the World Cup had missed that magical moment. You had to go on air the moment the match was over and Dhoni's six meant our work had just begun. But what missing out on seeing Dhoni dispatch it into the stands in real time did was give me a glimpse of people on the road as the celebrations were gradually beginning. It is a cliché to say adults behaved like children but if you really wanted to see thousands do so, the night of 2 April 2011 should be a stand-out case study. Most importantly, it did not matter if you were Hindu or Muslim or Parsi; if you were an Indian you had won the World Cup as much as those 11 men had at the Wankhede. People were kissing and hugging each other and, I am sure, nobody cared to ask if the person standing next to them was a Hindu or a Muslim. A city infamous for communal violence was throwing up a very different picture. Sudhir Gautam, by then the official emblem of Indian sports' fandom, was called into the dressing room by Tendulkar and given the World Cup trophy to hold and celebrate. '*Maine aajtak itna zor se shankh kabhi nahi bajaya* [I've never blown the conch this hard],' Sudhir said. Here was an Indian fan from a very modest background standing in the Indian dressing room with his hero and the World Cup in hand; only sport could make such a moment possible. In that instant, every conceivable boundary between mortal and immortal, rich and poor, privileged and underprivileged, icon and common man had broken down. The trophy was as much Sudhir's as Sachin's and that's what made the World Cup win even more significant.

Moments after he had entered his room in the hotel, Tendulkar danced to a Bollywood number with a flower in his ear. A sight such as that was inconceivable in normal circumstances from a conservative, disciplined traditionalist like Tendulkar. However, it wasn't a normal night. It was a night when boundaries were crossed and traditions were broken. The guard, finally, could be let down.

This was a very peculiar Indian modernity on show. Tendulkar was in the private confines of an ultra-luxurious five-star hotel, very Indian in symbolism and essence, and celebrating to a Bollywood number with a flower in his ear. Tendulkar, who loves Western music and is a connoisseur of sorts, preferred a more popular Indian number to anything Western that night. It might well be a coincidence but surely it's an interesting one. And this modernity was reinforced when Dhoni appeared before the media the next morning with the World Cup in hand but in a completely different avatar. The Indian captain, once known for his flowing hair, had given it all up to commemorate the victory. Wearing a full suit and standing in front of the Gateway of India with the World Cup trophy in hand, sporting a fully shaven head, there could be no better picture postcard of contemporary India than Dhoni. A small-town boy who had made it to the highest echelons of power and fame was certainly a success story for the ages; the culmination of the big Indian dream. He had won world cricket's highest prize in a stadium located only metres next to where there was once a sign that read: 'Dogs and Indians not allowed.' Furthermore, he was presented the trophy by an Indian boss of the ICC, inconceivable at the time the World Cup was first started in England in 1975, or when India won the Prudential Cup for the first time at Lord's in 1983. With an Indian tournament director running the show, this was the best example of a form of atypical globalization.

The Cosmopolitan Indian, Cricket and Globalization

As argued by Alan Klein, it might be helpful to think of globalization in the context of Indian cricket as a case of what he calls 'tough-love globalization: Which includes not only the cardinal features of contemporary globalization (for example, time and space contraction) but also a degree of decentralization of power'. Klein argues that tough-love globalization is inclusive of corporations and nations—encouraging the have-nots to enter into the matrix if they can—it stops short of institutionally seeking to distribute power and wealth. Tough-love is about merit, and though it opens the door to opportunity, it brooks no failure. This is not to be confused with a utopian vision, concerned primarily with distributing the benefits of globalization. Tough-love globalization merely allows entry to those who can take advantage of it, turning its back on all others.

Suffice to say that the Indian team, which had won the World Cup, had at its disposal all the ingredients necessary for success. India, under coach Gary Kirsten and captain M.S. Dhoni, was already the world's number one Test team with a proven track record of ODI success. And in some of the architects of the World Cup victory, Dhoni, Raina, Zaheer, all small-town men in yet another departure from the post-independence context, the team had elements of aggression that Indian sides of the past lacked. In Kirsten and Paddy Upton, the coaching staff, the Indian team had the best support on offer globally. To sum it up, the Indian team had the necessary 'merit' emphasized by Klein, besides the potential to take advantage of the opportunities afforded by globalization. Interestingly, in the Indian team referred to here there were two foreigners, going by strict markers of nationality. However, in the context of Indian cricket, they were as much Indian as anyone else, breaking down conventional nationalist paradigms as it were.

Kirsten's popularity in the country, at an all-time high with the World Cup win, was no surprise. All of India pleaded with him to extend his contract when it was known that Kirsten would return to South Africa in April 2011 to spend more time with his family. With cricket seducing the global Indian like nothing else, the treatment meted out to Kirsten was not unimaginable. For this assertive and more cosmopolitan Indian, cricket had replaced religion as a source of emotional catharsis and spiritual passion. It helped infiltrate memory, shaped enthusiasms and served fantasies. In a choice between sectarianism and success, Indians had opted for success, appropriating Kirsten for his professionalism and work ethic.

I have to conclude this chapter with a very personal anecdote. It was 4 April 2011 (a date now made very special as my only daughter's birthday, though she wasn't born then) and I had met Tendulkar at the Mumbai Cricket Association at the Bandra Kurla Complex to do an interview. Tendulkar, 48 hours after the triumphant night, looked relaxed. In the lead-up to the interview, he said to me rather enquiringly, 'Have you seen Arjun [his son]?'

I was startled. I hadn't; there had been no reason for me to see Arjun recently.

'He has grown taller you know. I was busy trying to win the World Cup for India and did not notice that my children had grown,' Tendulkar said.

Was he sad or was it a matter of fact statement? Honestly, I do not know. But it was indeed true that while Tendulkar had been busy doing his best to win the World Cup for India, Arjun and Sara, his two children, had grown up. Things in India had moved on, as they always do. There was life beyond cricket and it was important for all of us involved with the sport to realize and respect that.

PART FOUR

RANJI: LOVE, LIFE AND CRICKET

In one of the earliest of the many biographies written on Kumar Shri Ranjitsinhji, by the British author Percy Cross Standing in 1903, there is no mention of his disputed succession: That he had no real claim to the throne and would have struggled to mount a legitimate bid for himself had it not been for his cricket. Standing celebrates Ranji as a contemporary cricketing superstar, and what adds to his story is Ranji's exotic Oriental appeal. A sophisticated Cambridge educated Indian aristocrat topping the cricket averages in the England of the 1890s and scoring a century for the Queen's country was an important news headline and it had catapulted Ranji into the world of the high and famous. He was the perfect example of the success of the civilizing-mission ideology and epitomized all the good the empire had taught the Orient. His appropriation by British society had encouraged him to date British women in Cambridge—despite his financial troubles—and plot his way to the Jamnagar throne back in India. It was Ranji's prowess in cricket—rather than his lineage or administrative skills—which eventually won him the *gadi* (throne) in 1907. His is a classic case of a mesh between cricket and politics, and how the game was gradually assuming significance in the colonial

Indian imagination. Besides, his journey exemplified how the sport could be used as a ladder for social mobility and to secure personal ends. Ranji, India's first sporting superhero, was celebrated the country over and, time and again, bailed out of financial trouble by other native aristocrats and British bureaucrats who turned out to be admirers of the game in early twentieth-century India.

Schooled at Rajkumar College in Rajkot and, subsequently, Cambridge University in England, Ranji was one of the most written-about sporting figures of the time. Depicted in cartoons and featured in magazines and newspapers, he was a perfect page-three-celebrity, who loved the life in the limelight and, as a matter of fact, revelled in it. Dedicating *The Jubilee Book of Cricket* to the Queen Empress, in 1897 added to his growing clout and helped him woo the British administrators of his native state. He was the 'perfect colonial subject', if there ever was one.

The Ranji narrative is proof that the story of Indian cricket from inception was imbued with political significance, debunking the classic myth that sports and politics do not mix. As evident right through this book, Indian cricket and politics always went hand in hand, and the complex interplay played a role in shaping the future trajectory of the game in India. Ranji, a good cricketer, soon turned into a regal aristocrat with a voice in colonial Indian matters, normally reserved for men of affluence and pedigree. Ranji's was an acquired pedigree, earned in English county grounds during his stint as an England cricketer. He was an example of the success of the empire's quest for civilizing colonial subjects and turning them into compradors of the ruling British elite. These men, carefully nurtured and pampered by the empire, played a significant role in the continuance of British rule in India. While Ranji was more British than Indian, his legacy as a cricketer was appropriated by the Indians for nationalist needs and, in that sense, he was Indian cricket's first real superhero. An incurable romantic and a scheming politician, he is, however, best remembered for his supple wrists and for pioneering the leg glance, not to forget authoring one of the earliest classics of cricket, *The Jubilee Book of Cricket*. His appropriation in the annals of the Indian game was complete when, after a year of his death in 1933, the Indian national championship for cricket was named after him. This was the ultimate tribute to Ranji and made him immortal in India's cricketing pantheon.

There are two Ranji anecdotes that help capture the layered impact he had on contemporary British society. The first goes thus: As Ranji was coming out to bat in a game, a spectator pointed out to the person sitting next to him that here was the great Ranjitsinhji, an Indian aristocrat and one who had learnt the skills of the British game better than anyone else. There was an element of pride in the statement and it was as though he was flaunting Ranji as an empire success story. Ranji had been appropriated and, in the process of appropriation, very little agency had been attributed to him. It was as though he did what the colonial state wanted him to. As it happened, he got out for a duck in the match in question and the spectator immediately reacted, calling him a 'dirty nigger'. The extreme reaction is significant in that it clearly establishes the dichotomy in the contemporary thinking of the time. Ranji was British as long as he suited British ends. He was Indian if he failed to live up to expectations.

The best current parallel is Andy Murray. Murray is British as long as he wins Wimbledon and plays to potential in the grand slams. He is a boorish Scot the moment he loses a match he is supposed to win and cops more criticism than anyone else. Given Ranji's skin colour was different to that of Murray, the reaction in the former's case was more volatile and aggressive. There was an element of impatience in the spectators' behavior, symptomatic of British thinking at the turn of the century. There was never any real loyalty or affection. As long as Ranji delivered what was expected of him, he was held in high esteem. The moment he failed, he was discarded as a useless Oriental. Importantly for Ranji, though, he knew the reality well. He used his cricket to perfection and achieved both status and fame. He made up for his lesser status as a royal by scoring runs and, in doing so, became close to the British administration in India. While cricket wasn't an industry at the time, there is little doubt that Ranji was Indian cricket's first global brand.

A Life Little Known

'Cricket is a game of glorious uncertainties,' runs the old maxim. However, sometimes the lives of cricketers can turn out to be more gloriously uncertain than an exciting game of cricket. How else can we explain the fact that Ranji rented a whole train to take his love, Mary Holmes, to London for a holiday in the 1890s, even though he was deeply in debt, owing money to his tailor, bartender, grocer, newsagent and restaurateur in Cambridge? How can one explain his showering Mary with costly gifts—a diamond bracelet, an ivory necklace, a model of the Taj Mahal, a brooch—even as he was planning to live on friends, eating in their homes after inviting himself forcibly, to avoid destitution?

It is already known that Ranji played for Cambridge University and decided to make his cricketing career in England rather than in India, for Sussex and England. He played 15 Tests between 1896 and 1902 (in a period well before India had achieved Test status), all his matches being against Australia. Ranji had a first-class average of 56.37 and a Test average of 44.95, which is remarkable for the period. What is, however, not widely known is Ranji's colourful love life. This aspect comes alive from the 37 letters he wrote to Mary, rescued from oblivion in March 2002, 112 years after they were written. The letters are now housed safely in the Wren Library, Trinity College, Cambridge. There are more than half-a-dozen published treatises on Ranji. (Percy Cross Standing, 1903; Charles Kincaid, 1931;

Roland Wild, 1934; Alan Ross, 1983; Vasant Raiji, 1987; Simon Wilde, 1991; Mario Rodrigues, 2003). Yet, there is no mention of Mary Holmes, also referred to as Madge or Poly by Ranji, in these books. The discovery of these letters is a prize, one that opens up interesting facets about Ranji's life and character.

They came by me rather strangely. I was to present at a seminar at the South Asia Seminar Series at Oxford in February 2002. When the pamphlet announcing the series of papers to be presented that term was circulated, I got an email from Mariecke Clarke, granddaughter of Mary Holmes. She wrote: 'I have noted that you are giving a seminar on cricket in colonial India this term. I am not a student of cricket, but you may like to know that I have just donated a substantial number of letters written by Prince Ranjitsinhji to my grandmother to his old College, Trinity, Cambridge.' While interviewing Mariecke, I was told that Ranji had been close to the Holmes family since 1890.

It all started when Ranji was cycling past Bond and Holmes (established 1874), their huge grocery store on Cambridge's 57 Sidney Street. The two sisters, Mary and Minnie, saw the Indian prince for the first time. Finding him attractive, they dropped their handkerchiefs for Ranji to pick up. Once he did pick it up, the journey had begun. The next stop was the Holmes house, above their store. The eighteen-year-old Ranji soon became a regular. A few months later, he started calling Mr and Mrs Holmes 'mother' and 'father'. With Ranji living on 22 Sidney Street, it wasn't difficult for him to visit the Holmes house regularly, more so with indulgence from both the sisters.

Ranji's first letter to Mary, written in 1891 as a nineteen-year-old, was formal. However, it was reflective of his growing attachment to the Holmes family. 'My dear M.H., I was delighted to have your sweet note. I am sorry I was the unfortunate means of a quarrel between your darling self and your beautiful sister. The opera glasses, I hope, you will accept as a present from me to you. But if your sister is desirous of having a pair, I shall be most willing to provide her with a pair. I wish I could have your charming company sometimes here at teatime. I shall be delighted to be of any service to you if you want anything.' At the end of the letter, he expressed keenness to know her full name.

By the course of the third letter, the tenor of the writing had changed. 'Dear Madge, I am glad to say that I am not going away during the vac but am allowed to stay here. So I hope I shall have your company till the next term without a break. If you let me know when you can come today, I will manage [ensure] so that no one can come and see me. I hope your mother will let you and Minnie come.' In the next letter, Ranji was profusely apologetic for not being home when the two sisters had come. He also insisted he liked them more than he liked any other girl. 'Please do not think I like all girls because I seem to give them presents. I like you and Minnie best. I can do anything I can to please you and Minnie.'

Within six months, their affair had grown stronger, if the tone of Ranji's letters is anything to go by. 'I think of going to London from Friday to Monday. I shall miss you immensely but shall rejoice doubly to see you back again.' It's from this time that we know of another Ranji—the poet. In many of his letters, he wrote verses for Madge, urging her to write some for him. He claimed that all of them were either original, composed by him, or translated from the vernacular. He even copied Shelley's *Lines to an Indian Air*, claiming it had been written by an Indian poet and translated by him! On 1 April 1891, he wrote to her, saying, 'In the last verse I have asked you to guess [who I am referring to]. I think these are better than the last ones as they are made after thinking a lot and the rhythm is all right.'

> *Dearest Madge, Would my Poly know if I love let her take*
> *My last thought at night and the first when I awake?*

Let her think what odd whimsies I have in my brain
When I read one page over and over again
And discover at last that I read them in vain.
And lastly when summoned to drink to my flame
Let her guess why I never mention her name
Though herself and the lassie I love are the same.

In the next verse he did not leave anything to guesswork:

I loved thee once, I love thee still
And fell this world asunder
My loves eternal flame would rise
Midst chaos crash and thunder.
Two rubies on those lips of thine
Unrivalled in fresh glory
Happy is the man to whom
They whisper their love story.

A few days later, he wrote:

Good night my love!
The night is ill
Which shows those we should unite
Let us remain together still
Then it will be good night.

On one occasion, Ranji had tried to ignite Mary's passions by telling her how intimate he had become with a London girl. This was part of a plan his friends had made to tease her. Upon seeing the plan fail, and finding her determined not to speak to him any more, he wrote: 'I am so sorry to have offended you by letting you [know] about the beastly London girl. It was Hussain's [a friend who visited Ranji often] suggestion, when I told him that you had asked me whether I like any girl beside you and Minnie, to say what I did. I shall never forgive him for the trick. I am so awfully ashamed of acting accordingly but you must forgive me for doing so unless you wish to make me unhappy and sad. I love you only and I did not think I could be fond of anyone as I am of you and of Minnie. I hope you will forgive me.'

It's evident from the account of Christopher Neve, grandnephew of Mary Holmes, that Ranji often gave the girls extravagant gifts, bicycles and jewellery. He used to take them on picnics and expeditions. Once he had taken them to visit Wimpole Hall, where the Holmes had their farm, to see their grandfather William Clarke, referred to as W.C. in the letters. The most interesting thing about this expedition, however, was that they used a dogcart as transport.

In the letters, there is little mention of cricket, except to say, 'I am tired this evening. I have been playing cricket.' However, in the last surviving letter from him to Madge, dated 24 October 1905, Ranji briefly mentions his financial crisis and his plans of writing a cricket book, which he intended to sell as a last resort to alleviate his problems. He mentions that he had already secured 3,000 orders for a book he had started writing, entitled *Cricket Guide and How to Play Cricket*, and he planned to sell 5,000 copies in all. Clearly, Ranji, living like a prince, continued to live beyond his means on an annual allowance of INR 5,714 and was perpetually in debt. He gave away expensive gifts to the Holmes sisters on credit. His financial problems were only partly taken care of in 1898 when his friend, Pratapsinhji of Jodhpur, gave him INR 30,000.

What was most interesting, as suggested by Neve, was that while Mary married in 1898, seeing that her affair with Ranji was going nowhere owing to the difference in their skin colours, Minnie was deeply attached to him and preferred to stay unmarried all her life. This seems possible, for Ranji was in constant touch with Minnie even when he had not written to Mary from India. However, Mary had never forgotten her first love and had a large photo portrait of Ranji with his bat with her in her old age.

What we don't know is whether Mary, whose husband had

abandoned her with their six surviving children, and who was on the verge of destitution, received any support from Ranji after he became the Jam Sahib of Nawanagar in 1907. We will also not know whether Ranji would have preferred to stay unmarried to honour his relationship(s) with Mary and/or Minnie. This suspicion is strengthened when we hear about the statue of a British woman Ranji had erected in his native state in the 1920s. His biographers have wondered whether it was of Edith Borissow, daughter of the Chaplain of Trinity, the Rev Louis Borissow, who had looked after Ranji when he arrived in Cambridge. The discovery of his letters to Mary suggests otherwise. If that is assumed to be true, Ranji, Wisden Cricketer of the Year for 1897, never forgot the love(s) of his life.

A Life Well Known

Ranji, ruler of Nawanagar from 1907–33, had a disputed succession. Born in 1872 to a Jadeja family of Sarodar, Ranji had no legal claim to the throne. The Jam, Vibhaji, ruler of Nawanagar, made him heir apparent after he decided to disinherit his son, Kalobha—son of Dhanbai, one of the Jam's Muslim concubines—in 1877, on charges of attempting to poison the Jam. Having no other son, Vibhaji adopted Ranji, son of a distant relative, in 1878. Prior to Ranji's adoption, the Jam had adopted Ranji's elder brother, Umedsinhji, as the future heir. When Umedsinhji died within six months of adoption, the Jam made Ranji the heir apparent. However, when Janbai, sister of Dhanbai, bore the Jam a son in 1882, Ranji's claim to the throne was annulled. Under pressure from members of his zenana, Vibhaji appealed to the British government to accept Jaswantsinhji, the newborn, as the future ruler, because he was the Jam's own son. The appeal was accepted and Ranji was disinherited in 1884.

Despite this, Ranji did eventually become Jam in 1907. His succession to the throne would have been impossible had he not also been one of the world's best cricketers. His cricketing skills endeared him to the British administrators. Many of them were keen to meet him during his visit to Kathiawar in 1898–99. The following account by Charles Kincaid, judicial officer of Jamnagar, bears testimony to Ranji's status: 'After the end of Mr Stoddart's tour [to Australia] Ranjitsinhji paid a visit to Kathiawar. He stayed there for several months, and it was then that I first made his acquaintance. All the agency officials were anxious to meet the famous cricketer; but the situation was rather delicate. The King Emperor's representative at Rajkot was pledged to the support of the young Jam Jaswantsinhji. Fortunately, as a Judicial Officer, I was not so bound. I invited Ranjitsinhji to my house, and he cordially accepted the invitation. I expected to find a young man embittered by the decision of the government of India and his head turned by his cricket success. I found, on the contrary, a charming youth, who treated the viceroy's decision as a blow of fate to be endured, rather than to be rallied against, and who spoke of his prodigious cricket scores with the most becoming modesty. I took him as a guest to the officers' mess at Rajkot, and everyone was delighted with him. The Colonel afterwards remarked to me bluntly that he wished all his English guests had as good manners as Ranjitsinhji.'

For Ranji, friendship soon turned into support and many of the administrators wanted him to be crowned Jam, knowing well he had no legal claim to the throne. Kincaid's words, as recorded in his *The Land of 'Ranji' and 'Duleep'*, echoes this sentiment: 'In 1903 his [Ranji's] fortunes reached the nadir. In March of that year, Jaswantsinhji was formally installed as Jam of Jamnagar by the agent of the Governor. He was an unattractive figure. He had had every advantage—an English tutor, education at the Rajkumar College, constant coaching at cricket, tennis, polo, pigsticking, hockey, shooting. Yet, he never learnt to play any game properly. Nor did he ever show the least interest in sport. I, as an agency official, attended the ceremony of installation. I well remember my disgust when I saw this loutish bastard of a lowborn concubine seated on the throne of Jam Rawal; while my unfortunate friend, the lawful heir, had not even been invited to the investiture.'

The unequivocal support for Ranji was evident when, after Jaswantsinhji's death, the British resident accepted Ranji's claim to the throne in 1907: 'At last, justice prevailed. On 7th March 1907, Ranjitsinhji was installed on the throne of his ancestors to the delight of all save the corrupt clique that had fattened on the incompetence of Jaswantsinhji.'

In his struggle for the throne, Ranji also received support from powerful princes. This support too, Kincaid asserts, owed much to his cricketing abilities: '[In 1898] the young prince found the Jamnagar throne barred and bolted against him; so, after some little time, he returned to England. His kinsman, the Maharaja Pratapsinhji of Idar and Jodhpur, the Maharaja of Patiala and many other Indian chiefs helped him, for they were justly proud of his extraordinary success in first class cricket.'

With Ranji in dire financial condition at the turn of the century, many ruling princes came forward to help him, wishing to associate themselves with the world's leading cricketer. In 1898, Pratapsinhji made Ranji a Sirdar of Jodhpur, an appointment that carried with it an annual grant of INR 30,000. He also arranged for Ranji to meet the Nawab of Patiala, one of the wealthiest men in contemporary India.

Even when his appeal to win back the *gadi* was dismissed in 1899, Ranji's supporters did not lose hope. The Nawab of Patiala appointed him Aide-de-camp (ADC) during the visit of the viceroy, Lord Elgin, to Patiala, giving Ranji an opportunity to present his case to the viceroy in person. This opportunity proved useful, with the viceroy declaring the government of India wished to see all documentation submitted by Ranji regarding his claim to the throne. Ranji's case was strengthened by Lord Curzon's appointment as viceroy, chiefly because the latter was a keen cricket follower and an admirer of Ranji.

In 1895, Ranji accepted an offer from Blackwood and Sons to produce a book that included chapters on the techniques of playing cricket. The product was the *Jubilee Book*, published in 1897. The very next year, Ranji picked on the tenets of fair play, an intrinsically English virtue, to assert that he was the rightful claimant to the throne. He argued that the English, should return the throne to him. In fact, in a prayer he had written as a student at Cambridge, which later became required recitation at English public schools, he had already evoked the Victorian virtue of fair play: 'O Powers that be, make me to observe and keep the rules of the game. Help me not to cry for the moon. Help me neither to offer nor to welcome cheap praise. Give me always to be a good comrade. Help me to win, if I may win, but—and this, O Powers, especially—if I may not win, make me a good loser.'

When he was touring Australia with Stoddart's team in 1898, Ranji accepted a contract to write a column for the *Australian Review of Reviews*. Finally, when sued by his friend, Mansur Kachar, for non-payment of dues in 1904, Ranji decided to write another book, and called it *Cricket Guide and How to Play Cricket*, published in 1906. Kachar, a childhood friend, had lent him INR 10,000, hoping that Ranji would use his favourable relations with Curzon to advance Kachar's claims to become Raja of his state. However, Ranji did nothing to this end and Kachar finally sued him for fraud in 1904.

With Jaswantsinhji's death in 1906, Ranji once again had an opportunity to stake his claim to the throne. Of the claimants who presented their cases before the government for consideration, Lakhuba, son of Kalobha, the disinherited son of Jaswantsinhji, and Ranji were the most influential. Though Jaswantsinhji's queens claimed a right to rule, this was quickly brushed aside, making it a contest between the two strongest incumbents. Ranji had an advantage over his rival because of his cricketing prowess.

A comparative analysis of the petitions submitted to the British Resident by Ranji and Lakhuba would suggest that Lakhuba's claim to the throne was legal. In his petition, submitted to the governor and president in the Council of Bombay, Lakhuba asserted that he was the only surviving descendant of Jam Vibhaji and, hence, the rightful heir to the throne. He stressed that after the recognition of Jaswantsinhji as heir in 1884, Vibhaji had assigned to Lakhuba the status of a *'fataya'*, meaning 'cadet' or 'heir presumptive', and established him in that position through various rituals and ceremonies. Though probably stronger than Ranji's, his claims were summarily rejected and the government on 20 February 1907, announced Ranji as Jaswantsinhji's successor to the Nawanagar throne.

After becoming Jam Sahib, Ranji used cricket to further the cause of his state. By the time of his accession, his skills at the game were on the wane. However, he returned to Sussex in 1920, after World War I. He had lost an eye during the war years, making it doubly difficult for him to play as before. Rather than trying to demonstrate his cricketing skills, Ranji used his name to win concessions for his state. Harbouring an ambition of making his state a leading princely power, Ranji set about his task in England. Given its size, Nawanagar could not enjoy the status that, say, Baroda or Patiala had. Ranji capitalized on his fame as a cricketer, convincing the secretary of state for India, Lord Montague, to grant Nawanagar the status of a princely state. Subsequently, King George V's visit to Nawanagar further helped the cause. As eminent journalist and author, Mihir Bose writes, 'Ranji knew how well cricket and diplomacy could be made to work.' Even the charge against him that he did nothing for India and Indian sport should be seen as an extension of his diplomatic behavior. He did not hesitate in saying that 'Duleep [his nephew] and I are English cricketers.' Ranji could not have been more blunt. His opposition to the nationalist agenda, spearheaded by the Indian National Congress, intensified the charge.

The following narrative will demonstrate that his opposition to nationalism was driven by selfish considerations and, to that extent, the anti-nationalism was a stance projected to achieve his ambitions. He looked upon the Congress move to boycott British goods as an opportunity to boost Nawanagar trade. The anti-British campaign had had a disastrous consequence for ports like Bombay (now Mumbai), and Ranji made the most of the opportunity to improve the economic condition of his ailing state, spending a huge amount in developing the port of Bedi. On his last visit to England in 1932, Ranji publicized this economic advance, giving details of Nawanagar's profits. Addressing a meeting arranged by the Manchester Chamber of Commerce, keen to increase the volume of trade with India, he asserted: 'Over the last two or three years, we, in my state have trebled, if not quadrupled, the sale of Manchester goods because we felt that Bombay's stupidity was our opportunity.'

Again, the text of a speech delivered at the 1922 session of the League of Nations raises doubts regarding the charge that Ranji was an Anglophile unconcerned with the fortunes of his countrymen. On this occasion, he spoke against restrictions on the immigration of Indians to the colonies and criticized the empire's policy in South Africa: 'I should feel false to my fellow countrymen in India, and also to my fellow countrymen in South Africa, were I to neglect this unique opportunity of summoning to the assistance of their aspirations the spiritual power and the spiritual blessing of your sympathy. . . What is our ideal? What is our purpose? What is the very reason of our being? Let us have catholic justice and we shall have catholic peace.'

His speech provoked enormous displeasure among representatives from Australia and South Africa. He was also critical of the British government's efforts to set up a federation in India and fell out with Lord Willingdon on this issue. Using cricketing metaphors for the umpteenth time in his life he said, 'The princes of India have been very old members of Great Britain's team and they have tried their best to play with a straight bat for the empire.'

His refusal to allow Duleep to play for India, arguing that he was an English cricketer, may be explained in terms of the benefits on offer for cricketers in England. Ranji was aware that Duleep could earn a better living by playing for England. Though there was no match fee for amateurs in England, he could make money from writing on the game and receiving donations and gifts. Such opportunities were scarce in India.

Finally, Ranji did assist in the development of Indian cricket in ways that often pass unnoticed. To him goes the credit of spotting Ladha Amar Singh, an outstanding cricketer of the 1930s. He also shared cricket coaches, hired to train players of the Nawanagar team with other states, and captained the state team on many occasions. He promoted cricket in Nawanagar in an effort to attract the English monarch to his state, a strategy that proved successful.

It was only because of cricket that Ranji could earn the following eulogy:

> *O Statesmen, who devise and plot,*
> *To keep the white above the black;*
> *Who tremble when your bolt is shot*
> *Lest love and loyalty grow slack.*
> *There's not a deed of craftsmanship,*
> *There's not a thing Red tape can do,*
> *Shall knit the Hindoo to the Celt*
> *As much as this—the Cambridge Blue!*
>
> *No million acres of dispatch,*
> *No tanks of governmental ink*
> *Can force a native not to watch*
> *For days when England's star may sink.*
> *Build factories to weave the tape,*
> *Make tables for the rice and dew;*

Do all your best, and you shall miss
The binding force of Cambridge Blue!

An India gentleman today
Has staled your tortoise policy;
And thousand cheer to see him play,
A splendid batsman quick and free.
A game shall dwindle all your cares,
A clever catch and runs a few.
A Parliament may fool indeed,
But not the band of Cambridge Blue!

THE COLONIAL IPL
BOMBAY PENTANGULAR, 1892–1946

The first sign of cricket's commercial viability was evident as early as the 1920s. This was in Mumbai, and was linked to the emergence of the city as the commercial nerve centre of the country, with a concentration of capital. It was the economic potential and glamour associated with the Bombay Pentangular Tournament, the foremost cricket competition in colonial India, that made it an object of envy among rival sporting bodies, primarily the BCCI. Princely figures like the Maharajkumar of Vizianagram, who wielded great power in cricketing circles otherwise but had no place in the Mumbai tournament, soon emerged as detractors of the Pentangular. In short, the Pentangular, which was India's first professional cricket tournament of sorts, had emerged as the stage for a show of players' defiance of their erstwhile princely patrons.

Widely popular in colonial India, the Pentangular was controlled by the communal gymkhanas in Mumbai. It had its origins in the Presidency matches of the 1890s, initially played between the Europeans and Parsis but which grew over time to become the Pentangular, with the inclusion of the Hindus in 1907, the Muslims in 1912 and the 'Rest'—comprising mainly Christians and Anglo-Indians—in 1937. Despite considerable opposition, the tournament continued into the 1940s, before it was abolished in January 1946.

The eventual discontinuance, most argue, was the outcome of a prolonged agitation against the communal organization of the tournament. However, beneath this politically correct rhetoric may be detected the play of complex politico-economic forces.

Anything 'national', it is assumed in the Indian context, should be free of the vices of communalism. The communal organization of the game in Mumbai, it followed, was an obstacle in the path of an emerging secular nation. This assumption has given birth to the view that the Pentangular was abolished because its communal team structure was an anathema, given the evolving shape of Indian nationhood.

I would, however, argue that much more than communal antagonism, it was the diverse forces sculpting Mumbai society in the 1930s and 1940s that influenced the course of the game. It is recorded that in 1924, when the Muslims won the Pentangular (then the Quadrangular), the Hindus joined them in their victory celebrations. This was a period when relations between the two communities were at a real low in the aftermath of the failure of the joint Non-Cooperation/Khilafat agitation. Muslim representation in the Indian National Congress had reached dismal proportions after Gandhi called off the Non-Cooperation Movement in 1922, with severe communal discord culminating in riots and arson. Against this backdrop, Mohammed Ali Jinnah praised the brotherly feeling between the two communities on the sporting field of the Pentangular.

Things did not change in the next two decades. Assess the eyewitness account of the 1944 Pentangular by Vasant Raiji. The final of the 1944 tournament was a closely contested match between the Hindus and the Muslims, which the Muslims won with less than five minutes to spare: 'Unprecedented scenes of jubilation followed.

Ibrahim, the hero and architect of the Muslim victory [he had carried his bat for 137] was chaired by the and carried shoulder high all the way to the pavilion. Never before had the Brabourne Stadium witnessed a match so thrilling and exciting as this. Communalism was nowhere in evidence and everyone, including the Hindus, cheered the Muslim team at the end of the match. Merchant, the Hindu captain, went to the Muslim dressing room and hugged Mushtaq Ali warmly with the words, "Well played Muslims, you deserved to win. It would have been a sad day for cricket if you had lost."

Much more than clashes between imperialism and nationalism, between communalism and secularism, cricket has to be understood in terms of the practices of everyday life in colonial Indian society. Newly structured hours of work with increased leisure opportunities for workers, the emergence of the salaried middle-class professionals with a conscious investment in leisure, and the growth of a commercial culture shaped the fortunes of Indian cricket in the 1930s and 1940s.

That the Pentangular was a pivotal aspect of Mumbai life in the 1930s and 1940s is evident from the extensive coverage it received in contemporary publications. From the 1930s, coverage was mostly negative with protests having started in earnest against the communal organization of cricket. Somewhat strangely, relentless criticism was directed exclusively towards the Pentangular, ignoring other similarly structured tournaments in Mumbai city itself, in the rest of the province, and indeed, in the rest of India. It may be mentioned here that the popularity of the Pentangular and its commercial success had spawned a series of tournaments along similar lines from the second decade of the twentieth century. The Sind Quadrangular, later renamed the Karachi Pentangular, had started in 1916; a Central Provinces Pentangular had started in the 1920s; a Triangular had started in Delhi in 1937; in Lahore, too, there was a similar communal competition.

The singling out of the Pentangular makes it clear that reasons for the protests against the tournament has to be understood with reference to the changing political economy of Mumbai.

It was following the founding of the BCCI in 1928 and institution of the Ranji Trophy in 1934—under the aegis of the BCCI—that the movement against the Pentangular gathered momentum. Echoing the sentiments of the anti-Pentangular movement, the *Bombay Chronicle* of 27 November 1935 declared: 'Communal tournaments were, perhaps, necessary at a certain stage in the history of Indian cricket. Scarcely conducive to the growth of healthy nationalism, it is time they were given a decent burial.' J.C. Maitra, the paper's sports editor, consistently wrote in support of the Ranji Trophy and against the continuation of the Pentangular. J.M. Ganguly, a well-known sports journalist, propounded an identical view in his article 'Quadrangular Cricket: A plea for its abolition': 'When the Quadrangular matches were conceived and started times were different; the sports atmosphere was clear and unclouded by communal and sectarian feelings. . . Victory in the Quadrangular was not taken as a communal victory, but merely as the result of a better performance by the winning side, and which did not leave any rancour or mean jealousy. . . Those happy days are now gone, thanks to those self-seeking leaders who want to gain their ends by raking up communal fanaticism, and who would not rest on their oars after doing all the mischief they could in the political sphere but would go out in search of new fields and pastures green. Even the sacred field of sport they would not leave unmolested.'

Berry Sarbadhikary argued no differently: 'Communal cricket must be buried. That is as things stand today. There might not have been, at the outset, anything "communal" about communal cricket in the accepted sense of the word as Anthony S. De Mello submitted when the controversy had been raging fiercely and fully a few years ago. There may not be anything communal about it even today so far as the players and spectators are concerned as has been laboriously claimed with the aid of a whole heap of evidence. But the fact remains that once the controversy gathered the fierceness and the momentum it did, once communal cricket was dissected and decried or patched up and praised by politicians or cricketers, by the press and the public in the manner it was done, communal cricket became communal straightaway. Only communal cricket is basically wrong and although synonymous with the cream of Indian cricket once, it has now outlived its usefulness, to say nothing of its being not indispensable to Indian cricket any more.'

While these men come across as conscientious objectors, others like the Maharajkumar of Vizianagram 'Vizzy' and the Maharaja of Patiala, influential members of the BCCI and state cricket associations, used similar rhetoric to conceal ulterior motives.

The Heat Is On

The anti-Pentangular movement intensified with Mahatma Gandhi's pronouncement against the tournament on 7 December 1940. Close scrutiny reveals that the Mahatma's verdict had been selectively publicized by the opposing lobby to suit its ends. The text of the Mahatma's message has hardly ever been referred to in its entirety. On being met by a select delegation of the Hindu Gymkhana at Wardha, Gandhi had remarked: 'Numerous enquiries have been made as to my opinion on the proposed Pentangular cricket match in Bombay advertised to be played on the 14th. I have just been made aware of the movement to stop the match. I understand this as a mark of grief over the arrests and imprisonments of the satyagrahis, more especially the recent arrest of leaders.'

He went on to add: 'I would discountenance such amusements at a time when the whole of the thinking world should be in mourning over a war that is threatening the stable life of Europe and its civilisation and which bids to overwhelm Asia. . . And holding this view I naturally welcome the movement for stopping the forthcoming match from the narrow standpoint I have mentioned above.'

It was only after this statement that he went on to condemn the communal organization of the tournament, a denunciation given much publicity in the contemporary press. Even the headline in the *Bombay Chronicle*, reporting the Mahatma's stand, read: 'No Festival When World in Mourning'. It was a sub-heading that declared, 'Communal Code in Sport Condemned.'

Yet there was no waning of interest in the Pentangular matches. Confirming this, *The Times of India* reported the day after Gandhi's statement: 'With Bombay's great annual cricket festival only a few days ahead, the Pentangular fever is at its height, a height that has rarely been attained before. Large crowds watched all the three trial matches played over the weekend. . . Although rumours had been set afoot that there would be a serious attempt made by a large procession of students to compel the authorities to abandon the trial more than 500 enthusiasts gathered on Saturday afternoon for the start, and the number was almost doubled the next day.'

When a resolution was tabled at the Hindu Gymkhana, calling for a withdrawal from the tournament, it had the support of only 70 members of the Gymkhana. The total membership of the Gymkhana stood at 900. This led the sports correspondent of *The Times of India* to declare: 'There is a strong Hindu feeling, not only in the Gymkhana but in the city as well, in favour of the Pentangular being held as already arranged. I shall be extremely surprised if the redoubtable champions are not at the Brabourne Stadium on the morn of December 17 to begin their defence of an honour.'

Though this resolution was eventually passed by a small margin of 37 votes (280–243), particularly as a mark of regard for Gandhi, it generated serious ill-feeling among the members. A prominent member of the Gymkhana, who had supported the resolution, said later that the managing committee had been unwise in seeking Gandhi's opinion, but once it had done so it was duty bound to abide by it.

Gandhi's stand, too, seemed to lack consistency. His pronouncement against the Pentangular contradicted the avowed ideal of keeping sport away from political interference. His contention that amusements should be stopped at a critical juncture (in this case, World War II) reflected a clear 'politicization of sport', and was criticized in a series of letters to the editor of *The Times of India*. One such letter went as far as to denounce Gandhi for hindering democracy and the law and order situation: 'The Mahatma's argument against the continuity of the Pentangular cricket tournament in effect that it should be dropped because it is a form of amusement, and that too while a blood bath is going on, makes strange reading. Indeed one is tempted to ask whether it is fair on Mr Gandhi's part to embarrass and put obstacles in the way of democracies in general, and law and order in this country in particular, while this blood bath is going on, and to incite people to lawlessness and civil disobedience. I appeal to sportsmen and particularly to the Hindu players who are unlikely [after Gandhi's announcement] to be selected for the Pentangular to rise to the occasion by proving that political considerations do not stand in the way of sport.'

Gandhi's stand provoked considerable opposition from the small Hindu cricket clubs of Mumbai. Many of these clubs subsisted on the profits accrued from the Pentangular. They had already invested their meagre capital in securing seats at the Brabourne Stadium, the venue for the tournament. In the event of the withdrawal of the Hindus from the competition, interest was expected to wane to such an extent as to make the sale of tickets impossible. This would ruin the clubs. It would also, it was argued, be unfair in view of the wholehearted support accorded by the Hindus and Hindu clubs in Mumbai and the mofussil to the Hindu Gymkhana in times of crisis. These clubs emphasized that the Hindu Gymkhana could not overlook that it was a Hindu representative XI that was expected to participate in the Pentangular—and not a Hindu Gymkhana team. A decision that was expected to affect thousands of Hindus, it was agreed, could not be taken by just the 900 members of the Gymkhana. This body of opinion expressed surprise at the decision to consult Gandhi: 'We respect Mr Gandhi's opinion in politics as being that of a great statesman and patriot, but when he offers it in connection with cricket and the Pentangular, about which he himself pleads ignorance, we feel he has no local standing.'

A meeting convened by the Hindu cricket clubs adopted a series of resolutions supporting the Pentangular. The primary factor behind this support was the tournament's commercial potential: 'This meeting of the Bombay Hindu Cricket Clubs is of the opinion that the Hindus should take part in the ensuing Pentangular tournament, as the non-participation of the Hindus in this year's tournament will lead to serious financial loss to the Hindu cricket clubs in particular and the Hindu public in general.

'In the event of the P.J. Hindu Gymkhana deciding not to participate in this years [sic] Pentangular, this meeting requests the Bombay Cricket Association to reconsider the minimum charges fixed for the sale of tickets, and further requests the Gymkhana to fix its rates in consultation with the representatives of this Union.'

Within a couple of weeks of Gandhi's pronouncement against the Pentangular, the Maharajkumar of Vizianagram declared, 'Mahatma Gandhi has expressed unequivocally on communal cricket. He gave it as his considered opinion that communalism carried into the domain of sport is no happy augury for human growth. It is high time that we gave Pentangular cricket the burial it always deserved.' He was supported by the Jam of Nawanagar and the Maharaja of Patiala, who announced that no Nawanagar or Patiala player would be available for any match conducted on communal lines. Cricketers employed by these princes, it was expected, would not defy their orders. Following the princes, P. Subbaraon, the BCCI president, declared: 'I did not want to say anything about the Pentangular though the matter was referred to me as I felt that it might be said that I took this opportunity to achieve what I have in mind, but now that Mahatmaji has spoken, I feel free to say that the authorities will be doing the right thing if they abandon communal cricket.'

That such lobbying had a covert agenda was attested to by the following statement by K.F. Nariman: 'There was no opposition to this tournament from the official Congress; on the contrary, the Secretary of the BPCC had actually issued a statement on behalf of the organization, not to boycott the game, but some individual Congressmen desired artificial political demonstration, because they thought the natural popular enthusiasm was lacking, and hence, in spite of Gandhiji's aversion to such engineered demonstration, the annual fixture was sacrificed, under a false screen of communalism and nationalism.'

Significantly, it was around this time that the Congress government in Mumbai converted swimming baths in the city into communal ones, with separate bathing times for Hindus, Muslims and Parsis. The absence of protest against this measure makes it evident that the motives of the Pentangular's opponents, though couched in the politically correct idiom of secularism, were rooted in other considerations.

Interestingly, the cricketers remained vociferous supporters of the Pentangular. In November 1940, Wazir Ali, the captain of the Muslim team, issued a press statement asserting 'the tournament is not in the least anti-national and will and must go on in the interests of Indian cricket.' The next year, C.K. Nayudu issued the following statement against the pronouncements of the Maharajkumar of Vizianagram and the Maharaja of Patiala: 'There is no valid reason why the Pentangular tournament in Bombay should be stopped. On the contrary it is absolutely essential that it should be run in its present form if we do not want to see the funeral of Indian cricket.' Following Nayudu, Mushtaq Ali came out in support of the Pentangular: 'When politics are introduced into sport, which should never be the case, communal feelings are aroused. It is not the game played by persons of different communities, which give rise to such feelings. As for the Pentangular it has always promoted a very healthy spirit of rivalry and inculcated sporting spirit among players and the public. Ripples and roars of genuine applause have greeted good performances without distinction.' Vijay Merchant, Vijay Hazare and C.S. Nayudu, all cricketers of repute, expressed similar views.

The anti-Pentangular movement, therefore, emerged as the arena of contest between the players and their princely patrons. At a time when the political influence of the princes was on the wane, their efforts to retain social ascendancy led them to make desperate attempts to reinforce their control over sport. The strong arm of the Maharajas was palpable in the 1936 tour of England, when the best player, Lala Amarnath, was forced to return on grounds of 'indiscipline'. On the same tour, Shute Banerjee of Bengal was deprived of a Test place for defying an order of the captain, Vizzy, and refusing to abuse C.K. Nayudu at the breakfast table. Baqa Jilani, who carried out the order, earned himself a maiden Test cap.

The commercial potential of the Pentangular escalated tensions amongst the communal Gymkhanas that organized it. During the 1937 tournament, there was severe disagreement over the allocation of seats in the Brabourne Stadium, the new venue. The CCI, owners of the Brabourne Stadium, had allotted an equal number of seats to all the participating gymkhanas. This provoked opposition from the Hindu Gymkhana, which, with a membership much larger than its Muslim, Parsi and Catholic counterparts, preferred an allocation on the basis of the membership strength of each gymkhana. A larger share of seats would bring a larger share of the gate receipts. The distribution of population in contemporary Mumbai would make the Hindu stand appear logical. Hindus made up 68 per cent of the city; Muslims came next with 18 per cent. As the CCI and the other gymkhanas did not accede to this demand, the Hindus decided not to field a team in the competition in 1937.

The controversy over radio commentary was also indicative of just how much of a cash kitty the Pentangular was. Radio commentary from the Pentangular was banned and replaced by commentary of the less popular Ranji Trophy. In response, the All India Radio merchants came up with the following statement: 'The trade views this development with deepest concern. The trade is in the best position to judge the great interest taken all over India in these running commentaries of Bombay's famous cricket festival and views with apprehension a move that gravely affects its business.'

They urged a review: 'There is still ample time to arrange for the famous broadcasts and thus make available to the public of India the commentaries that are the most looked forward to radio events of the year by every class, community or creed.'

Even the *Bombay Chronicle*, arguably the most vocal detractor of the communal Pentangular, was unable to discount its mass appeal. While branding those who attended the Pentangular as alcoholics—they were apparently drawn to it as drunkards to a pub—the *Chronicle* itself failed to boycott the tournament. On 23 December 1940, when the anti-Pentangular movement was gathering momentum, the *Chronicle* reported Pentangular matches on the front page under the heading 'Rest to Meet Muslims in Final'. The Ranji Trophy, which was also being played in the city, was relegated to the sports page. In fact, protests against the 1943 Pentangular came to be tempered because part of the profits of that year's tournament was to be donated for relief operations in famine-ridden Bengal. Pushed onto the backfoot, the *Bombay Chronicle* reported, 'In view of this decision many of the opponents of the past have decided to allow the tournament as a necessary evil.'

The privileges enjoyed by the Bombay Cricket Association

(BCA) as organizers of the most popular cricket tournament in the country made it the object of envy of competing interests across India. Hostility towards Mumbai had become stronger after the establishment of the BCCI in 1928. The Board, cash-strapped since inception, soon realized where the real power lay. The Ranji Trophy, organized on a provincial basis from 1934, was not half as popular as the Pentangular. In its crusade against the Pentangular, the Board had the support of most other cricket associations of the country, which resented the Mumbai hegemony.

During the Pentangular matches, the Brabourne Stadium was often packed to capacity, while the 1935 Ranji Trophy final in Mumbai attracted a mere 1,000 spectators a day. In 1944, the number increased to 4,000, still way behind the 25,000 attendances at the Pentangular. This, it was argued by the Board and its allies, was reflective of an unhealthy attitude to the game; Mumbai seemed to prefer cricket played on sectarian lines. In comparison, spectators in less sophisticated centres, it was said, had learnt to enjoy cricket even in the absence of the communal influence. In his book *Indian Cricket Uncovered*, Berry Sarbadhikary complained: 'If Bombay and Madras were to play a championship match in Calcutta today, a capacity crowd would, I know, attend it. Madras, I believe, would do equally well for a Bombay and Bengal encounter at Madras. But not so in the home of Indian cricket! That is the pity.'

This faction also held that though the economic stability of the Pentangular owed much to the patronage of Mumbai's citizens, there were other factors that were often overlooked. It was argued the 'large body of headliners from outside Bombay have provided the bill of fare,' implying the popularity of the Mumbai tournament owed much to its all-India character. If leading cricketers from around the country, it was said, refused to take part in the Pentangular, public support for it would surely dwindle—the 'days were over when Bombay alone could stage the show'. Sarbadhikary summed up these views saying: 'The financial consideration has always played an important part in cricket. If Bombay could raise all the money from her domestic cricket—as, for instance, Calcutta could do from her football—and keep it to herself other centres would have nothing to say. But when the contribution of outsiders to the success of the show is deemed to be not inconsiderable, those centres to which the outsiders belong might very well claim to have some interest in the net proceeds for the general well being of the game everywhere and not for cricket in Bombay alone and, least of all, for communal cricket. Bombay should take into account the fact that, given the scope and the time, other centres can stage equally successful shows annually both from the points of view of cricket and money and are only too keen to have a shot.'

At the same time, it was alleged that Mumbai was failing in its duties as the richest member of the Board in that it ought to have helped the Board much more than it usually did. After the Mumbai–Holkar final for the Ranji Trophy at Mumbai in 1945, the host centre presented the Board a cheque of INR 1,500 only, amounting to 15 per cent of the net profits. For the indigent Board, charged with the duty of developing and promoting the game in the entire country, this was a meagre sum. It was also alleged that Mumbai had done little to promote the game in other parts of Western India. For example, resentment was high in Pune. It was felt that Mumbai had employed and exploited its best players—like Deodhar and S.S. Joshi—but had never given Pune anything in return.

Climax

The opposition to Mumbai reached a climax when the United Provinces Cricket Association passed the following resolution in 1942: 'It is felt on all hands that the time has come when concerted action should be taken to rid the country of the canker of communal cricket as it tends to retard unity and good fellowship in the country.

Is it not deplorable for Hindus to play against their Muslim brethren and vice versa? The cream of Indian cricketers participate in the Pentangular and these players belong to the various provinces which are affiliated to the Board of Control as the governing body. The Board, as constituted with these affiliating units, should come to a decision by which a player who participates in communal cricket shall not, for the rest of his cricketing career, be eligible to play for his own province or his country in any official match that may be staged or any tournament that is run under the auspices of the Provincial Association concerned or the Board.'

This resolution marked the beginning of a concerted campaign against the Pentangular. Eventually it led to the government threatening to intervene if the Pentangular committee continued with the tournament. The Board, which had favourable relations with the government, ensured that the protests against the Pentangular had official sanction. None of this, however, had any impact on the popularity of the Pentangular evident from the following extract from a report published in *The Times of India*: 'There appears to be no doubt as to the popularity of this season's cricket festival. Youthful picketers resumed their efforts to dissuade enthusiasts from entering the Brabourne stadium, but they were good humouredly ignored and an even bigger crowd than on the previous morning greeted the rival teams on the commencement of play, a crowd steadily increasing until it was somewhat in the vicinity of the 20,000 mark during the afternoon.'

Drawing on this popularity, Sir Homi Mody, presiding over the tenth annual general meeting of the CCI in 1944, strongly criticized the opposing lobby: 'We have a set of critics in Bombay who have no eyes or ears for the many communal institutions, which flourish in our midst and the many communal fixtures that are staged throughout the country. The gaze of these people is fixed upon the Pentangular and they return again and again to attack it. The sporting public of Bombay has given a most convincing and resounding answer to their charge that the Pentangular breeds communalism and radical ill feeling. Never in the whole history of cricket in this country have such enormous and enthusiastic crowds been seen.'

Unable to contend with the growing popularity of the tournament, the Board convened an extraordinary general meeting in January 1942 to obtain the support of cricket associations countrywide for banning the Pentangular. At the general meeting the following resolution was tabled: 'The Board considers that time has come when concerted action should be taken to rid the country of the canker of communal cricket as it tends to retard unity of good fellowship in the country, and as the first step in that direction it views with strong disfavour any tournament or match being played on communal lines and calls upon its affiliated associations to co-operate in this respect and take all necessary steps to stop such matches and tournaments.'

This resolution understandably provoked serious opposition from the representative of the BCA, H.N. Contractor. He retorted that the Pentangular, organized by the communal gymkhanas under the aegis of the BCA, was an autonomous tournament and the Board had no power to interfere with its internal management. He asserted that the guiding principles of the Board precluded it from tampering with the conduct of any tournament run independently, especially one that was in existence long before the Board was formed. Following Contractor's response, Pankaj Gupta, representing the interests of the Board, moved an amendment to the effect that the BCCI, on a matter of principle and in the larger interests of the country, resented any tournament/cricket match run on communal lines. The Board resolved to appoint a sub-committee to formulate schemes for an alternate tournament, if necessary.

At this Contractor again expressed doubt as to whether the Board had the authority to interfere in the activities of a provincial association, in whatever capacity that may be. He went on to threaten that if the Board enforced the resolution, it would lead to a parting of ways between the Board and the BCA. This clearly demonstrated the confidence of the BCA, in no way dependent on the Board for its well-being. Contradicting the main tenet of the resolution that communal cricket generated communal antagonism, Contractor narrated his experience of the 1936 Quadrangular. This tournament was played at a time when Mumbai was experiencing bitter communal riots. Despite such strife the Pentangular (then Quadrangular) did not cause a single unpleasant incident. On the contrary, Contractor claimed, the tournament had 'ameliorated the estranged feelings by smoothing the hot atmosphere and had actually ended the serious riots.' A.A. Jasdenvala and H.D. Kanga followed Contractor. Both of them complained of the attitude of some of the princes towards the Pentangular. These princes had banned players of their states, or those employed by them, from participating in the Pentangular. Kanga argued Bombay would not tolerate this.

In the face of opposition, Dr Subbaraon, the Board president, announced his decision to resign if the resolution was not passed. He justified the actions of the princes in the larger national interest. A rift between the Board and the BCA loomed large, and Pankaj Gupta appealed to the BCA not to oppose the Board. The representatives of the BCA, however, remained adamant. Failing to impose its decision on the BCA, the Board finally decided to withdraw the resolution and appoint a select committee to deliberate on the question of communal cricket. After much deliberation, the committee asserted at the next meeting of the Board, on 15 March 1942, that the controlling body was empowered to take any step deemed necessary to discontinue the holding of any tournament by any member association within its jurisdiction. It asked the member associations responsible for the management of communal tournaments to immediately discontinue these. At the same time, fearing the BCA might decide to break away from the Board, the committee was forced to make concessions, somewhat contradicting itself in the process: 'The structure of Bombay and Sind cricket being on communal lines, this sub-committee further considers that relaxation of the principle set forth above may be made in case of Bombay, Sind or any other association in order to follow the principle that there should be no interference normally in the internal administration of any member association, provided the tournament concerned is confined to players in the area of the association concerned on the lines of the rules of the Sind Pentangular.'

All concessions notwithstanding, Contractor continued to express dissent, declaring that the more the Board tried to legislate on matters beyond its jurisdiction and interfere in the internal affairs of a provincial affiliate, the more difficult would it become for the Board to retain its position as the apex body. The BCA, he asserted, had never intervened in the affairs of the communal gymkhanas that controlled the running of the Pentangular. Finally, he said: 'It is ridiculous to enunciate the principle that communal cricket is likely to lead to unhealthy communal rivalry, and in the same breath to allow Bombay, Sind or other associations to run communal tournaments, provided the players participating therein are local players. The profound fears of the committee come into play when players are imported. Conveniently forgetting the principle on which it lays so much importance, the committee establishes an "exception" to its principle and makes a laughing stock of itself. Is this playing "cricket" with Bombay?'

The conflict between the Board and the BCA did not abate, eventually leading to Mumbai's withdrawal from the National Championship in November 1942. This provoked a hostile reaction in many quarters because most of the other associations, less favourably endowed than Mumbai, had consented to participate. As reported by *The Times of India*, Mumbai's refusal to participate stemmed from the BCA's fear of financial loss. Even so, the decision had the support of the players. Vijay Merchant, captain of the Mumbai team, was the chief advocate of the move to stay away from the national championships, a stand that may have led to his suspension by the Board.

It is possible to read into this stance an attempt by the players to challenge the Board. That they were largely successful is established by the following statement by K.S. Ranga Rao, the BCCI secretary: 'The recommendations of the Bombay Cricket Association to abandon the Ranji Trophy for this year has been circulated to all associations for their views and a majority of them have expressed themselves in favour of holding the all India championships as usual.

'It is needless for the Board to stress how important the Ranji Trophy is for the furtherance of cricket in India, in view of its all India character. I am directed by the President of the Board to request such associations as have expressed their inability to participate in this year's championships to reconsider their decision and to extend their full co-operation and support as hitherto in the successful conduct of the championships.'

The growing ill-will between cricketers continued with Merchant accusing the president, Subbaraon, of trying to influence the outcome of the 1945 Ranji Trophy. He charged the Board president with conspiring against the Holkar side. Merchant expressed his disapproval of the Board president speaking to the umpires and conveying his displeasure over a number of decisions that had adversely affected Holkar (Bombay [now Mumbai], however, eventually won the match by 374 runs). In retaliation, the Board planned disciplinary action against Merchant, eventually rendered impossible for want of adequate evidence.

The anti-Pentangular movement also brought into focus the factionalism within the Board: A.S. De Mello, the first secretary of the Board, was vocal in his support of the Pentangular. From the early 1940s, there was growing ill feeling between De Mello and the Bengal lobby led by Pankaj Gupta, eventually leading to

De Mello's ouster from the Board in 1951. Since Gupta was an ardent detractor of the Pentangular, De Mello supported it, trying to enlist the support of the BCA by declaring, 'There is nothing communal (in the sense the word is used in India) about the Pentangular. It has for 25 years given India thrilling and top class cricket played in a very healthy spirit of competition.' De Mello appealed to the Board and patrons of cricket in India not to interfere with the Pentangular. If stopped, he argued, it would lead to an eclipse of Indian cricket. He declared that much money was required for the development of cricket in India and as the Pentangular provided this it was in the best interests of Indian cricket to allow it to continue and prosper. This stand, it needs to be mentioned, caused him much discomfort after he took over as Board president in 1946.

As emphasized from the start, the anti-Pentangular movement demonstrates the influence of vested politico-economic motives behind the projected ideal of secularism. Empty stands at the Ranji Trophy matches, contrasting starkly with attendances at the Pentangular, made the Board, patrons of the former, envious of the communal gymkhanas and the BCA. The BCCI and the princely patrons did their utmost to curb the mass appeal of the Pentangular. Yet their attempts failed to achieve their ends—as may be gleaned from the disappointment expressed over the lack of public support for the Ranji Trophy even after the Pentangular was stopped in January 1946.

Growing professionalism in sport, I would like to suggest, led to the forging of an unnatural alliance between the princely and nationalist lobbies. The analysis of the anti-Pentangular movement, proof enough of commercial potential of cricket and its role as a ladder for social mobility in early twentieth century India, also challenges the hypothesis that commercialization of cricket was a 1970s phenomenon. Signs of economic viability were visible as early as the 1930s and only increased manifold from the 1970s and 1980s onwards.

THE DEBUT YEARS AND THE
POLITICAL BACKSTAGE

India's international debut at Lord's on 25 June 1932 was in every way sensational. In front of a 24,000-strong crowd at cricket's Mecca, India had England reduced to 19/3 in the first hour of play, thanks to some excellent bowling and fielding. It was a clear statement that the colony was here to compete. The performance, which came as a surprise to many, was a testimony to the progress of the game in India and was indicative of the future of cricket in the country. Though the English won convincingly in the end, the Indians had done enough to merit a return visit from the MCC a year later, the first official Test tour on Indian soil.

If this was the state of affairs on the field, the turn of events backstage was no less fascinating. It was, quite simply, sensational stuff, packed with intrigue and rivalry, pride and guile, twists and turns, and a dramatic finale culminating in C.K. Nayudu going out to toss with Douglas Jardine at Lord's.

The two men who dominated the backstage were the Maharaja of Patiala and the Maharajkumar of Vizianagram, the two foremost patrons of the game in India in the 1930s. While neither was a member of the touring party that actually played at Lord's, they dominated the backstage and continued to do so for the next four years; a rivalry that culminated with the sending back of Lala Amarnath in 1936 on charges of indiscipline during India's second tour of England. This rivalry also resulted in the birth of the Ranji Trophy in 1934 and ended up doing much for the progress of the game in India.

By the early 1930s, the Maharaja of Patiala was among the most powerful princes in India. He controlled the newly formed BCCI, donated huge sums towards the building of the CCI in Mumbai and was the vice-patron of the Board, second only to Lord Willingdon, patron by virtue of being the viceroy. Patiala employed many senior cricketers and had supported Ranjitsinhji in times of financial crisis. However, it was beginning to become clear by the early 1930s that the Maharaja was falling out of favour with Willingdon, as a result of his involvement in numerous sex scandals. The situation was ripe for the emergence of a new power player in Indian cricket.

The challenge came in the form of the Maharajkumar of Vizianagram, the younger son of a ruler of a principality in modern Andhra Pradesh who had left his home in the south to settle in Benaras. He rose to prominence in 1930, by organizing a cricket tour to Ceylon and parts of India.

The political situation in India in 1930 was stormy. Mahatma Gandhi had announced the Civil Disobedience Movement, which resulted in the cancellation of the proposed MCC tour. Vizianagram (Vizzy to the world) capitalized on this opportunity by forming a team to tour parts of India and Ceylon. This team included, among others, Jack Hobbs and Herbert Sutcliffe, two legends of English cricket. The Indian stars were C.K. Nayudu, S. Mushtaq Ali and D.B. Deodhar. This tour catapulted Vizzy into a position of power, a position only strengthened by the praise showered on him by Sutcliffe. Commenting on the tour in the *Daily Express*, Sutcliffe declared, 'The Maharajkumar is a candidate for the captaincy of the Indian team to tour England, and if he is fortunate enough to be appointed, he will no doubt give an excellent account of himself for he has had a thorough grounding in the finer points of the game, and is a most capable leader.'

Vizzy used this newfound success to project himself as a rival to the Maharaja of Patiala and offered to sponsor India's tour to England in 1932. This is evident from the following report published in *The Times of India*: 'Nawab Liaqat Ali Khan, the retiring president of the Cricket Control Board interviewed by a press representative at Delhi station en route to Mumbai for the Round Table Conference made the following statement: The emergency meeting of the All India Cricket Board was hurriedly convened at Simla in view of his departure last week to consider three important questions: 1. Appointment of Officers, 2. The proposed tour to England, 3. The visit of the Ceylon team to India next winter.

'He was glad to say that he was in receipt of an offer to contribute rupees 50,000 from the Maharaj Kumar (of Vizianagram), which was welcomed by the Board. Mr De Mello, who was also present, said he had wired the Maharaj Kumar to get to Delhi as early as possible to meet the Board (officials) to discuss financial matters.'

Vizzy duly arrived in Delhi and after the meeting with BCCI officials, the following report was published in *The Times of India*: 'An important statement made after the meeting of the emergency committee held in Delhi on Friday was that all anxiety regarding the financial side of the tour had vanished as a result of the generosity of the Maharajkumar of Vizianagram who had written a letter to the Board marking a donation of rupees 50,000 to the Board of which 40,000 must be earmarked for the tour to England next year. The position now is that the Vizianagram donation should ensure a surplus for the benefit of Indian cricket.'

The correspondent concluded, saying, 'I understand the

Maharajkumar of Vizianagram will captain the Indian team [to England] next year.'

Soon after this meeting, Vizzy met Willingdon to discuss arrangements for the forthcoming English tour, beginning on 27 November 1931. This meeting was reported widely in the national press: 'The Maharajkumar of Vizianagram who is here in connection with the meeting of the Board of Control interviewed and discussed with the Viceroy the proposed tour of the Indian cricket XI to England. His Excellency, it is understood, evinced keen interest in Indian cricket, especially in regards to the forthcoming visit of an Indian XI to England next year.'

The struggle for supremacy between Vizzy and Patiala was thus out in the open before the 1932 tour of England. With Vizzy having won the first round, the Maharaja of Patiala came back to win the second by agreeing to sponsor the trials of the touring party. In the annual general meeting of the Board in November 1931, Patiala announced his intention to sponsor the trials, agreeing alongside to take care of the finances of the touring party for a whole month. This offer was too tempting for the financially impoverished Board to refuse, allowing the Maharaja to reinforce his supremacy over Indian cricket.

That both princes were vying for the captaincy of the touring team became apparent when cricketers from around the country started taking sides on the issue. In a letter addressed to the editor of *The Times of India*, an Indian cricketer of the past asserted: 'In the first place there was a report in *The Statesman* of Delhi some days ago that the Nawab of Pataudi had intimated his willingness to forego his qualification for Worcestershire county if he was selected to play for India. Of his selection of course, there is no doubt. Even with that case, with all due respect to the Nawab, he is far from an ideal skipper for the Indian team, as he would be lacking the necessary knowledge of the abilities of the men under his command, a necessity with which your correspondent agrees. In my opinion, the Maharaj Kumar of Vizianagram is obviously the best choice, and I put the Nawab of Pataudi, with his extensive knowledge of the conditions in England, as the second in charge.'

Within a couple of days of the publication of this letter, M.E. Pavri, the Parsi stalwart, wrote another letter to the editor: 'Sir, I quite agree with the "Indian Cricketer" from Karachi who had written a letter in *The Times of India* except about the captaincy. I beg to differ from him entirely on this question about appointing the Maharajkumar of Vizianagram in preference to the Nawab of Pataudi, who with his vast experience of English cricket conditions and with the opportunity that he will get of playing with the members of the team and so getting to know them during the trial matches and practice games, would be the ideal captain in the absence of Prince Duleepsinhji. The great sporting enthusiast, the Maharaja of Patiala, however, would be the most appropriate skipper, if His Highness can make up his mind to play all the matches in England.'

It was the hosting of the trials between 23 and 29 January 1932 that tilted the issue in Patiala's favour and he was appointed captain of the touring party on 4 February 1932. That this was the most likely outcome had already been reported in *The Times of India*: 'A popular item of discussion in cricket circles across the country is the official announcement of the selection, which takes place in the evening of February 4. The selection committee will meet at Montgomery Hall at 3.30 p.m. tomorrow and submit their recommendation to the Board of Control who will then select a captain, a vice-captain and a deputy vice-captain. Rumours are that the Maharaja of Patiala will skipper the All India side and the two other places are being filled by the Maharajkumar of Vizianagram and K.S. Ghanshyamsinhji, though their respective roles are not known.'

Patiala's election evoked mixed responses in the media. This is borne out by the publication of two contrasting reports in *The Times of India* of 6 February 1932. The first described the selection of the Maharaja of Patiala as a 'tribute to His Highness' long and devoted service to the cause of Indian cricket. The second, by contrast, declared, 'The selection of the Maharaja of Patiala as captain of the team is, however, a strange nomination, as it can hardly be claimed that he merits a place in the team on form alone. Neither can his tactical knowledge be considered very high.' It went on to suggest, 'It is very likely that he will be a non-playing captain and that Prince Ghanshyamsinhji will be skipper on the field itself.' The report concluded by saying, 'His Highness, the Maharaja of Patiala will undoubtedly be in his element in the social side of the tour and this is probably the reason for his official nomination as captain.'

Vizzy, the defeated challenger, was given the subordinate position of deputy vice-captain. He withdrew from the tour citing personal reasons and spent his time cozying up to Lord Willingdon. Saying that he was 'broken-hearted', Vizzy issued the following statement: 'I have just sent a letter to the President of the Board of Control for Cricket in India and I can hardly express how broken-hearted I am, but I am making this immense sacrifice for the future of cricket in India, for which I worked so hard for the past two years, and shall continue to do so in the future. The Board of Control has indeed bestowed on me a very great honour by appointing me Deputy Vice-Captain of the team that is to tour England next summer. I not only regret, but am very disappointed that I shall not be able to undertake this tour.

'I have not been well for the greater part of the current cricket season, and this has been responsible for my very bad form throughout and loving the game of cricket as I do, I keenly feel that I shall not be able to do justice to your selection and to the team if my present form continues and I fear that this will be so with my confidence so shaken after my recent performances.'

In the wake of Vizzy's statement, the Maharaja of Patiala

announced his decision to not tour. As *The Times of India* reported on 3 March 1932: 'The Board of Control for Cricket in India have now received confirmation from His Highness the Maharaja of Patiala that he much regrets his inability to accept the captaincy of the cricket team to tour England this summer as he finds that it will not be possible for him to get away.' Finally, the Maharaja of Porbandar was appointed captain of the touring team on 15 March 1932. Vizzy greeted his appointment with the following words: 'On the eve of my departure to Europe, I feel I must offer my felicitations to the Indian team under the Maharaja of Porbandar sailing early next month. I have had the hand in the formation of the side and I am proud to say that it constitutes the core and kernel of cricket talent in India. I shall watch its career in the West with deepest interest. I wish them the very best of success, and hope that they will prove [to be] true representatives of India, both on the field and away from it.'

Perhaps the worst player of the touring party, Porbandar wisely decided to leave the captaincy to Nayudu, arguably his best player. Vizzy, sensing an opportunity, made use of Nayudu's rise and his growing unpopularity within the team to plot against Patiala. He deliberately sang praises of Nayudu, who, by the end of the tour, was greatly unpopular with his teammates. The team that was initially united under Patiala's leadership was deeply divided by the end.

The Debut

The tour itself, however, was widely covered in the British press from the time the Indians stepped on British soil. In fact, even before the team arrived in England *The Times,* London, published the following report on 1 March 1932: 'We still play cricket in India. Political rough houses, communal riots, Congress hartals, Bengal terrorists, and the 10% cut in pay have all done their best to queer the pitch for us, but the game goes on. The Delhi Police may be having three sharp rounds with a rioting crowd in the Chandni Chowk, the crowded bazaar of the old city, but a mile or two away on the club ground set in the gardens that 400 years ago Shah Jehan built for his princess, a Roshanara side will be playing the Punjab Wanderers or an Army team from New Cantonments will be fielding in the white sunlight. . . .

'Here is the team for England:

'The Maharaja of Patiala, Captain [eventually withdrew in favour of the Maharaja of Porbander], K.S. Ghanshyamsinhji (Kathiawar), Vice Captain, Amar Singh (Jamnagar), S.M.H Colah (Bombay), Ghulam Mohammed (Ahmedabad), Joginder Singh (Punjab), B.E. Kapadia (Bombay), Lal Singh (Kuala Lumpur), N.D. Marshall (Bombay), J. Naoomal (Karachi), J.G. Navle (Gwalior), C.K. Nayudu (Indore), Nazir Ali (Patiala), S.M. Nissar (Punjab), P.E. Palia (Mysore), S. Godambe (Bombay), Wazir Ali (Bhopal).

'It will be seen that the team is composed entirely of Indians; the question of selecting Englishmen playing in India did not arise.'

And soon after the Indian team arrived in England on 13 April 1932, the *Evening Standard* commented on the socio-political significance of the tour: 'No politics, no caste, just cricket. This is the unofficial slogan of the cricket team that has come from India after a lapse of 21 years to try its strength against England and the first class counties.

'There has never been such a team of contrasts meeting on the common footing of cricket. The 18 players speak eight to ten languages among them; they belong to four or five different castes; some may not eat this and some may not eat that; a few are denied smoking by their religious laws; some similarly have drink proscribed; they are captained by a Maharajah rich beyond the dreams of county cricket treasurers and they have tradesmen who earn their living with their hands; some come from the plains where cold is almost unknown, and others from the hills where the climate has insured them even to an English summer . . .

'Caste demands that the Hindus do not eat beef or veal, and that the Mohammedans avoid pork, bacon and ham. So to prevent any difficulties at meal times the order has gone forth that these things must not appear on any menu during the tour. Instead the men will eat mutton, chicken and fish.

'The team contains six Hindus, five Mohammedans, four Parsees and two Sikhs. The Mohammedans forswear alcohol by religion and most of the others do so by choice. The Sikhs, who will play cricket in turbans, are similarly denied smoking. There are no training regulations but when serious cricket comes along there is a voluntary rule of 9 o' clock bed . . .'

The Indians played their first tour match against T.G. Trott's XI at Pelsham Farm, Pearmarsh near Rye, on 29 April 1932. Interestingly, playing against the Indian team in this match was Duleepsinhji. While the Indians acquitted themselves fairly well with Lall Singh, the Sikh from Malaya leading the way, it was on 22 May 1932, in the match against the MCC, that the world for the first time had a glimpse of what India's first home-grown legend, C.K. Nayudu, was capable of. (Nayudu, *Wisden* Cricketer of the year in 1933, smashed the first Indian century of the tour in style.) *The Star*'s headline on 22 May 1932 summed it all up: 'The Hindu Bradman in Form at Lords'. *The Observer* was equally eloquent: 'A brilliant not out innings of 116 by C.K. Nayudu was the feature of the first day's play between All-India and the MCC.'

However, it was in the first and only Test match at Lord's that the Indians shocked the English in the first half-hour itself. The MCC were reduced to a dismal 19/3 by some excellent Indian bowling and fielding. *The Birmingham Post* wrote: 'The All India cricket team has administered a few shocks to the dignity and confidence of England today. If there were among the 24,000 spectators at Lord's some who imagined that the granting of a Test match by the MCC to the tourists from the Indian empire was merely an amiable concession, then they had a very rude awakening before the close of play . . .

'It was an extraordinary start to the match. Sutcliffe and Holmes, Yorkshire's record smashing opening pair, united in a similar manner under the banner of England, went out full of cool confidence . . . But the first ball of Nissar's second over . . . was an inswinger and Sutcliffe, playing with the edge instead of the middle of the bat, diverted it into the wicket—and one of England's greatest batsmen was out . . .

'The disappointment was redoubled and revived when the last ball of the same over, a delivery perfect in flight, length and pace, sent Holmes' off stump spinning through the air, while the batsman was only half way through the stroke . . . Woolley and Hammond were now together . . .

'When he [Woolley] had got 9 in twenty minutes, he played a ball from Nissar to a point between short leg and mid-on. The stroke was worth a comfortable single and no more, but for some extraordinary reason an attempt was made to secure two runs. The fielder, the blue turbaned Lall Singh, threw in rather wildly, but even so the wicketkeeper had time to gather it and remove the bails while Woolley was still several feet from home. The wicket was thrown away by wild calling, and three men were out for 19 . . .'

Though India eventually lost the match by 158 runs, the courage and grit shown at Lord's clearly conveyed to the world that the Indians, in little time, would carve out a niche in the world of cricket.

The credibility the Indians had raked up on tour duly paid dividends when the MCC, taken by India's impressive Test debut at Lord's in 1932, sent a competent team to India in the winter of 1933. Most significant was that Douglas Jardine, born in India and master of Bodyline, was chosen leader of the party.

In the first ever Test on Indian soil at Bombay [now Mumbai], a match England won comprehensively, the teen sensation Lala Amarnath's batting overshadowed all else. No one who watched Amarnath bat in the afternoon of 17 December 1933 could ever forget the experience. Vasant Raiji, who watched the match at the ground, mentioned, 'Amarnath played some unbelievable shots and Indian fans just loved the experience of seeing the first hundred by an Indian on home soil.'

At the time the MCC tour was on in India, Vizzy was busy working backstage trying to cement his alliance with Lord Willingdon. He even donated a pavilion to the newly built Feroze Shah Kotla Stadium in Delhi, naming it after the viceroy. These efforts to curry favour were partly successful and, though Patiala was elected chancellor of the Chamber of Princes after Ranji's death in 1933, his influence, as Mihir Bose writes in his *History of Indian Cricket*, was declining: 'Willingdon's hostility to Patiala had coincided with the waning of the latter's cricket power. He had been the kingmaker of the 1932 tour, but in the winter of 1933-34 he was pushed to the sidelines. The emergency Board of Control meeting in Delhi on 1 May 1933 showed that the associations, which had once survived because of his generosity were now turning against him.'

Patiala, however, was not resigned to the situation. To make a comeback, he fell back on a trusted weapon—patronage. He entertained the MCC team lavishly when it toured Amritsar and, in return, the MCC cricketers showered generous praise on Patiala; and it was at Patiala that the MCC played the only four-day first-class fixture of the tour. During this match, the tourists were taken for shoots to the hills, and even Jardine, the captain, was won over. However, despite Patiala's success in reinforcing control over the game, Nayudu was retained captain for the Test matches against the MCC, overriding the Yuvraj of Patiala, an able cricketer and the Maharaja's son, whom he was trying to promote. Vizzy, expectedly, welcomed Nayudu's appointment. He, too, used the tour to good effect by leading his side to a significant victory against the MCC. This was the MCC's only loss on the tour and it may well have been the result of complacency. Whatever the reason, Jardine did Vizzy's cause a lot of good by proclaiming he had the potential to be a good captain. By the end of the MCC tour, therefore, the stage was set for a showdown between the two patrons of the game.

Patiala had an advantage because the game was once again confronted with a financial crisis and, and given his economic position, he was the only person capable of resolving it. With the Bombay Pentangular Tournament stopped for the time being, the moment was ripe for a national championship. Accordingly, at a meeting of the Board in Shimla in the summer of 1934, A.S. De Mello, the secretary, submitted the proposal for a national championship. He also presented a sketch of the proposed trophy, which Raiji describes as 'a Grecian urn two feet high, with a lid, the handle of which represented Father Time, similar to the one on the weather vane at Lord's'. As soon as De Mello mooted the plan, the Maharaja of Patiala stood up to declare that he would be pleased to donate the trophy and committed a donation of £500 (INR 6,667) at the prevailing exchange rate. He wanted the trophy to be named after Ranji. The Maharaja also declared his intention to present a miniature trophy to the winner of the championship, one that could be retained permanently. His offer drew considerable applause.

The connection between Ranji and Patiala was well known. Ranji had played for Patiala's team in 1898–99. While touring Bengal in 1899, Ranji and Patiala had been accorded a royal reception, the Kolkata Town Hall spending the huge sum of INR 3,000 on the occasion.

However, the official announcement to launch the Ranji Trophy was withheld for some reason and this allowed Vizzy to work his manipulations. He proposed that the trophy be named after Lord Willingdon instead of Ranji who, he argued, had done little for the game in India. An emergency meeting of the Board was summoned to discuss the renaming and Vizzy strengthened his case by donating a trophy himself. The meeting accepted the Willingdon Trophy as the national championship.

Reporting the decision, *The Times of India* declared that the Willingdon Trophy, specially selected by Lady Willingdon, had been gratefully accepted and placed on display. Despite being present at the meeting, Patiala could not prevent the acceptance of the Willingdon Trophy.

Following the acceptance of the Willingdon Trophy by the Board, newspapers such as the *Bombay Chronicle* and *Star of India* wrote in support of the Ranji Trophy. Writing in the former, J.C. Maitra argued: 'I wonder if by doing so [accepting the Willingdon Trophy] they ever thought of the sacrilege they were doing to the memory of the greatest cricketer ever born in India, whose memory is still cherished by thousands of followers of the game in all parts of the world. If such a move is made, the duty of all cricketers in this country is clear. They should rise in a body and oppose the sacrilege.'

Despite such protests, it was expected that Mumbai, the winners of the first national championship in 1935, would be presented the Willingdon Trophy. However, a surprise awaited Homi Vajifdar (standing in for indisposed captain L.P. Jai) when he walked up to collect the trophy a week after the final, at a function in Delhi. Lord Willingdon was present at the podium to give away the prize, but the trophy he handed out was the Ranji Trophy.

It turned out that Patiala had successfully outwitted Vizzy while touring England with the Board president, Grant Govan, in January 1935. The two had represented India at the Imperial Cricket Conference (now the International Cricket Council or ICC) meeting at Lord's, and it was during this trip that Patiala had turned the tables on Vizzy. The trump card was his promise to sponsor Jack Ryder's Australians, who were to tour India in October 1935. To Vizzy's dismay, the Willingdon Trophy was later presented to the winners of the Festival Cup played in Delhi.

The skirmish was over, not the war. Vizzy had the last laugh when he was appointed captain of the Indian touring team to England in May–June 1936. He won the vote by a 10–4 margin against Nayudu, after Patiala had withdrawn the candidature of his son, the Yuvraj. While Delhi, Bengal, Central Provinces, Maharashtra, United Provinces, Hyderabad, Rajputana, Mysore, Bangalore and Madras voted for Vizzy, Southern Punjab, Northern India, Sind and Mumbai voted against him. Central India and Gujarat did not vote and the Western Indian States nominee was not present.

Realizing Vizzy had outdone him, Patiala withdrew his invitation to host Ryder's tourists. Vizzy, of course, was an undeserving captain. The tour saw the sending back of Lala Amarnath, Patiala's protégé and the team's best performer, on grounds of alleged insubordination and in doing so triggered one of Indian cricket's most bitter controversies.

The Amarnath Fiasco

'I have the full authority to announce that a sensational decision to send Amarnath back has been made. He is aboard the *Kaiser-I-Hind*, which leaves Southampton today.'

—Cricket correspondent Edward Humphrey
Dalrymple Sewell in *The Times of India*

On one level, the Amarnath–Vizzy clash was evidence of a plebian–patrician divide in colonial India. As a controversy, it far outlived the 1936 tour, its mix of intrigue, corruption and power play continuing to fascinate to this day. The genesis of the story goes back to early 1936, a time when Vizzy was at his diplomatic best, determined to captain the team to England. However, victory in the election for captaincy against Nayudu was not enough. Vizzy was intent on isolating him within the touring party.

Soon after the tour began, Vizzy ordered Amarnath to stay away from Nayudu. In the words of Amarnath: 'While we were at our hotel prior to our match with Oxford University on May 6, the captain's servant came to call me. I went to the captain who straightaway asked me to join his side and not to mix with Major C.K. Nayudu and several others with whom I generally mixed. Up to this time I was not aware of any party feelings among the players. . . I told the captain that C.K. was a friend of mine, but I was not concerned with any particular party except that we generally went out together. I agreed to do what the captain thought best.'

Because Amarnath duly obliged his captain, Nayudu stopped talking to him. Vizzy, on the other hand, was pleased. He congratulated Amarnath for his century at Northamptonshire and, from then on, gave him regular rides to the ground in his car.

The matter should have ended there, but did not. A confrontation between Vizzy and Amarnath was triggered during the match against Leicester that was held between 20–22 May. Amarnath, bowling from the pavilion end, asked the captain to remove the third man fielder and place him between cover and point instead. Vizzy snubbed Amarnath, asking him not to waste time and ordered him to carry on. After the game, Amarnath made the cardinal mistake of discussing the incident with his mates, saying he had never seen a captain refuse to assist his bowler so curtly.

News of this got to Vizzy. He called Amarnath aside and told him that as captain he could do what he liked. When Amarnath retorted that captaincy did not include the right to insult colleagues. Vizzy brought the incident to the notice of the manager, Major R. Britton Jones, who ordered Amarnath to apologize. The young cricketer did so, as Britton Jones had promised to help him secure a professional contract in the Lancashire league. Vizzy, however, was not satisfied. In the match against Middlesex at Lord's, Amarnath was asked to field in the deep and was under-bowled even though he had returned an impressive figure of 6/29.

Amarnath answered this humiliation with centuries in both

innings of the following match against Essex, batting at number three. Vizzy congratulated him but was quick to add that had Amarnath not foolishly tried to score off every ball, he could have scored many more runs. In this match, as Amarnath later stated, 'I hurt my shin very badly and had to retire for 15 minutes and then took the field after putting on plaster. I fielded wherever I was placed.'

Before the next match against Cambridge University, held beteween 30 May and 2 June, Amarnath sprained his back at the nets. 'The pain was so severe that I cried in agony and was frightened that something serious might have happened,' he recalled later. But the manager ordered him to play, ignoring his plea for a much-needed rest. Amarnath went in to bat ten minutes before lunch and was out leg before, first ball. When India fielded, he was brought on to bowl first change and hurt himself again. 'I informed the captain and he told me to go to the pavilion. He also went with me and spoke to the manager. I put on my coat and stayed on to watch the match.' After an hour's rest, Britton Jones brought in a doctor who plastered Amarnath's back. Soon after, Amarnath was ordered on to the ground and was asked to tell Vizzy that he could bowl and field: 'I went to the field and gave the chit to the captain and told him that the manager had asked me to say that I could field and bowl. The captain said it was his own lookout. After 45 minutes he put me on to bowl and after bowling four or five overs the pain increased considerably and was unbearable. I went in the country to field and came back to bowl again.'

At lunch, Amarnath had a chat with teammates Amir Elahi, Baqa Jilani and others in Punjabi. Apprehensive of what he was saying, Britton Jones summoned him for a meeting. 'He had in his hand two letters, one addressed to the Nawab of Bhopal and the other to the Maharaja of Patiala,' Amarnath later said. 'These he exhibited threateningly to me, saying that he would post them and also that he would send me back to India as my behaviour was not proper and my language foul. It was obvious that these letters contained some complaints about me.'

Britton Jones offered to give Amarnath another chance. When Amarnath snapped back, saying that he had not offended anyone and that there was no reason to beg for another chance, Britton Jones accused him of presuming that he was indispensable.

Amarnath's shin and back had not healed in time for the next match against Yorkshire, but the manager insisted he play. In this match too, Amarnath was posted in the deep and had to do much running, aggravating his injury.

The already strained relationship only worsened when the manager accused Amarnath of being a womanizer. Amarnath refuted the charge, saying: 'Since I had arrived in England, I was always in bed by about 10.30 p.m. on match days and the latest by 11.30 p.m. on off days and I gave no occasion for anyone to reprimand me for late nights. I had gone to England to play cricket, which I liked much more than women. He could not have seen me behaving disgracefully or in a compromising way on any occasion and he was not in a position to make any such remark.'

This episode was followed by a week's truce during which Britton Jones repeatedly emphasized to Amarnath the need of befriending Vizzy. In response, Amarnath informed his manager: 'I have nothing against the captain and said that the captain should not make unkind remarks about me to others. If he was displeased with me in any way, he should speak to me directly.'

Things came to a head during the match against the Minor Counties, which started on 17 June. Amarnath was told he would be batting at number four. However, it was Amar Singh who was eventually sent in at that position. When Amarnath asked Vizzy when he was to go in, he was told the captain had not yet made up his mind.

Amarnath was finally sent in at number seven, ten minutes before the end of the day's play. 'In the meantime when one of the players asked the captain why I had been sent in so late he replied that he wanted faster scorers. I played out time and came back to the pavilion rather excited and while undressing threw my pads etc. near my bag in the corner. I felt quite disgusted and talked to several players in Punjabi. What I said was slang, words to the effect that I had not wasted four years uselessly but had learnt cricket.'

When Vizzy asked Amarnath whether he was speaking to him, Amarnath insisted he was not speaking to anyone in particular, nor did he wish to speak to anyone.

After the match, Amar Singh suggested to Amarnath that he apologize in writing to the captain for his behaviour in the dressing room. Amarnath refused, saying he had done nothing to offend his captain. Soon after, Britton Jones asked Amarnath to see him at 6 p.m. The manager produced a statement signed by several players testifying to Amarnath's misbehaviour. He informed Amarnath that he had decided to send him back to India in a week. An hour later, when Amarnath was in Wazir Ali's room, Britton Jones came to see him and ordered him to leave by the ship *Kaiser-I-Hind* the very next day. Amarnath begged for another chance but Britton Jones was adamant. Later that evening, many of the players, Cotah Ramaswami, Wazir Ali, Nayudu, Elahi and Dattaram Hindlekar, went to the captain and pleaded with him to reconsider the decision. Vizzy gave in on condition that Amarnath tender an unqualified written apology. This, Amarnath gave at once. It was then decided that Vizzy would meet Amarnath the following morning at 8 a.m. to give the final verdict: 'The next day the captain and I went to the manager's room, but I did not go in. The captain came out in a few minutes and asked me to go to Wazir Ali's room and wait. A little later Wazir Ali came in to inform me that the manager's decision could not be changed and brought back my written guarantee of good behaviour. I left by the *Kaiser-I-Hind*.'

Commenting on Amarnath's repatriation, *The Times of India* of 20 June 1936 declared: 'It is confirmed that Amarnath is leaving for India this afternoon. The manager of the team, interviewed by Reuter, said that Amarnath has been sent back as a disciplinary measure. The matter now rests with the Indian Board of Control and neither the manager nor the captain of the team would make any statement. It appears that Amarnath was warned several times for insolence to his captain and manager, and when reproved for his behaviour. . .he is reported to have said that no action would be taken against him, as he was indispensable to the team. After a lengthy meeting it was decided to teach him a lesson.'

Amarnath, dismally sitting in a reserved compartment of the boat train at Waterloo, told a bitter story to the *Star* correspondent: 'I am supposed to have been insolent and insubordinate. I did not mean to be rude. This is the end of the trouble that has been going on for some time. It reached a climax at Lord's. I did not like the way I was put on to bat. I had played hard, and was tired and flung down the pads. I told the captain that I could not play his way. Last night there was a conference between the manager and the captain who decided to send me away. All my team members have signed a document agreeing that I have been insolent. I do not think all the players are against me. There are a lot of reasons of an extremely private nature for their agreeing to my being sent away.'

However, Mushtaq Ali, in an article published in *The Times of India* on 23 June, stood by the manager and captain: 'I went home from Lord's last Friday hoping against hope that some way might be found out of the great difficulty wherein the captain and the manager of the Indian team had been placed by Amarnath's behaviour on Thursday evening. I feared the worst as Prince Victor of Cooch Behar had been in the dressing room when the incidents complained of took place, and I felt that the powerful evidence of a non-member of the team, which I knew had been given in support of the Captain and Manager, was likely to clinch matters. Next morning at The Oval I was told the verdict in simple words, "He will be soon on the boat for India" and I knew that the most sensational happening in the history of cricket tours had taken place. Since then I have become aware of facts, which left me no option but to agree with the drastic decision. The correctness of the decision, severe though some who do not know the facts may think it, was confirmed if the alleged interview [referred above] given by Amarnath in the train was actually given.'

The whole affair, Ali lamented, was a 'sad thing. Certainly it is not the fault of the captain or the manager that this has happened. I hold no brief for either. . . But on this occasion, both must and will have the sympathy and the support of every sportsman who understands what cricket means.'

Back home, Amarnath was whisked away from the Mumbai port soon after arrival and was not allowed to speak to the media. He was asked to go to Bhopal immediately to see the Nawab of Bhopal, the Board president. Following this meeting, *The Times of India* of 15 July reported: 'Amarnath is returning to England immediately, honourably forgiven and reinstated as a member of the Indian cricket team. He will land at the Croydon aerodrome on Thursday, July 23, and may play in the second Test match at Manchester on July 25–28.'

This decision, it was reported, was made by the Nawab of Bhopal after reading the lengthy statement given by Amarnath and after meeting him in person. The Nawab had instructed the manager to recall Amarnath, who had been ordered to tender an unqualified apology to the captain and manager. When informed of the Board's decision, Vizzy gave his consent saying he was extremely broad-minded and did not bear any personal malice against Amarnath.

However, soon after the publication of this report, the private secretary of the Nawab of Bhopal issued the following statement to the press: 'The attention of the President of the Board of Control for Cricket in India has been drawn to a broadcast message from England tonight announcing that news has been received from New Delhi that as a result of the intervention by His Highness the Nawab of Bhopal, Amarnath is returning to England by air to play in the Test match at Manchester. The President wishes to lose no time in informing all concerned that this announcement is wholly unauthorised and premature. No decision has been taken in this connection either by the Board or the President.'

Next, on 18 July, the office of the president issued another statement: 'On a private and confidential inquiry by the President, the captain and the manager having agreed to the return of Amarnath on certain conditions, the matter was being considered by the Board. Since then, intimation has been received by the President that his return is undesirable. The question of Amarnath's return has therefore been closed.' On the same day, Vizzy, too, distributed a statement to the press that stated: 'I am a strict disciplinarian. After agreeing to Amarnath being sent back on certain conditions, deeper considerations changed my mind, and I informed the Board to that effect.'

Upon being informed that he was not to be sent back, Amarnath criticized the Board for not being fair and impartial. He demanded that the Board conduct an inquiry. In an interview to *The Times of India* he said: 'I have no intention of appearing before the Board again, as I feel that it will serve no purpose. I am not indispensable to Indian cricket, nobody is, but if I am to come back to international cricket again, I demand that the Board should make an impartial inquiry into my case and obtain an apology from either me or the captain and manager, whichever party is considered guilty.'

He stated that till 1.20 p.m. on Saturday, 18 July, he was under the impression that he was to return to England to join the team. In fact, his trunk had been sent to Mumbai by a special messenger with instructions to send it overland from Marseilles as he was carrying a couple of bats, some flannels and his cricket boots with him. It was only after lunch that he received the message that he was not to go. When he telephoned the shipping office in Mumbai, he was told his luggage had been sent by the English mail steamer earlier in the afternoon.

Later the Beaumont Committee, appointed to deliberate on the controversy, found Amarnath guilty and supported Vizzy's and Britton Jones's action in sending him back. To strengthen Vizzy's position, the committee also declared that prior to the commencement of the tour, Amarnath had sent Vizzy a telegram asking for a loan of INR 6,000, which he received and this was proof that the captain had no malice against him. Amarnath denied these allegations and insisted that a third party, if at all, had sent the telegram. He accused Vizzy of introducing the story of the telegram to justify the unfair disciplinary action taken in England.

However, Vizzy emerged unscathed and won considerable social acclaim in independent India as a commentator and cricket patriarch. His patronage of the game won him a post on the selection committee and he remained in the limelight long after the other princes had ceased to matter. As president of the Uttar Pradesh Cricket Association, he rubbed shoulders with India's political leadership. His exalted position was evident from an interview to the *Sunday News of India* while on his way to a meeting with Sardar Vallabbhai Patel, the Union home minister: 'We should not forget what cricketers like Amar Singh, Ramji, Dr Kanga and Hindlekar have done for India. Let us as a mark of respect for Amar Singh's great services to this country call the CP Governor's match Amar Singh's XI versus the Commonwealth side. His Excellency Shri Pakwasa, will, I am sure, have no objection if the Nagpur Cricket Association approaches him; for His Excellency Shri Pakwasa belongs to Bombay and must have seen Amar Singh at his best some years ago. I shall pave the way by writing to His Excellency.'

'I shall pave the way by writing'—that one expression said it all.

CLASH OF THE TITANS

'Only noble souls can rejoice at the success of others. The attitude of cricketers who were antagonistic to Nayudu has its roots in jealousy, conceit, greed and indiscipline.'

—D.B. Deodhar

'C.K. Nayudu is India's greatest cricketer. Whether it was bowling, batting, fielding, captaincy, physical fitness, positive approach to the game, there will never be Nayudu's equal among Indians. . . The greater the crisis, the greater was Nayudu and I have never seen him being affected by nerves. It was a pity that during his time there were not many Test matches, otherwise his record in Test cricket would be second to none amongst our cricketers. Judge him by statistics and he was only moderately successful. Judge him by performances when the going was tough and he was our greatest cricketer. There has never been a greater entertainer in a cricket ground, and in my time the name of Nayudu was good enough to draw people from their offices and from their businesses to the Bombay Gymkhana to see him play.'

—Vijay Merchant

Imagine the same Vijay Merchant plotting against Nayudu, hand in hand with Vizzy and Amar Singh, that too during a vital match. It happened when Lord Tennyson's Englishmen were in India for an unofficial Test series in November–December 1937. Nayudu, by far the greatest cricketer of colonial India, was even edged out of the side through machinations of power play and corruption. In an age when the princes controlled Indian cricket, Nayudu, a commoner, had the courage to challenge them. In 1932, when India played their first ever Test at Lord's, the Maharaja of Porbandar was forced to step down from the captaincy in favour of Nayudu. Profoundly impressed, *Wisden* described India's first captain thus: 'Tall and well-proportioned, Nayudu is eminently fitted by nature to be a good cricketer and his doings for the Indian team fully bore out the accounts of him that had come to us by reason of his excellent performances in his own land. Possessed of supple and powerful wrists and a very good eye, he hit that ball tremendously hard.'

What received greater praise were his leadership skills:

'He. . .showed himself admirably suited for the duties of leadership in what were, after all, rather difficult circumstances.'

The Indian team returned home from this tour having left a favourable impression on their hosts. Nayudu later told the *Bombay Chronicle*, 'Every day, every way, we learnt some new lesson or other during our tour of England.'

In 1933–34, when Douglas Jardine's MCC toured India, Nayudu captained the Indians in the three Test matches at Bombay, Calcutta and Madras. Though this series was a disappointment for Nayudu, he was still a strong contender for captaincy for the 1936 tour of England. In the election to choose the captain, however, he won only four votes to Vizzy's ten. Vizzy, perhaps the team's worst player, was forever keen to humiliate Nayudu. Baseless charges flew about that Nayudu was not cooperating with the captain. Without recording Nayudu's evidence or even consulting him, the Beaumont Committee, appointed to probe the 1936 debacle, asserted, 'Nayudu held himself aloof from the team and did not offer any support to the captain.' As Vasant Raiji writes, 'Nayudu was not designated vice-captain nor was he briefed to play the role of advisor to the captain. Surely, Vizzy would have received Nayudu's whole-hearted co-operation had he approached him in the right spirit.' However, one of the worst controversies involving Nayudu was to occur a year later.

After a forgettable tour of England, the Indians faced Lord Tennyson's men at home in the winter of 1937. To everyone's surprise, Nayudu was dropped from the team for the first unofficial Test, allegedly because of a string of poor performances in domestic games. That the reason cited was only a cover-up is evident from the following report published in the contemporary press: 'The 1936 Quadrangular lacked the glamour of the earlier two years because of the absence of two superstars, Nayudu and [Mohammad] Nissar. In 1937 one more team, the Rest, was added and the tournament was now called the Pentangulars. The venue of the matches was shifted from the Bombay Gymkhana to the Brabourne Stadium where the wicket always favoured the batsman. . . Because of a dispute over the allocation of seats in the new stadium, the Hindus (who were to be captained by Nayudu) withdrew from the tournament.'

Thus Nayudu, absent from the premier domestic competition in 1936 and 1937, could hardly have been dropped for loss of form. There were clearly ulterior motives at work. Unfortunately for the men in power, India fared miserably without Nayudu. With public opinion firmly against them, the selectors, led by Colonel Mistry, were forced to recall Nayudu for the second Test. Little did they know that they would be forced to reverse their decision soon. In fact, the sequence of events that followed his recall can easily rank as one of the most disgraceful episodes in the history of Indian cricket.

After the selectors had picked the team for the second Test, an official letter was sent to Nayudu on behalf of the Board informing him of his inclusion in the All India XI that would meet Tennyson's XI in the second Test in Bombay. One of the selectors even remarked that Nayudu was the only cricketer capable of handling Alf Gover and Paul Gibb, the bowler–wicketkeeper pair who 'had become terrors for our Test team'. Nayudu accepted the invitation and duly arrived in Bombay in time for the match.

Commending his sportsman spirit, the *Bombay Sentinel* reported, 'A great sport that he is, he came here setting aside all the grievances and forgetting all the slanderous remarks hurled at him by the Beaumont Committee.' However, on the morning of 11 December, the day the Mumbai Test began, the public woke up to an official announcement in the newspapers about Nayudu's exclusion. To add insult to injury, Nayudu had not been informed and only learnt of the decision from the papers. He was dropped in favour of Mohammed Sayeed, about whose cricketing abilities not much is known.

Why did the selectors pick him in the first place if they were going to drop him later? Apparently, the letter was a charade, and the selectors had hoped that Nayudu would not accept the invitation. When he did, the 'enemies of Major Nayudu were nonplussed,' the *Sentinel* reported, in a reference to the princes, in whose hands rested all powers of decision-making. These enemies, it was speculated, also included Nayudu's teammates. Rumour had it that when Amar Singh, who had failed miserably with both bat and ball in the first Test, got to know of the invitation, he set about pulling strings. He received full support from Vizzy, by then the leading patron of Indian cricket having consolidated his position at the helm in the aftermath of the 1936 tour of England. Accordingly, those who had sent Nayudu the invitation were soon taken to task. Emboldened by Vizzy's backing, nine of the 14 players informed the selection committee they were unwilling to play with Nayudu in the team. Speaking of Nayudu's enmity with his teammates, Raiji argued: 'Amar Singh was not keen to play under Nayudu. [Sorabji] Colah and Amir Elahi became his enemies during the English tour and there was not much love lost between him and Vinoo Mankad. Nayudu was a superstar and it was but natural that some of his teammates resented the public adulation that he received to the exclusion of others who got relegated to the back stage.'

J.C. Maitra wrote in the *Bombay Chronicle*: 'It is an open secret that during the England tour of 1932 some of the Indian players threw all barriers of discipline to the winds. Keeping late hours and getting drunk were with them ordinary features of the day. Even when they did not restrain themselves before a Test match, C.K. Nayudu as their captain called them to order and threatened to keep them out of the Test if they did not behave themselves. He also appealed to them in the name of India's honour. This instead of acting as a restraining influence on them infuriated them still more. It is said there were squabbles and fights thereafter over this and the recalcitrant members pledged themselves to be after Nayudu's blood ever since.'

Further, as Raiji recounts, 'After the first Test against England at home in 1933–34, Amar Singh stated that he wanted to enjoy cricket, not to win at all costs. He liked to entertain the spectators and give them good value for their money but Nayudu made the game such a kill-joy pursuit that he just did not feel able to try. Can Nayudu be blamed for taking Test cricket seriously and not in a light-hearted manner?'

What was surprising was that Merchant, team captain and one of the three selectors, allowed this injustice to pass. Had Merchant desired he could have applied pressure on the selection committee, which consisted of himself, the Nawab of Pataudi and Colonel K.M. Mistry. But all that Merchant cared for was to establish himself as India's star batsman, and for his friend Amar Singh to get some wickets. Subsequently, Merchant duly came in for criticism. The *Sentinel's* correspondent voiced public sentiment when he declared, 'It is very doubtful if ever he will get back the popularity he once enjoyed.' When Merchant was dismissed cheaply in the Test, the *Sentinel* remarked, 'The curse of the 35,000 who had gathered to watch the match seems to have worked. . . I have yet to come across a man who was sorry at Merchant getting out early.'

This was clearly a prequel to what happened in Kolkata, in 2005, when the Indians under Rahul Dravid were beaten by South Africa. Rahul's team did not include Kolkata's favourite son Sourav Ganguly, who had been deliberately left out by coach Greg Chappell for reasons explained earlier in the book. Irate fans vent their anger by booing Chappell and supporting the South Africans.

In Bombay, too, cricket enthusiasts and the press were firmly behind Nayudu. A number of letters published in leading dailies expressed admiration for Nayudu and condemned princely interference in Indian cricket. One of these letters, addressed to Colonel Mistry, asked: 'If you were not sure of his inclusion in the team why did you at all call him? Was it to insult the veteran and disregard public opinion? Secondly, we have a strong doubt that it might be a player or group of players who threatened the selection committee that they would stay back if CK was included. If this be the case, leave out those players who have no sportsmanship and spirit of sacrifice.'

Just like Ganguly in 2005, Nayudu emerged from the controversy a greater hero than ever before. 'Attempts deliberately to insult and humiliate the Indian Jessop would only hasten the day when those at present in charge of Indian cricket will nowhere be near it,' thundered the *Sentinel*. There was also speculation that if Nayudu had played in the second Test, India would not have lost, as it tamely did by six wickets. What was ominous for the Board was that sections of the public felt they had been hoodwinked. Thousands who had arrived in Bombay just to see Nayudu play, taking advantage of the railway concessions provided for the occasion, felt cheated.

Some fans further demanded that Nayudu be made captain for

the third Test in Kolkata. The *Sentinel* led the charge, asserting, 'Let Major Nayudu skipper the team in the third Test and victory will be ours. This will to some extent go to compensate for the gross injustice done to him.' The *Star of India,* however, put it more bluntly: 'The public will not take the Nayudu affair lying down. It means more than what it superficially signifies. Nayudu humiliated means India humiliated.' Though Nayudu was not picked for the rest of the series, his popularity by the end of the tour was far greater than that of Merchant, who lost the series 2–3 to the second-string English side. To redeem himself, Merchant was forced to admit his mistake in public and apologize to Nayudu.

Nayudu did not play a single Test match after this but returned to captain the Hindus in the Pentangular of 1938. He played one of his best innings on his comeback. Raiji, an eyewitness, described the innings thus: 'In 1938, I watched Nayudu's beautiful cameo, an innings of 66 against Nissar. Nayudu batting against Nissar is the finest spectacle I have ever seen on the cricket field.'

Nayudu was felicitated with a reasonable purse by most cricket associations of the country on the occasion of his 25th year in first-class cricket in 1941–42. He was chief guest at various functions through the 1940s, a rare distinction for cricketers then. The esteem with which he was held becomes clear from the following description: 'In 1944-45 when Nayudu was fifty, his Golden Jubilee was celebrated with great éclat both in Bombay and Calcutta. In his honour a match between C.K. Nayudu's XI and the C.C.I. was staged in Bombay at the Brabourne Stadium. A purse was presented to him by the cricket loving public of Bombay on the occasion. In 1955, in recognition of Nayudu's services to Indian cricket, the President of India conferred on him the award of Padma Bhusan. In 1973–74 the Board of Control for Cricket in India named a tournament after him. The tournament is conducted on the lines of the Ranji Trophy for those under 22. The trophy was donated by the Bombay Cricket

Association from the funds collected to perpetuate the memory of the great cricketer. Nagpur, Nayudu's birthplace, honoured him by unveiling his bust in the square near the Vidarbha Cricket Association grounds and naming a street after him. Indore, the city to which he later migrated to serve Holkar and in which he lived for the rest of his life, erected a life size statue of their illustrious citizen at the entrance to the Nehru Stadium. The C.C.I. named their banquet hall after him.'

Nayudu was also one of the first Indian cricketers to endorse commercial brands. One of the earliest promotions for the Tea Market Expansion Board went thus: 'Major C.K. Nayudu, India's greatest cricketer, says, "I have always found a good cup of tea a great refresher during a game of cricket, hockey, soccer, tennis or any other game. It is a great stimulant of the mild and harmless kind. I strongly advocate this beverage to those who partake in any strenuous game. Tea is the only drink I love. I cannot do without my tea in the morning and evening."'

The people's hero continued playing first-class cricket into his sixties, captaining Holkar to four Ranji Trophy victories in the 1940s and 1950s. Today he is universally acknowledged as Indian cricket's first home-grown mega icon.

THE ROYAL BENGAL BATTLE

If it was between the Maharajas of Patiala and Vizianagram at a national level, the contest was equally fervent in Bengal between Nripendra Krishna Narayan, the Maharaja of Cooch Behar, and Jagadindranarayan Ray, the Maharaja of Natore, now in Bangladesh. Both were committed patrons of the game and spent serious monies in employing cricketers to play for their respective teams. Even before the First World War, the Maharaja of Cooch Behar had three proficient cricket teams under his employment. With the help of two Sussex professionals, Joe Vine and George Cox, and later Frank Tarrant, he had created a team which could hold its own against the well-known all-European Calcutta Cricket Club at Eden Gardens. The Cooch Behar team also performed reasonably well against the Jamnagar–Jodhpur combined team, captained by Ranji himself. In addition, a team which included A.C. Maclaren, also put in an impressive performance. As a result, local cricket in Kolkata flourished over the years.

The cricketing initiative of the Maharaja of Natore may be traced back to 1900. Jagadindranarayan had started promoting cricket to challenge his arch rival, the Maharaja of Cooch Behar. Soon after the latter had formed his team, hiring English professionals as coaches, Jagadindranarayan formed one of his own. Even after Nripendra Narayan had ceased to be a patron of cricket, Jagadindranarayan continued his patronage for a few years and established himself as the leading patron of the sport in the province. However, after Nripendra Narayan's death in 1911, Jagadindranarayan decided to withdraw support in the 1920s. The real reason, it can be conjectured, was the absence of competition from Cooch Behar. Despite the demise of Nripendra Narayan, Bengal cricket continued to be a significant presence in the country till the early 1920s. Jagadindranarayan was determined to improve upon the performances of the Cooch Behar side. He purchased 45 acres of land on Bondel Road, near Old Ballygunge in South Calcutta (now Kolkata), converting it into a cricket field. He also erected a pavilion on his private cricket ground, one that had all the necessary facilities. By his own admission, he had taken to cricket patronage having observed that the Maharaja of Cooch Behar's efforts weren't proving effective. To improve the standard of cricket in Bengal, the Maharaja of Cooch Behar, Shri Nripendra Krishna Bhup Bahadur, had undertaken a series of steps. He had recruited professional coaches from England together with professional European players from all parts of India to play for his team. He also arranged regular matches wherein his team could get valuable practice by playing against local and provincial sides of the country. However, because of a strong European presence in his team, whether his efforts contributed to improving the standard of native cricket in Bengal remained unclear.

Similar sentiments were expressed by noted contemporary writer Hemchandra Ray: 'At the time when the Natore team dominated Bengal cricket, the Maharaja of Cooch Behar had also formed a quality cricket team. However, we, Bengalis, could not rejoice at the victories of the Cooch Behar side. This was because Bengalis were a marginal presence in the Cooch Behar team and hence the credit for these victories went to the European players of the team.'

It was in response to this that Jagadindranarayan Ray decided to form a cricket team comprising Indians alone. He invited Saradaranjan Ray, widely seen as the father of Bengal cricket, to join him as coach, recruiting talent from all parts of the country. Saradaranjan had spent years in improving cricket at Vidyasagar College Calcutta as its principal and was a natural choice to lead the Natore project. To fulfil his ambition, Jagadindranarayan spared no pains, evident from his efforts towards Srishchandra Ray, an aspiring young Bengal cricketer who belonged to a poor family. Having observed Srishchandra's talent, Jagadindranarayan adopted him, paying for his expenses from the Natore treasury. Jagadindranarayan made no distinction between his own son, Prince Victor, and Srishchandra, giving them equal opportunity at cricket. However, Srishchandra, whose father was a clerk at the Natore court, fell ill and, despite the Maharaja's attempts, died within a week. The Maharaja, as established by contemporary accounts, was devastated.

Further evidence of the Maharaja of Natore's resolve to produce a top-class completely native cricket team came when he insisted on the inclusion of Mani Das in the Natore side and, later, of Kaladhan Mukherjee in the Bengal team that travelled to Rawalpindi in 1911. Kaladhan was the younger brother of Bidhubhusan Mukherjee, Bengal's leading batsman in the early twentieth century. Das, rated highly by the Maharaja, was born in a low-caste family and was not quite accepted by the upper echelons of Bengali society. The Maharaja, however, refused to attach any currency to such discriminatory factors. He asked Das to open the batting against the touring Gwalior side, an opportunity that changed Das's life as an aspiring cricketer. Jagadindranarayan described this episode in his memoirs: 'Among the current lot of Bengali players, Mani Das is one of the very best. I had sent him to open the batting against Gwalior. He wasn't willing to open and was afraid of performing poorly in front of his more illustrious teammates. Noting this apprehension, I called him and said, "We are Bengalis. In a predominantly Bengali cricket team, it is the duty of the Bengalis to take the lead." Upon hearing this, he touched my feet to take my blessings and went out to the middle to play an innings that proved invaluable for the team in the end.'

Kaladhan was in prime form in the 1909–10 season and was a prolific scorer for the Bengali schools against their Anglo-Indian counterparts. Yet, he wasn't included in the Bengal touring team, a decision that made the selectors extremely unpopular with the Maharaja. Henceforth the Maharaja decided to choose his own team and organize his own tours. This, he argued, would put him ahead of Cooch Behar and was a fundamental contribution to the development of the game in the country. He hired professional cricketers from Western India such as Palwankar Baloo, H.L. Semper, Palwankar Vithal and Ganpat, putting together one of the best cricket combinations in colonial India. The Natore teams' tours were a characteristic feature of Bengali cricket in the first decade of the twentieth century and did much to add to the Maharaja's national acclaim. He was soon recognized as a serious patron of sport, which, in turn, helped Natore, a relatively small principality in colonial Bengal, gain national recognition.

While taking on the Maharaja of Cooch Behar, the Maharaja of Natore was also trying to fulfil his other ambition—defeating the English at their own game. His own personal politics, often kept covert and unstated in view of the prevalent political environment at the time, equally influenced his decision to form a quality cricket team. The Maharaja was an ardent nationalist, having been an active member of the Indian National Congress for some years. Upon turning 18, he became president of the Natore Political Association at the request of Surendranath Banerjee, the founder of the Indian National Association. In 1894, he joined Banerjee and Anandamohan Bose as member of the Rajshahi municipality. After the partition of Bengal in 1905, he was a key figure in the protest movement, delivering a famous speech against the partition at the Kolkata Town Hall.

However, he differed from most nationalists in his modes of resistance. Till 1914, he used the cricket field to challenge the English and afterwards, helped foster the vernacular press. His success in evoking nationalist sentiment is evident from the following piece published in the regional press: 'Whenever the Natore XI defeated the European teams of Calcutta, our chests swelled with pride. Before the formation of the Natore XI, we Indians were losers on most occasions. But with the formation of the Natore XI, Maharaj Jagadindranarayan turned the tables on the English. Whether it is a fault of ours or not, we do not regard games as something simple, rather we are impacted by the results of these encounters. This is because this is the only arena where we are allowed to compete on even terms with the English. The English have always ridiculed us as "effete". It is on the sporting field that we may counter such false allegations. This is why we justifiably perceive a victory on the sporting field as a "national victory" against the British.'

The Maharaja's advocacy of cricket proved doubly effective because he appropriated the virtues—fair play and a sporting spirit—that were supposed to lend the game its distinctive 'Englishness'. These traits were in evidence when the Natore side played Presidency College at Natore Park. The college team was bowled out for a small total by the fancied Natore bowling, led by Palwankar Baloo and H.L. Semper. However, the college struck back, removing the frontline Natore batsmen cheaply. With eight Natore wickets down, the team was still 20 runs behind. At this juncture, rearguard action on the part of one of the Natore batsmen took the team to the brink of victory. Controversy arose when he hit a ball hard and thought it had crossed the boundary. In reality, it had not. When the fielder retrieved the ball and threw it to the wicketkeeper, the batsman was found short of his crease. The umpire correctly declared him run-out. The Natore team, with the Maharaja the only batsman remaining, protested that the other umpire had signalled a boundary. The team hoped the Maharaja, fearing he would have to bat in failing light against fast bowlers, would intervene on behalf of the batsman. Jagadindranarayan surprised everybody by declaring the umpire's decision final. The Maharaja came out to bat but with little time remaining, the game was drawn. After the match, he rebuked his players for questioning the umpire; the Maharaja of Natore was ever the gentleman cricketer. This incident serves as an example of how cricket was selectively appropriated by the local elite at a time of heightened nationalist activity in Bengal between 1900–10.

On another occasion, when the Natore team was playing the lawyers of the High Court, the umpire wrongly adjudged a Natore batsman out. The batsman had hit the ball towards the bowler, who had failed to stop it. When the ball hit the stumps on the other end, the umpire, presuming the ball had touched the bowler's hand, declared the batsman run-out. The bowler, Purna Ray, went up to the umpire and requested him to reverse his decision. The Maharaja, however, intervened saying that this was against the spirit of the game and the batsman was out. The umpire, frightened of the Maharaja's wrath initially, was reassured by the Natore ruler, who gently told him it was only human to err and umpiring errors were part of the game.

Yet, the very Maharaja so deeply involved in the game, so steeped in its culture and spirit, simply gave up on cricket patronage post 1914, soon after the death of Nripendra Narayan, the Maharaja of Cooch Behar. The premature death of his rival prompted Jagadindranarayan to shift his interest to the promotion of Bengali literature.

It is worth mentioning that cricket patronage by Jagadindranarayan followed a similar trajectory as that of Nripendra Narayan. Clearly, whatever the other motivations, peer rivalry was plainly the most important factor. As the Maharaja of Cooch Behar had established his cricket ground at Woodlands, in South Calcutta, it was essential for Jagadindranarayan to have his own ground, whatever the expense. He spent INR 1,00,000 on the ground in Old Ballygunge, an investment that almost depleted the Natore treasury.

Peer rivalries—notably the one between the Maharaja of Patiala and the Maharajkumar of Vizianagram and between Nripendra Narayan and Jagadindranarayan—had their positives. Each of these men played a role in improving the standard of Indian cricket. They also made the game more representative than is often realized, with the princely patrons seeking out talent, regardless of their social or economic background.

THE AMARNATH–DE MELLO AFFAIR

He was humiliated and sent back in 1936, with no one speaking out for him. He was treated with disdain by people with little or no talent as cricketers. He was denied an opportunity to play for India at his peak, despite having scored a hundred on debut against the MCC, in Bombay (now Mumbai), in December 1933. Many would have given up in the face of such adversity. But this was Lala Amarnath. He persisted and continued to play on in difficult circumstances and eventually got his reward when he was appointed captain of the first independent Indian touring team to Australia in 1947–48. More importantly, he managed to hold his own against Anthony Stanislaus De Mello, an administrator of prominence who played a leading role in the formation of the CCI, in a bitter fight for power in 1949. It was Amarnath who was instrumental in the eventual unseating of De Mello from the presidency of the BCCI, marking the beginning of a phase when cricketers started to hold their own in the cobweb of Indian cricket's power politics.

It was as sensational as it could get with De Mello, the president of the BCCI, preparing a list of 23 charges of indiscipline and misdemeanour against Amarnath. Of the charges, the most startling was that Amarnath, stand-in captain and selector along with Phiroze Edulji Palia and M. Dutta Roy, had accepted a bribe of INR 5,000 from officials and cricket enthusiasts in Calcutta (now Kolkata) to include Probir Sen of Bengal for the fourth and fifth Tests against the West Indies in 1948–49.

It all started when, at an extraordinary general meeting of the Board on 10 April 1949, De Mello charged Amarnath with serious breach of discipline and restricted him from playing any representative cricket for India or for any province in India. Soon after, De Mello, in an interview to the Associated Press of India on 14 April 1949, declared: 'The Board, at its meeting on April 10, was unanimous in its decision to take disciplinary action against Amarnath and it did not consider it necessary to hear him any more or any longer, as it had before it plenty of evidence about the veracity of which the members had no doubt.'

He also said the 'affair had caused him much disappointment' because he had 'at the sacrifice of many great friendships' brought Amarnath back into Indian cricket after the disciplinary action against him during the 1936 tour of England.

Amarnath hit back with gusto, saying he found it strange the Board had arrived at a decision without giving him an opportunity to defend himself. He warned 'the country will soon know the other side of the picture and will then be in a position to judge and decide as to whether the charges framed against me are correct'. He also said that he had 'sacrificed and suffered much—not only financially but in friendship as well—out of devotion and loyalty to the Board and its President'. He demanded that in the interests of Indian cricket, the Board should make public the charges made against him. 'While I do not expect any favour from the Board, I certainly hope they will play cricket.'

Amarnath found strong support from the Bengal lobby, mainly in Pankaj Gupta and J.C. Mukherjee, who declared Amarnath's suspension had been single-handedly pushed through by De Mello. Gupta revealed that he had, in fact, spoken against the motion, which had not even been on the agenda for the 10 April meeting: 'I yielded to none in the matter. I was not concerned with the merit of the case and the resolution at that stage but against the manner in which it was brought up and rushed through. Having spoken twice against the motion being placed on the agenda, I could not have been a party to passing of the resolution even as a matter of principle. It was indecent in my opinion to associate the INR 5,000 purse with the inclusion of P. Sen in the Test side. To connect the purse with P. Sen's inclusion was the thought, surmise, inference, and conjecture of persons, who perhaps, for reasons best known to themselves, lost the balance of judgment and good behaviour.'

Upset at being challenged, De Mello told *The Times of India* on 10 May 1949 that it was time to show Amarnath that even if most of the Board's officials did not take any action, the Board 'did have a dog that could bark and bite when indiscipline in Indian cricket was concerned'. He attacked Gupta, saying, 'Such rash statements are attempts at creating malice. The misdemeanour of captain Amarnath last season was seen, heard, and known throughout the country. I therefore had to submit the whole matter to the Board and did so at the full meeting on April 10 in a thoroughly constitutional manner. Discussions, in which all present participated for quite two hours were cool and cordial. At the end of the discussions, I submitted the phraseology of the resolution, which was unanimously passed. I can categorically state that there was no request for any revision or vote.'

Earlier, at a press conference held in the Governor's Pavilion of the CCI, in Bombay, on 4 May 1949, De Mello had issued a statement detailing the charges against Amarnath: 'Lala Amarnath's suspension from playing any representative cricket for India or for any province was the accumulated result of numerous acts of misbehaviour and indiscipline during the last season—acts which culminated in his blatant interview to a Lucknow newspaper, scathingly critical of the Board and its President, A.S. De Mello. That was the gist of Mr De Mello's explanations to representatives of the Press at a conference on Thursday afternoon in the Governor's Pavilion of the Cricket Club of India. The charges against the substitute skipper of India's Test sides for the series against the West Indies, together with all the correspondence relating to the unfortunate affair, were set down with exceptional detail in a statement, which was distributed to all present, and after this had been pursued, Mr De Mello invited questions and provided enlightenment on numerous points which were put to him. Twenty-three separate charges have been labeled against Amarnath, and the full list has been sent to him, while copies, along with relative enclosures, have been forwarded to the Vice-Presidents, the Honorary Secretary and the Honorary Treasurer of the Board of Control for Cricket in India, as well as to all its affiliated associations,' mentioned *The Times of India*.

These charges, as reported, also alleged Amarnath's negligence in his duties as captain, particularly his failure to organize net practice in good time before the first three Tests due to his late arrival at the venues; on a purported demand by him for additional payment made by him, as captain, for his out-of-pocket expenses in entertaining friends in his Delhi hotel; his last-minute decision to not captain the States' XI against the West Indies; his failure to notify the Board president of the injury that subsequently became a handicap to him and India in the second Test; his utterances against the Board and its president at receptions and to the press; his insult of the Board in not replying to two letters sent to him; and finally, his illegal acceptance of a purse of INR 5,000 against the promise to include Sen in the last two Tests against the West Indies.

In turn, Amarnath, on 5 June 1949, addressed a press conference in Calcutta where he distributed a 39 page, 27,000-word statement in an attempt to prove De Mello was out to settle personal scores. He replied to each of the 23 charges levelled at him, emphasizing that the Board, in effect De Mello, would never revoke the decision, nor make amends for the grave injustice done to him or to sport in general. Commenting on Amarnath's statement, the *Sunday News of India* noted: 'Amarnath has adopted the simple expedient of emulating M. Molotov as a convenient refuge from the numerous misdemeanours, which have been attributed to him. All he has said is a categorical "No" even in regard to utterances, which are alleged to have been made in the presence of a large gathering. According to Amarnath, his reported interview to a newspaper correspondent at Lucknow was a complete fabrication, the product of fertile imagination, though he has not bothered to suggest what could have been the object of the person responsible, one, moreover, who was obviously most sympathetic towards him. If one were to take Amarnath seriously, he would be left aghast at the injustices heaped upon his devoted head and the enormity of the conspiracy of which he is supposed to be the innocent victim. And, since everything can be placed at Mr De Mello's door, according to our blameless and long suffering substitute Test skipper, what could be more natural than a vigorous resort to mudslinging by the unfortunate aggrieved. Amarnath has tackled this in a really big way, with the quiet efficiency of a connoisseur, ignoring nothing that could smirch the antecedents of his accuser.

'To characterise this squabble between Amarnath and the President of the Board of Control for Cricket in India as an unfortunate affair, is, actually, an understatement. It has done the game in this country irreparable harm; and much of the responsibility for a most regrettable situation can be traced directly to the parent body, as well as to Mr De Mello himself. . . Those responsible for this ridiculous paradox will probably attempt to explain it away by declaring that the Beaumont Committee had, to all intents and purposes, exonerated Amarnath, and that subsequent honours extended to him were by way of reparation. Such an assertion would lead to the inference that

the Board of Control are incapable of making an appropriate choice
for key positions and that they ultimately display little confidence
in their own judgment, as well as that of their nominees. For one
reason or another, the swashbuckling Amarnath has been pampered
by Mr De Mello as well as by the Board ever since the first incident
[his sending back in 1936], and now he has struck back at one, who
himself claims to have been his benefactor.

'Dignity is the guiding influence for the controlling bodies of
all cricket playing countries in the world, but it does not appear to
carry the same importance for the Board of Control for Cricket in
India. When Amarnath was unceremoniously sent back to India
thirteen years ago, he sobbed out his misfortunes during a railway
journey to his port of embarkation. He has matured quite a lot since
then. Now, instead of weeping at his suspension from Indian cricket,
he has thrown out a veiled threat of legal action against the Board.
That was all that remained to complete the effect of a thoroughly
reprehensible business.'

In response to the charge that accused him of demanding
additional payment for himself, Amarnath said he had asked for
INR 150 for each Test player for eight days' stay at Test centres, which
he thought was a legitimate request. He also denied the allegation
that he had accepted an illegal purse in Calcutta, saying that he had
only accepted INR 5,000 from A.N. Ghose, honorary secretary of
the CAB, as a contribution to the Amarnath Testimonial Fund.
Ironically, this was a scheme mooted by De Mello for Amarnath's
benefit in 1947, when, in the interest of Indian cricket, Amarnath
had cancelled his Lancashire League contracts and turned down the
prospect of a contract with Sussex. In Amarnath's own words, 'The
Board, on Mr De Mello's initiative, had decided to try and help
me by reimbursing me partially [or the losses sustained].' As for De
Mello's aspersion that Amarnath had taken money to include Sen
in the team, Amarnath dismissed it, pointing out he could not have

got Sen into the side without the consent of the other selectors, Palia and Dutta Roy.

In response to the accusation that he dropped out of the States' XI match against the West Indies at the last minute, Amarnath pointed out he had informed the secretary of the Board eight days before the match, also drawing attention to the fact that the decision on his participation did not rest with him but with his employer, the Maharaja of Patiala. On his alleged unwillingness to reply to the Board's letters, dated 8 January and 21 February he said that he had responded on 14 January and 7 April respectively.

The *National Standard* published each of Amarnath's responses to De Mello's charges in 19 separate parts. The 19th and final rejoinder went thus:

I deny 'continued insulting disregard of the Board.'

Mr De Mello's charge number 21

Your continued insulting disregard of the Board by not replying to our first letter dated the 8th January 1949, and yet another letter dated the 21st February 1949, as given hereunder which was sent to you, 'registered-ack-due' and which was duly received by you on the 24th of February 1949.

Dear Captain Amarnath,

I returned to Bombay early this week and was surprised that there was no reply from you to my letter sent to you through the kindness of Mily, Secretary to H H Maharajadhiraj of Patiala dated 8th January 1949. To avoid unpleasantness and other difficulties I would appreciate a reply to reach me at the above address before the end of this month. There is also another inquiry to make. In a speech made by you after the fifth Test match at Bombay, you have referred to 'power politics' by the Board. Will you explain what you meant by the remark?

Captain Amarnath's reply:

I totally deny Mr De Mello's charge of 'continued insulting disregard of the Board'. I did reply to his letter of 8th January on the 14th of January—if you will look up its copy in reply to charge No. 17. I replied to Mr De Mello's letter of 21st February on 7th of April, which, Mr De Mello states, was received by him on 11 April that is the day after the meeting that suspended me. The delay in replying to Mr De Mello's letter (i.e. of February 21) was owing to my various preoccupations after the considerable time I had to devote to cricket for three months. My foot also had to be operated upon in Kanpur and besides I was positive I had replied to Mr De Mello's letter of January 8 on January 14, which would have served to inform Mr De Mello on the points he had raised.

Mr De Mello's charge number 22

Your interview to the *National Herald* dated 2 April 1949 charging me personally, the Selection Committee and the Board with intrigue against you.

Captain Amarnath's reply:

I deny categorically that I granted any interview to the National Herald or authorised its Editor or anyone else to publish any story quoting me. I possess conclusive documentary evidence to show that no interview could possibly have been given to the National Herald for publication on or about 2 April. This will also be borne out by the fact that as soon as my alleged interview to the National Herald came to my notice, I, under a registered letter, acknowledgement due, dated 4 April wrote to the Editor of the said journal contradicting the alleged statement that I had granted the interview. You will note that on 4 April when I denied giving the alleged interview I had no idea that there was any motion to suspend me on the 10th. I thus acted in good faith in writing the letter of contradiction. The question, therefore, of my charging

Mr De Mello personally, the Selection Committee and the Board with intrigues against me, does not arise for the simple reason that I have never made any such charges.

Mr De Mello's charge number 23

Your speaking disparagingly to all and sundry about what transpired in the Selection Committee thus depriving India of the best efforts of selected players.

Captain Amarnath's reply:

It is absolutely untrue that I spoke disparagingly to anyone about what transpired in the Selection Committee. Mr De Mello should at least remember that he himself often evinced keen interest in the proceedings of the Selection Committee meeting with such questions to me as, 'How on earth could so and so be chosen and how could so and so be dropped?' My uniform reply was, 'The Selection Committee did it. Don't ask me.'

It is amazing that Mr De Mello should bring this charge against me. I was a selector along with the Nawab of Pataudi and Mr V.M. Merchant in England in 1946 and again in Australia. Not one word was ever spoken against me on those occasions nor until the end of the West Indies tour. I have always known my responsibilities in the matter but Mr De Mello must have his own good reasons to have preferred such a vague and frivolous charge. I have nothing more to say.

The 18th installment of the series went thus:

Mr De Mello's charge number 20

Your statement at a lunch in Bombay on 9th February charging the Board with "Power Politics" was reported by the UPI.

Captain Amarnath's reply:

It is incorrect that I made any reference to "power politics" at a lunch in Bombay on 9 February, which I gave in honour of the West Indies cricketers. I did, however, give an interview to the United Press of India on February 11 in Bombay after the last Test was over. Almost the entire interview dealt with the technical aspects of Test cricket and an appreciation of the West Indies cricketers. In answer to a question on the organisation of our cricket with a view to India taking her rightful place in international cricket, I used the expression "Power Politics" in a very general way.

Public opinion was deeply divided over whom to support, and there was conjecture that De Mello's enemies within the Board would use the opportunity to oust him. Expressing this sentiment, *The Sunday Standard* issue of 3 July 1949 reported that 'there is no question that Bengal and Madras think alike on the Amarnath affair' and are determined to expel De Mello from the Board. It went on to predict, 'There is every indication that the suspension of Amarnath is going to be made the medium of a very big gamble for the control of Indian cricket.' De Mello, however, showed no signs of relenting and issued the following statement: 'Amarnath's statement of June 4 from Calcutta is as apocryphal as all others that he has continued to make once he attained the exalted position of substitute cricket captain of India. Reading through it, I can only remark that it is difficult to escape the conclusion that he and his hired assistants in Calcutta, like the proverbial mountain, have laboured really hard and brought forth a mouse. His statement is a veritable tissue of suppressions, misrepresentations and inventions. My return to India Today and this statement by me ring the bell for round 20 of this slanging match started by Amarnath and his advisers. I am not going to quote again that Amarnath did so and so at Delhi and Bombay and so on. I shall leave all that for the exhibition bout on July 31. But

I shall again emphasise that the matter was given full consideration at our meeting on April 10 and a unanimous decision was made at a dignified and cordial meeting. I cannot understand how all this malice and wearisome wrangling have since crept in. I shall name the culprits responsible for all this in our meeting on July 31. I am hundred percent confident that the Cricket Control Board of India will not permit Amarnathism to make a paradise for indiscipline in Indian sport and may I add that the game is more than the player of the game. . . It is not yet known and realised that Indian cricket, which has attained international manhood under me (1928–49), is my second religion and that with my eternal vigilance on her behalf I shall not tolerate indiscipline or nepotism of any kind in her ranks.'

To complicate matters, Amarnath announced his determination to go to court: 'Lala Amarnath told the Press Trust of India today that he had made up his mind to take legal steps against the Board of Control for Cricket in India for his alleged wrongful suspension by the board on April 10 as a last resort to vindicate his honour. Amarnath said that "the court of law was the only place where I can get justice." He said that he had already circulated his public reply to all those who counted in Indian cricket, and he felt that the statement of the President of the Board. . .characterising his reply as a "tissue of suppressions, misrepresentations and inventions" showed clearly that the President in the name of the Board was persisting in defaming him nationally and internationally.'

Soon after, influential commentators like A.F.S. Talyarkhan began rallying against Amarnath. In his column in *The National Standard*, 'Take it from me', Talyarkhan argued: 'Instead of threatening to go to court, Amarnath should boldly seek permission of the Board to attend its next meeting. He should ask to be permitted to appear in person, answer questions and generally satisfy everybody that the charges against him are false. If he is so adjudged he should ask to be reinstated. This to my mind is the only thing he can do as a cricketer against whom action has been taken. To go to court will mean that Amarnath will have to prove malice on the part of the Board. I dare say that those who were present at the meeting, which penalised him, will become the defendants to the suit. I was representing a province at that meeting and I, therefore, will also become an accused. Very well, at least I am ready to stand up to the Lala's charges. Let him prove that my vote for suspending him was based on malice, enmity, ignorance, or that I voted without the facts before me. As an individual and as a representative of that Board meeting I accept the Lala's challenge. Let him proceed. I will need no lawyer to defend me.'

On the day of the Board meeting, the *Sunday News of India* reported: 'Well! That fateful annual general meeting of the Board of Control for Cricket in India will be held this morning at the Cricket Club of India, and before another couple of days are over we will probably know whether those who are entrusted with the destinies of the game in this country have succeeded in extricating themselves from what can be considered as nothing better than an appalling mess. This mess revolves around the suspension of Amarnath and enough has been said on the subject to obviate further comment. According to a press report, Amarnath has sued the President of the Board of Control, A.S. De Mello, for defamation claiming a lakh of rupees as damages, and this suit will be heard at Calcutta, where the Lala evidently commands a great deal of support. It has also been stated that India's substitute Test skipper tends to drag the Board of Control itself into the Madras High Court after today's meeting.

'So if we accept De Mello's statement regarding his many kindnesses to Amarnath, it seems that the President of the Board of Control has sown the wind and now reaps the whirlwind.'

In the fateful Board meeting on 31 July 1949, a compromise was reached, which, in hindsight, can be best described as a temporary truce. Amarnath tendered a qualified apology to the Board and its president. However, the Board was forced to concede that its decision against Amarnath was ultra vires, since no advance notice had been issued and because no opportunity had been given to Amarnath to make his case. As a result, the Board was forced to delete the relevant portions from the minutes of the 10 April meeting.

That the animosity between De Mello and Amarnath wasn't buried after the compromise of 31 July was evident from the cricketer's statement in an interview prior to his departure for England in April 1950. Amarnath told *The Times of India*: 'De Mello has done me a lot of harm. But my reputation has been fully vindicated by no less a celebrity than Bradman in his memoirs. He (De Mello) had tried to drive me out of cricket, but without success. One day soon, I feel sure, he will come crawling to me, begging me to help him once again.' He added, 'They came in large numbers to give Hazare, Mankad and Umrigar a grand send-off when they sailed from Bombay a few days ago. Don't they know that I am also going to play in the Central Lancashire league? But, anyway, they will gather in their thousands to greet me on my return after the successful season that I anticipate for myself with the same club that Worrell served as a professional last year.'

Something of the sort did happen a year later. To quote *The Times of India:* 'De Mello was unceremoniously bundled out of the Board of Control for Cricket in India.' The Bengal lobby, led by Gupta and supported by Amarnath, unseated De Mello, who had held considerable clout in Indian cricket for the best part of the preceding 25 years. As a rude reminder to De Mello that he was no longer in power, Amarnath soon notified the Board that he was fit to play for India again.

However, Amarnath had still not won the battle. De Mello's attempted comeback the following year constitutes the final lap of the Amarnath–De Mello affair. De Mello needed to successfully

outmanoeuvre the Gupta–Mukherjee–Amarnath combine in the 1952
Board election. This is precisely what he set out to do. Buying and
selling of votes began in earnest. In return for votes, both sides held
out the lure of administrative posts, including managerial positions
of touring Indian teams. Both sides portrayed themselves as avenging
angels, intent on righting the wrongs done to Indian cricket during
the other's tenure. That De Mello had done much to develop cricket
in India was beyond doubt. He had contributed to the building
of stadiums and clubs, had organized tours and, above all, been
instrumental in the establishment of the Board in December 1928.
A section of the local English press was all praise for De Mello. In
fact, *The Times of India* once reported that, 'all that stood to the
credit of the parent body was the handiwork of De Mello and the
new office bearers would find it extremely difficult to emulate him'.
Some leading sports journalists, close associates of De Mello, were
critical of Gupta and Amarnath. Class and social status suddenly
turned important and De Mello's polish was preferred to the rusticity
of Gupta and Amarnath.

With elections round the corner, De Mello was the favourite to
win. Expressing this view, the sports correspondent of *The Times of
India* reported on 12 October 1952: 'As anticipated, the battle for
the Presidentship had developed into a clash between the Bengal
clique and that which supports my old and respected friend Anthony
De Mello, and so well had the latter conducted his campaign that
as late as on the day before the meeting there was a strong feeling
evident that Mr J.C. Mukherjee would certainly be dethroned by
the veteran administrator he himself had unseated.' Confident of
victory, De Mello had, in fact, arranged for celebrations at a leading
Kolkata hotel.

De Mello's task had been made easier by Gupta's absence, away
in England, in September, with the touring Indian team. Gupta
had only got back to Kolkata in October, just weeks before the

election. Amarnath had a special role in the drama and his selection as captain for the forthcoming tour of Pakistan had much to do with the determination to keep De Mello out. Commenting on the selection, *The Times of India* reported: 'Like a prima donna who bows numerous farewells, Lala Amarnath comes back and forth as India's captain. That is no reflection on him but on the pinchbeck Caesars of the Cricket Board of Control who unlike Caesar's wife never seem above suspicion.' It was also suggested that, 'The motivations which excite the choice of India's captain are many and mysterious. And the selection committee appears to change its mind as often as a Hollywood actress changes her husband'.

It was justly questioned why, six months after Amarnath had been discarded (he was dropped for the tour of England in the summer of 1952), he was suddenly invested with the duties of captaincy against Pakistan. Amarnath had done nothing in the intervening period to merit selection, let alone captaincy. It was not without reason that *The Times of India* asserted: 'There can be no doubt that the question of captaincy would play a big part in the ultimate result of the elections. No logical or practical explanation is possible in justification of the Board of Control's decision to dig Lala Amarnath from virtual obscurity and entrust him with the leadership of our representative side.'

That it was a tactical masterstroke was proved when on the morning of the Annual General Meeting, the Bengal clique was assured of a majority. Though the margin, 12–11, was as narrow as it could get, it was enough to keep De Mello out. Realizing the implications of defeat, De Mello withdrew his candidacy. It was poetic justice. The very methods used by De Mello to become president earlier had been deployed against him. That this was largely the handiwork of Gupta was evident from a report in *The Times of India* which noted: 'Tony's adherents, however, had reckoned [they would win] without that incorrigible pan chewing diplomat Pankaj Gupta, who, with his customary thoroughness and resource had utilised the appallingly few days since his return from England to such excellent purpose that on the morning of the AGM the Bengal clique was assured of a majority.'

In hindsight, the saga of De Mello's ouster seemed to have been orchestrated with poise by Gupta and Amarnath. It was all part of a meticulous plan, apparent from the tenor of Amarnath's statements before the media a few months earlier, when he was forthright in declaring that he would captain the team to England in the summer of 1952. That particular ambition might have gone unfulfilled, but Amarnath was back in favour for the series against Pakistan. His outrageous statement about captaining the side led the sports correspondent of *The Times of India* to assert: 'I have no hesitation in saying today that if the parent body succeeds in disproving that its choice of a skipper was engineered by the exploitation of party politics, as usual, the only conclusion that can be drawn is that it is hopelessly inept and unschooled in its duties.'

As for De Mello, Board president Mukherjee offered him the chair of the committee entrusted with arrangements for the celebration of the Board's silver jubilee. Unsurprisingly, De Mello declined. In a letter to the secretary of the Board he said, 'As one of the founders of the Board of Control for Cricket in India, I wish the silver jubilee celebrations great success but regret that owing to the uncertainty of my plans, I am unable to accept your invitation.'

This letter, written to stave off further humiliation, marked the end of De Mello's career as a leading cricket administrator. The ordinary Indian cricket fan of today is unaware of his many achievements—among them the establishment of the Asian Cricket Confederation in 1948. It was no great surprise then, that De Mello's birth centenary, in 2000, was allowed to pass unnoticed, except for a function at the CCI.

EGO VERSUS PERFORMANCE

At a time when Amaranth was involved in a no-holds-barred fight with Anthony De Mello, another Indian stalwart, Vinoo Mankad, fell out with the BCCI. This was yet another episode in the bigger story of control, with cricketers gradually coming into their own in the echelons of Indian cricket's corridors of power.

It all began when Mankad wrote to the BCCI in November 1951, informing the Board that he had received an offer to play as a professional for Haslingden Club, in the Lancashire league, the following season. With India scheduled to tour England in the summer of 1952, Mankad's assignment as a professional was not looked upon with favour by the BCCI. However, given his reputation, the Board would have found it impossible to drop him, and accordingly, he was advised to fly back from England to attend the trials for the forthcoming tour. It was surmised that the Board knew Mankad would have to rescind his contract with Haslingden to come to India to attend the trials. Hence it was all a ploy to keep Mankad out.

Upon receiving the invitation, Mankad agreed on the condition that his selection was assured—by no means an unjust demand from one of the world's top all-rounders. It seemed reasonable because Mankad, under contract with the Haslingden as a full-time professional, would have to forsake his only source of income to make himself available for the trials. Mankad proposed to the Board that he play in all four Test matches while assisting his club for the rest of the tour.

At first, the Board responded with sympathy, urging him to join the trials and leading him to believe that his selection was a formality. On 16 February 1952, things turned on its head. After a Board meeting, Mankad was told he was not needed for the tour. One of the selectors decreed that Mankad was not special and Indian cricket had dozens of players of his calibre.

Commenting on the Board's decision to drop Mankad, *The Times of India* wrote: 'The meeting decided that Vinoo Mankad's services, even if available for the four Tests in England this summer, should not be utilized. Mankad, it may be recalled, captured thirty three wickets in the series of Test matches against England in India, which is one of the finest performances in Test cricket of all time.' As there was much criticism of the Board's decision to drop Mankad, the president, J.C. Mukherjee, tried to justify the action in an interview to the cricket correspondent of *The Times of India*: 'It was pointed out to me by Mr Mukherjee that the proceedings of the Board's special meeting were incorrectly reported, and that, far from making any direct allusion to Vinoo Mankad, the controlling body had merely arrived at a decision on the policy that should be followed with regard to the tour as a whole. As experience had shown that much dissatisfaction and heart burning resulted when the services of players who were not actually in the touring side were utilised for Tests and other matches, it was resolved that the selectors of the team for England should be directed not to choose players who were not available for the entire tour. Thus since Vinoo Mankad had already intimated to the Board that his renewed agreement with a club in the Lancashire league for the coming season would make it impossible for him to assist the Indian touring side, it was obvious that the famous all-rounder could not possibly figure in the coming Test series against England. Much is being said by people who claim to be in possession of first hand information about the controlling body's refusal to meet Vinoo's demands in respect of an adequate guarantee and financial terms, but Mr Mukherjee gave information that strenuous efforts had been made to ensure Vinoo's participation in the tour.'

But as fate would have it, Vijay Hazare's team faced disaster at every step in England. The irony was completed by Mankad's rousing form, playing for Haslingden in the Lancashire league. In his first appearance, Mankad was unbeaten on 71 in a score of 118/5, and even before the start of the first Test at Leeds, 5–9 June 1952, Hazare was forced to turn to Mankad for assistance. This was after two players, Ghulam Ahmed and Dattu Phadkar, had got injured. However, their injuries were not serious and it was almost certain both would be fit for the first Test. Even if they weren't, Chandu Sarwate and Ramesh Divecha, both part of the touring side, were available for selection. Given these circumstances, the team management's SOS to Mankad seemed awkward. This is how *The Times of India* summed up the situation: 'Since last Saturday, when it became known that Vijay Hazare had cabled for the Board's permission to utilise the services of Vinoo Mankad in all the Tests, the sole topic of discussion among sports circles in Bombay appears to be the justification, or otherwise, of the touring skipper's action, an action which, it now transpires, has the full support of the team's manager Pankaj Gupta. Many are of the opinion that Hazare was driven to this recourse by the rapidly developing panic, which has engendered in him a premonition of defeat in the forthcoming Tests and the loss of prestige he feels he would suffer as a consequence. Others are definite that the Indian skipper was compelled to make this appeal by Pankaj Gupta, who, basing his calculations on what has happened thus far, is seriously alarmed at the disastrous effect an early defeat in the series would exercise on already unpromising gate receipts.'

In another report, the special correspondent of *The Times Of India* criticized the manager of the touring team, Pankaj Gupta, stating: 'I can find excuses for the skipper of the side, for, as I have always maintained, he has not been fortunate enough to receive the specialised grooming for the important position that has been entrusted to him by a notoriously inept parent body, but it is impossible for us to be tolerant with Pankaj Gupta for the part he has played in the creation of an appalling mess, nor can we condone the completely weak kneed attitude of the president of the BCCI, Mr J.C. Mukherjee, who had the power to put a stop to all the nonsense that was brewing and yet did not exercise it.'

What made the actions of Gupta look worse was the demand that Mankad be released by Haslingden not just for the first Test but for all four Tests. As *The Times Of India* remarked: 'Vinoo Mankad should have been a certainty for this tour, but for reasons best known to the Board of Control for Cricket in India he was not included in the touring side. Furthermore, any question of his services being utilised in the Tests was placed completely beyond the bounds of possibility by a resolution passed by the parent body to the effect that only those players who were available for the entire tour would figure in the Tests. It is extraordinary that Pankaj Gupta, who was one of the most fervent supporters of the resolution, should have taken the lead in a move, which is intended to make a farce of it.'

On its part, Haslingden Club was apprehensive about releasing Mankad, knowing it would affect both the club's championship prospects and its revenues. Accordingly, it initially refused permission and India was forced to play the first Test match without Mankad. They lost the game by seven wickets.

Before the start of the second Test, the club, under intense pressure, reversed its decision. Mankad's release, it was surmised, was perhaps facilitated by Sir Herbert Merett, a leading Welsh industrialist and president of the Glamorgan County Cricket Club, who made a cash offer to Haslingden. This, he said, was to demonstrate to the Indians how much Welshmen admired their pluck as cricketers.

Merret's gesture, *The Times Of India* reported, was greeted warmly by the Indian manager, Pankaj Gupta, stating: 'This is a very fine gesture and one which we expect from Wales, where we have many friends. We want Mankad for all the remaining Tests and I have told the Haslingden Club that we want him without any special conditions being imposed.'

However, when confronted with an agency message from London containing Gupta's statement, Mukherjee, the BCCI president, expressed his ignorance about the attempt to bring back Mankad. Referring to news that Merrett had made a cash offer to Haslingden, Mukherjee felt such a move would not be appreciated in India and that the Board would most likely refuse to have Mankad on those conditions.

Against Mukherjee's wishes, Mankad was included in the team for the second Test, with Haslingden consenting to release him for the rest of the series.

The second Test, which India lost by eight wickets, is still best known as 'Mankad's Test'. He scored 72 and 184 respectively, and also took 5/196 in the first innings. Even after this performance, the BCCI did not honour Mankad and he was forced to return to Haslingden later that month. The club wanted to give him a hero's welcome, but Mankad, disappointed by the treatment in India, turned down the offer of a red-carpet reception. As T.B. Hargreaves, mayor of Haslingden, said: 'We would dearly have liked to accord Mankad some civic reception, but we are respecting his wishes that no fuss should be made.' Haslingden, he went on to add, was proud of Mankad for placing the town on the cricket map. His signing had increased the club's membership to nearly 1,400, a record for the club.

Back in India, *The Times of India* expressed disgust at the manner in which the BCCI and the team management had conducted themselves on the Mankad issue: 'Principles have gone by the Board, solemn decisions which were based on the experience of past tours have been blithely ignored, and the manager of our side has not only condescended to accept for Indian cricket what is tantamount to pity and charity but also, to all intents and purposes, demanded that consideration.'

In turn, Gupta condemned the Indian press. Pointing out patriotism was nobody's monopoly, he declared, 'I have always had the prestige of the country in mind and despite whatever the Indian tinpot critics might say in the matter, I maintain that by bringing in Mankad I did not barter away India's prestige but enhanced it considerably.' He also stated that, 'Anyone who thought India would win in the Tests against England should have found a place in a lunatic asylum. If we could not beat the second English team under Nigel Howard on our home grounds, how could we, without Merchant, Amarnath and Mushtaq Ali, hope to succeed on a wet English wicket with the opposition at full strength?'

As for Mankad himself, saddened at the treatment meted out to him, he confirmed his decision to retire from Test cricket at the end of the English season. Hearing this, the Board acted promptly and persuaded him to change his mind. Mukherjee conveyed this at a press conference on 17 December 1952, stating: 'Vinoo Mankad has decided to reconsider his decision to retire from Indian cricket. It will be recalled that some time ago Vinoo Mankad had declared in Ceylon that he would retire from Indian cricket. Vinoo is an outstanding cricketer and has still got a lot of cricket in him. It would be a great loss to Indian cricket if he ceased to play for India. I am very glad to say that he has, at my special request and that of some of his friends, agreed to reconsider his decision. It is indeed very good news for us that he has placed his services at the disposal of the Board.'

Mankad was finally felicitated on 23 December 1952, for having achieved the fastest double—100 wickets and 1,000 runs—in Test cricket, breaking the record of Monty Noble of Australia. He was presented with a purse of INR 12,501 in Bombay, an amount that reflected the state of cricket's finances in 1950s India. Commenting on this occasion, S.R. Tendolkar, the president of the BCI, deplored Mumbai's poor response to the appeal to raise a substantial purse for Mankad.

Compared to the niggardly response to the purse in the home of Indian cricket, Bombay, other centres responded with zest to the effort to honour the country's leading cricketer. While Justice Tendolkar received contributions from all over India, including distant parts of Bihar, Mankad was feted by the members of the Nagar community, to which he belonged, at a public function.

PART FIVE

THE PRESENT INTO THE FUTURE
VIRAT KOHLI AND A BILLION DREAMS

It was around 11.15 p.m. in Dhaka on a muggy evening in March 2012, and Virat Kohli had just played one of the most incredible 50-over knocks of all time. He plundered 183 against Pakistan, demolishing Saeed Ajmal, who was at the time hailed as the world's leading spinner. Through that knock Kohli had given the Indian journalists in Dhaka enough to write about. At Mirpur, the press conference enclosure is right across the dressing room on the other side of the ground, and each of us had been eagerly waiting for Kohli to come and answer our questions. To our surprise, however, he stopped midway into his walk towards the press conference area. To his right, a section of the crowd had still been lurking around, close to 45 minutes after the match had ended and was screaming his name when all of a sudden the star of the night started walking towards them. He spent a good 10 minutes with the fans, signing autographs, and then almost sprinted across to see us at the presser venue. Soon after he had taken his position in front of the microphone, he offered an apology for the delay and said to the fairly large media contingent that he felt it was his duty to spend a few minutes with the fans.

He added that if any of us had a deadline to meet, he was sorry to have kept us waiting.

All of a sudden there was a hushed silence in the room. The statement had come out of the blue and none of us had been anticipating it. Here was a man known to be brash and aggressive, passionate and temperamental, and the last thing we had been expecting was to hear Kohli speak like a statesman.

To our surprise, he did so and to the few of us who had been tracking his career from its inception, it was a sign of the things to come. His transformation from being a match-winner to contemporary cricket's biggest brand had only begun.

Soon after the press conference was over, I remember walking up to him and telling him that we, the Indian television media present in Dhaka, wanted him to speak to us individually. It was not the norm, but given that it was a night like no other, a request like that wasn't out of line. An Indian cricketer had just scored 183 against arch-rivals Pakistan and we had every reason to be celebrating Kohli. In terms of broadcast journalism, we much needed this elusive 'exclusive' for the routine press conference wasn't enough. The media manager Satish was non-committal and had left it to Kohli to say a 'yes' or a 'no'. Much to our surprise, once again, he agreed. 'Please ensure no one asks me more than three questions. I am really tired,' was all he said as a prelude to the presser. For the next hour, he patiently did nearly 10 media interviews. It was enough indication that Kohli was working on an image makeover and it was a sign of things one could expect from him in the future.

Between March 2012 and May 2016, Kohli, the batsman, had made gigantic strides towards seeking immortality. He took over India's captaincy from M.S. Dhoni across formats in course of time, scored four centuries and seven fifties in the 2016 edition of the IPL, then groomed himself into arguably the best limited-overs batsman in the world, and has been the hottest brand in Indian sport by a distance for some time now. Through these years, Kohli, in a run chase had been fast becoming a subject of folklore, and for a journalist, he was the interview every sports scribe was keen on doing.

Kohli and I had been in touch all through and I had covered almost every game he had been a part of. We discussed things on WhatsApp, and it was only after he had singlehandedly beaten Australia in the World T20 in Mohali in March 2016 that I requested him for an interview at his convenience. It was batting of a very different quality, and I really wanted to understand how his mind functioned under pressure while hunting down huge totals.

Sourav Ganguly had deftly summed up Kohli's unbeaten 85 against Australia. 'Sheer class,' he said when asked to decode Kohli's prowess in a chase. 'If it's a run chase, he just has this uncanny ability to take his game a few notches higher. Pacing innings after innings beautifully and soaking in all the pressure, India's talisman is also India's single biggest match-winner in ODI and T20 cricket,' an overjoyed Ganguly had said.

'What is it that makes Kohli so special when chasing herculean totals? How is he different to others, and is he the best white-ball batsman in the world on current form?' I asked him.

'The last question is the easiest to answer. It is an overwhelming "yes". No A.B. de Villiers, no Joe Root and no Kane Williamson come near Virat in the 50-over format. In T20 it is ABD and him,' reasoned Sourav.

Ravichandran Ashwin, Kohli's biggest match-winning weapon in Test cricket, puts it even better. 'He just knows some grounds like no one else does. He can work out strange angles when batting and place the ball at will. He hunted down the Australian score in Mohali with the asking rate touching 13, something that we have very rarely seen in cricket.'

In trying to analyse what's extraordinary about Kohli's batsmanship, one is forced to single out his confidence and ability to soak in pressure. The context, however big it is, doesn't faze him and he goes about his business in a manner he has mastered over the years. Knowing well he can accelerate at any time, the asking rate is never a concern with Kohli and the self-awareness allowing him that extra bit of cushion to pace his innings. Importantly, he allows the batsman at the other end to bat freely, and to their liking, they do so without ever feeling the pressure. Considering Kohli's running between the wickets is inevitably top notch, most batsmen can revolve around him without having to look at the scoreboard.

It wasn't so, however, in January 2012 in Australia. Mired with self-doubt after multiple failures in Melbourne and Sydney, Kohli had receded into a cocoon trying to answer the hardest question for himself—'Was he good enough to belong at the highest stage of all?' A gritty 75 in the second innings in Perth on a pace-conducive pitch at the WACA restored a measure of his self-confidence but it was the century in Adelaide that left him changed as a cricketer forever. 'I finally felt vindicated that I did have the ability to score runs on the big stage,' is how he had summed up the innings to me in a longish phone interview, soon after the team was back from Australia.

The year 2016, however, turned out to be a memorable antithesis. Self-doubt and introspections were a thing of the past and, by then, he had become the first Indian captain to score four consecutive Test hundreds against Australia in Australia in 2014–15.

As an analyst of the game, I needed to make sense of the transformation of Kohli if I had to make sense of Indian cricket going forward.

Knowing that Kohli was to be in Kolkata in May 2016 for the game between Royal Challengers Bangalore (RCB) and KKR, I asked him for a time to conduct the interview. I was apprehensive if he would readily agree or not. A detailed television interview will mean a clamour for more interviews from rival networks and, as Indian captain, it might well be impossible for him to say no to a few others who have closely tracked him over the years. Hence, a refusal would have been understandable and I had prepared myself for it. To my delight, however, Kohli agreed. We decided to fix the exact time closer to the date.

RCB had not started the season well and lost five of the first seven matches, needing six wins from the last seven to make it to the playoffs. Time was running out for Kohli and my interview, too, hung in the balance. How could I ask him for it when his IPL season was on a downward spiral? The stars, it seemed, were conspiring against me. That's when I got a message from him late one night reconfirming the interview and suggesting that we meet at the ITC Hotel at 6 p.m. on the designated date. When I called him the next day to finalise the plan, it seemed he wasn't remotely worried about being knocked out. All he was talking about was the need to win the next few games and for him it was the only thing possible. Losing, for Kohli in May 2016, wasn't an option. This was a very different Kohli to the one I had seen and met in Australia in 2012.

I hadn't informed many in India Today Television, the channel I have a consultancy with, about the interview because I was still unsure how things would eventually turn out. This was because I have, forever, believed in promising less and delivering more. Maybe the video quality of the interview could have been better if I did apprise the crew of the same earlier. The set-up and the equipment, too, could have been better. However, to be honest none of it was of any real consequence to me. As an analyst of the game, all I wanted to do was decode the mind of Indian cricket's presiding deity, to understand him better and get closer to his craft.

I called Kohli at 5.45 p.m. to tell him I had reached the venue. 'I will be there by 6 p.m., as discussed. I just need to arrange for security to get to the part of the hotel where you have set up,' he said. 'I need security'—his words were a very matter of fact statement as far as he was concerned. But, isn't it hard to picture? He needed protection to walk across the lobby to come and do an interview inside a five-star hotel where he was staying! This was a first in my life. In my career I have interviewed the very best and the most popular of the sportspersons, and this man was clearly in the same league to be faced with this level of curiosity and fan adulation. He arrived a minute before 6 p.m. and looked totally relaxed in his black rimmed spectacles and a grey round neck t-shirt. I asked him how much time he had for I would formulate my questions accordingly. 'You said you wanted to do it nicely and go deep. I have an hour and more. So don't worry and let's start.' Even before the interview had started, Kohli had scored a boundary. He made me feel comfortable and relaxed and I was no longer in a hurry.

For the next hour-and-a-half I asked him all I wanted to ask. And he answered each and every question in detail. Speaking on possible comparisons with Sachin Tendulkar, he said, 'It is unfair on Sachin. He played for 24 years with amazing consistency and I have just completed five,' was his candid response. Clearly, here was a man who was at peace with himself. Indian cricket, more importantly, seemed to be in safe hands.

And then I asked him about Test cricket and whether he still considered it the format to excel in. He was, till May 2016, a better limited-overs player than he was in Tests, and knowing so, I had deliberately tried to bowl him a doosra. 'There is no doubt I need to do better as a Test cricketer. That's what we are remembered for and I am no different. Getting a Test hundred for India is the most special feeling of all,' he had dismissed the delivery with a simple swat of the bat. Yet again it was apparent to me that Indian cricket, going forward, could not be better placed.

The 12 months, between May 2018 and June 2019, with tours to England, Australia and the 50-over World Cup scheduled, will define Kohli's legacy as a captain. Seeing Kohli up close I feel a real sense of hope and anticipation.

As the clock neared an hour, I asked him my most important question. How could he deal with the kind of pressure we put on him day in and day out? To what extent does it entail being left with no 'me time' at all? Is it impossible to be living a life dictated by having to deal with the 24x7 news media, who want to know everything about his private life?

Kohli, it seemed, was ready for the question. He said to me with a smile, 'I try to be like a monk living in a civil society, you know and I don't have any regrets.' Here was a twenty-eight-year-old national icon speaking to me with the maturity of a forty-year-old. I had got my headline, and the statement resonated all over the media for the next few days. But it had a far deeper effect. It helped me understand Kohli better than I had ever done. Here was someone so deeply invested in his craft that all things happening in and around were of little consequence to him. He could cocoon himself from it all and do what has been asked of him—lead the Indian cricket team with infectious passion in all formats of the game.

His 'monk in a civil society' comment, however, would come under real test in June 2017, when in the aftermath of head coach Anil Kumble's resignation, he was the subject of a severe social media backlash. And, to be honest, it did test him and his resolve. While he has not spoken on the issue as mentioned earlier in the book, people in the know have confirmed to me that Kohli did feel let down and disappointed; more pained than anything else. He had been held guilty without being heard.

Until February 2017, Kohli could do no wrong. Four double hundreds in the Indian home season between September 2016–January 2017 and winning back-to-back series against the West Indies, New Zealand and England, Kohli was the media's blue-eyed boy all round. Not one to hold back in press conferences, he would give the media what they wanted, and journalists welcomed the onset of the 'Kohli era' in Indian cricket with open arms.

And then came the dip in form against Australia in the last leg of the home series, followed by the injury sustained while fielding at Ranchi in the third Test which sidelined Kohli from the first few games of the IPL. RCB finished at the bottom of the table in the 10th edition of the tournament, but with the Champions Trophy around the corner, many felt India's talisman would soon be back to his flamboyant best. And if the start of the Champions Trophy was any indication, things did seem to have fallen back into grove for captain Kohli. A match-winning innings against Pakistan and thereafter another half-century against South Africa in a run chase, leading India to the semi-finals before hammering Bangladesh with panache, batsman and captain Kohli could again do no wrong.

Debate over the rift between him and Kumble, a reality of Indian cricket for a while, was pushed to the background, thanks to strong on-field performances taking centre stage. So much so that officials and players could brush aside talk of the rift without the media forcing their hand. All of this before the much-awaited final against Pakistan.

And once India lost, and lost badly, things started to unravel for Kohli. A dressing room exchange, with Kumble giving Jasprit Bumrah a dressing down moments after the loss did not help and then the very next day Kumble resigned as coach making matters worse. The media, which was all in Kohli's favour, all of a sudden started questioning the Indian captain and his conduct. He was subsequently perceived as the big bully and the man who had let success get to his head. Unable to defend himself with the BCCI's media gag in place, Kohli suddenly had become the big egotist who had forced out the legendary Kumble to take control.

How can a legend like Kumble be treated like this, was the common refrain and some even went on to suggest that Kohli was perhaps becoming too powerful to the detriment of the sport in India. A couple of media reports also suggested that Kohli had taken the biggest risk of his life by pushing the ego tussle against Kumble as far as he had. The overwhelming sentiment was that he should have backed down and made peace with Kumble.

It is important to state that the media bashing, often unfair and unfounded, was good for Kohli in the long run. Without knowing his side of the story, the media had gone after him and sided with Kumble. In cricket, it is the captain and not the coach who is the ultimate boss and it is Kohli's team, no matter what the media said or says in future. With India playing away from home over the next 12 months in England and then Australia, Kohli would have the most difficult year of his life as captain. This hardening in the aftermath of the Kumble saga should only help him in these tough times. His honeymoon as captain was clearly over by June 2017 and he knew what to expect from the media in difficult circumstances. He also knew that it was to be his bat and bat only that could/ can save him and speak for him the long run. His series wins and hundreds are his legacy. All he needs to do is conquer those 22 yards like he has done so often until now. Once he starts winning, and does so away from home, all talk of treating Kumble poorly will go out of the window. The very same people who called him a brat will then say he is the best thing to happen to Indian cricket in a long time.

If the Indian captain needed a reality check ahead of his most difficult tenure as skipper, with the Kumble saga he got it in full. It only made him stronger and got him further ready for the grind. Whoever the coach is, it is Kohli who will have to face up to Anderson and Broad and Starc and Cummins. It is his bat that will have to save games and set totals for his bowlers to defend. He is in the hot seat for good and bad and he is aware of it every second of the day. Maybe one day he will defend himself. And give out his side of the story. But by going after him in the manner that it did, a section of the social media may have inadvertently done Indian cricket a big favour—getting India's captain and best player battle ready; and perhaps hungrier than ever.

Is Kohli aware of the enormity of the task at hand? Does he know what failure in the next 12 months might even lead to? Two separate news items, both involving Kohli in the last week of October 2017, both of which consumed a lot of newsprint, tell me he indeed does. While the first celebrated Kohli as one of the world's leading sports brands, the other, yet again, speculated on his then prospective marriage with actor-partner Anushka Sharma. What is interesting in each of these cases is how Kohli was being consumed and appropriated in the media. First, anything Kohli does is news—whether it's right or wrong. That he might get married to Anushka was considered breaking news. Wonder why? But it was and that's the ground reality. And once a news platform puts something out in India, it just gets copied and multiplied, without being given a thought to what Kohli might feel or what his opinion might be on the issue. A concern for his privacy is the last thing in the mind of the media. It is, as if, his life, public and private, will have to be played out in front of the gaze of the 24x7 news media and he, Kohli, will have no agency in controlling things going forward.

'What can I say to this,' he wrote to me when I asked him about the media play. 'How many people can I personally go and correct? This is their way of selling news,' he said.

This is an alarming trend. While it isn't new, its strength is getting multiplied by the day and with a flippant social media machinery behind it, there is no mediation anymore. Icons are deified in India by the minute and in the very next instant they are trolled or abused. Their private lives aren't a protected domain and that Kohli wasn't issuing a statement on the wedding story was considered a failure on his part. Social media, more and more, thrives on being flippant and violating privacy, and if you are an icon of the stature of Kohli, you are public property.

What is further alarming is that perception, more often than not, seems to be shaping reality in India. During the fall-out with Kumble, social media, as I have emphasized, had branded Kohli arrogant even without knowing his side of the story. How can a super-rich, tattooed, hugely successful man with a beautiful actor girlfriend (now wife) not be arrogant was the notion. The die was cast. He was hung without a trial. #ArrogantVirat was trending on Twitter and yet again there were thousands of tweets attacking his relationship with Anushka. Kumble, older and considered more mature, was wronged by this brash upstart was the sentiment. Without getting into the right or wrong, the moot point here is that in the media deluge, his voice was the last thing anyone wanted to hear.

The same thing had happened when India lost the 2015 World Cup semi-final against Australia in Sydney and the trial by social media had adjudicated Anushka's presence in the stands as the primary reason behind Kohli's failure to score beyond a run. The jingoistic outpouring, rather obnoxiously I must say, targeted Anushka for Kohli's failure and yet again social media was on the boil for days. How she could have impacted his run-scoring, rather failure to score, wasn't ever given a thought. Intemperate comments were flying around thick and fast, and within minutes, Kohli, the deity, was a fallen hero.

The Kohli–Anushka affair—Virushka as it became known to us all in 2017 when they got married in Italy—it must be stated, is entirely a private matter of these two individuals. The media, page three or otherwise, has no business trying to interfere and arriving at conclusions on them. In the least, such conclusions need to be verified before being put out for public consumption and a thought spared for what the person concerned might feel about the issue. It is a moral and ethical issue at a certain level. An issue of conscience and probity. Of media accountability and uprightness. Anything Kohli can't be peddled as news. He can't be our hero at our convenience;

we cannot worship him when he scores a hundred and criticize him for not telling us if he is indeed getting married or not. It is his will for god's sake and we, the media, have no right in trying to interfere and speculate.

Kohli, commenting on such inane speculations, himself puts it best: 'Everyone makes choices. You choose what you do. Some choose good some choose bad. Bad is easier.'

His concluding statement is, perhaps, most revealing: 'I am a hero at personal convenience.'

For the sake of Indian cricket, we need to leave Kohli, the married man alone. As captain of this talented Indian cricket team he will need every bit of media support in England and Australia. The media, like in the West, will have to back him up as captain. If the goings-on don't change, Kohli will find it impossible to trust the media and confide in them. Take them into confidence and consider them partners. Of course, we must criticize Kohli for his failures on the cricket field. And hail him for scoring hundred after hundred and winning series after series. No captain has won more bilateral ODI series than him on the trot. But as far as his private life is concerned, it is time we leave the man alone. We must allow him his space for that's key to him seeing the media as a support system and not otherwise.

The last words on Kohli have clearly not been written. Will he be hailed in five years as India's greatest batsman and captain, or will he go down as an autocrat who treated legends unfairly? Again, will it matter to him how we label him? Does Kohli, the person, really care anymore? I guess, he doesn't, for he is at peace with himself, in his gym, at training, in marriage and most importantly in the coveted 22 yards. He is at peace in giving up multi-crore endorsement contracts because he doesn't believe in the products he is being asked to endorse. He is all alone when he bats and when he trains. A passionate robot with single-minded determination. Much like the team he now leads. He is happy to take responsibility for his failures just as he is keen to enjoy his success, he said to me in an interview in Delhi on 8 September 2017. And Indian cricket, so far, has benefitted. He will continue to polarize opinion but give us results. And, in sport, it is winner takes all. And Kohli, no one can dispute, is a winner.

UNFINISHED BUSINESS

It was around 8.45 p.m. India time on Saturday, 27 January 2018, when Mohammed Shami ran into bowl to Lungi Ngidi searching for his fifth wicket in what was shaping up to be a match-winning spell in Johannesburg. There was chirping all around with the Indians sensing a famous come-from-behind win in the third and final Test of the series. Social media was abuzz with Indian fans starting to express themselves and the Indian dressing room was on edge. Ravi Shastri, India's head coach and his bowling deputy Bharat Arun, were busy chewing their fingernails and the sense of anticipation had been multiplying with every ball. Indian captain Virat Kohli, passionate and expressive as ever, had marshalled his troops dextrously, reducing South Africa from 124/1 to 161/9 in a 241-run chase that had seemingly been on course to culminating in a 3–0 whitewash by the hosts.

For Kohli, it was a moment of reckoning. India, having been defeated in the previous two Tests and staring at a whitewash, had all of a sudden given themselves a crack at redemption. The series may have been lost, but pride wasn't. Credibility stood to be restored and, with it, a renewed sense of hope that this team is capable of doing well overseas as well—and consistently so. At the start of the Wanderers Test, many had pegged it as a dead rubber. It was, however, anything but dead. On a treacherous pitch, which was subsequently rated 'poor' by the ICC on account of making 'batting extremely difficult and hazardous' and as the match progressed, with four South African fast bowlers steaming in, the Proteas had done everything to make the most of home advantage. Determined to avenge 2015 and complete a 3–0 clean-sweep, it was yet another no-holds-barred contest. India, under Kohli, was committed to pulling one back and reignite faith. Kohli himself had excelled as a batsman and had time and again proved his class in the series but, as captain, he had to win the third and final Test to demonstrate that he was leading a team which had the potential of winning Test matches away from home.

The series, played at the back of less than ten days' practice in South African conditions, had not gone according to plan for India so far. While the bowlers had done well right through, the batting was a let-down. Chasing 208 for a victory in the first Test, India failed to complete the task at hand, resulting in the same old lament that the Indians were poor travellers. The captaincy may have changed but results hadn't, was the refrain. Kohli, clearly, was smarting. He had looked good with the bat in the second innings of the first Test, at Newlands, before playing the wrong line to Vernon Philander. With the talisman out, the rest of the batting unit collapsed in no time and it was, yet again, a tale of what could have been. Kohli, however, could not just be competitive and lose. He had to win to make a statement; prove that his team deserved to be called the best in the world. He had an opportunity in the second Test on a relatively easier pitch at SuperSport Park and, yet again, his batsmen squandered it away. The captain with a valiant 153 batted like a lone colossus and was understandably distraught at the end of the match. An altercation with the media did not help and going into Wanderers, Kohli and his team were under enormous pressure, with the impatient Indian cricket fan already starting to call them names. Wins at home were starting to be scorned at and all the achievements of 2017 suddenly weren't enough any more.

And finally, when Kohli opted to bat on a green Johannesburg surface, having picked an unprecedented five fast bowlers in his side, he faced the ire of many. Experts like Shaun Pollock doubted the call on television and it seemed that Kohli, the captain, was still far from being in the league of Kohli, the batsman. This belief was reinforced within the first 30-odd minutes of the Test, with K.L. Rahul and Murali Vijay both out to false strokes. South Africa had their tails up and Kohli walked in to bat with a possible ignominy staring at him if he failed. Cheteshwar Pujara, one of Test cricket's best advertisements, and one with the patience of batting for days if need be, was at the other end and scored his first run only off the 54th delivery that he faced. Pujara, and the dressing room, were all smiles. The message was loud and clear. While the captain was determined to dominate, Pujara was determined not to get out. It was a fight for survival and the Indians were gradually starting to find feet. Kohli, eventually got out for a well-compiled half-century, having made a serious statement about batting overseas in the most difficult of conditions. And, to his credit, not once did he complain about the pitch being played on. Pujara's 179-ball vigil, not always the best to look at, but effective nonetheless, was proof that the Indians weren't just flat-track bullies. Buoyed by the twin-fifties from Kohli and Pujara, and a lower-order cameo from Bhuvneshwar Kumar, India scored 187, which was a par score on the surface. With the bowlers doing the job for the team one more time, the match was finally reduced to a second innings shoot-out. It was all about the ability to soak in the pressure, the hunger and the zeal to win, and do so amidst adversity.

That's when the batsmen finally stepped up. It started with a small but effective cameo from Parthiv Patel of only 16 runs but, on a pitch like the one on offer at the Wanderers, it was as good as a 40. Murali Vijay and K.L. Rahul then stitched together a plucky 34-run stand, which Kohli would have been proud of. Then Vijay/ Kohli followed by Kohli/Rahane contributed with partnerships that tilted the match in favour of India. Every few overs the batsmen were getting a knock on the fingers and on the body by deliveries coming in at speeds of over 145 kmph; they weren't pleasant, to say the least. The Indians, to their credit, did not flinch. There was no running to the umpires or no throwing in the towel. With a dressing room cheering every single run, it was a batting display that was enough to redefine India's poor overseas record, and prompt experts like Nasser Hussain to laud Kohli and his team. On a pitch where people could get injured and end up with broken fingers and ribs, the Indians did not back away. They wanted the game to go on. Rahane, playing his first Test of the series, got hit on the elbow but refused medical attention. He remembered the uneven pitches in Mumbai and batted on. Clearly, he wanted to be out there—for himself and, most importantly, for India. And he said it at the post-day press conference reiterating what Kohli and Shastri have been saying all along: The Indians were ready to play in any pitch given to them. Yes, there were soft dismissals and dropped catches but the intensity, which Kohli keeps talking about, was there for all to see. It was there when Shami, not the best tail-ender, smashed Morne Morkel for a six over mid-wicket, in a shot that spoke volumes about India's ticker on display. Not only did it add six runs to the total, but also had a never-give-up attitude written all over it. Here was Shami, on a surface where every ball had a death warrant signed to it, smashing one of South Africa's premier fast bowlers for a six. Understandably, the dressing room was all upbeat. A statement was made and intent declared.

Finally, it came down to the bowlers for one last time. They had picked 50 South African wickets on the tour already, but it would all come to nothing if they did not nip out these final 10. Shami, at the back of a good batting cameo, started the process by picking up the first one, but then there was Hashim Amla. He may not have been sold at the IPL auction but he was definitely the best South African batsman on view on an immensely spiky track. Playing with an exaggerated shuffle, Amla blunted everything the Indians threw at him. All of a sudden the pitch looked less menacing, and South Africa was back in the hunt. Already 2–0 up and, at half an hour to tea on day four, the possibility of a 3–0 outcome in favour of South Africa was starting to look likely. There was every reason for the Indians to give up with a 100-plus-run stand staring at them, and with Dean Elgar and Amla looking good against the softer old ball. There was every reason for Kohli to lose patience and make mistakes on the field. There was reason for the bowlers to look sluggish and fielders to concede easy runs. None of it, however, happened and the Indians kept finding their way back into the match. The visitors kept at it until Amla finally made a mistake. He flicked the ball in front of the pitch slightly uppishly to mid-wicket and Hardik Pandya, who was having a horrendous Test match until then, plucked the ball out of thin air. He had breathed life into the Indian bowling effort and the game was far from over for either side. In came the great A.B. de Villiers, and soon enough hit a boundary to a rare bad delivery from Ishant Sharma. Half an hour of de Villiers and the match was done. Young Jasprit Bumrah, the find of the series, and one who wasn't carrying any baggage of expectations, however, had other ideas. He made the old ball jump off a length and a hapless de Villiers could not do much but watch the catch go to India's most reliable fielder Ajinkya Rahane at gully.

The slide had started. An inspired bowling change in giving Shami another go followed and soon South Africa were on the mat. Vernon Philander, Kagiso Rabada and the rest failed to offer much resistance and the Indians emerged deserving winners by a substantial margin of 63 runs. The win, more than anything else, was testimony to what the team was capable of. It was proof that competing overseas isn't an impossibility, and with proper preparations, India can justly claim the tag of being the 'best in the world'.

While the win at the Wanderers was indeed a huge sigh of relief, it was also indication of what I call 'unfinished business'. India isn't a team any more to bask in the glory of winning one good overseas Test match in a year. Instead, they can make winning overseas a habit and can give good teams competition on their turf. There is enough substance in this team to redefine the history of Indian cricket, break barriers and conquer frontiers. This is a bowling unit that is well capable of picking up 60 wickets in three away Tests and a batting unit that scores runs on a surface where even the South Africans were feeling unsafe to bat on. It is a team that wants to set new standards. And, thereafter, raise the bar yet again. Pujara isn't afraid of playing 53 dot balls before scoring and Kohli isn't afraid of bossing the cover drive off Vernon Philander on a pitch where driving on the up is like picturing India win 10 gold medals in the Tokyo Olympics in 2020. The first happened. The latter probably will not.

As this book goes to press, I sense hope, renewed energy and positivity. It is not only about the IPL and the big money and the glamour that lies at the core of it. So what if Pujara and Ishant don't have an IPL contract? They will still turn up for India in England and try and fulfil a collective national yearning. There is more unfinished business, and Kohli and his boys know it well. They have a chance in England and they will have another opportunity in Australia during the end of 2018. Wanderers is proof that India have the goods to stamp their authority overseas, just as deftly as they do it in their own backyard. There is, however, a gap between potential and reality and Kohli is well aware of that too. He knows he can't afford to take a chance in England come 1 August 2018, and will do all he can to make winning on foreign soil a habit. This is what matters to Kohli the most and it is only a matter of time before his infectious enthusiasm bonds a team that has one motto and one dream—to rewrite history and win away from home with aplomb. There is unfinished business no doubt, but there is also hope that it will soon be done. Under Kohli and his new India.

POSTSCRIPT
THE INDIAN CRICKET TEAM AND NOT
THE WOMEN'S CRICKET TEAM

When we left Mumbai to play in the World Cup there were hardly any journalists who had come to the airport to see us off. But when we returned to India on 25 July having made the final, there were close to a hundred journalists at 2.30 a.m. in the morning. I was surprised to see so many journalists and must tell you the flashes just did not stop. This was something totally new. Since then all of us have been flooded with interview requests and offers. We have been invited to events, have been felicitated and celebrated the country over. Today people stop to greet us and recognize us. I have been playing for India for 18 years now and this has never happened before. So in that sense 2017 has made a huge difference to our sport.

—Mithali Raj (Captain, Indian team)

This book is the story of the men's game in India. Not for once, however, do I wish to suggest that the women's story is any less significant. The only reason I haven't touched upon the women's story is because I don't think I am equipped yet to do justice to it in all its complexities. It is a book for another day. And it is indeed a story no less thrilling.

Sample this: Barely a dozen journalists were present at the press conference where Indian captain Mithali Raj outlined her plans for what was the to be the biggest tournament of her career, before leaving for England in June 2017. On 26 July, more than 60 journalists and cameramen flocked to the Grand Ballroom of the JW Marriot in Mumbai, where Raj and her girls fronted the felicitation presser, less than three days after coming second-best to England in a closely contested World Cup final. These are facts confirmed to me by Annesha Ghosh, an *ESPNcricinfo* journalist, who has been my research associate for a long time. She is among the few reporters who was present on both occasions and also at the Chhatrapati Shivaji International Airport, where the World Cup finalists were greeted to a rousing reception at 2:30 a.m.

Yes, you read that right: In the dead of night, the Mumbai airport was teeming with fans, junior cricketers, policemen and the media, who couldn't seem to get enough of the Indian team. Here's what Annesha writes on the arrival in an *ESPNcricinfo* piece titled 'India Women Revel in Unmistakable Buzz': 'Through that one hour [after landing], it appeared as though the media had taken upon themselves to expiate for the sins of an entire nation that had conveniently chosen to be oblivious to the existence of nearly four generations of women cricketers. Raj, having endured non-recognition for the larger part of her career, like her peer Jhulan Goswami, however, didn't fail to acknowledge what the reception meant to the team.

'"Obviously, it's quite overwhelming to see such kind of a reception. It's first of its kind for all of us," Raj said. "I did face something similar [in terms of our outcome in the final], not exactly similar, but a little lesser in 2005. But then there was no BCCI. At that time, I was wondering had we been under BCCI, what kind of reaction we would have or what kind of feedback we would have got back home. But today I can actually feel it's such a huge thing. It's just the beginning of good times for women's cricket.'"

Even when Goswami landed in Kolkata the next day, there were no fewer than 50 journalists present at the airport. The team was awarded INR 50 lakh each by the BCCI and other hefty monetary rewards and commendations were subsequently conferred upon them by the state associations and the Indian Railways. Raj herself was gifted INR 1 crore and a house plot by the Telengana state government and also a BMW by sports enthusiast V. Chamundeswaranath. It was a final like no other and has indeed changed how the women's game in India was perceived.

The build-up to the final on 23 July 2017 had started early in the morning. Queues of Indian fans began making their way into the stadium well in advance of the start of play—a sight so very common whenever India plays at Lord's. Only this time it wasn't Virat Kohli and his boys. It was Raj, Goswami, Harmanpreet Kaur, Punam Raut and 11 other women, who had finally forced the Indian cricket fan in London and beyond to come to Lord's waving the tricolour and hollering for the blue brigade. Back home, the build-up was no less momentous. All India Radio, in a rare gesture, had organized live commentary in multiple languages and the host broadcaster was showing the match across eight different channels. Not to be left behind, news channels, which play a key role in generating buzz, had multiple shows right through the day. Suffice to say, it was the biggest news event in the country on the day; a fact proved beyond doubt when Aarti Dabas, Head of Media Rights, Digital and Broadcast, at the ICC, tweeted staggering Star Sports viewership figures for the final.

Furthermore, even when the team lost, the buzz did not diminish. From the prime minister of India down to other high-profile politicians, sports stars and Bollywood celebrities, social media was ablaze, celebrating the achievement of Raj and her team. The sport, it was apparent, was no longer an also-ran. The team had done enough to lift it out of oblivion and shove it right at the centre of public discourse. Each of the players, stars in their own right, have been celebrated since.

There were no television cameras in 1983 when Kapil Dev smashed that 175 against Zimbabwe and rescued India from the depths of despair. While the world missed out on seeing the heroics, for his teammates the knock had the effect of making them feel that a miracle was indeed possible. A dream that few dared to speak, or even think about, turned into a reality in the next two weeks. Prior to the 1983 World Cup triumph, India's victories, few and far between, were hardly accorded the recognition they merited. With 1983, it all changed.

Harmanpreet Kaur's unbeaten innings of 171 against Australia in the semi-final, which was broadcast live across the world, has equal potential and more. Kaur, trending ahead of the newly elected president of India, Shri Ramnath Kovind, had broken through as the emblem of a blue billion that dared to believe. Every six that came out of Kaur's bat was a statement in itself—pushing the need for more recognition and better pay, telling corporate honchos what this team is capable of, stating in unequivocal terms that the BCCI needs to do more for women's cricket in the country and do so immediately. So what if the opposition had Meg Lanning and Ellyse Perry, Raj and her blue brigade were out there to seek immortality. The anger Kaur vent at nineteen-year-old Deepti Sharma for running slow towards the non-striker's end was not so much because Kaur's 100th run was at stake, but, as she later explained, was due to the significance she attached to Deepti's wicket in the context of the game. Kaur, a senior member of the side, and the vice-captain, was aware of the enormity of the occasion. Her outburst was as much a testimony to the currency she attributed to every run that was to be scored or conceded in the match by India as it was an outpouring of the collective angst of Indian sportswomen, who, for the longest time, have been discriminated against. The World Cup—for Kaur, Raj, Goswami and the other girls—was an opportunity that they couldn't afford to let go. Even though they fell nine runs short of lifting the trophy, they had done enough to ask the BCCI for equal treatment and demand their fair share.

On 14 August 2016, Dipa Karmakar, the young gymnast from Tripura, made the world sit up and take notice of what an Indian is capable of when pitted against the best in the business, including the likes of Simone Biles, who took the gold for USA at the Rio Olympics. She was followed by Sakshi Malik, who helped lift the growing gloom in Rio and was bettered by P.V. Sindhu, who gave further impetus to an Indian badminton revolution that was begun by Saina Nehwal in London in 2012. Sindhu, for the record, was the second-highest earning Indian sports star in 2017, after Kohli. If the multiple brand-endorsement deals, appearances on television shows, cover shoots for magazines and an unprecedented spike in social media following in the wake of India's World Cup campaign is anything to go by, Raj can surely be expected to emerge as a close competitor.

Going back to Kaur, her innings of 171 had done far more than just take India to the final of the World Cup. It had given women's cricket a new identity that it so badly needed. More importantly, others who nurtured a silent ambition to be the next Kaur or Raj, but stopped short of saying so due to familial and other pressures, found a new voice.

On 23 July 2017, 11 Indian girls stepped on to the hallowed turf at the Lord's cricket ground, knowing they were on the cusp of history. Rather, they were shaping history. Some years down the line, a history of women's empowerment in India will have to include a very determined Kaur, who took on and defeated the mighty Australians, world champions several times and considered unbeatable by many. Battling a finger injury and a shoulder strain, she fought on, and in doing so, wrote a new preamble for any history of Indian women's sport. In a country starved of sports champions, this women's team came through as a whiff of fresh air, leaving an indelible imprint in tough overseas conditions and against quality opposition.

Moments after the final came to a close, Abhinav Bindra, India's lone gold medal winner at the Summer Olympics, tweeted saying, 'Shit happens'. Bindra, for the record, came the closest to a second-time podium finish at the Olympics in Rio, before eventually losing out in a tie break. It was the closest one could get to a medal and yet not win. Was it pressure or was it just that moment? As Bindra says, it just happens. In that moment, when Veda Krishnamurthy played a cross-batted slog trying to clear the infield and go big, she must have backed herself in doing so. Until then, she had been hitting the ball cleanly and there was no doubting her ability. But that particular shot did not work. And she knew it the moment she had hit it. A slight shake of the head as she set off for the single was proof of what she must have felt.

And then, there was the teenager Deepti. For her, this was as hard as it could ever get. The pressure of a World Cup final and the pressure of a billion expectations is not something one has to deal with every day. Deepti, it must be said, will never face anything tougher in her whole life than what she felt on field that day. A charge to lift the ball over the bowlers head for a boundary and it was evident she had the mettle. But could she finish the job that all of her seniors wanted her to do? Seeking immortality is one thing but to achieve it is difficult. Deepti did her best at Lord's. In front of a packed stadium, she looked anything but a nineteen-year-old. Interestingly enough, Deepti was only two years of age when Raj made her debut, in England, and on the day of the final, Deepti was India's last hope. How can I best explain to my readers how difficult it was for these girls? I have to go back to the 1990 football World Cup or to the more recent penalty shootout involving Argentina and Lionel Messi. At home, in front of a legion of Italian fans, home star Roberto Baggio stepped up to thunderous applause to take a key penalty. He had won hearts that tournament and was the next big Italian superstar. Baggio, most felt, could never miss. He did. And so did Italy. Can Baggio ever come to terms with what had happened that instant as he took that shot? Does he replay it in his mind? It will be a huge surprise to me if he doesn't.

And then there is Messi. The Argentine superstar has come close to achieving immortality numerous times in his career. He came close in 2014 against a raucous German side that had thumped Brazil 7–1 in the FIFA World Cup semi-final. Could he go past them and, once and for all, close out the comparison with Diego Maradona? Could he prove to the world that he was as good as the Argentinian legend? Unfortunately for Messi, he wasn't able to. The trauma was such that he even contemplated retirement. While Raj and Goswami may have to go away from the game knowing they were as close as one could possibly get, Kaur, Deepti, Krishnamurthy and the others are likely to have another crack in the future.

Real Impact of the Campaign

With several months having gone by, and with the felicitations from men and women of prominence completed, the most important question is: Have we lost sight of the real goal?

For the record, India won 101 medals at the 2010 Commonwealth Games and it was our best showing ever. It was followed by an impressive performance at the 2010 Asian Games, with our boxers winning multiple medals, including a very important gold by Vijender Singh. The surge continued in London in the 2012 Olympics and

India ended up with six medals for the first time in history with podium finishes in boxing, shooting, wrestling and badminton. These athletes, toast of the nation, were celebrated and rewarded. But soon enough it all went back to square one. With the Indian Olympic Association suspended for corruption and mismanagement in December 2012, the entire momentum was lost. India was down to 64 medals at Glasgow, 2014, from the 101 in 2010; we won half of what we had won in 2010 at the 2014 Asian Games, and had to settle for only two at Rio 2016. Inability to capitalize on hard-earned success to make more profound structural changes in the sporting realm means that Indian Olympic sports continue its struggle for corporate support.

That's what we don't want for women's cricket. While it was admirable to gift Raj a BMW, maybe Chamundeswaranath, a former cricketer and administrator, would have done better in giving this money for hosting women's camps across the state. The BCCI, unfortunately, has not been too gung-ho about ringing in change right away. While plans of formulating a Future Tours Programme (FTP) for women cricketers have made headlines, that India has not scheduled any international fixture over six months since the World Cup final is not how the Indian Board should have dealt with the momentum generated by the team's transformative performance.

Besides, is it not high time to start thinking of more camps for girls at the National Cricket Academy and elsewhere? Will there be considerations for an IPL-style tournament or exhibition games that can be held alongside the men's IPL, as Snehal Pradhan, former India-international-turned-freelance-journalist, had suggested in the months following the World Cup?

With the women's World T20 only months away, it is time to get behind the blue brigade one more time. Not the Indian women's cricket team, but the *Indian* team. Kaur, the T20 captain, leading an Indian team out in the Caribbean, will yet again galvanize the nation and corporate India will be forced to take notice. The women, lest we forget, are equal stakeholders in the decision-making as the men.

There is indeed enough momentum for a revolution. Only it should not get stymied by our penchant for not effecting structural change.

And yes, there is enough for a gripping story to be written about women's cricket in India. As I said earlier, maybe another day, another time.

I will leave the last words of this book, which has been my sincerest labour of love, to my friend and highest wicket-taker in the world, Jhulan Goswami. 'When older siblings [implying male siblings] needed one more person to play with, I was called upon to make up the numbers. After they finished playing, I practised all by myself because that was the only time I had access to the bat and the ball. From Chakdaha to Lord's has indeed been an eventful journey.'

Is there a story there? I would certainly say so!

EPILOGUE

It was time for the mid-innings break in one of the IPL matches in its 10th season at Eden Gardens. To be honest, the tedium of it all had started to get to me. Match after match was turning into a blur. Yes, the crowd loved it and I was part of a minority—an aberration. Instead of wasting the ticket, I decided to walk out of the comfort of my seat in one of the hospitality boxes in the L enclosure and quietly leave the stadium. I needed some fresh air and the whole cosmetic atmosphere of Eden Gardens, with the loud music, was starting to feel suffocating. Just as I walked out of the gate, some 15 people who ran up to me to ask if I had tickets. I did. I had my own and one extra ticket. I handed them over to a young boy as I crossed the road to try and walk back to my car as soon as possible. The boy, who had literally snatched the tickets out of my hand, couldn't believe his luck. He darted towards the gate, where a cop told him, 'I saw what you did'. For a second I thought of going back and speaking to the cop about the boy. He was entitled to go in and there was no reason for the cop to stop him. But then I felt drained and just left the boy to his own devices and kept walking. That's when she approached me.

'*Dada, chinte parchen*? [Hey, brother, do you recognise me?],' she asked. The voice sounded familiar. Like someone I may have known closely in my past but who had now faded from my mind. Each one of us have had this experience at some point. I was glad the lady came to my rescue. '*Dada, bhalo achen? Aapni aamar theke awnek toffee kinechen jakhan Test khela dekhte aashten aar Mohun Bagan maathe football dekhte ashten.* [You bought a lot of candy from me when you came to watch Test cricket and local league football at the Mohun Bagan grounds].' Instantly, it all came back to me. She used to sell candy when I was growing up and used to be a permanent feature of the Maidan. Whether it was football or cricket, she was always there. All smiles, in a saree. And, here she was—still selling candy. Twenty years earlier, there had been no IPL, no T20 cricket, no cheerleaders. She, however, was there. For the few people who came to watch Bengal play the Ranji Trophy at Eden Gardens, she was there—flashing a radiant smile. And even as the IPL took over, she continued to sell candy. The riches of the T20 league had not made her bottle of candy—merely a rupee each—passé. She was like a link between the past and the present—a thin thread of continuity. From the time when cricket was a mere sport to now, when cricket is a billion-dollar industry. I am a relic too: Someone who loves Test cricket but has been reduced to a minuscule minority. But it did not matter. Just as the 60,000 people inside were/are the story of Indian cricket, so were we, the two of us, an extricable part of the narrative. Different constituencies, but, yes, part of the same story. And there is no moral judgement here. I wasn't better than anyone inside the stadium; nor were they any better than me. We were both constituents of Indian cricket and, in a manner, it was our community.

As I looked at her in appreciation and awe, she said to me with a smile, '*Khaaben*? [Do you want to have one?]' I had not had a candy in ages. But this was much more than just a candy. It was a slice of my childhood—my bond with cricket. My world, where the sport was different but the same sport nonetheless. I agreed to have one, and as she handed it to me. I gave her a 100-rupee note and requested her to keep it. I wanted to give it to her but not out of sympathy. She had given me free candy all my childhood and here I was, seeing her again after nearly two decades. It was the least I could do. She, however, refused it right away. She just wouldn't take money. I felt as if the sport itself was telling me that it wasn't always about the money. It can never be. Regardless of the IPL and all its riches, there will always be Test cricket; and Virat Kohli, I'm certain, will still prioritize the five-day format over anything else. It does not matter to him whether or not people watch the format any more, or if 60,000 spectators dance to his sixes like in the IPL, but not to his straight drive when playing in whites. For Virat and many of his ilk, the straight drive is their legacy—was, is, and always will be. That lady selling candy was a reminder of the time when cricket was a sport, not an industry; a time when 100,000 people would stand in serpentine queues for tickets to watch Test cricket at the Eden Gardens. Back then, there was no online system; no website to book tickets at the click of a button. Did I feel old? Alien? No, I did not. Just as there is an Andre Russell, an IPL star in the real sense, there is a Cheteshwar Pujara, who India turns to when playing the five-day game. Both have a place in the game's pantheon and both have their domains carved out. While I will watch Pujara ten times out of ten, thousands will prefer watching Russell hit those towering sixes for KKR to Pujara toiling it out for singles. How does it matter who watches whom? Both are playing the game and adding to the story of Indian cricket at home and beyond. Shouldn't that be enough for the lover of the sport?

I got back home that night all charged up. I had never played the game at the highest level but I did play—for school and my *para (gully)*—kept wickets, did some good stumpings, and batted decently as well. I could never hit the ball out of the park but I had managed to put a price on my wicket a few times. In that sense, I was more like Pujara than Pandya. It was time to go back and see some *para* cricket again, just to see if I could identify with it any more. I knew no one would recognize me as a player—journalist and newscaster, yes, but not a player. And that's what I wanted to do. Go play. Stand behind the wickets and try and take a catch one more time. I wasn't confident of playing with the leather ball, but that did not matter. For the moment, tennis-ball cricket was good enough. As soon as I woke up the next morning, I changed and walked to the YMCA opposite my house. Every Sunday a game of cricket is played there and that Sunday was no different. It was a seven-a-side match and they were missing an umpire. That's when a young kid recognized me and asked me if I would stand as umpire for that game. I was happy to. In fact, I was just happy to be out there on the pitch and be involved with the game in some way. Not to analyse, not to speak about it on television, not to write another column. Just be a part of the action and soak it all in. To think that a few hundred such matches were being played all over Kolkata at that very instant and that a few thousand young boys and girls (hopefully!) were playing the sport we all love was good enough for me. Maybe none of them would ever go on to play for India. Or maybe, one or two would. But for each of them playing that morning, the intensity was no less than anyone playing an IPL game in front of a packed crowd at Eden Gardens.

Players at the YMCA came in all shapes and sizes. Some were completely unfit like I was. But it did not matter. It was a game of bat and ball and the perfect start to a Sunday. Seeing a really young kid walk into the YMCA with his kit bag, as big as he was, my mind went back to Sachin Tendulkar in the year 1987. No one knew then that he would be *the* Sachin Tendulkar—the best batsman in the world and a Bharat Ratna awardee. All he knew was he loved the game; that he wanted to score runs and keep playing. Like any other kid playing at the YMCA that day. It was not about records broken or money earned. Not about IPL contracts or big endorsements. It was all about playing for the simple love of the sport. These kids who turned up and played every single day of their lives, often with no end in sight. More often than not with no audience to watch them play. There was no Star Sports or Sony television crew covering the match, no cheerleaders to entertain the audience, no anchors walking into the crowd to drum up the excitement. It was literally a throwback to the game as it used to be 100 years ago. Just a game played between two teams for the sake of it, with no frills attached. And this was as much representative of Indian cricket as a Lalit Modi or a M.S. Dhoni. Thousands still turn up in Kolkata and Mumbai and Chennai and Bangalore to play the game for the sheer thrill of it. Hundreds of matches are still played at the Azad Maidan on a national holiday. Nothing has changed since Tendulkar batted there for the first time in 1987. Yet everything had changed. Cricket is no longer just a sport. It is quasi-religion—a huge money-spinner. Success at cricket is now a ticket to deification and immortality.

Writing and talking about cricket is my profession. I do it for a living. But it also gets boring on occasions; dull and monotonous sometimes. And that's when I run away to the Maidan, to the YMCA, to county cricket if I am in Oxford, or to the Sunday afternoon *para* game if I am at home in Kolkata. I don't need to write or commentate or analyze any of these games. No one is interested. And this obscurity is often pristine. It represents a part of cricket's romantic past that is now lost. But it does exist. It exists in these inconsequential matches played across the country, in schools and colleges, in joint family courtyards and in small club grounds. And the intensity generated in these matches make the game what it is—a national aspiration for the discerning Indian. Every second Indian wants to excel at cricket, bat like Kohli and bowl like Ashwin. We are, still, largely a single-sport country. Yes there is badminton and shooting and tennis but cricket, it has to be acknowledged, is the undisputed leader.

And then there is the BCCI, a body that has little credibility left but one that still fetches INR 20,000 crore for IPL rights for five years.

In the last three years, the BCCI has repeatedly been castigated by the apex court of the country. Its office-bearers have been shamed, thrown out, summoned and rebuked. They've been called names and questioned.

And at the very same time, Indian cricket on the field has grown from strength to strength. Within a month of the spot-fixing scandal in May 2013, India won the Champions Trophy in England. As the the BCCI president was being forced to step aside in March 2014, India made the finals of the world T20 in Dhaka. When the Lodha Committee was tasked with the responsibility of cleaning up the mess created by the BCCI, the Indian team was playing some outstanding cricket in Australia and New Zealand at the 2015 World Cup. Finally, when the judicial order was passed by the Supreme Court in July 2016, asking for a fundamental overhaul, on the field of play, Indian cricket had its best home season ever and consolidated its position at the top of Test rankings.

It is a story of on-field achievement marred by off-the-field disgrace. A story of officialdom tarnishing the brand nourished and elevated by Virat Kohli and his team.

Do we need a BCCI that day after day continues to hurt Brand Indian Cricket? What is the one tangible contribution that the office-bearers can be proud of and showcase when questioned by the Supreme Court? How do they justify the millions spent by them, since it is public money they are dealing with? Do the administrators exist for the players or it is the other way round? Why should the Indian cricket fan have to tolerate people whose only ambition is to oppose reform and hold on to power? How, and in what way, are they helping Indian cricket?

No matter what the answers are, the truth is, they are as much a part of the story as Kohli and Shastri and the *para* cricketers in Mumbai and Kolkata—for better or for worse. And that's the story I have tried to capture in these pages. A story of ecstasy and agony, of adversity and triumph, of corruption and cleansing and, most importantly, of obscurity and intense public scrutiny.

It is time I go back to the lady at the Maidan one final time and complete the story. Yes, she did eventually take the 100-rupee note I gave her. Rather, I forced her to. It was my way of telling the Indian cricket world that we exist, she and I—the fans and the stakeholders. We are the billion Indians who make the 11 gods what they are. We are as much part of the canvas as Tendulkar and Kohli are.

I'll leave the final words to her. Rather, to a story she told me and which I will never forget. '*Dada, ekta IPL khelay Sourav babu amake ticket diyechilen. Club house lower tier. Duto ticket. Uni amake KKR r player der sathe dekhao koriye diyechen. Ami jantam na ke tabe chhobi tulechi. Ekhon seta amar barite ache. Janen oi ratre mone holo ei eto bochor ja korechi sammaner sathe korechi. Ar amio ei jagat tar ekta angsha* [Dada, for one of the IPL games, Sourav babu [Ganguly] gave me two club-house tickets. Lower tier. And he also got me to meet the KKR players. I don't know who they were but I posed for a picture. I have the photo at home. It was a night that made me feel that my 30 years at the Kolkata Maidan had gone towards something special. And I am also an important part of this world.]'

To me, however, it was something more. It was a rare frame where the deity had met the disciple and posed with her. And the meeting had been facilitated by arguably India's greatest Test cricket captain ever. A moment when the two worlds, distinct from each other in every possible way, had converged. It is a moment that explains the game in India. Did she offer the player a candy? I could not ask her the question for she had already found a customer and left to sell her last remaining stock.

And, in the meanwhile, the game continued at Eden Gardens to the chants of *Korbo lorbo jeetbo re . . .*

ACKNOWLEDGEMENTS

The first cricket match I remember reasonably well is the one I watched as a five-year-old at the Eden Gardens in January 1982. India was playing England and Geoffrey Boycott was caught out by Syed Kirmani early in the innings off Kapil Dev. Or so I think. I remember the delight I felt although. I understood little except that something special had happened. People around me were ecstatic, and so was I. It was the start of a love affair that continues unabated. When I am at my lowest I watch India play. Live at the stadium, on television, or on YouTube. When I am on a high, I watch India play. It is an addiction and the ultimate acknowledgement has to be attributed to the game that a billion in India consider religion.

To Sachin Tendulkar, Sourav Ganguly, Virat Kohli, Harbhajan Singh, Virender Sehwag, Ravi Shastri, Deep Dasgupta, Michael Clarke, Andrew Symonds, Nasser Hussain, Mohammed Azharuddin, Madan Lal, Kapil Dev, Bharat Arun, Suresh Raina, Ravichandran Ashwin and Rohit Sharma—thanks for answering my questions from time to time.

Sourav, a special thanks to you, for the many lunches together at your house during the writing process.

Gautam Bhattacharya, Jeet Banerjee, Vikrant Gupta, and Kushan Sarkar, for your insights and for sharing your experiences.

Vinod Rai, for the many hours of phone calls clarifying my doubts and answering my questions.

Justice Lodha, Justice Mudgal, Vidush Singhania and Gopal Sankaranarayanan—I enjoyed discussing the game and the challenges faced by you all in trying to cleanse and reform the BCCI.

Shashank Manohar, Amitabh Chaudhary, Rahul Johri, Diana Edulji, Ratnakar Shetty and the late Dr MV Sridhar—for the many hours of discussion and debate.

Lalit Modi—for your time in London discussing the IPL.

Avishek Dalmiya—my understanding of the BCCI was shaped at your house when your father was around. Thanks for giving me a look-in at all the papers.

Debabrata Mukherjee and Abhinav Bindra, for reading the chapters at the draft stage.

To my colleagues at India Today and Aajtak—Rahul Rawat, Aswin Kanumarath, Manoj Prasad, Arefa Sultana Hussain, Yash Grover, Shobhit Mittal, Ateet Sharma, Gagan Sethi, Dharmendra Kumar— you all have been incredible to work with in the last five years.

Supriya Prasad—I don't think you ever said no to any idea I have pitched! Thanks as always.

To the many sources who want to remain anonymous, I appreciate the need to be discreet.

Sanjiv Goenka—coffee at your office is the best and the insights into the running of an IPL team, revealing.

Vikas Singh and Nalin Mehta—for the hours of discussions in Delhi and Kolkata.

Kalli Purie—for all the stories and more we have done together. I appreciate your unstinted encouragement and support. Wish you all success in your new role as vice-chairman.

Joyneel Mukherjee—for the many *adda* sessions addressing my questions. I sincerely appreciate all your help.

Harshvardhan Neotia—for partnering with me in setting up the Fanattic Sports Museum, which has helped in ways impossible to document.

Ramesh Pandey and Satyendra Prasad—we have loved doing the events at the museum, haven't we?

Malavika Banerjee—there is a sports book in you and I am convinced about it!

Raghav Gupta—you listened to all my stories without never sounding bored! And I will forever value your support as a younger brother. Rajneesh Chopra—I know legally I am in safe hands!

Annesha and Umakanta—appreciate your efforts as always. Annesha, maybe you need to step up to writing the story of the women's game in India sooner than later.

Dharini—I wanted to do this book all my life. It was your push that eventually forced me to get going.

Sayantan—for all the work you have done to make *Eleven Gods* a reality.

Debasis Sen—for the cover photograph without which this book wouldn't have been complete.

Rochona—for all our discussions on the title and more.

To my mother and everyone at home for suffering through my moods.

Aisha—for the hours you have played alone as your father looked blankly at his computer struggling to document this story.

Finally, Sharmistha . . . I've said it all to you for over two decades now!

INDEX